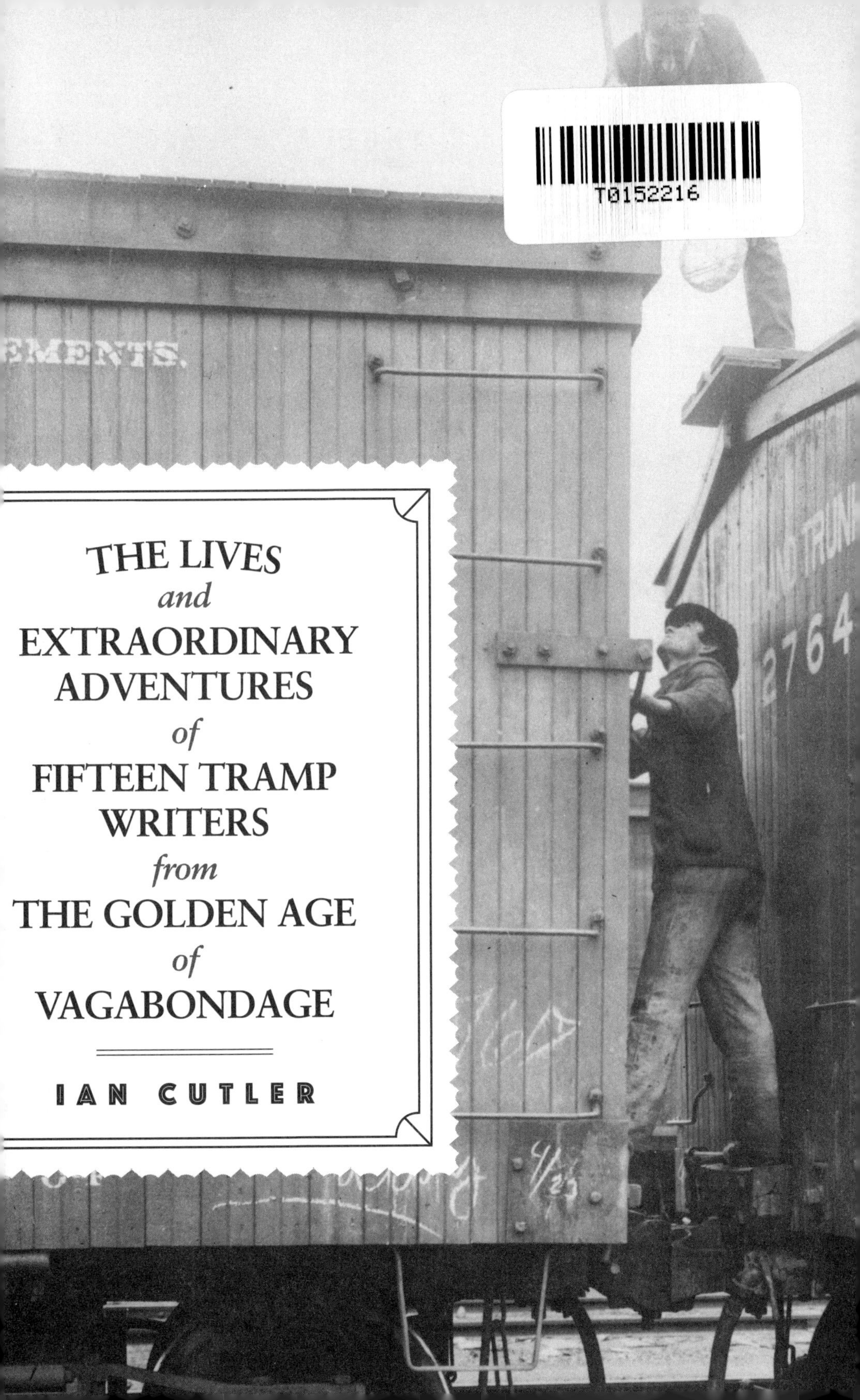

THE LIVES *and* EXTRAORDINARY ADVENTURES *of* FIFTEEN TRAMP WRITERS *from* THE GOLDEN AGE *of* VAGABONDAGE

IAN CUTLER

FOR ANGELA

WHO HAS TRAMPED

THROUGH LIFE WITH ME

AND IS ADORED

– P.v –
A Philosophy of Tramping

– P.1 –
Thomas Manning Page
(1841-1900)

– P.15 –
Morley Roberts
(1857-1942)

– P.29 –
Bart Kennedy
(1861-1930)

– P.59 –
Trader Horn
(1861-1931)

– P.101 –
Josiah Flynt
(1869-1907)

– P.121 –
Jack Black
(1871-1932)

– P.145 –
William Henry Davies
(1871-1940)

– P.167 –
Leon Ray Livingston
(1872-1944)

– P.201 –
Jack Everson
(1873-1945)

– P.219 –
Jack London
(1876-1916)

– P.243 –
Stephen Graham
(1884-1975)

– P.267 –
Jim Tully
(1886-1947)

– P.295 –
Jim Phelan
(1895-1966)

– P.327 –
Tom Kromer
(1906-1969)

– P.351 –
Kathleen Phelan
(née Kay Newton)
(1917-2014)

– THE END –

★ ILLUSTRATIONS by MAX CUTLER ★

N.Y. POLICE DOG TREEING TRAMP 8-12

Introduction
A Philosophy of Tramping

by IAN CUTLER

What made the vagabond so terrifying was his apparent freedom to move and so to escape the net of the previously locally based control. Worse than that, the movements of the vagabond were unpredictable; unlike the pilgrim or, for that matter, a nomad, the vagabond has no set destination. You do not know where he will move next, because he himself does not know or care much.[1]

Zygmunt Bauman

Bauman identified an age-old distrust of tramping, a suspicion that can be traced back centuries to fears of wandering strangers, escaped slaves and runaway servants. The periods in history when numbers of homeless and jobless drifters swelled to epidemic proportions mirror the enactment of various vagrancy laws in both Europe and the New World, fueled as they were by a perceived threat of idleness in the population and breakdown of the social order. One of the earliest such laws in Britain dates back to 1349 following the Black Death, others followed prolonged military campaigns, such as the Napoleonic Wars in Europe which gave rise to the 1824 Vagrancy Act in England and Wales, and the "tramp scare" following the American Civil War which triggered "Tramp Acts" in many states (and also "Black Codes" in the South to control freed slaves). Former soldiers, used to a harsh outdoor life, long marches and little thought of anything but their immediate needs, joined other economic migrants, and those who adopted tramping as an alternative lifestyle choice.

Parallel crises can be traced back to ancient times. Following a great gathering of Cynics from all parts of the Greek-speaking world at the Olympic Games in 167 A.D., it was reported that many of the humbler classes in Rome and Alexandria were turning Cynic in such numbers that alarm was expressed at the prospect of work being brought to a standstill. The philosophy of Cynicism itself, which emerged five hundred years before the Cynic scare of the second century A.D., may have been the first recorded organized "movement" of tramping as a positive lifestyle choice. The philosophy of Cynics, and also that of the modern philosopher Friedrich Nietzsche, will be referred to frequently throughout this book because of the direct parallels between their philosophy of tramping and asceticism, and that expressed by the tramp writers whose lives and thoughts are recorded in the pages that follow. But for now, let us stay with the negative portrayal of the tramp, as illustrated by the long list of (mainly) pejorative terms below:

Beggar
Bindlestiff
Boomer
Bum
Derelict
Dingbat
Down-and-out
Drifter
Floater
Flopper
Gonsil
Hobo
Indigent
Itinerant
Jocker
Jungle Buzzard
Landloper
Loafer
Mendicant
Moocher
Padder
Panhandler
Peripatetic
Piker
Plinger
Postman
Punk
Rambler
Ranger
Roamer
Rover
Scatterling
Shellback
Shuttler
Stewbum
Stiff
Stroller
Tatterdemalion
Tramp
Transient
Traveler
Vagabond
Vagrant
Wanderer
Wandering Willy
Wayfarer
Wheeler
Wobbly

and, less frequently but more affectionately, Gentlemen or Knights of the Road, and the British tramps' designation for each other as Sons of Rest.

Many attempts have been made to classify these terms, some of which have several meanings. Most frequently quoted is the work of former hobo and radical activist Dr. Ben Reitman, husband of the anarchist Emma Goldman. Reitman wrote at a time when sociology's obsession with classification had reached absurd proportions. In Reitman's study of women tramps, *Sister of the Road: The Autobiography of Box-Car Bertha*, he provides an appendix with over 30 pages classifying women tramps alone. Reitman started riding trains as a hobo from the age of 12, after being abandoned by his Jewish immigrant father. He later qualified as a medical doctor but continued to work with Chicago's burgeoning hobo community, and also with the prostitutes enticed there by the parallel local economy. This came in the form of transient workers returning to the city from other parts of the Midwest where they spent significant sums of money in Chicago's "Main Stem" from harvesting, logging, mining, and construction work. Reitman was also an early advocate of birth control and abortion, for which he received a six-month jail sentence. The title of the book, from which the passage below is taken, provides adequate testimony to Reitman's achievements: *The Damndest Radical: The Life and World of Ben Reitman, Chicago's Celebrated Social Reformer, Hobo King, and Whorehouse Physician.* In his role as a sociologist, Reitman classified vagrancy into three main divisions:

> A tramp is a man who doesn't work, who apparently doesn't want to work, who lives without working and who is constantly traveling. A hobo is a non-skilled, non-employed laborer without money, looking for work. A bum is a man who hangs around a low-class saloon and begs or earns a few pennies a day in order to obtain drink. He is usually inebriate.

One-time hobo and Chicago sociologist Nels Anderson was even more obsessed with classifying tramps. A study he commissioned (from other tramps) included five main divisions with 30 subdivisions, further subdivided again. Unlike Reitman's 30-page appendix of women tramps, Anderson cites James Moore ("The Daredevil Hobo") who included women as a subdivision of "Other Classes" along with Cripples, Stew Bums, Spongers, and Old Men, only further subdividing women into three groups: prostitutes, dope fiends and drunks, and mental defectives.[2] Tramps, Reitman and Anderson may have been, but partly due to the coincidence of Chicago becoming a hobo mecca at the turn of the last century, and the birth of the Chicago School of Sociology (responsible for popularizing "urban sociology" as a specific research area), many of these works on tramping concentrate on sociopolitical and historical investigations rather than getting underneath to the very essence of tramping itself.

This book will deliberately avoid "scientific" explanations of tramping, rather allowing the phenomenon to be explored directly in the words of those who lived and wrote about it from personal experience. The available literature on tramping, written by actual and self-proclaimed tramps from the middle of the 19th century, is surprisingly rich and abundant. Yet it is difficult to ignore the classification of tramping altogether, as will become obvious from the tramp writings in this book that started to appear within a decade of Charles Dickens penning the following quote from his satirical classification of tramps, *The Uncommercial Traveller: A Tramp Caravan* (1860):

> THE "EDUCATED" TRAMP ... the most vicious by far, of all idle tramps ... is more selfish and insolent than even the savage tramp. He would sponge on the poorest boy for a farthing, and spurn him when he had got it; he would interpose (if he could get anything by it) between the baby and the mother's breast. ... this pitiless rascal blights the summer road as he maunders on between luxuriant hedges; where to my thinking, even the wild convolvulus and rose and sweetbriar, are the worse for his going by, and need time to recover from the taint of him in the air.[3]

One can only question whether Dickens would have singled out the "educated tramp" as the most undesirable of the species, had he had the privilege of reading the literature that started to emerge shortly before his death and is presented in the following pages. Interesting to contemplate also is just how these same tramp writers would have responded to Dickens' description of them. This book will hopefully rescue the "educated tramp" from Dickens' condemnation of them. *The Golden Age of Vagabondage* covers the hundred-year story of tramping between the approximate dates 1874, Josiah Flynt's first tramp at the age of five, to 1972, the publication of Kathleen Phelan's story of her solo tramp through nine Arab countries from Casablanca to Iran and on to Nepal—something nearly impossible for any European vagabond today.

A chance combination of three major events heralded a golden age of tramping in America (and also in Canada, which is less reported): the end of the American Civil War, the development of the railways, and the financial crash of 1873. At the end of the Civil War in 1865, thousands of former soldiers, well used to an outdoor life and tramping, found themselves homeless and certainly ill prepared for the domestic responsibilities of home and civic life. With the first transcontinental railroad opening in 1869, followed by the first of a series of catastrophic international financial crashes and associated "depressions" (1873, 1893 and 1930), it is not surprising that, through choice or necessity, large numbers were thrown into and maintained a transient life, forced to roam the continent, surviving on whatever resources came to hand. This episode of tramp history has been comprehensively reported in two major studies published two years apart: Tim Cresswell's *The Tramp in America* (2001) and Todd DePastino's *Citizen Hobo: How a Century of Homelessness Shaped America* (2003). Both DePastino and Cresswell drew from numerous first-hand studies and accounts of tramping, many by former hobos.

Between 1870 and America's involvement in World War II at the end of 1941 (which provided a distraction and alternative occupation to many former hobos), tramping developed into a significant parallel culture, one that was about more than simply homelessness and joblessness. From the mainly white male hobos of the late 1800s, through the organized political tramp movements, black, Latino and Chinese work gangs, and "Okie" migrant families of the Dust Bowl era, to the "skid row" bum between the two World Wars, what emerged for thousands of individuals caught up in the Depressions (aside from simply meeting the basic need for food and shelter) was a philosophy and way of life for those alienated from, and dispossessed by, the rest of society—a society drunk on the capitalist dream.

DePastino notes that in a 1930s census, Nels Anderson put the population of those sleeping in public shelters and out of doors in America at 1.5 million, excluding the millions more sleeping in cheap boarding houses. Periodically gathering together for relief in the major cities of America, with Chicago as its cultural and entertainment capital, the hobo created urban centers of their own, with up to 75,000 in Chicago's "Main Stem" alone, an area centered for half a mile in every direction around West Madison Street.[4] This city within a city included cheap saloons, restaurants, flophouses, whorehouses, gambling dens, clothing, cigar and drug stores, but also bookstores, theatres, missions and meeting halls, thus providing evidence that the tramp army included those from cultured as well as the laboring classes. Indeed, these tramp cities also became a regular destination for those seeking temporary thrills and escape from mainstream society. Before drawing some parallels between the American hobo and the ancient Cynics, it is worth mentioning one further hobo statistic. DePastino reports that during the five-year period from 1901 to 1905 alone, nearly 25,000 hobos lost their lives, and many more suffered horrific injuries, riding trains. Not only from jumping into moving boxcars, but riding on the roofs, couplings and, most dangerously, on the rods beneath the carriages. The Welsh author of *The Autobiography of a Super-Tramp*, W.H. Davies, whose story is told in Chapter 7, was fortunate to escape jumping a train with the loss of only a foot. In spite of the well-understood risks of riding the trains without buying a ticket (and Davies actually did have more than sufficient money at the time, which in the event was spent on doctors' bills instead), many who rode the trains describe an exhilaration and freedom in tramping that was addictive, even when personal circumstances meant it was no longer a necessity.

This introduction will now attempt to establish the idea of "a philosophy of tramping," a useful starting point for which is to make some further comparisons between the ancient Greek Cynics and the rise and fall of "hobohemia" in America, before going on to acknowledge the modern cynic philosopher Friedrich Nietzsche's contribution to tramping.

Trains aside (although the Cynics would no doubt have ridden trains had they been available) there are clear parallels between hobohemia and ancient Cynicism. As with Chicago's Main Stem, the Cynosarges, a gymnasium and temple dedicated to the worship of Hercules (proto-cynic and mythical tramp par excellence) just outside the ancient walls of Athens, became a regular gathering place, not only for Cynics but others who felt exiled within their own community. A law passed in the fifth century B.C. prohibited "bastards" (defined in Athenian law as including anyone with an Athenian father but whose mother was a slave, a prostitute, or a foreigner, as well as those whose parents were not legally married citizens) from exercising in the gymnasiums, but for some reason this law did not extend to the Cynosarges. It thus became a regular gathering place, not only for official bastards, but also "self-proclaimed bastards," a definition of which provides a description that could equally apply to the hobo: "men and women who were or felt illegitimate and foreign everywhere, and who lived ill at ease within the established civic community."[5] A major distinction, though, between ancient Greece of 300 B.C. and America of the late 19th century, was the way in which these two different societies regarded the tramp. Both cultures shared some cosmopolitan features and also multi-ethnic populations, yet, unlike America, ancient Greece showed a tolerance to tramping not enjoyed by the hobo. So much so that Alexander the Great showed a respect and admiration for Diogenes' lifestyle, even when the Cynic showed contempt for the king's interest in him by asking him to stand out of his light while sunbathing in a public park.

It is interesting to note that, although both hobos and Cynics distanced themselves ideologically from mainstream society, both claimed the city streets as their natural habitat, scavenging out an existence like stray dogs on the margins of "civilized" human activity—a society that the tramp, in turn, views as imprisoned by their own possessions. The term cynic is derived from the Greek *kynicos*, adjectival form of the noun for dog, and is a literal reference to the dog-like appearance and behavior of the followers of this sect: fornicating and defecating in public, scavenging for scraps of food, etc. Where others used it to deride the Cynics, they themselves embraced the term as a positive choice of lifestyle.[6] Unencumbered by what they regarded as the trifles of civilized society, hobos and Cynics were free to claim their own sovereignty of the city streets. It might be the cosmopolitan nature of cities that provides the attraction, or the ability to more easily blend into the landscape, or the greater mobility that cities provide; either way, tramps were easy targets on the move between larger centers of population. It would have been natural, therefore, even for those who preferred solitude, to occasionally seek out the companionship and security of other tramps, particularly when the need for food, shelter, security or rest became critical. And so although homelessness is a central feature of tramping, the need for habitation, to claim dominion (often illegally) over some dispossessed scrap of terrain, whether it be Diogenes in his barrel, an abandoned doorway, or the hobo "jungles" and "main stems" of America at the turn of the last century, remains a fundamental human need.

How and why those who chose an ascetic lifestyle became objects of fear and loathing will be explored further in this book, but it is worth noting that, paradoxically, one such ascetic, Jesus of Nazareth, remains the spiritual leader to millions of conventional hobophobic Americans who have forgotten his mortal tramping beginnings and worship him today as a deity. The hypocrisy between what Jesus originally stood for and the mischief carried out in his name was noted by Friedrich Nietzsche in Germany, at the very same time that hobos were being persecuted across America. Nietzsche well understood the way that morality had been used throughout history as the justification for the tyranny that humans inflicted upon other humans, carried along under the banner of improving and enlightening peoples. And Nietzsche expressed just how much he thought humankind had lost their way when he argued that: "As a moral code it [Christianity] produces dull, static and conformist societies that dampen down human potential and achievement."[7] It was just such a social vacuum in late 19th- and early 20th-century America that the tramp army filled: a demand for a simpler, more meaningful way of life.

Expounding on the virtues of tramping and the deceit of Christianity with equal vigor, Nietzsche was greatly influenced by the Cynics as his sister Elizabeth confirmed in a letter: "There is no doubt that . . . my brother tried a little bit to imitate Diogenes in the tub; he wanted to find out with how little could a philosopher do."[8] This imitation can be seen in Nietzsche's obsession with self-discipline and testing himself against the elements. Living on his meager pension, Nietzsche embraced the minimum necessary for life as a strategy for survival. The tiny rented room where he lived and worked in the Swiss alpine village of Sils-Maria, devoid of decoration or comfort, has parallels with Diogenes' tub.[9] His typical day would start at five o'clock in the morning where he would write in his room until midday before tramping up the surrounding peaks, eventually retiring early to bed after a snack of bread and ham or egg, alone in his room. An examination of Nietzsche's work reveals many examples of this testing himself against the elements, raging against comfort in all its manifestations: physical, intellectual, and moral. But further credentials as a tramp philosopher come from his cosmopolitan convictions and rejection of German culture and religion. The following lines from Nietzsche underscore the central motif of this book and motivation for the true tramping spirit: "Why cling to your bit of earth, or your little business, or listen to what your neighbour says? It is so provincial to bind oneself to views which are no longer binding a couple of hundred miles away."[10]

But what justifies describing tramping as a philosophy? The branch of knowledge we describe as "philosophy" in the West was hijacked by Plato, Aristotle and their successors from the view of the world held by Socrates, and further embraced by the ancient Cynics, over 2,000 years ago. Until Plato introduced scientific logic based on first principles (the view that still dominates in the West today), the human world was explained either through gods and other myths, or in the way that "lower animals" experience *their* world: feeling it through the senses rather than through intellectual and scientific reasoning. That most genuine tramps and cynics veer toward this more existential view of the world—choose to experience and *feel* what is important in life, rather than write or read scientific theories on the subject—is why tramping has a right to be viewed as a philosophy as well as a way of life. And it was the Cynics who insisted that one must *live* their philosophy.

The definition of tramps in this book, what distinguishes them from the rest of humankind, and what drives them to abandon "civilization," is not helped by the long list of terms provided above, and may *never* be defined precisely. It is the intention of this book that a clearer understanding of a philosophy of tramping will emerge from the following chapters by posing questions such as: Does the tramp feel exiled from their own communities or do they feel, as Nietzsche suspected, that it is the rest of us who have lost touch with what it is to be human in our quest for some higher moral purpose? It would not be surprising, then, if some of those who chose a tramping lifestyle did so from their own moral sense of purpose, a rejection of wider society's misguided morality that the tramp finds difficult to reconcile with. But is there also a part of the tramp that perhaps *wants* to belong? Does he or she feel envy for the metaphysically innocent: those for whom slavery to a tribe, a religion or a state is a source of pride? Or is the tramp above such inconsequential preoccupations? Do they, like the Cynic, regard themselves as "citizens of the world," free to roam wherever they feel the fancy, adopting any customs and habits that suit their needs? Is a tramp born a tramp, through some endogenous but unexplainable sense of "not belonging"? Or conversely, "belonging" to the world in a different way to his or her fellows; is it something the tramp actually chooses to feel at all?

Perhaps the tramp, as with the philosophy of the Cynic Crates, has a sense of a "republic," but one not restricted to a geographical place, an ethnic group, religious or cultural traditions, rather, a republic without boundaries or social distinctions. The tramp fully accepts the risks that such a lifestyle brings, but whether or not this is motivated by any external cause, especially political, is not at all certain. Nevertheless, the tramp would seem to live out their apparently existential existence, in most cases, without the sermonizing or sentimentality one associates with some others who choose alternative lifestyles, such as the hippie or new-age traveler. Even the Cynics, who did engage in an exhortation of sorts, practiced "anti-philosophy" rather than an alternative ideology; they stood *against* what they saw as human arrogance and hypocrisy but offered no alternative belief system to put in its place. Neither did they seek to persuade others to join their movement. One feature of tramping, however, unites all of the disparate characters discussed in this introduction and in the chapters that follow. Asceticism is the lifestyle choice of the tramp, whether hobo, ancient sage, "son of God" or university professor. It is a position sought in direct contradiction to those who regard the acquisition of money and possessions as the key to a better life. The ascetic's belief is that "freedom from unhappiness" (a more realistic goal than happiness itself) is more attainable through independence from material desires than striving to fulfill them.

So what definition is used in these pages to describe a tramp? It does not rule out the itinerant worker (one definition of the hobo) where this mode of existence is a lifestyle choice rather than purely an economic necessity. Neither will the definition of tramping be confined to walking. The call of the road, the view around the next bend or hill, the need to put distance between one's narrow provincial surroundings and succumb to the lure of the unfamiliar and the exotic, is timeless and compelling. And so if the means to satisfy wanderlust involves hitching a ride in an automobile, jumping a train, or stowing away on a ship, one is no less a tramp for that. Then again, we are all familiar with our local wayfarer who pounds the same streets day after day, a creature of habit whose dominion is the local neighborhood; he or she is just as much a monarch of the road as those who tramp further afield.

Some of Samuel Beckett's vagabonds even tramped in their imagination from a bed or other confined space, others yet in the pages of books. But the fictional and screen tramp, like Chaplin, will have to wait for another book; this one chronicles the lives of those who, at some point in their lives, turned their backs on family and community and set off into the world as self-imposed exiles from humdrum or abusive lives in search of adventure. For the purposes of tramp writing, there is a fine line between biography and fantasy, which means that one must accept the autobiographical in fiction and the fictional in autobiography. What the stories that follow reveal, though, is that the facts are often even more extraordinary than the fiction.

We have adapted more than any other animal to survive as a species. It's what makes us human. But our explosion in numbers means that, for most of us at least, we have had to abandon our genetically programmed role as hunter-gatherers to live in vast metroplexes, governed by increasingly complex systems of laws and conventions in an attempt to impose order and control out of what should be a natural state of chaos and caprice. In the urban landscapes of North America, the domestication of human life has reached such a state of evolution that walking in the suburban sprawl, much of it too scattered and dispersed to make public transport viable, has long since given way to the exclusive use of the automobile as the only acceptable means of moving around. Rebecca Solnit in *Wanderlust: A History of Walking* describes how more than 1,000 pedestrian crossings were removed in California, quoting an announcement from Los Angeles planners in the 1960s that "The pedestrian remains the largest single obstacle to free traffic movement." And in New York, Solnit describes the scenario where then-mayor Rudolph Giuliani ordered police to start citing jaywalkers, and fenced off sidewalks in some of the busiest areas of the city.[11] But it was wannabe hobo and beat poet Jack Kerouac who first observed modern America's intolerance to tramping in an essay he wrote in the 1950s, "The Vanishing American Hobo." He noted that the aggressive implementation of vagrancy laws, backed up by intensive police surveillance, including the use of helicopters, meant that "you can't even be alone anymore in the primitive wilderness":

> In America camping is considered a healthy sport for Boy Scouts but a crime for mature men who have made it their vocation. — Poverty is considered a virtue among the monks of civilized nations—in America you spend a night in the calaboose if youre caught short without your vagrancy change. ... They pick on lovers on the beach even. They just dont know what to do with themselves in those five thousand dollar police cars with the two-way Dick Tracy radios except pick on anything that moves in the night and in the daytime on anything that seems to be moving independently of gasoline ...[12]

If tramping was tough for Kerouac's hobos, how much tougher nowadays for the tramp, with the ubiquitous CCTV and electronic databases that analyze even our shopping habits. To remain under the radar today, without money, a registered address or ID, requires no little skill and a strong possibility of being admitted to the local psychiatric institute. The following pages present a very different epoch in which, though frequently despised and criminalized, the tramp still represented an honorable tradition as an explorer and pioneer of the (un)natural world and the human condition.

ENDNOTES

1 Bauman, Zygmunt. *Life in Fragments: Essays in Postmodern Reality*, Oxford: Blackwell Publishers, 1995, p. 94

2 Anderson, Nels, cited in Cresswell, op. cit., p. 83

3 Dickens, Charles. *The Uncommercial Traveller: A Tramp Caravan*, Cambridge: The Riverside Press, 1869, p. 157

4 DePastino, Todd. *Citizen Hobo*, The University of Chicago Press, 2003, p. 72

5 Navia, Luis E. *Classical Cynicism: a critical study*, Connecticut: Greenwood Press, 1996, pp. 15–16

6 Cutler, Ian. *Cynicism from Diogenes to Dilbert*, Jefferson, NC: McFarland & Co., 2005, pp. 12–23

7 Cited in Robinson, Dave. *Nietzsche and Postmodernism*, Cambridge: Icon Books, 1999, pp. 26–27

8 Cited in Niehues-Probsting, Heinrich. "The Modern Reception of Cynicism: Diogenes in the Enlightenment," in Branham & Goulet-Caze (eds.), *The Cynics: The Cynic Movement in Antiquity and Its Legacy*, Berkeley: University of California Press, 1996, p. 359

9 Cutler, Ian. *Cynicism from Diogenes to Dilbert*, op. cit., p. 71

10 Nietzsche, "Thoughts out of Season, Part II," in *Complete Works,* London: George Allen & Unwin. 1909, p. 25

11 Solnit, Rebecca. *Wanderlust: A History of Walking*, London: Verso, 2001, p. 254

12 Kerouac, Jack. "The Vanishing American Hobo" in *Lonesome Traveler*, op. cit., pp. 149 & 155

Thomas Manning Page

(1841–1900)

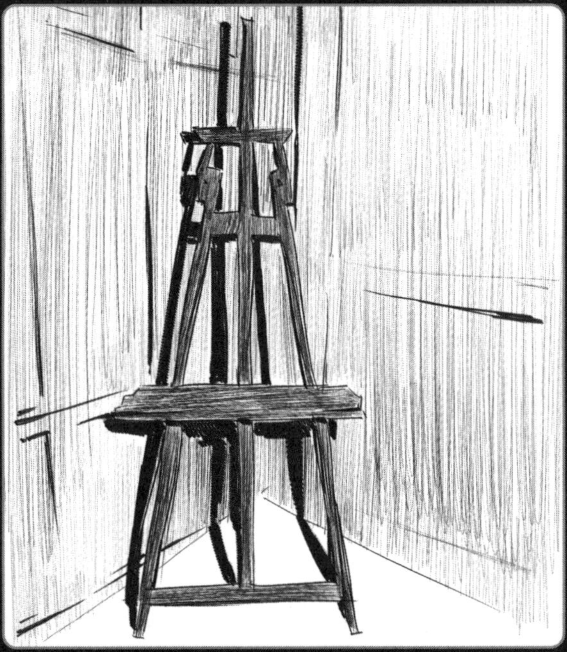

... on one occasion, while smarting under a well merited but none the less offensive reprimand, left the maternal cot, in Wheeling, Va., ostensibly for school, and having deposited my books and slate in the coal-shed, proceeded to the wharf and hid myself on board a steamer plying between Wheeling and the, to me, remote and romantic port of Steubenville, Ohio.[1]

Thomas Manning Page, *The Autobiography of a Tramp*

The enigma of Page is compounded by no existing image (photographic or drawn) being unearthed; this in spite of scrupulous research and evidence proving that Page spent time working as a bohemian portrait artist in Paris and New York and died the president of a mining company.

Preamble

Before even getting so far as Chapter 1 of Page's book, *Bohemian Life; or The Autobiography of a Tramp*, it is clear that this writer is a cynic par excellence. In the upside-down world that defines cynicism, satirical irony is there from the book's opening, as Page deliberately defies literary convention by opening with a postscript that contains a diatribe against prefaces.

> The custom of writing prefaces is a servile one that has come down to us from those good old days when authors had to choose between the alternatives of starving in garrets or else procuring patronage by fawning like spaniels on such vain, noble personages as were willing to pay for the pleasure of seeing their grand names and mythical virtues embalmed in fulsome print.
>
> When, in the progress of events, it ceased to be necessary to cringe before such beneficence, the literary craftsmen, at a loss by force of habit of something to propitiate, bethought him of the expedient of cringing to the reader; grotesquely ignoring that a book worth the reading needs no apology, and that to a volume of the other sort it is superfluous to add an extenuating which, in the na ture of things, is necessarily an enlargement of the offence.[2]

Taunting other writers, his publisher, critics and his readers, Page continues in this vein, but at least describes the purpose of his work: to introduce Bohemianism to an American audience, even though William Makepeace Thackeray had popularized the term in *Vanity Fair* some 36 years earlier. To press home his satirical comments, Page adds in the following apology to his readers for having to produce a second edition so soon after the first:

> APOLOGY FOR THE SECOND EDITION
>
> The only excuse that can be offered for this quickly flooding the country with another large edition of these chronicles is the sordid one, of unexpected wealth in bank hastily by first edition, which easily gotten gain has instigated the mercenary publishers to peremptorily command another edition to immediately come forth.
>
> Under such circumstances, all that a helpless author can do, besides repudiating all other responsibility, is what has been faithfully done, by diligently revising the text and multiplying and improving the illustrations.[3]

Even a thorough reading of Page's book does not make it entirely clear how much might be fictional and how much autobiographical. Page wrote in the first person without naming himself, or other family members,[4] and so there are no clues that the hero of the book was not necessarily the author. To be sure, below the book's dedication, in handwriting, is scribbled "Willie Wagtale." Given the absurdity of the epithet, one might ignore this as the joke of a previous owner of the book. It is not until well over one hundred pages in that the name is revealed as belonging to the book's narrator. And so, commencing a reading of *The Autobiography of a Tramp*, in the full belief that Page is both author and narrator, it is easy to be baffled why nothing is given away about where or when our hero was born. Page simply teases his reader that he was born "in the usual way," at an early age, and from a mother.[5]

On contacting the book's publishers and the archivists of digital copies, none had any autobiographical information on Page, assuming that the work was the actual autobiography of its author. It was only on contacting a genealogist in Wheeling, West Virginia, birthplace of the book's hero (but a significant distance from Page's hometown of St. Louis—did Page's family move to St. Louis from Wheeling?), that some factual information about Page came to light. A newspaper article from the *St. Louis Republic* dated April 19, 1900, announcing Page's death from a heart attack, did provide some brief autobiographical information. This was later augmented on acquiring two hundred digital pages from Page's probate documents. These revealed no more about the man or his writing than that the contents of his house included a library of over a thousand books. Then a librarian from the St. Louis Public Library unearthed the newspaper report below that, far from clarifying Page's biography, only further adds to the mystery surrounding the enigma that is Thomas Manning Page. There is a brief entry about Page in the *Encyclopedia of the History of St. Louis* (1899), but this also revealed very little. The newspaper report from the *St. Louis Post-Dispatch*, dated March 29, 1884, opens as follows:

> There will be published from a local publishing house next week a book which will no doubt attract a great deal of public attention from the reading public ... It is by an anonymous author, whose identity, however, is known to the artists and literary men of the city, many of whom have been given a glimpse of its pages.

The article further reveals that Page's book "is the story of the wanderings of a Bohemian by a Bohemian, the author being a well-known and comparatively opulent artist, who travelled through Europe on foot." Page himself describes it as "the story of a tramp by a tramp." The article continues that Page's book is "the story of the life of an artist, a poet and a scholar, who, obeying his vagrant impulses, has loitered in the paths worn by the feet of those who love the beautiful." And so we do have some evidence that Page might have been a Bohemian artist, even if the report underplays his characterization as a tramp. Strangely, a further edition of Bohemian Life was published in 1886, this time under the new title *Tramp Life: of Roving Adventures in Europe and America.*

But let us continue with Page's story and leave it to the reader's imagination as to what may be fact and what fiction. What must be considered on reading this work is that Page wrote his "autobiography" before any of the works mentioned in the succeeding chapters herein would have been available to him. Furthermore, following a reading of the chapters that follow, all of verifiable authenticity, Page's writings on tramp life are so accurately described that they must have been based on some intimate knowledge of tramp life. In this sense, *The Autobiography of a Tramp* provides an important prototype for all the tramp literature that follows. Even if Page's book *were* in large part fictional, that only renders the books discussed in later chapters all the more remarkable, as their authors' adventures far exceed any told in Page's book.

It can be established from Page's obituary that he was born on May 7, 1841, enrolling in the Confederate army at the age of 20 and serving in the 4th Tennessee Regiment with, according to the article, some distinction. He was wounded several times and captured at the battle of Chickamauga, then released in an exchange of prisoners and was fighting with General Robert E. Lee when the Confederate Army finally surrendered at Appomattox in April 1861. At the completion of the war, Page returned to his hometown of St. Louis where he took up journalism and writing. Page's obituary refers to him as writing "several books," although only *Bohemian Life* seems to have survived. The manuscript of a "World History" by Page was destroyed in a fire and never rewritten. On his father's death, Page took over the presidency of his father's business, the Page and Krausse Manufacturing and Mining Company of St. Louis. Page was an only child, never married, had no children, and there are no close surviving relatives.

The paradoxical, upside-down style of Page's writing has already been referred to. Discovering that Page was a Confederate cleared up at least one anomaly in his writing. Why, one might wonder, did the hero of Page's autobiography, a child soldier in the Union army, express so many sympathies with the Southern cause? This is just one example out of many literary strategies employed by this unconventional author into prompting his reader to ruminate on their understanding of the text.

So why include what could be a fictional autobiography (in part at least) alongside actual autobiographies? Apart from a view that all fiction is autobiographical to some extent, and all factual histories contain a degree of fiction, it can be asserted that myth and legend are equally as instructive, sometimes more so, than so-called historical accounts. The particular style and content of Page's book certainly qualifies him as a tramp writer. It is also interesting to note just how closely the early events in Page's book parallel those of other tramp writers in this book, even though Page predates them all. As with several of those other writers, Page's hero loses his father (who also beat him) at an early age, is a rebel, spends time in a reform school, drives his loving mother to distraction, and has adventures as a child tramp. But perhaps this was a more common scenario in the 1800s than looking back from our present age seems likely. In any event, what follows is the first tramping adventure of Page's protagonist.

On the occasion of a beating from his father, our hero "left the maternal cot, in Wheeling, Va., ostensibly for school." After depositing his school books in the coal-shed, he proceeded to a nearby wharf and hid on a steamer plying trade between Wheeling and Steubenville, Ohio. Wandering the streets of Steubenville for some hours, he then informed a local innkeeper that he was "a friendless waif from Pittsburgh." After feeding and comforting the lad, the innkeeper asked him a series of questions, "all of which I answered with a seeming frankness that forestalled suspicion of guile." The next day his patron offered to send him to school but was assured that the boy had already spent enough time in school and would rather earn an honest living blacking boots in the hotel. That position already being occupied, he was then offered, and accepted, the role of a newsboy, to which he applied himself with "energy and profit for two days," winning the confidence of his benefactor into the bargain. Eventually the child tramp confessed the real reason for his arrival in Steubenville and the innkeeper, after much fatherly advice, put him under the care of the captain of a package steamer to return him to his family. On the return of her son, his mother "threw up her arms, and almost fell upon me in her haste to hug the wicked boy whose undutifulness had graven some fresh, deep lines of grief, which joy could not disguise, on her sad, sweet countenance."[6]

Shortly after this adventure, the family moved to Cincinnati where, with the help of his older brother (two other siblings had died at a young age), the young tramp's mother tearfully deposits him at a reform school. The events told here very closely mirror the experiences of Josiah Flynt's (Chapter 5), Jack Everson's (Chapter 9) and Jim Tully's (Chapter 12) cruel treatment at the hands of their jailers. But a year later, after a prison riot, our hero is able to persuade his mother and brother to rescue him from further abuse and he is discharged home again.

Soldier, Sailor, Tramp

The end of the young tramp's failed schooling coincides with the outbreak of the American Civil War in 1861, and, although his mother does not give the parental consent required, he joins the 83rd Regiment of the Ohio Volunteer Infantry (of the Union Army) as a drummer boy. The adventures told by Page here provide a fascinating account of the Civil War and help put into some context the phenomena described in the introduction, in which a legacy of that war was to create the raw material for the golden age of tramping in the United States.

Josiah Flynt (Chapter 5) was one of many commentators to describe how the war had created an army of men well used to traveling around the country and sustaining themselves on a minimum of food and shelter, in fact all the skills required to survive without working. Many ex-soldiers were simply unaccustomed to the responsibilities of domestic and civil responsibilities, and continued the way of living they had been trained to endure. In any case, with the outcome of the economic collapse in 1873, only eight years after the war had ended, there was little prospect of work even for those so inclined.

Following his short army career, Will, for by now that is how he prefers to be addressed, engages in various adventures, including working on the paddle steamers serving the Mississippi and its tributaries. After rescuing a damsel in distress from a sinking steamer which had caught ablaze (note Jack Everson's almost identical escape from a burning steamer in Chapter 9), our hero gives up paid employment and, through circumstances rather than choice, finally becomes a tramp—but not until 150 pages into the book. Will lost most of his money in the river and provided the damsel, for whom he had developed an attraction, with the remainder. Tramping his way back to Cincinnati he encounters a fellow tramp (with the moniker of Sorrowful Sam) over a woodpile, the chopping of which being one of the hobo's standard means of earning a few cents in hard times. Will ponders on what his tramp companion might have been "before tramping became a fine art in America," and asks him why he is averse to working to fund an easier life. The reply he gets is: "Work ... has wasted more human life and happiness, and cemented the foundations of more inhuman wrong, energies of war, physic, and bad whisky—and yet you, a reading man, and a thinker, ask me why I do not work!"[7]

With a $2 bill in his pocket to prove they are not vagrants, Will's companion teaches him all manner of deception to secure a meal or a bed for the night, without having to part with the money. "I was to some extent fortified, if not swayed, by his confidence in the sojourning virtues of the two-dollar bill. I let him carry it during the remainder of our journeying together, and he never let the sun go down upon our supperless, shelterless souls."[8] It is not clear, thus far at least, where Page acquired his in-depth knowledge of tramping, at a time when there must have been few written accounts of tramp life. He next describes the carved signs tramps use to communicate with each other which, in this case, lead Will, his companion Sam, and a third tramp with the moniker Fishing Jake, to a tramp "jungle" (camp). By this time Will is starting to express some comfort and pleasure with the tramping lifestyle:

> Reclining luxuriously on the brown and yellow leaves, in the glow of the ash-white, smoldering log, surrounded by a unique assortment of utensils which doubtless had been "lifted" from farms not many miles away, I listened to the hum of voices and looked through the towering limbs at

> the sun-paled ghost of the gibbous moon, while a feeling of unmixed, exquisite joy expanded within me.[9]

The tramp "chapter"—a kind of vagabond freemasonry—that Page describes in this encampment appears to be an extended family of those who have chosen to tramp and congregate together for ideological reasons rather than the hobo jungles of necessity. Whether Page is portraying a golden age of tramping that existed following the end of the Civil War (but prior to the first of the major depressions that heralded the hobo epidemic), or whether he is simply exercising his creative imagination, is for the reader to decide. Certainly, his allusion later to Jesus as the ultimate leader of an itinerant tramp movement provides some helpful clues. At any rate, on debating whether or not to resume his travels alone, our hero is subjected to a speech that has the all hallmarks of a fraternal tramp brotherhood, with internal rules and conventions, and an elected leader rather than a random collection of wandering vagabonds. "For the next hour considerable pressure was brought to bear, to shake my purpose of resuming my journey immediately. The Chairman of the Convention ... in a low voice assured me that many halcyon days like that we were then enjoying would follow each other."[10] As Page continues his description of this tramping fraternity, one might suspect him of ascribing to vagabondage's civilizing qualities—whether for literary or ideological effect—both the rejection and imitation of mainstream society's codes of behavior. It is of further interest to note, in the passage that follows, the use of self-imposed injuries to secure charitable benefits, similar to those described later by Jack Everson in Chapter 9:

> It is a curious fact, well known but commonly disregarded in the medical profession, that tartaremetic ointment will speedily produce an eruption almost indistinguishable, to an expert physician on his guard, from that of variola. And, owing to the prejudice against small-pox that always prevails in all populous places, we have only (provided we have been well vaccinated) to select our city, annoint [sic] ourselves and at the proper time appear at the dispensary, to secure free quarters of a most desirable kind, for an indefinite period, with the further alluring certainty of receiving new apparel in which to encounter the vicissitudes of the ensuing season.[11]

In and Out of Work

In any event, our hero decides to leave his comrades to their own devices and strike out once more alone. Following a period as a bicycle salesman in Cincinnati, the entrepreneur heads for Chicago where he opens a very successful business manufacturing and selling lamps and "chimneys." With several thousand dollars in the bank and his prospects blossoming, he then credits one of his own lamps for starting the great fire of Chicago in 1871: "the following night a melancholy cow, disgusted with her diet, kicked over one of my non-explosive lamps and shot it, after the indestructible chimney, into a pile of hay. … by the following night Chicago was a mass of incandescent ruins."[12] Needless to say, having by this time got the drift of Page's narrative style, he loses everything in the fire but the clothes on his back, and is forced to tramping once more. There then follows a series of fortunes and misfortunes in New York City, too numerous to mention here, although it is interesting to note that Page uses Washington Irving's nickname, Gotham, for that city. This is followed by an unnamed illness caused by the stress of his misfortunes, which prompts another change of direction. On being helped back to health with the providential assistance of a certain Dr. Robert Taylor, Will then has to attend to his rekindled wanderlust: "as soon as I was able, and before I was really fit for work, I solved its first equation by shipping as pantryman on the steamship *Cortez*, then loading for New Orleans."[13]

Disembarking in New Orleans in a state of exhaustion, our penniless and starving vagabond finds himself outside a local YMCA. Only sheer desperation drives him to throw himself on the mercy of God's disciples; the consequent failure of which enterprise produces a highly entertaining and lengthy satire on misplaced Christian charity. But to return to his arrival at the mission: "I had often heard of 'The Young Men's Christian Association,' and seen, sometimes in my urban rambles, chaste signs of that eminently virtuous collection of alleged immature specimens of the masculine gender." Into a prayer meeting the starving tramp wandered, lured by a sign to "walk right up," convinced that on sight of his presentation as "sick and needy, distressed by hunger and sufficiently naked" that they would "delight their Redeemer by giving my famished stomach one good fill and shake-down." The initial reception lived up to his expectations. He was grasped by the hand and drawn into a seat by a young man "whose bald spot indexed mature juvenility," then by another who asked him whether he "loved the Savior," yet another who inquired after his "stony heart," and finally by a fourth who presented him with a pamphlet entitled "Milk For Babes" and then offered to pray for him. What follows is a long and highly amusing account of Will applying all his guile to get a square meal inside him, while his new hosts, oblivious to his earthly predicament, were focused only on saving his soul. Finally, in desperation, the starving tramp clapped his hands over his belly and started groaning aloud.

> At this outburst of inward agony the petitioner redoubled his earnest eloquence; and as he prayed hot tears, or drops of some sort, rolled down his cheeks; while two of his youthful brethren hastened to my assistance and comforted and strengthened me, by telling me that if I died in my

> existing condition I would certainly be damned, and warning me to flee in terror from the wrath to come.[14]

His patience finally exhausted at this crude attempt to frighten him into heaven, but not before agreeing to kneel and pray with his would-be liberators in one last attempt to receive some physical nourishment, this latest convert to Christianity was forced to leave the mission in the same miserable condition he had entered it. Page's sharp-witted satire on the stupidity of people who worship gods, and his further portrayal of Jesus as the ultimate tramp leader, is worthy of the best philosophical treatise on the subject, including Friedrich Nietzsche's, with whom Page may well have been familiar. As with Page's earlier description of the tramp brotherhood, we are presented here with parallel worlds in which the God-fearing, civilized majority of humans seem unaware that there are among them those who prefer to exile themselves from all the dubious benefits that religiously-minded model citizens enjoy.

The Bohemian Artist in New York and Paris

In spite of a bewildering diversity of talents, Will only remains briefly in any occupation, mistrusting success even when it presents itself. Following the unproductive prayer meeting, he finds casual work on a steamer that feeds him and then deposits him in St. Louis where, having discovered a new talent on the steamer, he sets up in business as a portrait artist (we know this to be Page's primary occupation for the major part of his life), before returning once again to Cincinnati where he continues to ply the same trade. Convinced that he should now train as a professional artist, Will responds to an advertisement as a companion for an invalid Englishman bound for Liverpool, from whence he intends to proceed to Paris and realize his new occupation in what he believes to be the principal center of that vocation. One suspects here that the transmutation from itinerant worker to Bohemian is now about to take place.

The next hundred or so pages describe our hero's initiation into life as a bohemian artist in Paris, his friends and his adventures. This whole section of the book also describes the protagonist's equal and unconsummated love for two different women. The one is the damsel he rescued from the burning steamboat and whose acquaintance he resumes, the other is a dancer who lives in the same boarding house and becomes his model. Hopelessly in love with both women, he yet refuses to respond to their attentions, not wishing to be unfaithful to either one; this may explain why Page went to his grave a childless bachelor. Page displays a significant knowledge of art, and going through his probate documents, there was mention of several paintings in his possession including a crayon self-portrait of Page himself (sadly no longer surviving). The following passage concerning the fictional hero setting himself up as the stereotypical starving artist in his (New York) garret, suggests that Page may have been a frustrated romantic other than in his relationships with women:

> To love art thoroughly one should suffer for it; since nothing else tests and toughens the fiber of an affection too strong to snap in the ordeal, like the prolonged agony of physical discomfort. For months and years I clung to the feet of my mistress [art], often shivering, sometimes famishing, but always refusing to be repulsed into any of the numerous ignobler callings in which I had never known either hunger or privation.[15]

Nonetheless, Will, or Page, seems to have spent an entertaining and enjoyable number of years as a struggling New York artist, in the company of other artists, writers and musicians, with whom he established a private "Bohemian Club."[16] The description of the activities of this motley society, their buffoonery, feasting, and drunken poetry readings, has parallels with the Dadaists and the Beats. That the milieu described by Page took place at the end of the 1870s (40 years before the emergence of Dadaism, and 80 years before Beat arrived on the scene), reinforces that such "movements" are not a unique product of a particular historical era, but a timeless reaction to the banality of "civilized" society. The view of the Avant-Garde as a fixed point in art history has been challenged previously by the author of this volume (*The Golden Age of Tramping*) as follows:

> By employing the label neo-avant-garde we have undermined what avant-garde stood for: challenging, subverting, overturning, and undermining the clichés that former artistic styles and images had come to represent. ... it is avant-garde as an ongoing movement rather than as an artistic style that concerns us. In this context, we can regard avant-garde as the cutting edge that defaces the currency of false or defunct ideas, styles, and customs in the world of Western art—the compulsive cynical act of keeping art awake and on its toes. ... Cynical art, then, is represented in two complementary ways. It is iconoclastic: rupturing and smashing images and ideas, and it is avant-gardist: creating new images and ideas. If it is to work in this way it must push aside the tired images of its own creations as much as those it identifies as the work of others.[17]

End of avant-garde digression.

Further European Travels— Observations on Life and Romance

By March 23, 1882, the vagabond artist's wanderlust had returned; he abandoned the Bohemian Club, and set forth on a steamer bound for Germany. But he did not tarry long in that country. After meeting a fellow artist of acquaintance, they decided instead to tramp to Paris, visiting several German cities along the way. On arrival in Paris there follows an interesting observation about the drinking habits of various nationalities that is as true today as it was 130 years ago. After noting that the average wine consumption in Paris is equivalent to a pint of wine daily for every man, woman and child, and that the statistics for beer in Germany are even higher, Page observes, "what does all that prove? Only, that the wine of France is cheap; and that in Bavaria the beer is good." He then goes on to make the further observation that English and American alcoholic beverages are adulterated and that "inebriety is an enormous social ulcer." By contrast, in France and Germany, "thanks to the purge of light, pure beverages, it is a sporadic pimple almost invisible and virtually unfelt."[18]

There then follows a lengthy diatribe against art critics in which Page observes that "the cook who compounds a rare pudding, and the cobbler who constructs an exemplary shoe [do not] have to employ a self-elected fraud, who calls himself a critic, to instruct them in the mysteries of pudding and shoe excellence." Until they do, he asserts, art criticism will continue to be a joke with an easel at one end of it and an *esel* [idiot] at the other.[19] But the main reason for the diversion to Paris was abortive. He fails to meet up with his former friends, in particular the two women aforementioned. He gets news of Estelle from an old acquaintance. She was last heard of having ended the season of 1881 as a singer of grand opera in London, following which success she then toured the world, "adding to her slowly but surely growing reputation, in Bombay, Hong Kong, or Melbourne, or some other seaport under our feet."[20] Page has a reason for reintroducing the female infatuations at this point in the text. The final chapter of *Bohemian Life* is a satire on the purveyors of plots and happy endings, especially of the romantic kind. So without giving the "ending" away, a literary nicety that Page is determined to subvert, the following passage is included simply to give a flavor of Page's literary circumlocutions:

> BUT WHAT—the romantic skipper will exclaim, or at least wonder, on fluttering this thin, final chapter—has become of Est—or is it Ada?
>
> An embarrassing question, truly; to which there is no truthful answer more pertinent than the short one, that all proper to be known about that interesting young being will be found out when her biography is published. This is the autobiography of a very other person; wherein an engaging young woman must, of necessity, appear and disappear.[21]

Returning to Paris, Estelle was dismayed to hear that she had missed her friend by six months, whereupon she penned a letter to several addresses that might reach their intended recipient. It is while reading this same letter that Will is moved to consider which of his two loves is the most intense. He acknowledges that by a slow process of time, "the same that removes mountains and casts them into the sea," his increasing partiality to Ada steadily undermined his fondness for Estelle. Yet later, and by the same slow process, his affections for Estelle were rekindled and his infatuation with Ada declined. Ever the cynic, Page goes on to observe that "the conventional idea of the silver chord that vibrates between the sexes is an abstraction which has no shape or form, other than that of a figment of the unphilosophic imagination." Then proceeds a lengthy lecture on the subject of love, concluding that a lifetime of one romantic attachment attacking and destroying another—to and fro with the same two women in his case—can result in twin attachments evolving that in the course of the average lifetime, "may not supply sufficient time for the struggle to determine which, in itself, is evolution's choice."

In spite of his lengthy sermons on the subject, Page is clearly not qualified to offer any helpful advice on the subject, other than to conclude that for his own sanity he should give up on the struggle and "lie down and rest," even though he is not as yet "aged or infirm." Here is also a hint that he has done with both tramping and attachments to women. For by this time, and clearly a confirmed bachelor of independent means, he notes about himself (we presume) in the third person, that given he is able to "riot at home in peace and luxury, there is little romantic interest left in him."[22]

Afterword—From Clippings Provided by the Missouri History Museum

One commentator writes in 1917 that *Bohemian Life* was the only book that Page ever published but lists many other publications to which Page contributed articles, essays, sketches and poems, under the pseudonyms of "Sydney Harrington," "The Hornet Poet," and "Comet John." The writer also noted that "Page was a bachelor, with many marked peculiarities, one of which was his invariable rule to read one library book each day." He also notes that Page traveled through Europe incorporating his experiences during this time into the only volume he published. Though clearly an avid reader, it is further acknowledged here that Page was never known as a writer, "He was by profession a crayon portrait artist and a good one in that line, but nothing more."[23]

The following extract provides confirmation that Page became president of the Page and Krausse Manufacturing and Mining Company sometime after 1886 and the death of his father—and only a few years after *Bohemian Life* was published in 1884:

> ...the Page and Krausse Manufacturing and Mining Company['s] ... extensive plant is located at Nos. 408 and 410 Valentine street and 411-413 Poplar street. This is an old-established and highly successful concern ... The firm was incorporated under the Missouri laws in 1884, two years before the demise of Mr. E.B. Krausse. Subsequently the decease of Mr. William M. Page occurred, and since that event the sons of the two former owners have constituted the company and operated the business. Their premises consist of a large three-story brick building, accommodating office, factory and stock rooms, the factory being supplied with all the best apparatus and paraphernalia applicable to this special branch of manufacturing industry. The scope and manufacture comprises the production of refined and floated barytes ... The individual component members of the company are Messrs. T.M. Page, president and E.B. Krausse, secretary, both of whom are native St. Louisans of the younger and more progressive generation of businessmen.[24]

ENDNOTES

1 Prior to the Civil War, West Virginia was part of Virginia.

2 Page, Thomas Manning. *Bohemian Life; or The Autobiography of a Tramp*, St. Louis: Sun Publishing Company, 1884, front matter

3 Ibid.

4 Page's obituary in the *St. Louis Republic*, April 19, 1900, gives his parents' names as William Masters Page and Eliza Jacquith Page.

5 *The Autobiography of a Tramp*, op. cit., p. 1

6 Ibid., pp. 6–8

7 Ibid., pp. 161–162

8 Ibid., pp. 170–171

9 Ibid., p. 176

10 Ibid., pp. 188–189

11 Ibid., pp. 190–191

12 Ibid., p. 203

13 Ibid., p. 226

14 Ibid., pp. 230–236. For further reading on the theme of Jesus as a tramp, see Bart Kennedy's discussion on this subject in Chapter 3.

15 Ibid., pp. 376–377

16 It cannot be determined if Page's "Bohemian Club" has any connection to the Bohemian Club founded in San Francisco during the same decade, and with the same original foundations.

17 Cutler, Ian. *Cynicism from Diogenes to Dilbert*, op. cit., pp. 131–133

18 *The Autobiography of a Tramp*, op. cit., p. 424

19 Ibid., p. 430

20 Ibid., p. 433

21 Ibid., p. 441

22 Ibid., pp. 443–451

23 Breckenridge, James Malcolm. *William Clark Breckenridge: his life, lineage and writings*, Fulton, MO: Ovid Bell Press, 1932.

24 *St. Louis, Queen City of the West* (St. Louis, MO: Mercantile Advancement Co., 1898–99)

Morley Roberts

(1857–1942)

What happens when the people are plastic and their circumstances rigid? What when the people are rigid and unyielding, and their surroundings fluent and unabiding?

Morley Roberts, *A Tramp's Notebook*

Preamble

London-born Morley Roberts was one of the most prolific tramp writers, with over 80 published novels, plays, essays, biographies and verse to his credit. Yet apart from Roberts' biography of his close friend and fellow novelist George Gissing—thinly disguised as fiction in *The Private Life of Henry Maitland*—Roberts' work is sadly even more obscure today than Gissing's. Gissing himself is best known for his cynical critique of the writing profession, *New Grub Street*. Although both men were born in the same year, Roberts would outlive Gissing by 39 years. But it is Roberts the tramp, not the novelist, who is the subject of this chapter, best established from his travelogue *A Tramp's Notebook* (1904). There are other autobiographies by Roberts, such as his debut novel, *The Western Avernus* (1887),[1] penned with Gissing's encouragement and weekly support, but *Tramp's Notebook* probably best conveys Roberts' own philosophy on tramping. The book consists of a series of memoirs and travelogues, not in chronological order, some describing Roberts as a professional tramp and others when tramping as a paid journalist. Yet, like W.H. Davies (Chapter 7), even following his success as a writer and able to pay for his passage and lodgings, Roberts often preferred to rough it, the better to appreciate the land and the people he encountered in his travels. In any case, the work Roberts acquired to survive, including stockman and miner in Australia and the Americas, often involved harsher conditions than simple tramping or begging.

A Tramp Education

Roberts describes his early life and education purely in tramping terms. Like many of the other tramp writers discussed in this book, he experienced feelings of wanderlust from an early age. Son of a government functionary and a family constantly on the move, Roberts mentions feelings of boredom and restlessness if the family had to stay in any English town more than two years: an itinerant lifestyle, he acknowledges, was a sound training to complement his endogenous wanderlust:

> Such a youth was gipsying [sic], and if any original fever of the blood led to wandering, such a training heightened the tendency. To this day even, after painful and laborious travel, Fate cannot persuade me that my stakes should not be pulled up at intervals. ... I could only read at eight years of age, but from that time until eleven I read a mingled and most preposterous mass of literature and illiterature. It was a substitute for

> travel, and, in my case, not a substitute only, but a provoker. ... With the child I knew best it urged him on and infected me with world-hunger and roused activities.[2]

Reading, then, would not have the effect on Roberts that his teachers intended. For rather than make of him a model student with respectable career prospects, it only reinforced that his destiny remained elsewhere and that his hunger for true knowledge was being suppressed. Rather than provide a true education, Roberts describes his teachers as his jailers, whose only interest was the acquisition of knowledge for its own sake and the passing of examinations: "the opinion is rooted deep in many minds that to surrender one's wings, to clip one's claws, to put a cork in one's raptorial beak, and masquerade in a commercial barnyard, is to be a very fine fowl indeed."[3]

For Roberts, reading would set him on an altogether different trajectory. He was saved from following in his father's footsteps as a civil servant by his "spirit of revolt." At the age of 18 he exchanged the university education at Owens College, Manchester (where he met Gissing) for what he described as his "new university," four months' steerage passage on the 1,600-ton sailing ship *Hydrabad*, bound for Australia. Roberts relates how the journey to Melbourne on board ship was his first introduction to "world realities as distinct from the preliminary brutalities of school." It gave him an authentic view of the world as opposed to "the substitutes for vision favoured by ... schoolmasters, professors, and good parents. How any child survives without losing his eyesight altogether is now a marvel to me." Those who survive at all, Roberts says, retain only a dim vision that permits them to "wallow amongst imitations." His *real* professors he found on board the *Hydrabad*, and they taught him the art of seeing things the way they truly are.[4]

Roberts describes the 102 days sailing from Liverpool to Melbourne as very harsh, with poor food and dirty cramped quarters. But to add to what Roberts describes as "an astonishingly fertile trip for a young and green lad who was not yet nineteen," his education was further enriched by time spent with crew members drawn from across the Asian continent. Knowing nothing of the East, he was now immersed in "an Oriental microcosm." The ship's bosun was "a gnarled and knotted and withered Malay, who took rather a fancy to me." Roberts would sit with him in his berth, sharing a pipe of tobacco, where he learned the wooden tallies for the sails from the sail-locker. The ship's cooks also became his friends and frequently supplemented the usual meager steerage fare by giving him extra rations. He got to know every man in the crew by name and sometimes joined some of them on the lookout. "So far as I remember the languages talked by the crew included Malay, Hindustani, Tamil and, oddly enough, French."[5]

Roberts' Philosophy on Education

In the chapter "A Graduate Beyond the Seas," Roberts' critique of education becomes satirical when he presents the following parodic examination paper on tramping, a paper he is by now well qualified to formulate based on his experiences as an American and Australian tramp. Roberts' satire highlights the absurdity of formal academia, at the same time forcing a reevaluation of the unique experiences and competencies of the American hobo:

> ... though I lack any learned degree earned by examinations, and may put no letters after my name, I maintain I passed creditably, if without honours, in the hardest schools of the world. ... My early work in New South Wales seemed to me then like sport. America was real life; it was for ever putting the stiffest questions to me. I can imagine an examination paper which might appal many fat graduates.
>
> 1. Describe from experience the sensations of hunger when prolonged over three days.
>
> 2. Explain the differences in living in New York, Chicago and San Francisco on a dollar a week. In such cases, how would you spend ten cents if you found it in the street at three o'clock in the morning?
>
> 3. How long would it be in your own case before want of food destroyed your sense of private property? Give examples from your own experience.
>
> 4. How far can you walk without food—(a) when you are trying to reach a definite point; (b) when you are walking with an insane view of getting to some place unknown where a good job awaits you?
>
> 5. If, after a period (say three weeks) of moderate starvation, and two days of absolute starvation, you are offered some work, which would be considered laborious by the most energetic coal-heaver, would you tackle it without food or risk the loss of the job by requesting your employer to advance you 15 cents for breakfast?
>
> 6. Can you admire mountain scenery—(a) when you are very hungry; (b) when you are very thirsty? If you have any knowledge of the ascetic ecstasy, describe the symptoms.

> 7. You are in South-west Texas without money and without friends. How would you get to Chicago in a fortnight? What is the usual procedure when a town objects to impecunious tramps staying around more than twenty-four hours? Can you describe a "calaboose"?
>
> 8. Sketch an American policeman. Is he equally polite to a railroad magnate and a tramp? What do you understand by "fanning with a club"?
>
> 9. Which are the best as a whole diet—apples or watermelons?
>
> 10. Define "tramp," "bummer," "heeler," "hoodlum," and "politician."
>
> This is a paper put together very casually, and just as the pen runs, but the man who can pass such an examination creditably must know many things not revealed to the babes and sucklings of civilisation. From my own point of view I think the questions fairly easy, a mere matriculation paper.[6]

Roberts exposes an attitude toward formal education that is shared by many other writers in this book. This includes the wanderlust articulated by many of these other tramp writers and philosophers and their strong desire to avoid the "civilizing processes" that most humans subject themselves to, and further fueled by a desire to hang on to the childlike innocence and illusions that those who do submit to "growing-up" relinquish. Roberts, whose *Tramp's Note-Book* was published four years after Friedrich Nietzsche's death, certainly concurred with that philosopher's belief (albeit written from within the hallowed world of academia) that real education is a far cry from the art of passing examinations which, as Nietzsche says, "produce merely the savant or the official or the business man":

> Imagine a young head without much experience of life, being stuffed with fifty systems (in the form of words) and fifty criticisms of them, all mixed up together—what an overgrown wilderness he will come to be.[7]

Knowledge, Nietzsche says, taken in excess without hunger, and contrary to desire, has no effect of transforming external life and remains hidden in a chaotic inner world. Importantly, tramps like Roberts, like the Cynics also, appreciate more than anyone else how best to reconcile the external and internal realities of being human, even if such a lifestyle choice comes at the cost of alienation from mainstream society. The contemporary German philosopher Peter Sloterdijk refers to this conflict as "inner emigration" because cutting oneself off from the fundamental values of society leaves one on the horns of a dilemma: "Get out or collaborate? Flee or stand firm?"[8]

So if there is something childlike about the compulsion to reject the perceived wisdom of others, as Roberts freely admits he does, the term "childlike" should not be viewed here in its pejorative sense. As Nietzsche also acknowledged, there is something that the child sees and hears that others do not, and that something is the most important thing of all.[9] Roberts admits to this desire for perpetual youth when stating that "without illusion one cannot write," and that (and herein lies a perfectly expressed manifesto for the life of the professional tramp), "When the Queen of Illusion illudes no more youth is over. ... The only illusion worth keeping is that anything can be useful. So far my youth is not ended."[10] End of digression on education.

Roberts' Tramping Adventures and an Encounter with Christianity in San Francisco

Roberts spent three years tramping Australia and working principally in sheep stations and mining camps. When he returned to London he made some attempt to settle to conventional life, including—in spite of the aversion to his father's profession—a spell as a civil servant at the War Office and the India Office. But wanderlust is an irresistible force and by 1884, now aged 27, Roberts bought himself a passage to America, initially heading for Texas where his brother was working on a ranch. Roberts then worked his way to Chicago on a cattle train, back to Texas (from where he adopted the tramp moniker Texas Charlie), then up to Iowa, St. Paul, and north across the Canadian border to Winnipeg. He tramped west through the Rockies on foot to Vancouver from where, after securing some work to raise further funds, he walked most of the way back across the American border to Washington and then on to San Francisco arriving penniless in 1885, where, as he put it, his second great university education took place.

The story that follows is testimony to Roberts' resilience and independence of mind and spirit. We are treated once again, as we are in other chapters of *A Tramp's Note-Book*, to a polemic on misplaced Christian charity. But here, Roberts exchanges open satire for profound candor and tenderness. The first chapter, "A Watch-Night Service in San Francisco," aside from the obvious target of its invective, is a marvelous exposition on friendship and maintaining one's integrity in the face of seduction. The vulnerability Roberts exposes himself to in this piece of writing cannot fail to endear him to his reader—a full reading of which is highly recommended. Roberts arrived in San Francisco with a quarter in his pocket. "Starvation and sleeping on boards when I was by no means well, broke me down and at the same time embittered me." On the third day he encountered some hobos inspecting a bill on a telegraph pole on Kearny Street. It contained a religious advertisement announcing that if out-of-work and starving men attended a prayer meeting they would be given a meal. "Having been starving only some twenty-four hours I sneered and walked on. My agnosticism was bitter in those days, bitter and polemic." After starving for a further 24 hours, "ill-clad and wet," Roberts attended the service, if for no other reason than the warmth of the room. He noticed that the place was half full of "out-o'-works" as he sat by the door. On observing that the preacher was "a man of a type especially disagreeable to me," Roberts left the mission, only to return a short time later.

"I went up to him and told him brutally that I disbelieved in him and in everything he believed in, explaining that I wanted nothing on false pretences." The preacher, taken aback by Roberts' forthrightness, yet surprised Roberts by offering him something to eat. "I took it and went, feeling that I had no place on the earth."[11] By New Year's Eve, after more days of starvation, friendless and alone in the world, Roberts found himself back with the preacher whose offers of salvation he had previously rejected. He took a seat in the middle of the hall that was soon filling up with worshipers and hungry hobos. When the service commenced, Roberts did not rise from his seat or join the singing. A few others acted likewise and when one of these caught Roberts' eye, his feelings of isolation started to wane. The hymns and prayers continued with the minister surrounded on stage by a dozen adoring young women whose faces, Roberts observed, exuded a "religious fervour." The time dragged on interminably and it was past 11 p.m. when the congregation rose to sing yet another hymn. This time the girls came down from the platform to offer hymn books to those who yet resisted singing; some took them shame-faced, others continued to decline. After more hymns, followed by silent meditation, Roberts turned to observe his new friend still sitting with arms folded and clearly not yet converted to the greater love of God. As the congregation started to leave their seats, fewer than 12 hungry non-believers remained seated awaiting some nutritional evidence of Christian compassion. And now the preacher addressed them personally, aided by the "girl acolytes" who appealed and prayed directly for those souls still in need of being saved.

> They were not beautiful perhaps, but they were women. We outcasts of the prairie and the camp fire and the streets had been greatly divorced from feminine sweet influences, and these succeeded where speech and prayer and song had failed. As one spoke to me I saw hard resolution wither in many. What woman had spoken kindly to them in this hard land since they left their eastern homes? Why should they pain them? And as they joined the singing band of believers the girls came to those of us who still stayed, and doubled and redoubled their entreaties.[12]

As the hair of one of the girls brushed Roberts' cheek, the hand of another lay upon his shoulder, and yet a third beckoned to him, "long-repressed emotions rose in me, I looked round like a half-fascinated beast," He caught the eye of the man he had noticed earlier. They were the only ones left sitting there, the rest having now risen and joined in with the singing. In that moment, each encouraged the other in what had become "an emotional struggle, and deeper than all a queer bitter amusement, that said plainly, 'If you fail me, I fall, but I would rather not play the hypocrite in these hard times.'" They acknowledged each other's resolve. "I knew if I yielded I was yielding to something founded essentially on sex, and for my honesty's sake I would not fail."[13]

Roberts spoke kindly to the girl nearest to him, "My child, it is no use," and removed her hand. But still they continued to sing and would not leave him until the first stroke of midnight sounded from the clock on the wall. Then one by one they left and rejoined the congregation. Turning to the other man, they looked at each other, "and being men, were half ashamed that another should know we had acted rightly according to our code, and had won a victory over ourselves." Now they were truly outcasts; no one spoke to them and the preacher prayed as they continued to sit in their seats.

> Perhaps in their [the young women] souls was some sense of personal defeat; they had been rejected as women and as angels of the Lord. We two at any rate sat beyond the reach of their graciousness; their eyes were averted or lifted up; we lay in outer darkness.
>
> As they began to sing once more we both rose and with a friendly look at each other went out into the streets of the hostile city. It is easy to understand why we did not speak. I never saw him again.[14]

More Tramping Memoirs and Wisdom

The fundamental activities of hoboism, such as riding the rails, eating in jungles, doing time in jail, and strategies for begging, are discussed in more detail in other chapters. This portrait of Roberts will be confined to those unique experiences that contribute to the character of the man himself. But before reviewing further chronicles from *A Tramp's Notebook*, it is worth noting Roberts' overall impressions of the United States, not least because of parallels with the world today, and in particular, the legacy that Europe has inherited from America's love affair with free market economics:

> America is a hard place, for it has been made by hard men. People who would not be crushed in the East have gone to the West. ... The rougher emigrant, the unconquerable rebel, the natural adventurer, the desperado seeking a lawless realm, men who were iron and men with the fierce courage which carries its vices with its virtues, have made the United States. The rude individualist of Europe ... has little pity, little tolerance, little charity. In what states in America is there any poor law? Only an emigration agent, hungry for steamship percentages, will declare there are no poor there now. The survival of the fit is the survival of the strong; every man for himself and the devil take the hindmost might replace the legend on the silver dollar and the golden eagle, without any American denying it in his heart.[15]

On Reading and Mountaineering

As other tramp writers have noted, Roberts observes that the full-time tramp "finds little time and little chance to read." For this reason, Roberts acknowledges, he always combined wandering with working. On one occasion, for instance, after tramping 8,000 miles in seven months and arriving in British Columbia with only 25 cents in his pocket, he took a job in a sawmill near the town of New Westminster which had a small public library. As often as Roberts was able, he would go to the library after work, but not enough to satisfy his appetite for literature. But because the work in a sawmill was so exhausting, he had little energy left to read, until winter arrived at least. Once the river froze up the logs in the "boom," the saws in the mill became silent: "I was free to plunge among the books and roll and soak among them day and night."[16]

One of Roberts' observations from time spent in the New Westminster public library is of particular interest: his scorn of books on mountain adventure and exploration, which he describes as "machine-made bits of description which are as inspiring as any lumber yard," and his depreciation of the "Alpine writer" whom he describes as using "pumped-up admiration." There is something about Roberts' attitude to mountaineering that is akin to his dislike of religion. Not that Roberts has no appreciation of nature. The target of his cynicism here is the vainglory of adventurers who exalt the virtues of "conquering" nature, elevating themselves vertically from the rest of the human herd, rather than exiling themselves horizontally (and anonymously) in the world, as does the tramp: "very little above the snow-line is truly beautiful. It is often desolate, sometimes intolerably grand and savage, but lovely it is very rarely. It is perhaps against human nature to be there at all."[17]

In *The Western Avernus*, written 17 years before *A Tramp's Notebook*, we are given some insight behind the more measured cynicism expressed both in the passage above and also in the account of the church service in San Francisco. As Roberts admits, the nearly three hundred pages of *The Western Avernus* were written in four months, "without notes, without care, without thought." What *Avernus* exposes more than *Tramp's Note-Book* is an acknowledgement and explanation of the raw emotions that fueled Roberts' cynicism:

> I was raging, nihilistic, anarchist, a mutineer against gods and men, a sneerer, a scoffer, atheist even as to Nature and Loveliness; a misanthrope, a misogynist, a reviler of all things, a Sadducee, a Philistine. For the iron entered my soul. And I walked like a whirlwind, with a pestilence and despair in me, self-contained and wrathful. I ate in silence or went hungry in silence. I rose up in starvation, and lived on apple orchards like a bird of prey forced to hateful fruits, lacking blood and flesh. I passed men on the road and spoke not. If they spoke to me I did but stare at them, and went by in strange quiet.[18]

"Veldt, Plain and Prairie"

In the chapter of this title, Roberts expands on his philosophy of asceticism, as though to reinforce his disdain of those constantly staring heavenward to discover the truth. He finds his own truth in the flat, barren wastelands of South Africa, America and Australia, and questions the relationship between humans and their environment: "What happens when the people are plastic and their circumstances rigid? What when the people are rigid … and their surroundings fluent and unabiding?"[19]

As with all true Cynic philosophers, Roberts criticizes those who seek truth through scientific discovery. Truth, he says, will always elude those who search for it: "The real observer is he who does not observe, but is gradually aware that he knows." And in answer to his own question about racial characteristics, he indirectly expresses the same "citizen of the world" sentiments as did the Cynic Diogenes. Those who seek truth will always find differences between peoples, while those who position themselves outside the civilizing process remain open-minded, aware of what is common in humanity. Roberts admits to encountering this wisdom amongst the flat places of the planet, answering his own question of what is different between the peoples of the bush, the plains and the prairies that he has tramped and ridden on three continents: "There is much difference; there is little difference; there is no difference. The great difference is racial, the small difference is human, the lack of any difference is animal and primaeval." For, Roberts continues, wherever we are in the world, and whoever descends from our shared Neolithic ancestors, we at least *arrive* into the world with the same "unconscious curiosity and faith in Nature."[20]

Roberts describes how his own particular truth dawned on him in South Africa when he came upon the veldt one night in the darkness halfway between Krugersdorp and Mafeking. Walking in a state halfway between sleeping and waking, he felt an "infinite peace" envelop him. In that moment, his solitude became a source of the utmost contentment and the necessities of civilization were necessities no more. He cared nothing for luxuries or news of the outside world. "The lack of small urgent stimuli, the barren growth of civilisation's weedy fields, left me to the great and simple organic impulses of the outstretched world."[21] Roberts is, of course, expressing his own personal philosophy, but it is not difficult to imagine how the same lure of anti-civilization would entice many a tramp looking for the same kind of inner contentment. Roberts hits the tramping nail on the head when he acknowledges that the essential character of the true wanderer has sunk so deep within him that he is unaware of it. And so the true tramp has no option but to tramp; he is born an exile. Or as Roberts puts it: "He belongs not to this age, nor to any age we know."

"Round the World in Haste"

Roberts was to retrace his steps several times, and at the age of 36 he would do so in spectacular style by embarking on a tramp around the world for reasons not fully discussed in this chapter of *A Tramp's Note-Book*. In any event, he was able to partly fund his trip by publishing an account of his adventures. Sailing to New York, he made his way to San Francisco, recollecting how he had previously made his way by jumping trains rather than paying his fare. Roberts' philosophy of the practical side of tramping was never to plan in advance but let each stage of his journey take care of itself: "Too much forethought is fatal to progress, and if I had really considered difficulties I could have stayed in England and written a story instead."[22]

Roberts arrived in San Francisco with insufficient funds to pay his steerage fare to Sydney, on top of which he picked up a cable from his London agent to say that the writing deal had fallen through, and so once more he had to resort to hustling. Having by now some reputation as a writer, he was able to pen some copy to fund the continuance of his trip. Roberts had never sailed that section of the Pacific and while he greatly enjoyed being in the tropics, he was vexed that his funds did not allow him a stopover in Honolulu. He did however manage to go ashore on the island of Upolu, home of Robert Louis Stevenson, and spent several hours in Stevenson's company. There is an entire chapter of *A Tramp's Note-Book*, "A Meeting with Robert Louis Stevenson," devoted to that encounter, more remarkable for the fact that Stevenson died later that year. Roberts was captivated by Stevenson, the man, to the point that any references to his works thereafter conjured up not the image of the text but of "a sweet-eyed, thin, brown ghost of a man whom I first saw upon horseback in a grove of cocoanut palms by the sounding surges of a tropic sea." Roberts acknowledges that many writers' works are a pleasure to read but meeting them can be a great disappointment, "almost an unhappiness, to be in their disillusioning company." These others give the best of themselves to the world. Robert Louis Stevenson's best was himself.[23]

> He spoke like an exile, but one not discouraged. Though his physique was of the frailest (I had noted with astonishment that his thigh as he sat on horseback was hardly thicker than my forearm), he was alert and gently eager. That soft, brown eye which held me was full of humour, of pathos, of tenderness, yet I could imagine it capable of indignation and of power. It might be that his body was dying, but his mind was young, elastic, and unspoiled by selfishness or affectation.[24]

Arriving at Sydney, Roberts had just enough money for the cost of the mail train to Melbourne where he planned to renew acquaintances from his teenage tramping debut and spend a year in Australia writing a book. But on his arrival he received a cable demanding his immediate return to London. His round-the-world trip would be completed in haste: by sea to Naples via Adelaide, Colombo (Sri Lanka), the Red Sea and Suez Canal to the Mediterranean and Naples. Roberts made London overland from Naples in four days.

Three years after this trip, in 1887, Roberts married Alice Bruce Hamlyn, a widow with three children. Sadly, one of his stepdaughters died in 1909, and Alice herself died from cancer two years later in 1911. Although Roberts continued to travel, including a return trip to British Columbia 40 years after his first visit, his time was now increasingly taken up with his writing—even if his reputation as an author had diminished—and his role as a raconteur in literary London. After Alice's death, Roberts was cared for by his stepdaughter, Naomi. Naomi died in 1941 and Roberts died in London the following year, aged 84.

ENDNOTES

1 "Avernus" is the entrance to hell in Virgil's *The Aeneid.*

2 *A Tramp's Note-Book*, op. cit., pp. 51–52

3 Ibid., p. 52

4 Ibid., p. 53–54

5 Ibid., p. 42

6 Ibid., pp. 57–59

7 Nietzsche, Friedrich. *Thoughts out of Season*, op. cit., p. 190

8 Sloterdijk, Peter. *Critique of Cynical Reason*, London: Verso, 1988, p. 119

9 Nietzsche, *Thoughts out of Season*, op. cit., p. 40

10 *A Tramp's Note-Book*, op. cit., p. 60

11 Ibid., p. 6

12 Ibid., p. 13

13 Ibid., p. 14

14 Ibid., p. 15

15 Ibid., pp. 3–4

16 Ibid., p. 74

17 Ibid., p. 217

18 Roberts, Morley. *The Western Avernus, or, Toil and Travel in further North America*, London: Smith, Elder & Co., 1887, p. 249

19 *A Tramp's Note-Book*, op. cit., p. 95

20 Ibid., p. 100

21 Ibid., p. 103

22 Ibid., p. 144

23 Ibid., p. 80

24 Ibid., p. 84

Bart Kennedy

(1861–1930)

Man is more of a man in the social state that is called savage and uncivilised. Civilisation is but a vast, theatric, backward step in the social life of humanity.

Bart Kennedy, *A Tramp's Philosophy*

Preamble

This chapter will attempt to reconstruct aspects of Bart Kennedy's tramping career from autobiographical elements of four of his published works. It will also summarize his philosophy on life, principally from *A Tramp's Philosophy.* Biographical information on Kennedy is very thin, and most of what is gathered from those of his texts discussed here is devoid of dates or chronology. *A Man Adrift* and *A Tramp in Spain* are available in digitized form, but rare hard copies had to be obtained of *A Sailor Tramp* and *In a Tramp Camp* as they are unavailable electronically and out of print. Interestingly, a 1922 silent movie version of *A Sailor Tramp* is still available. *Who's Who Online* describes Kennedy as having "picked up education in knocking about the world [and that he] drifted into writing." In the *New York Times* obituary of Kennedy[1] he is described as "the tramp novelist ... pioneer of the staccato method of short story writing," and *The* (U.K.) *Times* obituary[2] describes his works as "written with vigour, but in a curious jerky style." Below is Kennedy's bibliography so far as it can be established from several different sources:

Darab's Wine Cup, and other tales, etc. (1897)
The Wandering Romanoff (1898)
A Man Adrift (1899)
London in Shadow (1902)
A Sailor Tramp (1902)
In a Tramp Camp (1902)
Stone Fishing (1902)
A Tramp in Spain (1904)
Slavery (1905)
The Green Sphinx (1905)
Wander Pictures (1906)
The German Danger (1907)
A Tramp's Philosophy (1908)
The Hunger Line (1908)
The Vicissitudes of Flynn (1909)
The Human Compass (1912)
Soldiers of Labour (1917)
The Voice in the Light: tales of life and imagination (1917)
Thought-Coin (1921)
Brain-Waves (1923)
Golden Green (1926)
Footlights (1928)
Founder and proprietor of *Bart's Broadsheet* (a weekly started in 1921)

How Kennedy Became Accepted as a Sailor

Bart Kennedy was born in Leeds of Irish parents, Patrick (a shoemaker) and Catherine. According to the 1881 census, at the time Kennedy struck out alone for America, there were six younger brothers living with Kennedy in the family home at 145 Pollard Street, Manchester: John, Thomas, Phillip, James, Patrick and Joseph. It is not known whether Kennedy kept in touch with any of his family following his adventures as a tramp.

Working from the age of six in Manchester factories, at around the age of 20 Kennedy arrived in Liverpool with one shilling in his pocket, and so began his career as a tramp. He had dreamed of sailing ships since he was young, but this was his first sight of them, "just like the pictures I had of them in my mind ... so calm and strange; their tall, straight masts and their furled sails and rigging looked so fit and beautiful." To the fledgling tramp, these ships represented travel and great distances. "You felt that they had come from places a long way off, and that they were going to places a long way off. About them was something magical, fine, and strange."[3]

Having been well and truly smitten with the wanderlust, Kennedy then relates some of the practicalities of securing his passage on board one of the vessels that so seduced him. He is shown to a lodging house, not fully understanding the reason why he is provided with free board and lodge. The mystery is soon cleared up as every man who ships gets an advance note for two pounds that is redeemed by the boarding-house master when the ship, and the new recruit, are safely at sea.[4] This system ensured that the inn keeper got a regular supply of paid lodgers and the merchant ships a reliable stream of new recruits—albeit they were not always willing parties to the contract. The ship Kennedy signed with was the *John Gough*, a large steamer bound for Philadelphia, carrying freight and passengers with an average crossing time of 12–14 days.

Like several of the other tramps in this book, Kennedy was something of a fighter, employing his pugilistic skills at times to subsist as well as survive. Here he recalls his first fight out of England. Having been victim of the scam to enroll him as an able seaman, he was soon to find out just how cruel and inhuman the treatment of new recruits by veteran sailors could be. Just a few days into the voyage, in spite of being so seasick that he could not eat and only barely walk, he was nevertheless expected to put in a full day's work. The following story illustrates not only the hardships suffered by Kennedy, but also the elation of being a free spirit out for adventure with nothing to lose but one's life—as seems to be the thrill of many carefree and penniless tramps. The regular crew acted brutally toward him, having to take on his share of the work until he became skilled. On one occasion he fell and one of the sailors started kicking him. Too weak and ill to retaliate, he still managed to turn around to identify his assailant. Kennedy's illness lasted over two days, during which time he was unable to eat, yet he still had to do his four hours on and off with the rest of the watch. Sometime later, the same brutal crew member struck Kennedy in the face and blackened his eye. He could hardly stand up at the time, but looked the man steadily in the eye and said: "You shouldn't hit a sick man. Besides, this sick man will get well."

And Kennedy did get well, crediting the thoughts of getting even with his tormentor as aiding his recovery. The feeling of power returning to his limbs emboldened him, and whenever he met the man, he would look him straight in the eye and smile. Six days out to sea, and halfway into the crossing, Kennedy was now used to the motion of the vessel and quicker at his tasks. "The strong air of the ocean was putting a vigour of life into me such as I had never felt before. It was a wonderful sensation, after being shut up all one's life in a dull, sodden, black town, to be out in this vast open of moving waters." On the seventh day out, Kennedy was fit for anything and decided to settle matters with the sailor who had struck him. During his watch below in the forecastle, his eye still sore and black from the blow, Kennedy noticed the man standing near his bunk. He walked up to the man and said, "You struck me when I was sick and not able to do anything back. Now's your time to strike me again." The rest of the watch, who were sitting around talking, looked up and became silent in anticipation of what was about to occur; greenhands never addressed seasoned sailors in such a manner. "And you kicked me, too, when I was sick … Come on. Don't be afraid." Kennedy then pushed the sailor with his open hand and backed away a couple of paces. When the sailor went for Kennedy, he backed off again, sank down a little to the left, and then reached out with a feint. When the man followed over on that side, Kennedy turned to the right and landed a heavy, lightning blow to the side of his face, made all the more effective by the ship lurching at just the right moment. The sailor staggered back against the side of a bunk and Kennedy closed in on him, pounding his face and ribs. Down in a heap and his face covered in blood, Kennedy dragged him up by the collar and asked him if he had had enough. Clearly he had, and on dropping him again, Kennedy turned to face the rest of the crew and said quietly, "I'll fight the best man in this watch."[5] There was no response, neither was he bothered for the rest of the trip.

Many of the chronicles Kennedy relates, such as hand-to-hand combat with Indians, rescues and gales on the high seas, and his desperate escape from the desert riding the rails, read as though straight from a *Boy's Own* magazine adventure story. In turn, the stories that Kennedy listened to from sailors on his first sea voyage further fueled his own sense of adventure.

On Becoming a Tramp in America

On his arrival in Philadelphia, Kennedy writes that he had not a penny in his pocket, but tramped the streets in a state of elation at the prospect of having a whole new world before him. "After many days tramping," he says, "I found myself in the city of Baltimore. Here I shipped on an oyster-boat to dredge for oysters in the Chesapeake Bay. The wages were fifteen dollars a month, and one had to ship for a month at least."[6]

Kennedy had more fights and near-death experiences during his time as an oyster dredger, including being washed overboard from the schooner in a hurricane and having his yawl surrounded by ice in the Chesapeake Bay. One of his friends was less fortunate. His yawl had capsized in one of the sudden squalls that come up in the winter and he died fighting in the cold waters. The chapter is also a discourse on friendship: "Dredger though he was, tramp though he was, though he had known the inside of prisons, I am proud of having known him, of having taken his hand, of having been his friend."[7] Having grown tired of dredging and concluding that work "had brought me nothing but hardship and degradation," that he had "worked the blood and muscle out of my body to create wealth for others," and had "lived in the midst of absolute filth in a place not fit to kennel a dog in," Kennedy resolved to become a tramp.[8]

So off Kennedy headed, on dry land for Baltimore, soon afterwards falling in with an older tramp, Billy, whom he describes as "an English gentleman who had drifted away from his bearings, and come down in the world just a piece of human wreckage." Billy and Kennedy became partners, tramping and looking for work together, sleeping in the same haystacks, and sharing the little money they got from doing odd jobs. "When things were absolutely tight, we shared the food that we begged from the farmhouses we passed on the road." Kennedy never discovered anything about Billy apart from his name. "He came suddenly into my life, and went out of it in a like way." What Kennedy *did* get from Billy was the beginnings of an education: "At the time I met Billy I was all but an illiterate man—being hardly able to read and write. ... It was Billy who first gave me the idea of trying to educate myself." What struck Kennedy was the way Billy "knew things" and could express himself with confidence. Kennedy started to feel that if he could possess such qualities himself, he would have a chance to "raise myself in the world."[9]

Kennedy's education started out with a grimy, dog-eared 10-cent dictionary he carried in his pocket. With Billy's help, he started by learning to pronounce "big words" with the right pronunciation, repeating them over again until he got them right. Billy also taught Kennedy about the history and different nations of the world, the origin and mysteries of religions, and how geologists had wrested from the earth and rocks their dim secrets. "These days were for me wonderful days."[10] And Kennedy must have been a fast learner, for the first book he read, while still with Billy, was Goethe's *Faust*. In this fashion their tramp to Baltimore continued.

The pair eventually arrived in Baltimore tired and hungry, with only $1.75 between them. But Billy knew a boarding house where they could get a bed for 10 cents and a meal for 15. At this point of the book it becomes difficult to follow a chronology of events. Chapters follow separate episodes of Kennedy's American tramping exploits, but also themes, such as a whole chapter titled "Shovelling" which Kennedy describes as the most trying and monotonous kind of laboring work there is. Kennedy's essay starts in Columbus, Ohio, shoveling gravel on railroad tracks, moves to digging sewers in Cincinnati, then continues as follows:

> Perhaps the hardest shovelling of all is the shovelling of sand. I had an experience of this in British Columbia. I worked there for four days unloading sand-scows in the harbour of Vancouver. The pay was thirty cents an hour, a rate of three dollars a day. After the first day's work I was so tired that I felt as if I could lie down and die. I had a strained, sore feeling all over my body. I was hardly able to eat my supper.[11]

If the reader wishes to understand the finer points of the art of shoveling, a full reading of the text on the subject is strongly recommended in pages 94–105 of *A Man Adrift*. Next, we find Kennedy working in a mine, an 18-mile walk outside of New York City. Although Kennedy describes the work in detail—the drilling, dynamiting and shifting rocks—he does not tell us what they were mining for. The work started at seven o'clock, when down the mineshaft in a cage full of other workers Kennedy traveled to his daily toil. He describes random information such as the mechanism of the lifts in some detail, including how "If the wire broke to which the cage was suspended, a powerful spring suddenly pushed out two immense steel claws or catches, which fastened on to the big wooden beams lining the shaft. Thus the cage was held, and the men were saved from being dashed to death at the bottom."[12]

In Prison

In the chapter "In Prison" Kennedy provides a fascinating description of New Orleans and some very happy times he had there in good company with abundant good food and musical entertainment—a theme consistently echoed by other tramp writers in this volume. Unfortunately, Kennedy and some friends were arrested on a trumped-up charge of vagrancy because the police had been ordered to clear the streets prior to a local election for fear that vagrants would be recruited to vote by the opposition party. They were locked up with some 20 others, black and white, in a calaboose on the levee, yet none seemed overly concerned at the situation, being "comforted by the curious philosophy that goes with poverty and misfortune." None had the requisite 10 dollars required to ensure their liberty, so they made the best of it. Kennedy sent out for some beer with the two dollars he had, and a good time was had by all. "It is easy and natural to make merry with people who are in the same boat as yourself. We told stories, compared notes, and sang songs."[13]

Instead of spending just 24 hours in jail and then being released, Kennedy got into an argument with the judge for being falsely imprisoned and received a one-month sentence for his trouble. It was during this month in jail that Kennedy started to formulate his philosophy on crime and the justice system that he developed later in his *Tramp's Philosophy.* In this chapter of *A Man Adrift*, he discusses the effects prison has on a convict's mental state—although we cannot be sure that his own experiences were commonly shared. "Shut off from the world outside, the whole of his mind as it were passes in review before him. He sees into its most obscure fold and depth. His imagination becomes freer, more powerful." As with Jack Black's (more considerable) experiences of prison life in Chapter 6, Kennedy's spirit was strengthened rather than broken by his prison experience and being categorized as a convict: "The reason for which he was made to suffer had no effect upon him in the way of making him downcast." Further observing that "The partition that separates the criminal from what is called the honest man is made of the thinnest tissue paper imaginable."[14]

Kennedy further observed the way in which society inside jail mirrored that of the outside world. There were about 50 men in the block in which he was incarcerated, and they had their own codes and laws that had been handed down by custom and practice in the same manner as that governing countries and civilizations, "modified, of course, by the surroundings." Among the prisoners there existed a president, a judge, a sheriff, and other officers. "The warders never interfered with the laws of the prisoners."[15] But Kennedy also notes that the formal laws of the prison itself were far more brutal than anything meted out by prisoners to each other. Although discipline in the prison was lax, the breaking of the few prison rules that did exist was harshly punished. "Men were bound up and tortured in a contrivance called the stocks." This was a rack against which a man was tied and then tortured by means of stretching and twisting the joints of his legs. Kennedy never actually witnessed this torture firsthand but was witness to the groaning and screaming that resulted from it.

> The effect upon us as we listened to it in the yard was awful. We stood in groups, cowed and disheartened, for no one knew whose turn would come next. The cries of the tortured man seemed to get into the blood, and affect the beating of the heart. The cowed negroes and whites would look at each other fearfully. In these horrible moments even the sense of distinction of race was lost. We were fellow-prisoners before we were negroes or whites. After being tortured the man would be taken to the hospital.[16]

In another anecdote from Kennedy's first prison sentence he describes the pleasure he got from attending the prison chapel, not because he was religious, far from it; Kennedy had nothing but contempt for organized religion. Rather, Kennedy sought inspiration from Jesus as a fellow tramp and lawbreaker. On Sundays he attended "Divine Service," something the prisoners looked forward to, if only for an hour a week, because it allowed them to feel men once more, kneeling before the altar on the same terms as other men. And here Kennedy reminds his reader that, like himself and the other inmates of the prison, Jesus was also hard up and despised and would have absolutely identified with and understood their situation. "The Man whose name would live while the world lasted had been a tramp and a criminal."[17] Kennedy further asserts that our society was and continues to be based on theft, not the petty theft of those he shared the prison with, no, the meanest and worst criminals got off scot-free. "To conquer the world, cunning, fraud, and underhand violence had to be used." This included ministers of religion who, according to Kennedy, appropriated and misrepresented the teachings of Christ in order that they and the state might profit. Maybe, to follow out the teachings of the Galilean as decreed by him was impossible. "Could it be that cowardly theft and meanness, and lying, and underhand violence was the right thing after all?"[18]

It is of interest to note that Kennedy's eventual release from prison coincided with a similar flooding of New Orleans as that in 2005 caused by Hurricane Katrina. Due to the flooding, the only way out of New Orleans was by a narrow strip of hill-land which ran to the north up into Texas. The ways to the south, east and west were impassable. 'Water, water was everywhere the yellow water of the Mississippi. The big river had made a twelve-hundred-yard crevasse in the levee below New Orleans.'[19]

Kennedy's Canadian Adventures

The story now proceeds to Kennedy sailoring on Lake Ontario and tramping around Toronto, before deciding to make the 3,000-mile trip to the Rockies. This could be done by train for only a dollar, as experienced seamen—which by this time Kennedy was—were in short supply in British Columbia. Kennedy talks of the grueling monotony of that five-day journey, describing the prairie as more desolate than the ocean and wishing that he could have replaced the endless grinding of wheels for the roll of a ship. Arriving at Fort Donald in the foothills of the Rockies, Kennedy found work building "snow sheds" at $1.50 for a 10-hour day, less $3.50 a week for his board and lodging. After two months and with $30 in his pocket, Kennedy set out on a 30-day tramp to cover the five hundred miles to the Pacific coast.

He started out on a clear, bright morning in the middle of June, glad to get away from the monotonous labor of erecting cabins. His outfit consisted of a pair of blankets strapped across his back, a pannikin (drinking cup), biscuits, bacon, coffee and sugar. He also carried a .44-caliber revolver with 50 cartridges and a broad sheath knife because, he notes, he had to sleep out every night and take his chances on being set upon by Indians or wild animals.[20]

Here Kennedy shares some similarly negative observations concerning the so-called beauty of nature to that which Morley Roberts describes in the previous chapter: "to tell the truth, at that time the scenery impressed me but little. It was great and wild and finely coloured. But I had had enough mountain scenery to last me a lifetime." Working hard in the middle of it for two months had knocked the poetry out of it. "Neither will fine scenery impress a man when he's hungry, alone, tired, and wondering if he'll get out of it alive." Alone in the wilderness, Kennedy also had time to take some stock of his life—such as it had been so far.

> These frightful, lonely mountains made me think. I was face to face with things face to face with myself. I used to listen to the tramp, tramp of my feet, and wonder where I was going, and why I was going. I knew I was going to the Pacific Coast but what then? I had been going ever since I was a lad. And I was so tired of it all. What had I done that I should be a pariah and a labourer and a vagrant?[21]

The desolation of being alone in the Rockies had clearly put Kennedy in a very bad way, to the point that he describes in some detail how he wrestled with the notion and the practicalities of taking his own life. He recounts how one day he unslung his revolver, "determined to take a rest for good and all." Having witnessed how men shot through the brain jump violently, then sink down with a look of peace on their face, he mapped out the scenario in his mind then placed the muzzle of his revolver under his right ear, "so as to get the base of the brain."

> But just as I put my finger on the trigger I began to think in a way I had never thought before. My whole life, and everything I had done in it, suddenly came up before my mind. Everything was so clear and vivid. I seemed to see things from many sides at once. This is the way that men think when they are drowning, I thought. And I brought down the muzzle of the revolver. But I intended to kill myself nevertheless. However, I'd try and analyse my feelings first. And I sat down on a log and wondered.[22]

Why shouldn't he kill himself, he thought, what was there before him "but misery and hard knocks." People say that everyone in the world gets a break sooner or later but he could not, in all honesty, recall having been offered such a chance. "I had been born in the mire, and I had stayed in the mire ... moulded and crushed to a certain shape by circumstances." Not that he regarded this as a personal failing: "I was no more to blame for being what I was than the Indian was to blame for being what he was." But instead of pulling the trigger, Kennedy stood up and "cursed the earth and everything in it," thinking to himself that one day "the time would come when men of my breed—men from the gutter—would get even with it." Once more he put the muzzle of the revolver against his head but in that moment something came over him, a feeling he was unable to name. "It wasn't fear; it wasn't remorse. I just wanted to live just wanted to live for no particular reason."[23]

And so Kennedy continues his journey to Kamloops where he worked for a while laying rails—not without more adventures and another near-death experience—before continuing on to Vancouver. Here we learn that he actually had a passable baritone voice and spent some time on the stage. But the following chapter finds Kennedy on a ship heading from Yokohama to Vancouver, after which he decides to try and make it rich at gold prospecting in the Similkameen valley, some four hundred miles east of Vancouver, half of it a treacherous trek through forest-clad mountains proceeding at only 12 miles a day, with a companion, Bob. Here again, Kennedy mixes feelings of the futility of the whole expedition with those of elation and a carefree attitude toward his own mortality. Such is the existential existence of the tramp where the past and the future give way to the passing of the present. One's destiny, if it exists at all, is no more than reaching the next bend, a mouthful of food or simply the arrival of one's death, or denial of death.

Two Very Different Encounters with Indigenous Canadians

Kennedy describes the wild, hard country of the Chilkat Indians, "who always kill." The going was slow, fighting along mile after mile through the clouds, but a worthy achievement, Kennedy insists, to climb across an almost inaccessible mountain chain to the Similkameen, whether they found gold or not. "If we died well, other men had died before us! Other men's bones had lain whitening." They were not the first to have grappled with danger in search of treasure. "If Fate willed it that we were not to come back, what of it? It was as good to die one way as another."

> How glorious and terrible were the mountains! And how silent. The distant roar of the torrents seemed but to make more clear this strange,

> universal silence. We passed through gloomy, terrifying, vast canyons. We saw glaciers hundreds of years old giving forth the rays of the sun in a shimmering blaze of wonderful colours.[24]

After arriving at Similkameen, Kennedy and his friend Bob staked a claim and began their first placer mining enterprise, sieving out the gold deposits from the sand in and around the creek. For the first time, Kennedy actually experienced joy in shoveling. The pair did not make the fortune that gold prospectors dream of, but, with the assistance of Bob's luck at gambling, they came away with a respectable $4,000 after having been relieved of half that amount for provisions during their stay. The pair then headed back by a different route to try their luck at the Fraser River. On their journey they met two Canadian prospectors who warned them of reports that the Chilkat Indians were in the area. Kennedy's account of that escapade has a direct bearing on his treatise on war and killing in his *Tramp's Philosophy*. The American military eventually massacred large numbers of the Chilkat with the aid of Gatling guns to remove any threat to white settlers and prospectors.

But to return to Kennedy's own close encounter with the Chilkats, as the four prospectors trekked through the forest, Bob suddenly threw himself to the ground shouting for his comrades to do likewise, "barely in time to miss a volley that seemed to come from everywhere." They were in the open with little cover but neither could they raise themselves up to get to cover. There then followed "a most horrible whooping and screeching … enough to upset one, but by this time we had got a hold upon ourselves." From hardly 20 feet away, an Indian then appeared to spring up out of nowhere rushing full at them with a yell, but one of the Canadians dispatched him with his Winchester rifle.

> The knife he had brandished shot out of his hand towards us, and Bob grabbed it. "Up! Up!" I shouted and we were up to meet the rush, back to back. They came for us, yelling wild, savage-faced men, clad in skins and leggings. They had dropped their guns, and were on us with their knives. It was then that I found out that there is no weapon like a revolver of big calibre for close, sharp work.[25]

The whole thing was over in moments, and although they had made enough noise for a hundred men, their attackers numbered no more than a dozen. One of the Canadians was among the dead, having been knifed at close range, unable to defend himself with his rifle. That particular Chilkat had put up a tough fight, managing also to stab Bob in the shoulder before Kennedy shot him with his revolver. At the death of this particular Indian the remaining Chilkats fled.[26]

Questions have been raised as to the geographical and ethnological accuracy of Kennedy's encounters in this part of British Columbia. The modern-day literary vagabond, traveler and artist, Jim Christy (see *Jim Christy: A Vagabond Life*)[27], who has himself tramped the same area of the Canadian Rockies as did Kennedy, is doubtful of the accuracy of some of that writer's geography as he describes in the following email to the author:

> I like Bart Kennedy's writing, though his British Columbia geography is way off. It's about 150 miles from Van. to the Similkameen and the mts. he crossed were the Cascades — which are 450 miles west of the Rockies. Cascades are, however, just as rugged. There were never any Chilkat Indians anywhere near the Similkameen Valley. They've always been located in coastal areas of Alaska. The Indians Kennedy would have encountered were Interior Salish.

Regardless of any geographical confusion on Kennedy's part, and in spite of the aforementioned hostilities with whichever tribe it was that he encountered, Kennedy went on to have very agreeable relationships with indigenous Canadians as will be discussed below. But to return to our story: after stitching up Bob's shoulder with needle and thread and having to leave the dead Canadian behind, the remaining trio set off, first for Fort Hope and then, because Bob was ill and needed rest, back to Vancouver to rest and recuperate. But in no time at all, the pair had run out of funds. As Kennedy put it: "Making valiant efforts to relieve the Saharan thirst of bar-room crowds soon eased us of what we had brought from Similkameen." It seems to be the custom of most of the tramps encountered through these writings, that although any money they get is often very hard-earned, when they do have it they are compelled to share it with those down on their luck—a custom that is nearly always reciprocated, thus providing the tramp with a built-in insurance against hard times.

And so it was to be, for the pair arrived broke in the coal mining town of Nanaimo on Vancouver Island. Kennedy managed to raise $14 singing in a local tavern and so cheated destitution once again. After narrowly escaping being shanghaied, the pair then headed off for Departure Bay where they spent time with people Kennedy describes as the Siwash Indians of that region. (It should be noted here that "siwash"—from the French *sauvage*, savage—became a generic insult for indigenous Canadians, although that is clearly not the way Kennedy intended it at the time.) Kennedy recalls below the hospitality he received with the Siwash, a generosity that outmatched even that of the tramp, and an experience that made him question again the "uncivilized" European races, a theme he is to return to in his *Tramp's Philosophy*.

After they got fixed up in a shack in Departure Bay, Kennedy and Bob were invited by the Siwash to assist in a ceremony Kennedy describes as a "potlatch."

This consisted of a big feast that individual members of the community would lavish on the rest, following years, sometimes a lifetime, of denying regular comforts in order to acquire rifles, blankets, fishing nets, knives, ammunition, et cetera, but also money, in order to become rich enough to give the feast to which everyone would be invited; "it mattered not whether they were of the tribe or not, it mattered not whether they were strangers, friends, or enemies."

Everyone received presents and feasted for days until the last of the person's wealth was gone. Kennedy and Bob were given presents of blankets, ammunition, and other things they needed for their shack. The reward the person giving the party received came from "the knowledge that he was honoured by his tribe as a good and generous man. ... The religion of the Indian taught him to amass wealth so that he might give it to others."[28]

A feeling of shame came over Kennedy during the potlatch, the knowledge that people of his own race had tried to thrust their religion on these people whose own religion far surpassed the way Christianity was practiced in thought and deed. He describes the local missionaries as "a lot of loafing hypocrites, who corrupted the Indians, and who tried to spring a religion upon them that was not so good as their own!"[29]

Further Adventures and Thoughts on the Tramp in America

The Siwash tried to persuade Kennedy to stay and settle with them, and although the simple life impressed him, his wanderlust had returned. He was missing city life, and headed to San Francisco with a notion that he would embark on a stage career, arriving in that city with $4.50. Bob stayed with the Indians and Kennedy never saw him again. Kennedy did go on the stage for a short spell. We learn that he had been a big fan of the opera since childhood and studied reading music while mining in New York. But frequent fights with conceited members of the cast lost him his job. Nevertheless, Kennedy stayed for a long spell in San Francisco and has much to say about the agreeable climate and lifestyle he enjoyed in California. In one adventure, a friend from the opera house asked Kennedy to act alone as both captain and crew for his yacht, an escapade that, although it had its pleasures, again sees Kennedy facing more than one near-death experience. The chapter titled "Lounging Through Sunshine" is an homage to the virtues of Southern California, yet at this point of *A Man Adrift*, Kennedy pauses to write "a word as to the tramp in America."

"He is a man who has come to the conclusion that hard, sustained labouring work is bad for his general health. A little of it now and then is all right; but to keep at it for a month or a year is not to be thought of."[30] Kennedy reasons that after a man becomes a tramp (he never refers to women tramps) and travels from place to place, he gradually develops a philosophy on the subject of work—adding that, given the vastness of America, his reader should not get a false idea that the tramping only involves walking. "No, he is too clever for that. ... Walking it would smack of the nature of toil." So the tramp "presses the railway companies into his service ... [taking] advantage of the resources of civilisation." Neither is the tramp particular about the accommodation he occupies on trains, whether this be the cow-catcher of the engine, the front of the blind-baggage, boxcar, bumpers, or even under the carriage lying across the rods. "And when the brakesman tells him to get off he does when the train stops. But he gets on again when the train starts." Kennedy is at pains to point out that true tramps have an inherent sense of honesty and would rather perish than "rob any poor man out of a day's work."[31]

Kennedy maintains that the tramp only resorts to paid labor when he is weak enough. "But this weakness doesn't last long. He soon resumes his wonted vigour." The tramp's true vocation, Kennedy continues, is begging, and he goes at some lengths to emphasize just what a skilled and difficult profession begging is.[32] By his own reckoning, then, Kennedy must have frequently found himself in just such a weak position, given the number of times he himself resorted to paid employment. Or are we to take it that Kennedy was either averse to begging or not sufficiently skilled in the art? It is difficult at this point in his writing to separate out autobiographical references from those of the external observer—albeit informed by his own experiences of tramping.

From the Land of Sunshine to New York, and back to England

On Kennedy's return to San Francisco, he managed to join another comic opera company as first bass, singing in such productions as *Der Fledermaus*, *Boccaccio*, *The Beggar Student* and *The Pirates of Penzance*. This company toured the whole of the U.S. Pacific coastline, often without making enough to pay the cast their wages, but it was a happy time for Kennedy and he put his tramping skills to good use for his fellow performers when times were hard. There were also occasions when things went well, such as getting paid at the end of a particular month in Los Angeles and the landlord of the hotel where they were staying giving the whole company a champagne supper. "I was sitting next to the prima donna, and I was astounded to hear her tell the waiter that she wanted beer instead of champagne... . I afterwards found out that the worst beer is better than the best Californian champagne."[33]

After leaving this company, Kennedy claims that he dined and performed with Sarah Bernhardt for a season at the Baldwin Theatre: "I looked quite critically at the great actress to see if she were as thin as the report said. She was not. I suppose she had picked up somewhat." A short time later Kennedy took an engagement to sing ballads in the Eureka Music Hall on Kearny Street, where at least he received regular pay. But following a string of similar engagements, including failing as an actor, Kennedy became weary of the Californian sun and way of life, and determined to travel to New York.

On Kennedy's arrival in New York, he took lodgings just off the Bowery, and his chapter of that title, in contrast to his eulogy of California, is a delight for the abject and thoughtful characterizations he sketches of that district. By now Kennedy was beginning to weary of America altogether, and longed to return to England, specifically to try his luck in London. The final chapter of *A Man Adrift*, titled "No Place to Sleep," is a lyrical contemplation of being down and out in London at night. We learn nothing further of Kennedy's adventures but are instead transported into the soul of the man. Here are Kennedy's fears, fascinations, sorrows, regrets, and the objects of his anger, fused into a 13-page lament for the homeless man or woman, alone in (at that time) the largest city in the world:

> The hour of midnight tolls out and London becomes strange and quiet. It becomes at once alive and dead. The people leave its streets. And soon there is nothing left but shadows. Gigantic, weird shadows. Nameless shadows of the past and present. Monstrous, changing, weaving.
>
> In the waters of the old river are reflections of a strange and glorious beauty mingling with shadows foul, black, and unspeakable. Terrifying shadows. Forbidding, louring; and waving and moving into frightful shapes.
>
> London of the shadow. Formless, distorted London. Silence, blackness and dim light unite. Everything is vague, uncertain, and elusive. Here is mystery. Here is darkness and sadness and the unknown.
>
> London in shadow.[34]

From the same piece, and in the same style, there is a critical reflection on the hypocrisy of Christianity and those who profit from it, a critique that complements Kennedy's all too brief reference to Christianity in *A Tramp's Philosophy*.

In a Tramp Camp

The abstract of "In a Tramp Camp," published by *Wide World Magazine*, provides the following introduction:

> In the course of his wanderings the author came across a curious tramp settlement, where a couple of hundred tramps of all kinds and nationalities were gathered together ... he describes the daily life of this strange fraternity of work-haters, and the final catastrophe which brought about the break-up of the camp.[35]

The camp, with similarities to other camps and jungles described elsewhere in this book, was in Maryland, a mile from the state border with Delaware (and its much harsher tramp laws), and within sight of peach orchards that provided a plentiful supply of nourishment for the tramps. Sometimes they worked at picking the fruit to earn money for coffee, tobacco and other essentials; at other times they just helped themselves. A railway siding nearby, full of empty boxcars, made comfortable sleeping quarters. Kennedy had heard of the camp from a tramp he had met some 20 miles away and acknowledges to having enjoyed a "lazy but idyllic" time there during his stay. "We were composed of broken-down Continental counts, 'tired' labourers, scallywag English gentlemen, broken-down professional men, men who have made mistakes, and men who in all their lives had never made the mistake of dallying with toil."[36]

Most of the piece describes the various characters Kennedy met and the nature of the community with its own cliques and fraternity: "We were what might be called a democracy that declined work." A daily ritual at the camp was the roasting of a pig, driven to the camp from various places several miles away so as not to draw attention to the camp. Chickens were also in plentiful supply, but given that there were two hundred in the settlement, they took it in turns to eat meat. But all good things come to an end, and in this case not just because of the end of the peach season and the arrival of colder weather. A posse of police rode into the settlement to advise the tramps that if they did not break camp, the state governor was preparing to send in troops to clear it. A combination of local farmers no longer requiring the tramp labor and protests about a series of thefts in the locality, even if they were not all down to the tramps, resulted in the community hastily breaking camp and moving on. In this way did one of the happier moments of Kennedy's tramping adventures end as abruptly as it had begun.

A Sailor Tramp

A Sailor Tramp (1902) has been described as one of Kennedy's few autobiographical works. Yet, unlike *A Man Adrift* or *A Tramp in Spain* in which Kennedy is clearly chronicling his own travels and adventures, a reading of *A Sailor Tramp* shows that it is rather an autobiographical fiction. Although heavily informed by the author's own experiences, here Kennedy is able to fully exploit both his imagination and his personal philosophy in what is a very fine literary novel.

A word of caution though: For readers who are unable to cast off the strait-jacket of political correctness that defines our current age, and appreciate this text for what it is, this book may offend. Yet if one is able to approach this book free from the cultural canvas of our time, it should be acknowledged as an undiscovered and sadly overlooked treasure on many levels.

A Sailor Tramp is an unsentimental essay on the brutality of human life, a critique of deprivation, desperation, physical and spiritual survival. It also concerns longing and desire. For through his principal character, Sailor, Kennedy exposes the human face of the tramp, even his ambivalence to tramping itself. An example of this vulnerability can be found in the one romantic interlude of the book, where Sailor is wooed by the daughter of a wealthy businessman he is chopping wood for. She sees something authentic in him that her father and his rich, conceited friends lack. He desperately wants the love of a woman but realizes the hopelessness of his situation: "Being a tramp was sometimes well enough, but the great drawback about the life was the fact that a man was closed out altogether from knowing women. The conditions under which he had to live made the knowing of them impossible."[37] But for most of the book, Kennedy voices the harsh and unsentimental spirit of tramping. A resolve that turns its back on the comforts of steady work, a home or female companionship: "When men know how their bread is to come from day to day the time at last is at hand when they are no longer men. They are either slaves or parasites. They have become weak and puerile, for it is not given to man that he can stay at one point."[38]

The book opens with Sailor and five other tramps, having made a tortuous journey following the railway line on foot through the desert from New Orleans, eventually arriving in the Texan port of Galveston (where a large part of the story takes place) before finally being thrown out of that town and making the perilous tramp back to New Orleans. We know that Kennedy was a fighter and not averse to helping himself when the need was upon him. Whether or not he ever mugged anyone during the torment of hunger we shall never know, but the chapter titled "The Highway Robber" deals with the morality and anguish of Sailor, near to starvation, deciding to hold up a prosperous-looking drunk he sees staggering out of a bar.

Desperate situations require desperate measures, and Sailor wrestles with his conscience only to steel himself to the task. He approaches the man head-on rather than sneaking up behind him. He is prepared to kill or be killed in his desperation: "It was the way of the world. Was he to lie down and die of hunger like a dog? Not much!"[39] Sailor is fortified by Kennedy's philosophy on human hypocrisy. Nations plunder other nations with impunity and ruling cliques rob and murder their own citizens—"yes, it is the way of the world." Having relieved his victim of a roll containing $150, Sailor does not enjoy his first meal. He is haunted by guilt and the possibility of being caught and serving a long jail sentence. And when he does start to justify his situation and make plans to use the money to change his life, over $100 of his remaining spoils are in turn stolen from him and once again he finds himself begging for food (see also Tom Kroner's discussion on mugging out of desperation in Chapter 14).

Another brutal life-or-death moment occurs later in the book when Sailor, along with some other tramps, are arrested for vagrancy and then left by marshals at the edge of the desert with warnings not to re-enter the town. After several days tramping the sun-baked railway line, he and two companions arrive at a water tower knowing that if they do not jump the next train through that stops for water, they will die there in the desert. When the train stops, two of them climb up on the cow-catcher at the front of the engine while a third boards the blind carriage behind the engine. When the conductor threatens to club them from their perch, Sailor thrusts the muzzle of his revolver in the man's face and Kennedy's dialogue proceeds as follows:

> "We're goin' to ride on this train," he shouted. "We're goin' to ride—me and my partner and the Norwegian. We're goin' to ride—by the livin' God."
>
> "You—you will!"
>
> "We will! And I tell you that in any case I'll ride, if it's only to go for a trial and a rope at the end of it. I'm not goin' to stay in this desert because of a cruel hound like you. I'll lay your brains out here on the track. I will by God!"[40]

Once again Sailor's resolve pays off and the rest of their journey is uninterrupted, by the conductor at least. Kennedy's description of the rest of the ride is chilling, and the following chapter well illustrates his ability to switch his writing style and voice to fit the occasion:

> The hard, sharp wind pressed and cut into them and almost froze their blood. It came on—this wind—keen and sharp as a sword ... If they died here on the front of the engine it would still be better than dying in the desert...
>
> ...
>
> The men began to lose sense of themselves as men. They began to be lost in a chaos of wind and smoke and fire and motion. They began to lose even the sense that the whole thing might be an illusion. A vagueness and blankness came upon them.
>
> And at last their minds were gone from them altogether. They had gone back to the primal life-stage when all life was but motion. ... And

> now a train was rushing thunderously over the desert. On the front of it were crouched two peering things with blanched faces.[41]

Sometime later the train stops and the fireman, by now in wonder at the tramps' tenacity, pleads with them to step down and complete their journey in the carriage:

> Their faces were blackened, and holes were burnt into their clothes with the flying and dropping sparks.
>
> But they did not answer. They could not hear him. The eyes of the bigger man stared at him vacantly.[42]

As much as the fireman pleaded with the tramps to come down, they were frozen to their perch on the beam above the cow-catcher. They continued their journey until the sun came up the next morning and gradually life returned to them.

Many similar such train rides are described in later chapters, but to return to Kennedy's writing, as well as switching from first-person to third-person narrative, *A Sailor Tramp* also allows Kennedy to stand outside his storytelling altogether for the purpose of expounding his philosophy, such as the following episode where Sailor and others are arrested for vagrancy. Not a grave crime, Kennedy observes, but it was a crime nonetheless: "the chief basis of all crimes—Poverty." Kennedy continues by noting the absurdity that in a society based upon the acquisition of money and material possessions, "that man should be discovered guilty of the possession of nothing." Given then that tramps are "unsuccessful thieves" only reinforces that the tramp is "unfit to hold up his head in the halls and habitations of smooth, effective thieves."[43]

Kennedy's wider philosophy of tramping is reinforced in a chapter titled "Tramps and Outcasts." He describes tramping through the world without aim, plan, ambition or care for the morrow as a fine thing. Comparing tramps to upright citizens who daily commit crimes under the pretense of law, morality and virtue, who is to deny that the tramp's philosophy is not more potent? "Tramps and outcasts. Be easy with them. For it may come to pass that they will be held up to honour as the brave rebels and pioneers, who guided men up the tortuous path of intelligence and happiness. Be easy with them."[44]

Here we have also Kennedy the tramp prophet, further evidence of which is to be found in his *Tramp's Philosophy*. Note in particular his claiming of Jesus as a tramp, and how the corruption of Jesus (as deity rather than sage) by Christians, means that if one such as Jesus were to appear in our city center streets today, he would indeed be rejected and treated just as any other tramp. But just as with the ancient Cynics, Kennedy does not present himself as a philosopher or a prophet; he is too self-deprecating to pump himself up in that way. He simply holds up a mirror to corruption and stupidity, speaking his own truths with the passion of one who cares what a mess human beings have made of the world. As with Kennedy's prophecies about the banking crisis and the bankrupt state of education, here, from *A Sailor Tramp*, is a prophecy about humanity itself: "Man must go back to the earth if his race is not to become extinct in the world. He must leave the horrible, crowded noisome cities and go back to the earth. If not he will shrivel up and die out."[45]

A Tramp in Spain

The account of Kennedy's life now jumps to some future date when, clearly an older man and a writer of independent means, our hero embarks on further tramping adventures. The difference on this occasion, although making most of his expedition on foot, is that Kennedy has the means to pay for his board and lodgings. Even so, he does experience hardships and dangers on the way. For the most part, *A Tramp in Spain* (1904) is a travelogue in which Kennedy describes his journeys, adventures, and the places he visits, just as any tourist would, albeit from the standpoint of an experienced tramp. Rather than dwell on the usual tourist attractions such as going to a bullfight, the theater, art galleries, climbing mountains, et cetera, here are highlighted those passages from the book that relate to Kennedy the tramp and his contemplations on tramping.

The book opens with Kennedy on board a steamer entering Gibraltar Harbor from where he crosses the bay to the Spanish port town of Algeciras. His intention was to tramp the country on foot in a zigzag fashion from southwest to northeast, taking in Granada, Jaén, Madrid, Guadalajara, Zaragoza, west to Lleida in Cataluña, and from there north through the mountains into Andorra and the French border. Kennedy entered Spain with only a revolver, passport, knapsack, and no knowledge of the language. In the end Kennedy made the first leg of his journey, from Algeciras to Seville, by train in order not to miss the bullfighting season, "then I was to go on as my fancy led me. I was bound to the wheel of no plan." The fact that Kennedy was planning to explore Spain with no knowledge of the language was regarded by him as an advantage: "No one would be able to tell me this or that or the other thing. I would have to use my eyes. ... I would see things from an absolutely outside standpoint. And this was what I wanted."[46]

Kennedy is prompted to reflect again on the misfortunes of those who are down on their luck when he comes upon a homeless man at night in a square in Seville. He criticizes those who maintain that if someone is destitute it is their own fault. Such a viewpoint, he says, comes from ignorance: "Circumstances may force the mightiest man to the gutter." He proposes that all people should be put to the test of hunger, cold and loneliness as part of their education in order to learn the real meaning of life. Only then would they "know enough not to condemn."[47]

One notable and highly entertaining incident from Kennedy's Spanish tramp was his arrest in Granada for firing his pistol during a brawl. Kennedy had been drinking with some acquaintances he had made while in that city—even though he still understood little Spanish and they no English—when a fight started between Kennedy's friends and another group of men. When one of the other men threw a knife that only narrowly missed Kennedy, he decided to prevent anyone coming to further harm by drawing his pistol and firing a shot at the ground in front of his assailant. This action had the desired effect of clearing the street outside the bar, but the loud report brought the police to the scene and Kennedy was arrested. After spending an amicable night in jail in the company of police and jailers, Kennedy attended court the following day and was released on payment of a fine. As none of the police had witnessed the shooting, Kennedy was advised by his interpreter and counsel to confess that the gun had fired by accident when he was showing it to his friends, as firing a gun "with intent" was an altogether more serious affair. Following the trial, the judge asked Kennedy if he was satisfied with the trial—an experience entirely foreign to his experiences of British and American justice. He replied that he was very satisfied indeed and delighted to have had the honor of meeting the judge. "I managed to make the judge understand—as I shook his hand for the second and last time—that I hoped to see him again soon—in London!"[48] That night a long party was held in Kennedy's honor, following which he departed from Granada for his next destination, Jaén.

On the road to Jaén, Kennedy came across a tramp of around 60 years, making his way to Madrid. The two fell in with each other and a bond quickly developed even though they did not share a common language. Though not hungry himself, Kennedy joined him for a meal, as the tramp had obviously not eaten for some days. "I would have liked to have found out his view point of men and of things and of the world. He must have had a philosophy of his own concerning life just as all men have." Kennedy watched the man's expression change as he started drinking his wine. "What memories were coming up before him? Did the wine bring back to him some feeling of the magic of his youth? … We could hardly even exchange a word. And still—and still there was a link between us."[49] There then follows a commendation of the way in which Spain treats its beggars in contrast to the Anglo-Saxon races:

> They don't shut up their beggars as though they were lepers. There are places of shelter to which they may go, but they may please themselves as to whether they stay in them or not. They are allowed freedom. … The giving of freedom to the beggar of Spain is a fine and a humane piece of statesmanship.[50]

The rest of the book is an entertaining and interesting historical and sociological record of Spain in the early part of the last century: of the food, the housing, the people and their customs, including comparisons between the different regions Kennedy tramped through on his way. The only other significant tramping adventure was Kennedy's departure from Spain across the Pyrenees on foot that nearly marked the end of the adventurer himself.

On leaving the capital of Andorra, the innkeeper where Kennedy had spent the night warned him not to attempt to cross the summit of the Pyrenees' mountain pass in one day, a nine-hour tramp. He had been told to spend a night in the village of Soldeu with a friend of the innkeeper, before making his final push across the French border the following day. However, Kennedy was in a particularly buoyant mood and ignored the advice, imagining he could easily make the nine-hour journey in one day. On nearing the summit a blizzard set in that covered the trail both in front and behind him; he was now lost. After crossing a river, whereupon his shoes and trousers froze solid, he was fortunate to come across a conical stone shelter where he spent a freezing and sleepless night until it stopped snowing and the sun came up the following morning. He would later come across the party of drovers that sensibly *had* slept the night in Soldeu, arriving safely in the French border station of L'Hospitalet in time for breakfast.

Later Life

Kennedy married Isabel Emma Priestly (daughter of a Major Arthur Gore Priestly) at Holborn, London in 1897, the same year that he published his first book, *Darab's Wine Cup*, and when the tramp author was still only 36 years of age. Isabel Kennedy was born in 1865 in Langar, India. The 1911 U.K. census gives Isabel Kennedy's employment as journalist and editor, although there is no further information as to whether this was in relation to her husband's writing or an independent career. After some time at an address given as Cambray, Sandcross Lane, Reigate, Surrey, the couple moved to an affluent 14-room house at 20 Devonshire Place in Brighton. Two years after their marriage, the couple's only child, Rolf Darab Kennedy, was born. It is interesting to note the link between his son's name and the title of his first book published two years earlier. Kennedy's son, a second lieutenant with the 23rd Squadron of the Royal Flying Corps, aged only 19, was sadly shot down and killed flying a Spad SV11 over the Western Front on March 27, 1918. He had been stationed at La Louvie Airfield in France.

We do not know if Kennedy's tramp through Spain took place before or after his marriage, but given that he seemed very close to his wife, that his son was born two years later, and that he had published seven works between marrying and the publication of *A Tramp in Spain* in 1904 (five years after Rolf's birth), it is a fair assumption that the Spanish expedition occurred prior to Kennedy's marriage in 1897. This still leaves the largest part of Kennedy's married life and literary career unaccounted for. All that is able to be established are the three locations where Kennedy lived between his marriage and his death in 1930, and the contradictory facts that although he was able to occupy a 14-room house in one of the most prosperous neighborhoods in Brighton, sometime between the dates of 1912 and 1926, he had clearly fallen on hard times.

In a continuing search for a photograph of Kennedy, The British Library unearthed information that Kennedy had made several applications to The Royal Literary Fund, established in 1790 for "the provision of grants to writers in distressed circumstances" (the same mission it continues to this day). In his applications, Kennedy gives his occupation as "tramp." Details of his applications and amounts received are: Dec. 15, 1912 (£100), Aug. 28, 1923 (£75), Oct. 31, 1924 (rejected), Oct. 27, 1926 (£50). Kennedy's case file from the Royal Literary Fund contains 43 items of correspondence. It appears that after his wife's death aged 61 in 1927, Kennedy gave up any further interest in life, eventually being taken to the Brighton County Borough Mental Hospital in Haywards Heath, Sussex, in the summer of 1930. A friend found him there dying without food and ambivalent to life or death. Kennedy died on Dec. 6, 1930, at the age of 69. Such is the enigma of Bart Kennedy's later life.

There is an interesting obituary on Kennedy from the *Ottawa Citizen* dated Dec. 10, 1930, which states that: "Bart Kennedy had a curiously mixed career. Probably it would best be described as being built upon sand. But in any event Kennedy obviously enjoyed every minute of it until two years ago, when his wife died."

An Afterword on Bart Kennedy's *A Tramp's Philosophy*

It would require a further chapter to do justice to Kennedy's significant treatise on tramping as a philosophy. Yet this book covers more than simply tramping; it is a demolition of human civilization in the true Cynic and Nietzschean style. But as *The Golden Age of Vagabondage* is primarily an account of the lives and adventures of the tramp writers presented here, a full reading of *A Tramp's Philosophy* (1908) is recommended to fully acquaint oneself with Kennedy's thoughts and ideas on the range of issues summarized below. Sadly, the book was out of print and not available in electronic text. There was a used copy on Amazon U.K. for £199.75 but in the end, the grand sum of four pounds was invested to track down and borrow a copy through the British Library network. *A Tramp's Philosophy* has now been rescued from obscurity by Feral House and will be republished in 2020.

As with Nietzsche, Kennedy applies the term "cynicism" in both its popular negative form as well as in its positive role of denouncing human dogma and stupidity: "It is good to be cynical. It means that the scales have fallen from your eyes."[51] Like Nietzsche also, Kennedy both disconnects himself from *and* associates himself with "the masses," using multiple instances of irony and the form of the diatribe—albeit often softened with mock deference. Kennedy reflects on his ironic and satirical writing style in the final passage of his book when he says: "I often say hard things against the world, but even I must admit that it has a sense of humour. Its humour is a humour that has a bite in it, but better this humour than none at all."[52]

This chapter will conclude by reproducing just a few of Kennedy's comments on a range of topics covered in *A Tramp's Philosophy*.

On Education

> It pains me to say what I am going to say, for I revere the race of beings to whom I have the honour of belonging with the strongest and most powerful kind of reverence. But a fact is a fact. And the fact is that men get more stupid as they grow older. The human being starts with a good bright mind. As everyone knows, children are famous for their straight and apt and acute way of viewing things. But the child's mind is soon, alas! dulled by the process that is called education. Schools and colleges and other brain-benumbing institutions kill the mother-wit that the human began with.[53]
>
> When I say masses, I also include those who have suffered the disadvantage of having received an expensive education. In fact, this select portion of the masses is composed of bigger fools than usual. And if they had to earn their living without favour, they would be nowhere. Public schools and colleges are essentially brain-chloroforming institutions. Of course we get our rulers from them. Of course.[54]

Concerning Art and Artists

> I fear that the professional art critic is as other professional critics. He is an authoritative, exacting person, who can do nothing, and who feels that he is dowered with a divine right to tell the earth all about something just because he knows nothing about this something.[55]
>
> I like artists, for, taking them by and large, they are the nicest of

fellows. But I wish they had more sense of humour. I wish they could see that the grass would still grow even if they stopped producing masterpieces. ... It is a merry and comic world, my good artist lads. A world where it doesn't do to get too much vexed. Especially when one has so soft and easy a time as we artists.[56]

From the chapter titled "Cynicisms"

In the old, ancient, moss-covered days he [ancient man] had a distaste for expert advice regarding the problems that confronted him. ... It wasn't so easy in those good old ancient times to slap a king or an emperor on the back—if I may use so daring a metaphor—and tell him a thing or two about running his show. ... The old ancient mossy days were sorry days for the problem-solvers. But now happily all this is over. The world brims with exact advice about everything. If you are an emperor, and things don't go like clockwork, all you have to do is peruse the writings of some noble and thoughtful person, and you will receive tips of the most invaluable character.[57]

On Civilization and Human Nature

No social system or state can be really worth anything where the paramount aim is not to allow the individual to develop to the fullest, both mentally and physically. And this aim has never been the aim of any civilised state. ... The aim of all civilised states has been to keep the masses in subjugation for the benefit of cliques. And this is as true of republics as it is of autocracies. ... The money clique that rules America is more oppressive than is the Grand Ducal clique of Russia. It has a far worse effect on the American character.[58]

I must say that it makes me tired when I think of the way that the world has been insulted, and is still being insulted, by irresponsible ruffians who are called men of genius. ... Men of genius ought to be locked up. ... The truth of the matter is that human nature is now as it was in the days when it lived in the cave. It has exactly the same ideas.[59]

On Politics

And so, after the election is over, you sit down and rest easy ... A glow of satisfied pride steals through you. You are glad and thankful that you have done your poor suffering country a bit of good. ... For years things have not gone well with England. The traitors who were so long in power had done their deliberate best to ruin the country! ... The main point is that you have now put into Parliament a powerful and virile man who by the force of his personality will make himself felt as a power for good. ... you dream ... How this lion of debate will thunder forth if anything goes wrong ... hear the swelling tones of his resonant and reaching voice ... see his eyes flash, as his opponent wilts and withers before him. The bewigged Speaker listens to him with awed respect. Sleepy members shake themselves from their sleepiness as he grandly denounces Wrong and sets up on its pedestal, Right. His wit pierces as a sword. By the force of himself and his eloquence he sets things going as they ought to...

A beautiful dream, but alas, alas, only a dream.[60]

On Crime, the Law and Killing

There are many human acts, specified upon the statute-books of the world as crimes, about which there is a difference of opinion as to whether they are crimes or not. There are many human acts that at times are crimes and that at other times are not crimes. Killing is not a crime in times of war. Neither is theft.[61]

Of course, they don't go to war themselves. It would be too common place and too vulgar a thing for them to get in the firing line themselves. They might get shot—and then how would the people whom they govern get on? What a dreadful calamity it would be if the Prime Minister of a country, or a foreign minister, or any other sort of governing official, were to be killed in a war they had created. ... Such an awful thing would never do. ... They have the patriotic thoughtfulness to see to it that they keep well out of harm's reach.[62]

On Capitalism and the Economy

This foolish proceeding cannot, of course, last. Man may be many things, but he is not by nature an idiot. Nations will repudiate these absurd things that are called national debts. Indeed, nations will have to do it whether they like it or not, for the strain that it puts upon Labour to satisfy these unjust calls will in the end be too much. Nations will become bankrupt. In fact it only requires one to become bankrupt for the rest to follow.[63]

Concerning Work and Tramps

They [animals] are not skilled in book philosophy, but they have brains enough to know that the sun was given to them to bask in, and that the world generally is not half such a bad place if you will only take it as it is and not be forever trying to displace things and trying to get hold of knowledge that in the end means less than nothing.... Of course they have not the intelligence to work, you say. True they have not. And I might add that they are not particularly ambitious to possess such intelligence.[64]

Security is at best a cowardly word. I know men who are "secure." I know men who have plenty of money. And, taking it all round, they don't get as much out of life as those who live from hand to mouth.... The fine glamour of the unexpected! It shines into the life of the tramp. As he goes along he wonders what will turn up next. He is faced with the mystery of the changing, inscrutable face of life. Life holds for him an interest that it holds for no one else.[65]

I must dispel here an illusion that some people have to the effect that the tramp is a danger to the State. Never was their illusion more baseless. The tramp is too much of a philosopher to be a revolutionist.[66]

He [the tramp] knows that trouble will come to this civilisation, but not from men like him. It will come from the idiot slaves whose ideal is to be as well off as their masters.... He is the only honest shirker of work in the world. He is the pioneer of a finer and calmer life. He wanders along, a real philosopher.[67]

A Final Word

> The longer I live the more I am inclined to doubt the all-magic of the human mind. Believe me when I assure you that the other animals know a thing or two that we don't know. They neither write books nor build motor-cars, nor do they make foolish guesses about the planetary system. But they know enough to let one and other alone as much as possible—a thing that we with all our alleged wisdom have yet to learn. And they know things that neither you nor I nor any other man know anything about. They are wise enough to know that to live is in itself the highest and most absolute thing of all. They are wise enough to know that if they do this they do everything.[68]

ENDNOTES

1 *New York Times*, Dec. 10, 1930
2 *The Times* (London), Dec. 10, 1930
3 Kennedy, Bart. *A Man Adrift*, Chicago: Herbert S. Stone & Company, 1900, p. 2
4 Ibid., p. 7
5 Ibid., pp. 27–31
6 Ibid., p. 43
7 Ibid., pp. 62–63
8 Ibid., pp. 75–76
9 Ibid., pp. 85–86
10 Ibid., p. 87
11 Ibid., p. 101
12 Ibid., pp. 108–109
13 Ibid., p. 126
14 Ibid., p. 127
15 Ibid., pp. 130–131
16 Ibid., pp.133–134
17 Ibid., p. 137
18 Ibid., p. 138. For further reading on the theme of Jesus as a tramp, see Thomas Manning Page's discussion on this subject.
19 Ibid., p. 144
20 Ibid., pp. 159–160
21 Ibid., pp. 160–161
22 Ibid., p. 162
23 Ibid., pp. 162–164
24 Ibid., pp. 200–201
25 Ibid., p. 219
26 Ibid., p. 220

27 Cutler, Ian. *Jim Christy: A Vagabond Life*, Port Townsend, WA: Feral House, 2019

28 Ibid., p. 241

29 Ibid., p. 243

30 Ibid., p. 287

31 Ibid., pp. 288–289

32 Ibid., pp. 291–292. The art of begging is described in detail in other chapters and so will not be repeated here.

33 *A Man Adrift*, op. cit., p. 300

34 Ibid., pp. 330–331

35 Kennedy, Bart. "In a Tramp Camp," in *Wide World Magazine*, Vol. IX, London: George Newnes Company, May to October 1902, p. 119

36 Ibid., pp. 119–120

37 Kennedy, Bart. *A Sailor Tramp*, London: George Newnes Ltd., 1902, p. 175

38 Ibid., p. 129

39 Ibid., pp. 25–26

40 Ibid., p. 143

41 Ibid., pp. 145–147

42 Ibid., p. 147

43 Ibid., p. 114

44 Ibid., p. 106–107

45 Ibid., p. 111

46 Kennedy, Bart. *A Tramp in Spain*, London: George Newnes Ltd., 1904, pp. 4–5

47 Ibid., p. 48

48 Ibid., p. 131

49 Ibid., pp. 143–144

50 Ibid., p. 255

51 Kennedy, Bart. *A Tramp's Philosophy*, London: John Long, 1908, p. 226

52 Ibid, p. 317

53 Ibid., pp. 255–256

54 Ibid., p. 245

55 Ibid., p. 72

56 Ibid., pp. 81–85

57 Ibid., pp. 231–232

58 Ibid., p. 249

59 Ibid., p. 45

60 Ibid., pp. 167–169

61 Ibid., p. 33

62 Ibid., pp. 175–176

63 Ibid., p. 306

64 Ibid., p. 315

65 Ibid., pp. 13–14

66 Ibid., p. 11

67 Ibid., p. 16

68 Ibid., pp. 315–316

Trader Horn

(1861–1931)

My travels are not yet over. I have been travelling since—well, since I can remember. The wanderlust is highly developed in some people; so is it in me. I suppose I shall just go on wandering until I go to Mars and join the wanderers and the angels there![1]

Trader Horn, *Harold the Webbed*

Preamble

Trader Horn, alias Zambesi Jack, and several other monikers, was born Alfred Aloysius (Wish) Smith in Preston, Lancashire, England on June 21 (Saint Aloysius' day in the calendar of Catholic saints), 1861. It was his editor and literary collaborator who chose the pen name Horn, allegedly to protect the reputation of his family. In the same way, Horn disguised the names of many of the "characters" in his books, often with the same character being given several different names, although perhaps this was as much from Horn's own confusion as any deliberate attempt to confuse his readers.

Horn does not quite fit the mold of the other tramp writers featured in this book. His early years were as an adventurer rather than a tramp, having chosen employment as his primary existence over vagabondage, even if such employment included piracy, hostage-taking and highway robbery—as well as a short spell as a police officer. In contrast to many of the others featured here, Horn's tramping—as well as paid vagabondage—occupied his later adulthood, including beating trains in America. Had he not been "discovered" in his sixties by the novelist Ethelreda Lewis, he would likely have starved to death a tramp in a Johannesburg dosshouse. Most of the content of this chapter is drawn from Horn's three published works:

Trader Horn: A Young Man's Outstanding Adventures in Equatorial Africa (1927)
Harold the Webbed or The Young Vykings (1928)
Trader Horn in Madagascar: The Waters of Africa (1929)

In order to try to establish a more complete chronicle of Horn's life and adventures, a debt is owed to Tim Couzens for his exceptional and comprehensive piece of detective work, *Tramp Royal: The True Story of Trader Horn*. Couzens retraced many of Horn's steps in search of his remarkable story, speaking to descendants of Horn as well as getting access to many original letters and documents that reveal information not deducible from the enigma that is Horn's published works.

Trader Horn would yet have been just another unknown tramp and adventurer had he not arrived, in the spring of 1925 at the age of 64 (although looking and claiming to be considerably older), peddling handmade kitchen implements, at number 26 Loch Avenue in the Johannesburg suburb of Parktown. At first, the novelist Ethelreda Lewis was not sure what to make of her uninvited visitor, but a natural curiosity, combined with a shared interest in Viking history, soon turned into a remarkable literary partnership that within only two years would make Trader Horn an international celebrity. As with fellow tramp writer W.H. Davies, who received the patronage of George Bernard Shaw for his first book, Horn's success was partly attributable to the attention and a foreword for his first book from the (later Nobel Prize-winning) novelist John Galsworthy.

At first Lewis was perplexed by Horn's repetitious and digressive ramblings, primarily of his adventures in what is now Gabon in former French Equatorial Africa. Horn was only 17 years old when he signed up as a rubber and ivory trader with the company Hatton and Cookson, yet by the time he left Gabon only four years later he was, in addition to being a formidable trader, also an accomplished sailor, navigator, diplomat and military strategist. The disjointed accounts of these early adventures, as told to Lewis in their first few meetings, are centered around the "Ogowe" (Ogooué) river and include repeated references to friendships with cannibals and a white goddess, not to mention encounters with gorillas, elephants and French colonialists, the latter of whom Horn clearly despised.

Horn's Writing Process

It took many repeated weekly visits for Lewis to start making sense of the old man's rambling anecdotes and nearly two years to collect from Horn all of the material necessary for the three volumes published, plus other unpublished material. But it is the manner in which Lewis collected Horn's stories, and the form in which they appear in print that make this literary partnership remarkable and unique. Lewis quickly realized that the most productive way of unlocking Horn's memory and collecting his stories was to let him write down his own stories on paper (which he delighted in doing in his lodgings). He would then spend his weekly visits to her home discussing his week's work, at the same time engaging in lengthy conversations. These "conversations" (presented in the trilogy as a monologue with Lewis' voice excluded) were collected by Lewis in notebooks while her husband Joseph, a civil servant and doctor of science, typed up Horn's handwritten tales, faithfully including his idiosyncratic spelling, punctuation, grammar and misapplied capital letters.

The laboriously recorded conversations are printed in the published editions of Horn's books following each chapter of the primary text. The conversations reveal Horn's reflections on the writing process itself, interspersed with digressive and repeated ramblings concerning his adventures and contemplations on life. Many will find this the most fascinating element of Horn's writings. In some ways, it seems, Lewis encouraged Horn's aspirations as a writer of fiction the better to extract from him as much of his personal thoughts as she was able in the time available. As she confirmed, she did not write the book for the adventure it contained, but for "an old man's rich and sane philosophy of life ... his grand feeling for Nature and his love of the African native."[2]

Lewis well understood that Horn's writing was not only the product of his imagination, it also *activated* his imagination. In the second two volumes of the Trader Horn trilogy, the conversations often exceed the prose written in Horn's own hand which Lewis herself dismisses as "those banal, anxious, old man's attempts in the Victorian style." Remarkably—given Lewis' literary ambitions on Horn's behalf, not to mention the obsession publishers have for amelioration—both Lewis and the publishers left all of Horn's considerable spelling and grammatical mistakes unedited, adding to the charm and authenticity of the work. As for the conversations, Horn expressed surprise and admiration when encountering these passages following publication of the books. Caught up in his fantastic imagination, at times Horn seems blissfully unaware that his own life story is more remarkable than that of his "fictions," while at others he needs little encouragement to boast about his personal achievements. Lewis describes Horn's writing as follows:

> Mr. Horn has an enviable gift of speaking as if his characters really existed. The line between truth and fiction is but a shadow line with him. He casts the net of fiction over truth and of truth over fiction, enmeshing the listener by the same dexterous throw.[3]

If Horn has the gift of speaking as though his characters existed, it is because many of them *did* exist. Often modest in his autobiographical ramblings, there is, paradoxically, more truth in much of what he relates than he has been given credit for, or gives himself credit for, including facts that were only verified long after his works were published. The novelist William McFee wrote in his foreword to *Harold the Webbed*, "it is the author's complete obliviousness of all modern literary technique which evokes in us an almost breathless fascination."[4] In fact, the Trader Horn books *were* targets of criticism in their day, in spite of high sales, and are still sadly overlooked today. Horn and Lewis were even accused of being charlatans and faking the whole project. That Horn's work was not taken more seriously by the literary establishment was not helped by the melodramatic Hollywood movie made of his first book, ensuring his place as a curiosity rather than a serious writer. But Horn had his admirers as well as his critics, and the following passage from McFee's foreword, both validates Horn's writing style and impugns those who cried hoax:

> When reading, our pleasure is derived in the first place from seeing the story-telling faculty, reduced to its simplest components, operating in full view of the reader. ... Neither Dickens nor Dostoevsky ever cut so cleanly or so deep to the very quick of the poverty problem as does Mr. Horn ... we who write have to admit that Mr. Horn has the knack of stating our problems with the horrifying clarity of a precocious child.[5]

McFee's last observation corresponds with Nietzsche's maxim that there is something the child sees and hears that others do not, and that this something is the most important thing of all. As Horn tells Lewis in the conversations from *Harold the Webbed*, "If I am childish it's surely pleasurable to be a child in my own portion of earth, where you could walk blindfold." And so, perhaps it is high time that Horn's contribution to literature was reassessed. Not that we should concern ourselves on Horn's behalf—the prosperity he achieved in old age as a result of his celebrity status probably gave him far more pleasure than acceptance in literary circles would have done. Horn continues an honorable tradition of storytelling from the Vikings on down (of whom he claimed to be a direct descendent), a tradition that has no truck with facts, and, as in Horn's case, weaves myth and legend into the story of one's own life. He deliberately obscures the names of people and places, and as for dates he has nothing but contempt: "I've never burdened me memory with dates. A brain's given you for thoughts, not dates."[6]

> Dates? ... Excuse me sounding impatient, but I'd say my books are built on facts, not dates. ... When you're here there and everywhere for seventy years you can't be as neat as a lawyer's ledger. A man's got to choose between being a bit o' nature and being chained to the office calendar.[7]

Horn's first book, *Trader Horn*, was mainly autobiography embellished with fiction. His last book, *The Waters of Africa*, was fiction embellished with fact. *Harold the Webbed* was Horn's attempt at writing a purely fictional adventure story. Even so, some of the most implausible of Horn's tales are rooted in fact and some of his most innocent assertions are fiction—such is the joy and roguishness of this entire literary project. As Horn says in his third volume: "Beauty of fiction is you can suppress anything that's not convenient."[8] This includes even fictionalizing biographical information that readers normally take for granted. Published in 1928, the subtitle of *Harold the Webbed* reads: "*... written by ALFRED ALOYSIUS HORN at the age of seventy-three, and the life with such of his philosophy as is the gift of age and experience, taken down and here edited by ETHELREDA LEWIS*." Horn was in fact aged 67, not 73, when the book was published.

Harold the Webbed

Before moving on to discuss Horn's life and adventures as recorded in his other two volumes, it is worth briefly discussing the second book in the Trader Horn trilogy, if only for some of the interesting biographical references it contains. The "conversations" excluded, *Harold the Webbed* is a fantasy adventure of the 16-year-old son of a Viking chief from the Faroe Islands who is born with webbed hands and feet—a feature considered to bring good luck. The story opens with Harold participating in games and sports, including water sports—in which he naturally excels—all washed down with copious amounts of beer served up in horns. When his father, with a fleet of Viking ships, sets out to challenge Julius Caesar who has just landed on the southern shores of Britain, Harold and a group of his friends give their mothers the slip and set off in their own ship with Harold in command. Interestingly, Horn would have been a similar age to Harold when he first embarked on his own adventures. After a series of escapades, and much drinking and pillaging, the youthful sailors meet up with Caesar, whom they impress with their skills at archery and set off homewards laden with treasures acquired on the way. In this fictional boy's adventure tale, Horn mixes history and legend from different historical periods. Of particular interest in *Harold* is Horn's demonstration of his own knowledge of seamanship and navigation, something he displayed in his first volume with his use of Viking battle tactics in his nautical encounters with cannibals on the Ogowe River.

Couzens recounts a conversation between Lewis and the Oxford historian Winifred Holtby, in which the latter expressed some amazement at reading Lewis' notes of Horn's Viking stories, passed down to him orally through generations and not known to her from any books written of the period:

> "You may be the very first person to set down in writing some of these queer bits about Vikings. That bit about the Viking wife having always to sleep with the bowstring round her waist next to her naked skin so that it would be supple from the natural oils of the skin and ready for use at any moment. This may be recorded somewhere but I have never seen it."[9]

Lewis reports Holtby's further reactions to the coincidence of her (Lewis') meeting with Horn in her introduction to *Harold* when Holtby remarked, "There's something supernatural in an old man with a viking complex coming to your doorstep. Why should he come and babble of vikings to you of all people?"[10]

Trader Horn's School Days

Horn was enrolled at St. Edward's College, Liverpool, at the age of 11, which according to Couzens, "had buccaneering origins of which Aloysius could only have approved." In the conversations from *Harold the Webbed*, Horn described sailing as being in his veins:

> My great-uncle Bill, him that had landed in Jamaica and was the last of the privateers, and my grandfather John Horn, started the firm Hamlin, Horn and Hamlin. Know it? Aye, the world knows it. All, me uncles

> and cousins I've ever had are in it, same as they were in the Alabama syndicate. My uncle Richard was killed in the fight off Galveston.[11]

There are other references to pirate relatives throughout Horn's conversations with Lewis, but as they match up at best very loosely, we must either question Horn's veracity or memory of his actual ancestry, or embrace them as fantasy:

> There was me greatuncle Dick that was the last of the buccaneers and had a house in M— Road, Hyde Park. Property in Savannah [Georgia, USA]. ... And there was me greatuncle Horn. Stone blind. Always siting in a little chair by the fire. ... An old-style viking, me greatuncle Ralph. He asked his father for two ships to go privateering, but his father said no, one'd be enough if properly rigged for warfare.[12]

A more significant influence on Horn was the school's cosmopolitan milieu: "I believe the old idea of mixing the British youngster with his brothers of every clime was to make him cosmopolitan, and naturally we learned each other's language."[13] St. Edward's took in the sons of fee-paying politicians, businessmen and royalty from around the globe, including a figure that was to become a long-term friend of Horn's and semi-fictional character in his writing, "Little Peru, son of the Peruvian President." That Horn also describes Peru's father as: 'the son of an Englishman who had wandered to Peru and married an Inca chief's daughter and become the owner of a famous silver mine,'[14] seems to confirm that at least part of Little Peru's heritage must be fictitious, if not the entire character. At any rate, Horn claims to have received regular correspondence and gifts from Little Peru throughout his time in Equatorial West Africa, and Peru dramatically appears in the final scenes of Horn's first volume. Following publication of his writing, one of Horn's fellow pupils from St. Edward's noted that Horn's friends would have recognized in his books the enthralling stories he told them in school, and his pleasure that Horn had realized the dreams of his youth. The school friend had no doubt that Horn was more than capable of achieving his adventures, "even the wildest he has seen and lived."[15]

Couzens writes that Horn was expelled from St. Edward's College in 1878 at the age of 16, for being an untamed and troublesome boy "always on the roof," and that the principal, Dr. John Fisher, remarked, "I'm sorry for the Smiths, that lad's so wild."[16] But Couzens also acknowledges that Horn's behavior was the result of a certain malady (one common to all the tramps in this book) when he quotes from *Harold the Webbed*, that like Harold, Horn was "sick at heart and longed to see the world." Couzens further observes that, unlike Horn's two brothers who were trained for the priesthood, Horn took after his father and grandfather in his wildness, responding to his father when Smith senior expressed a wish to see him settled down: 'Settled down? ... You've bred me and you've bred me wild. Now you talk of settling down. 'Tis yourself opened the cage before I was born, and you'll not keep me in it now.'[17]

Just turned 17, and with the consent of his parents, Horn signed an apprenticeship with the Liverpool firm Hatton and Cookson to work for that company in equatorial West Africa's ivory and rubber trade at an annual starting salary of 40 pounds plus free board and passage on the SS *Angola*.

Trader Horn in Africa

Before commencing Horn's first African adventure, it would be useful to provide a potted history of the Congo basin, not least because of the minute part that Horn was to play in it—being a friend of Pierre de Brazza and later saving the life of Cecil Rhodes. De Brazza was to share information with Horn that he denied Henry Morton Stanley as part of his bid to colonize the area north of the Congo River for the French.

Horn's arrival in Africa at the end of 1878 coincided with the start of an international scramble for influence and power in one of the last unmapped regions of the world, one that promised considerable economic benefits from huge reserves of unexploited resources. The principal protagonists were the Portuguese, Belgians, French, Dutch, Germans and British. Stanley's second Congo expedition started the same year as Horn's arrival, this time as envoy of King Léopold II of Belgium. Léopold had set up the Brussels Conference in 1876 to enlist European cooperation in opening up the Congo Basin for trade and "civilizing" its population. But Léopold's plans were a cover for his personal ambitions for power in the region that, once exposed, initiated a frenetic land grab between the interested parties. The French dispatched the explorer Pierre de Brazza and in 1881 claimed what is now the Republic of the Congo, Gabon and the Central African Republic, at the same time challenging the Spanish over the borders of Equatorial Guinea. In 1884 the Belgians claimed the Congo Free State (now Democratic Republic of the Congo), and the Germans took over the Cameroons. The Portuguese had, of course, already been firmly established in Angola for two hundred years. Symbolically, Brazzaville was established (initially as a garrison) on the opposite bank of the Congo River from Léopoldville (founded as a trading post by Stanley in 1881—present-day Kinshasa) to prevent any further incursions from the Belgians. The two cities on opposite banks of the Congo River continue as the capitals of the two independent Congo states today, making the initial meeting between their respective founders, Stanley and de Brazza, much more significant than the legendary meeting between Stanley and Livingstone. To set the scene for Horn's own adventures, in spite of the territorial claims by the French and Belgians, throughout this whole period, British, German and Portuguese traders continued their profitable enterprises both along the coast and up Gabon's seven-hundred-mile Ogowe River (first explored by de Brazza between 1874 and 1878).

The story of Horn and de Brazza comes later, for now we must return to Horn as the new recruit of Hatton and Cookson. Having completed the first year of his apprenticeship at the end of 1879, it was into the Ogowe River that Horn sailed on the heavily armed old paddle steamer the *Pioneer* (previously owned by Livingstone) and the adventures that would be the subject of his first book began. At the time of Horn's introduction to the Ogowe, Portuguese and native slave traders, some of the latter also involved in piracy, were still very active in the region (slavery in Brazil did not end until 1888, and in the Congo Basin until 1890). It was into this hostile environment that Horn would carve out his new career as a trader, supported and encouraged by his mentor, the company's agent, a Mr. Carlisle, based further north on the Cameroon coast. Carlisle had told Horn that he was the youngest trader on the coast, that his chances of success in life were far beyond what Horn could imagine, and that he would personally make sure Horn had "every opportunity for forging ahead."

The secret of Horn's success was a combination of his skills as a sailor and navigator, his courage in the face of adversity, and, most importantly, the sophistication of a natural diplomat based on an understanding and respect for the local inhabitants: "Always had that *modus operandi* about me that I could follow the edicts of my surroundings."[18] This ability to absorb alien cultures and embrace their way of living marked Horn out from most of the other colonialists he came into contact with. Although retaining some romantic notions about the country of his birth, Horn shared the general attributes of the true tramp and cosmopolite: those who carry their home with them comfortably adapt to whatever natural environment they find themselves in, but most importantly, are able to adopt the customs of any culture that suits their purpose. In Horn's case, this included several occasions where he availed himself of the services of witch-doctors (including for gunshot and spear wounds) rather than Western medicine, a fact that also probably explains how Horn survived the often perilous environment of equatorial West Africa (The White Man's Grave) when so many of his contemporaries did not.

The Ogowe River

It would be helpful here to provide a summary of the terrain Horn had now entered in his own words from Chapter 1 of his first book:

> The Ogowe River empties into the Atlantic Ocean one day's sail south of the equator, and from this river came the most valuable cargoes of ivory, as much as 50,000 pounds weight being shipped in one season.

> The elephants are mostly hunted by the M'pangwes, Fans, and Ashiwa who speak the same language. These tribes inhabit the North bank of the Ogowe river nearly to its source and are all cannibals. I lived among them for many years, but for safety sandbanks and islands were the only safe camping grounds. Boys were supplied by the firm I represented ... and we were all well supplied with rifles ... Always kept handy in case of surprise attack, and we were frequently called on to defend ourselves...[19]

Horn describes many friendships he had with these people, to some of whom he also owed his life. But, as we shall see, Horn also *took* lives. Life was certainly cheaper on the Ogowe river and its tributaries than his Catholic upbringing in Lancashire had prepared him for. He describes, for instance, his shock at witnessing for the first time the practice of throwing an old woman, who had outlived her usefulness, into the rapids to be drowned or eaten by crocodiles: "they'd gather a few friends together and chuck somebody's old mother or granny into the river, at an age when in Lancashire she'd be just right for a shawl and a good cup o' tea."[20] But Horn soon became used to the ways of the people with whom he now lived and was completely captivated with the exoticism of the natural environment around him. Below is part of a description of Horn's first visit to Lake Azingo on one of the Ogowe's many tributaries, a lake Horn was to describe as the most beautiful of all the lakes he had seen in the world:

> The creek leading to the lake is arched over by vines, from which hang all kinds of vegetation which was simply crowded with flowers of all kinds of shape and hue. As the trees on both banks were high, there was lots of space between this natural archway and the water and terra firma, which was one mat of varied coloured vegetation. Birds of all descriptions flitted to and fro. Now the beautiful crested crane would rise and fly away and kingfishers of all kinds disturbed would follow them. The most beautiful bird in the world, the pippin, which is one mass of green and gold, finds a home here. ... As we neared the mouth of this enchanted waterway ... I saw three gorillas, one big fellow and two smaller ones.[21]

Horn's first trip up the Ogowe in the *Pioneer* did not immediately reveal the region's natural beauty. The first habitable spot with any land protruding above the mangrove swamps was 30 miles upriver. The village of Angala marked the beginning of the territory of the Nkomi people, and a further 25 miles upriver was the town of Chief Njagu. Fifteen miles further on again was the town of Ngombe, where Njagu's brother Isagi was chief. This same Chief Isagi plays a significant part in Horn's later adventures. Further on again Horn describes a fork in the river, the northern route going to Lake Azingo, described above, which joins the main southern fork again near the present-day city of Lambaréné. At the time Horn arrived, this confluence of the rivers some 130 miles from the sea included Lambaréné Island, a German trading company run by a Herr Schiff, the Kangwe Mission built and run by the Protestant missionary Robert Hamill Nassau, and Hatton and Cookson's own factory run by their agent, a dour Scot named Thomas Sinclair.

All of these characters are important to Horn's first volume, but Robert Nassau's contribution was his diary in an obscure book named *My Ogowe* which Couzens would eventually track down. The missionary's testimony provided valuable verification of much of Horn's story, something that Lewis herself had never succeeded in doing. This new evidence even included a description of the trading post that Horn had tried to establish further up river on the island he called Isange: "Three miles beyond Njoli was Assange Island, where a white man, Smith [Horn], had attempted to locate; but the lower tribes compelled him to leave."[22]

Trader Horn and the White Goddess

The first task Horn was given in his new job was to survey the Ogowe for a hundred miles further upriver, but not until he had taken soundings near the river's mouth to establish the safest channels for vessels to navigate. It was while engaged with this work that the most fanciful part of Horn's tale emerges, that part of Horn's early adventures central to the later Hollywood movie of the book, below as abbreviated as possible without compromising Horn's literary embroidery. Horn was invited by Chief Isagi to visit his temple and be initiated into a ceremony Horn calls the Egbo:

> On entering the temple, which had an ornamentation of human skulls … I was confronted by a row of masked objects hideous to behold. I was then seated bareheaded on a small seat composed of leopard skins. There were two objects the chief called my attention to, one was a square piece of crystal, the other was peg-top shaped and pointed at one end. He told me to place my hand on these objects, and that one represented fire (the red one) and the other water. … I came to the conclusion it was a ruby of great value. After this there was a great vociferation from the building, supposed to come from the spirits behind. … Now everything in the temple began to sparkle and placing his hand on my head, which I bowed low, he announced in a loud voice the entrance of Izaga. … The chief then ordered me to stand up and approach the centre mask. … There stood the God that Never Dies, the most beautiful white woman I had ever seen. Her eyes were

> wide and had a kind of affectionate look. Although I thought there was pity in them they had a magnetic effect on me.... Her head was auburn and was plaited in circles and pressed onto her temples. Two ringlets ornamented with gold and green tassels fell down on each side of her shoulders, whilst high up on her forehead the hair formed a diamond-shaped coronet. A short leopard-skin kilt ornamented with snakeskin and dainty fur sandals with black straps formed the rest of the dress of this Izaga.[23]

Extravagant as this tale at first appears, it is grounded in a surprising degree of fact. Both the skull-house and the religious rites of Egbo are described independently by Robert Nassau; and a raid on the same temple led by Nassau's stand-in, an ex-soldier named Dr. Bacheler, to rescue a convert to the mission chained to a post in the village (for revealing the secrets of their society to the missionary), adds further credence to Horn's stories. The raid and subsequent freeing of the Christian convert can be dated exactly to November 26, 1879,[24] and the chain that came with the victim was subsequently displayed in the Mission's museum at 156 Fifth Avenue, New York. Lewis was entirely convinced that Horn had been initiated into the Egbo, and Horn himself, who made repeated visits to the Joss House, gives credit to his initiation into that society for saving his life on several occasions. Horn had first become aware of the skull-house after witnessing a canoe taking a young woman to her execution there, after being accused of bewitching Chief Isagi.

Though the description of a white goddess is almost certainly a fictional creation to tease and entice his future readers, even this character may be based on someone known to Horn. As is the multilayered approach to his writing, the goddess (fictional or factual) is given several aliases to obscure her identity. Horn uses a host of different names for the goddess of the Joss House, such as Lola D—, but she is most frequently referred to as Nina T—. Horn's explanation to Lewis for why he avoids providing Nina's true identity was, "if I have to gather together all that I know of Nina T— and her father into a ponderous mass all in one chapter ... it would sure be an indigestible result."[25] Later Horn suggests to Lewis how timely the publication of such a story would be: "There's been nothing novel lately since Rider Haggard. One of the biggest mythologizers in the world, that feller. But mine'll be facts. You can weave a lot out of that."[26]

The reference to Rider Haggard is telling. Haggard's story *She*, which parallels Horn's tale of a white goddess in the African jungle, was published some 10 years after Horn's alleged adventure with Nina T— and so could easily have colored Horn's artistry, even his recollections of actual events. Horn was also very aware of the Franco-American explorer Paul du Chaillu's research, both on the Congo Basin and Horn's other obsession, Vikings. Du Chaillu provides his own description of female goddesses in the region. Who knows that Horn did not believe his own fantasies so long after the event? This makes Horn's assertion that his own story is based, in part at least, on fact, all the more intriguing. Fact or fiction, one has to admire the way Horn throws in credible clues to tease his reader.

We are told eventually that Nina T—'s father had a plantation on the coast near the mouth of the Ogowe. On his death he freed all his slaves who married each other and became what Horn describes as "a peaceful colony of natives." Horn claims that the chief of this colony showed him a mother-of-pearl inlaid casket which Horn later acquired from the chief for four bottles of rum. It contained two faded photographs, one being T— himself, "and the other was a lady that might be his mother."[27] The box also contained a letter from T—'s mother begging him to come home but Horn adds, "the content of this letter I shall never divulge for conscience sake." Horn does reveal that T—'s family "held a prominent place amongst the British aristocracy," mischievously adding several pages later that "there'll be great curiosity amongst the English aristocracy to know who George T— was."[28] T—'s marriage certificate identified that he married his wife (described by Horn as an octoroon) on Prince's Island (presumably the one in the Gulf of Guinea, not the one off the coast of Istanbul), noting that Nina was T—'s only heir, her brother having been killed with a party of nomads by a British patrol on the Lake Chad Road in northern Nigeria (a fact Horn claims to have later verified). Horn further claims that after T—'s death, his widow married a local witch-doctor, a connection that fits neatly into the narrative of the young Nina ending up (goddess or servant) working in the skull-house. The casket also contained a copybook indicating that T— had taught his daughter to write. "This I found later was correct, as far as reading went, so that I could always smuggle in a short note to the goddess when I used to visit the temple to make a wish."[29]

The chief also pointed out George T—'s burial place on a small island off the coast, but on visiting the site, Horn claims that the headstone was broken and the grave opened. Horn then says he moved T—'s remains, minus his missing skull, to the center of the island so as not to be washed into the sea. One legacy of this tale within a tale is that others, including Couzens, have continued searching for clues that might lead to the identity of, if not the goddess herself, the woman who inspired her, and the identity also of Little Peru (Horn was at school with two brothers, William and David Lewis from Callão, Peru) who at the end of Horn's first book is married to Nina by Captain King of the *Ruby Queen*. The existence of both Captain King and the *Ruby Queen* have been verified as fact. And just to confuse things further, Horn claims that the captain of the *Angola*, a Charlie Thompson from Birkenhead, was able to later verify what happened to Peru and his wife as they made regular trips to Liverpool. Couzens tells us that Horn eventually confided to Lewis that Nina's real name was Nina "Travers,"[30] and Couzens unearthed from Nassau's diary that a trader called Travis (a close similarity to Travers) had arrived on the Ogowe as an assistant of Sinclair around April 1875, some three years before Horn himself arrived. Further indications are that Travis was moved once more to Hatton and Cookson's factory at Fernan

Vaz on the coastal delta, something that could also explain Horn's invention of T—'s island grave. The trail goes dead in Nassau's diary but is picked up again in the diary of a Reverend William Walker. Walker discusses, as Horn does also, the habit some expatriates had of taking native wives, and Couzens closes the speculation about the identity of Nina T— with a diary entry from Walker dated May 26, 1882: "Mr Travis from Fernan Vaz going home on 'Angola'. Mr T. father of Mary yi Ngwange. But he has made no communication with the Mission. Some of these foreigners are oblivious of their connection with the natives."[31]

Perhaps the abandoned Mary explains the identity of Nina, but here let us simply abandon further speculation and leave the final word to Couzens when he says, "the jury must hand down a verdict either way as Not Proven. We must suspend judgement and leave a little mystery surrounding Trader Horn."[32] And so now let us continue with the rest of Horn's adventures—real or imagined.

Battles with River Pirates

Horn's personal friendship with Isagi and Nina was not to protect the company's cargoes from attacks of piracy by this same tribe. On his way back up river, Horn was able to impress the ship's new captain with his skills both as a pilot and military leader when the *Pioneer* came under attack from 20 of Isagi's war canoes. The *Pioneer's* crew were able to drive Isagi's warriors off and escape upstream. The second part of Horn's mission was to explore the Ogowe's large tributary, the Ngounié, upstream from the company's factory to the Samba Falls and beyond. The principal trade of the Akele tribe of the region, named by Horn the "Okellys," was rubber, although they continued to capture and trade in slaves also. Later Horn would be involved in a battle between the "Okellys" (their chief Iwolo had been befriended by Horn) and another tribe he calls the "Oshebas." Horn describes how they were guarding the carcasses and ivory of a rogue elephant tracked and killed by the Okellys, when they found themselves under attack from the Oshebas in full war paint and armed with rifles, crossbows and spears. With the help of Horn and his own fighters, the attack was repelled and the meat and tusks brought safely to the Okellys' town.[33] It will be related later how Horn was to nearly lose his life in another battle with the Oshebas. Beyond the falls was the territory of the Ivilli people to whose king it was customary to pay a toll of one-sixth the value of goods being taken from the region, although Horn also won favors with the old man by supplying him with whiskey. It was at Samba Falls that Horn witnessed the drowning of the old woman.

Horn also makes much mention of the fact that on two of his trips up the Ngounié, he had as his passenger a young Presbyterian woman missionary with whom he provided, as was his style, the alias Miss Hasken. Miss Hasken caused a great deal of interest, for, as Horn admits, "They'd never seen a white woman. And what a sweet face that soul had!" On his second trip upriver with Miss Hasken, Horn acknowledges that he was permanently on his guard to protect his guest; his anxiety, he admits, being due to the fact that "There was nothing so suitable for voodoo as a white woman's body."[34] With the help of Nassua's journals, Couzens later identified the mystery woman as a Susan Dewsnap who died of a tropical fever at the age of 41 in Gabon. Horn was one of only two whites at her funeral in Baraka in central Gabon on August 22, 1881, and, Couzens informs us, her headstone can still be seen in the cemetery there today.[35]

Horn was by now a seasoned trader, diplomat and river pilot. He had surveyed further upriver than any previous trader, and also identified the key to controlling the waterways into the interior and dominating the ivory trade. His strategy was to build a new factory on the island of "Isange" (Asange) but he had underestimated his old foes, the Oshebas, who launched an attack on Horn's expedition. While paddling his canoe inshore to enjoy some breakfast, Horn says, "I was hit on the wrist from a spear thrown from ambush." Taken by surprise, Horn and several of his crew reached the bank and commenced firing. When two of the Oshebas attacked Horn he was able to shoot the first with his revolver, only just managing to thrust aside the gun of the second. As Horn jumped back to fire at the second of his attackers his trigger refused to move. He managed to save himself only by throwing his revolver, "hitting him squarely in the nose, which I badly split." But the man was up in an instant and, to cut a long story short, the pair ended up in the river in hand-to-hand combat. Horn only survived by being able to draw his hunting knife and killing his attacker, but ended the affray with two bad wounds. "The last one had gone through my left hand and was a bad shot wound and had nearly torn my thumb off."[36]

This incident would cement Horn's friendship with the "Okelly" chief Iwolo, grateful for again helping him defeat his enemies. Horn's hands were saved by Iwolo's medicine, for after putting nine stitches in the spear wound, Iwolo packed Horn's torn thumb several times daily with a white substance squeezed from the bodies of black crickets and wrapped in a cotton from the underbark of a tree. The wound closed up and healed over time but Horn would always have one thumb shorter than the other, which he would display as a trophy of this escapade.

Sometime after this incident, Horn claims he hatched a plan with Peru to manufacture a fake ruby which Horn would exchange for the real one in the Joss House. The whole thing was meticulously planned, and Horn met Nina and the witch-doctors and "made myself as congenial as I could." After many pleasantries Horn said that he wanted to make a wish at the Joss House and "was ready to pay any favours I received from their ceremony." In the middle of the same ceremony as described earlier, Horn carefully switched the fake ruby for the real one and following the ceremony they all retired to enjoy each other's company once more. Presents were exchanged, including dresses and shoes for

Nina that had been sent by Peru. "I do not think they ever noticed the change I had made in the rubies. If they did they never showed it at any time and were always glad to see me when I called."[37]

The original ruby, Horn says, was sent to Peru who had it valued at Tiffany's in New York and Hatton Garden in London. He does not say what price it sold for. Later Horn would hatch an even more daring plan, together with Peru, to rescue Nina from her bondage as a goddess, thereby ending his friendship with Chief Isagi for good. However, following this adventure, Horn navigated the *Pioneer* all the way to Samba Falls with a full and valuable cargo. The vessel's new skipper was at first unhappy to give Horn control of the ship as he looked too young for such a hazardous task, but eventually conceded on witnessing Horn's skills as a pilot and authority with the crew. They stopped off again at Chief Isogu's town but as the river level was falling fast, Horn had to explain to the old sea captain that things could get perilous. "Chief Isogu on one side and Rengogu on the other, both notorious river pirates ... a place we could not afford to stick for long with a valuable cargo. If they saw us well-stuck they would attack us in a minute."[38]

A little further upstream they did get stuck on a sandbank and started to prepare themselves for the inevitable attack. But a canoe came alongside with Nina, the headman, and a couple of witch-doctors:

> Nina spoke to me first. She was nattily dressed in the European togs I had given her and spoke in a firm voice which I understood. Come and see us at once and you will receive protection. If not, you will be attacked and surely die.[39]

But Horn chose his responsibilities to his employer over his personal safety and stayed to defend the ship. With his heavily armed crew and personal war general Iwolo, Horn first saw off Isogu's war canoes and shortly afterwards 20 of Rengogu's canoes from the opposite bank. Having been victorious in battle and with the river rising once more, Horn weighed anchor in Isogu's town to press home his authority, not by mentioning his victory in battle but by thanking the old chief for the power of his ceremonies that had granted Horn his wishes. Isogu confided that he had not agreed with the plan to attack the *Pioneer*, and their friendship was renewed (with the help of several cases of gin) even though Isogu's son had been killed in the attack.

Trader Horn's Meeting with Pierre de Brazza

Horn describes how Hatton and Cookson had instructed their traders on the Ogowe to prepare for a visit from Pierre de Brazza and do all in their power to help him. "Count de Brazza was a tall gentleman of what seemed middle age, although not thirty, and was a pensive man who never joked or smiled." De Brazza stayed with Horn until his large canoes arrived and the pair soon formed a great friendship. De Brazza promised to assist Horn in any way he could if Horn would help him establish his trading posts. "He also told me he intended to put up the French Flag at Stanley Pool, and there he made his town which is Brazzaville today."[40] In this way Horn became party to information which de Brazza had kept from Stanley. He watched de Brazza's fleet of canoes sail away on their mission to take the north bank of the Congo for the French, "which we all knew was made to cut off any chances of Leopold's annexing both sides of the Congo," all the while lamenting the fact that the British had shown so little interest in the region.

It is interesting to note that, in spite of his expressed patriotism for his native country and his intense dislike of French colonialists, it was with de Brazza, not Stanley, that Trader Horn would form a close friendship. Horn acknowledges that none of the traders in the region cared for Stanley, and that his interest in trying to meet up with Livingston "'Twas nothing but newspaper ambition. Always wanted the spotlight turned on him."[41]

Horn's Venture as an Independent Trader and Final River Battle

It was around this time also that Horn's relationship with his boss Sinclair started to show signs of tension. Horn had no respect for Sinclair whom he described as cowardly, always putting his personal safety first and driven by a distrust of those around him. Sinclair was a fanatically religious man whose main concern was to return safely to his wife in Scotland, and, as Horn describes with some sarcasm, he spent a good deal of his time staring at her photograph. Horn clearly felt that without Sinclair he could have succeeded far better in his ambitions both as a trader and at having personal influence in the region. "If I'd been Sinclair I would have owned the country. In Britain's name of course. ... I thought myself as big as de Brazza." He was certainly better armed than de Brazza and better skilled at diplomacy with the indigenous peoples. "If I'd sent home for proper backing I'd have got clear of Sinclair's timidity and photo worship. Rhodes knew the power of home backing."[42]

And Horn could yet have played a major role in developing the region. He had his admirers and backers, including Hatton and Cookson's chief agent Carlisle, the German agent Herr Schiff, many of the local chiefs, and not least, de Brazza himself. But let us remind ourselves that at this point of an already eventful career, Horn can have been little over 20 years of age. Who knows what he might have achieved had circumstances been different. As Couzens comments: "It was Sinclair who pulled him back from his great adventure, from his flirtation with creative freedom, from his place in history."[43]

Yes, it was the wretched Sinclair who ended Horn's ambitions in Gabon. Horn had already become very close friends with Chief Apekwe of the Bakele people up the Angani tributary, and had purchased Asange Island from the chief for a bottle of rum. Here Horn planned to establish his own trading business but at the time was still under contract to his employers. With support and encouragement from others, Horn built his stockade at the east end of Asange Island and, not allowing any weapons to be brought inside, for a while Horn's trading post became a safe free-trade zone for the otherwise warring tribes—the M'pangwes and "Oshebas" from the north shore, and their enemies the "Okellys" (Bakele) and "Oketas" (Bakota) on the south. For a while, trade in rubber and ivory was bustling. Horn's own traders made successful forays up-country, while Horn made several uninterrupted trips with full cargoes downriver to Lambaréné.

However, several months into this enterprise, a valuable shipment coming upstream from Lambaréné to Horn's camp was captured by an M'pangwe tribe now hostile to Horn's enterprise. The chief of this tribe, Ngogudema, made a deal with Sinclair that he would return all of the captured consignment and prisoners, and furthermore cease any further hostilities against traders, if Sinclair promised to recall Horn from Asange Island. Horn was furious at what he regarded Sinclair's cowardice and betrayal. Without further supplies his venture was doomed. Horn chose not to abandon his camp, instead calling in his debts and seeking help from his friend and ally, Chief Apekwe, in preparing for the inevitable attack from the M'pangwe. A fleet of war canoes was sent upriver to attack Horn, and also a large regiment of warriors by land. But Horn was well prepared for the attack and describes in detail the strategy and naval tactics employed in defeating Ngogudema and regaining control of the river.

Details of the battle and the events that preceded it were later confirmed, according to Couzens, in a written account by a French traveler, Leon Guiral, on his way downriver in 1881, following a visit to de Brazza and shortly after the events just related. Guiral interviewed a local chief and also visited Horn on Asange Island. Guiral, who knew and respected Horn, offered him assistance in returning downriver but Horn declined, needing to settle up his affairs and collect his debts. The victory was in any case a hollow one as in order to placate the defeated Ngogudema, the traders from Lambaréné sent an envoy to the chief confirming their intention of removing Horn from his island camp. Couzens here refers to William Walker's final diary entry regarding Horn, dated January 18, 1882:

> Mr Smith was routinely taking his boat up the Estuary to Azya on the Rembwe. His contract may have come to an end soon after his patience did with Sinclair. In any case, he had, he said, "made up my mind to take a trip home to the old country as my folks in the old home in Lancashire were continually writing for me." ... Apekwe [whom Horn describes as "my bosom friend in whom I could confide and he never betrayed me"]

> and his followers lined the shore, crying, "Come back to us we shall always be thinking of your return." ... Herr Schiff said that if Aloysius wanted to return as an independent trader he would supply him with any goods he wished ... and would back Aloysius to any amount.[44]

Horn could still have been no more than 21 years of age at the end of his Ogowe adventure, yet he was already a seasoned trader with a formidable reputation. His parting from Carlisle, Hatton and Cookson's chief agent on the coast was equally magnanimous, but it seems there was no attempt to encourage Horn to continue his work in Gabon and, in any case, Carlisle himself was on the point of retiring. The drawn-out climax of Horn's Ogowe fiction, if not his actual story, was, in the company of Little Peru, the dramatic rescue of Nina T— from the Joss House, ending with Peru and Horn tossing a coin to decide which one of them would take Nina for their bride. It seems that Nina would have been happy to marry either of her rescuers but it was Peru who won the toss.

Testimony of Albert Schweitzer

An interesting postscript to Horn's adventures on the Ogowe River are the memoirs of Nobel Peace Prize winner Albert Schweitzer. By a strange coincidence, after completing his medical degree, Schweitzer arrived in Lambaréné in 1912 to set up a hospital near the site of Hatton and Cookson's factory on the Ogowe river. Being a German in a French colony during the First World War, Schweitzer was put under surveillance and in 1917 sent to an internment camp in France. Although freed soon after, he did not return to Lambaréné until 1925. As Couzens observes, Schweitzer became intrigued by Horn's first volume after its publication in 1927, just as he was moving the site of his hospital to the spot formally occupied by Hatton and Cookson: "So in those (earlier) years, Trader Horn was at home on the spot now occupied by my hospital." Fascinated by the Trader Horn story, Schweitzer conducted his own research from interviews with those on the river who still had memories of Horn. Couzens' transcripts of Schweitzer's memoirs add to the authenticity of Horn's Ogowe River story and further illuminate the animosity between Horn and his boss:

> Whereas the memory of the chief, Mr Sinclair, still lives in the land, there are but few old people who can remember his subordinate of that time. What they still remember is that he was very young, that he wanted to trade according to his own ideas and on his own account and was therefore constantly at variance with Mr Sinclair ... Apart from trifling discrepancies, Trader Horn's description of the country and its inhabitants is accurate.[45]

Horn's Return to England and Further Adventures

Horn's return to his home in Lancashire in 1882 was met with mixed events and emotions. Firstly he discovered that his grandfather, John Smith, had died at the same time that Horn made his last trip up the Ogowe, and so Horn was denied the pleasure of relating to the old man his adventures on water and land. But Horn was also reunited with his childhood sweetheart Amy Knowles. In his conversations with Lewis throughout his first volume, Horn refers to a blue-eyed, ringleted Lancashire lass who clearly remained in his heart and dreams throughout his time on the Ogowe. Amy's mother died in August the same year and she turned to Horn for comfort.

But after only a short time in Lancashire, Horn's wanderlust returned. Through the coincidence that an acquaintance of Horn's family was married to an old friend of Charles Dickens (the parliamentary reporter and master of Hansard, George Bussy) Horn decided to try his luck in London. Initially he just carried out odd jobs for Bussy but was soon a reporter in his own right. Clearly an important mentor and influence, Horn frequently refers to Bussy's wisdom in his writings. While working as a reporter, Horn also rediscovered a former interest in painting, no doubt stimulated by a young artist named Charles Evans and his wife Ellen, with whom Horn had taken lodgings.

Husband, Father and Scotland Yard Detective

Amy must have remained in touch with Horn because on discovering that her father was to remarry a disagreeable spinster, Horn returned to Preston in June 1883 and the couple eloped. Amy simply left a note for her father on the table saying that she was leaving to marry Aloysius Smith. Amy's 18-year-old brother had forged the marriage consent and the couple were married in St. George's Catholic Church, Southwark, London, on June 13, 1883. Couzens speculates that another inspiration for Nina T— could well have been Amy, and so in this sense it would have been Horn rather than Peru who won the toss of the coin. On the marriage certificate, Horn records his occupation as a reporter and the 16-year-old Amy lied that she was 17. We are told by Couzens that the only reason we know the details of the couple's elopement, is that Amy's half-sister May (from her father's second marriage) was still alive to give the details in 1983, aged 99. Just over nine months after Horn and Amy's marriage, on March 22, 1884, Horn's daughter Marie Louisa Smith was born.

By this time, Horn and his new wife were living above an antique shop in Lambeth where Horn did some work and also continued his painting, further inspired by his friendships with the cartoonist Phil May, and also with the artist Henry Scott Tuke, who on occasion stayed with the couple in their Lambeth apartment. For a short period Horn immersed himself in the bohemian culture of London, although he also seems to have made a trip to New York with his new family as part of an assignment as a journalist for *The Times*. America was to leave a great impression on him as we shall see. Shortly afterwards, Horn decided that he needed to provide greater security for his family, and so on October 27, 1884, signed up with the Metropolitan (London) Police service, later passing his exams as a detective. As a Scotland Yard officer, Horn worked primarily with the poor and dispossessed in central London, spending a good deal of his time with street traders in coffee stalls and pie shops. At the same time, Horn and his friend Phil May also took up boxing at a gymnasium in Lambeth. For a more detailed account of the times Horn spent in London, one must read Couzens' *Tramp Royal* which draws from Horn's unpublished work *Buddha's Other Eye*, and is amply illustrated with cartoons and sketches by May.

To America with Buffalo Bill's Wild West Show

But Horn was already showing signs of his true tramping nature, as he was to later observe: "London was panorama enough for a time but hardly suitable for a feller likes change." He was also too soft-hearted to survive as a police officer, identifying closely with the causes rather than the consequences of crime. And like many of the other tramps in this book, he was already starting to associate marriage with captivity: "There's some women you could drag about ... But there's not many you'd care to have hampering your freedom. No getaway where there's a woman."[46]

As has been acknowledged, the trajectory of Horn's tramping career is the reverse of others discussed in this book, for unlike those child and adolescent tramps who became more settled toward the end of their lives, Horn starts off trying to embrace conventionality even though suppressing strong instincts to the contrary, and only later follows the true tramping impulse. The new call for adventure came from a most unexpected arena. In 1887, as part of Queen Victoria's Golden Jubilee celebrations, Buffalo Bill's Wild West Show came to London, and after discussing it with Amy, Horn resigned from the police and sailed to New York for a second time. Horn's daughter Marie, who Couzens says wrote down her memories shortly before she died in 1956, recalled how the family lived in a tent, variously in Nebraska and Denver, and that her father worked as a horse handler for Cody and also a sign and façade painter. She also recalls Horn teaching

Indian women to paint on the reservation. Horn's son William was born at this time, allegedly delivered by Mrs. Cody. But Amy's health started to deteriorate, forcing Horn to leave the Wild West Show and take up work again as a journalist on regional newspapers. Horn's trail goes cold here as it seems he dragged the family around in an attempt to survive, laboring when he could but also panning for gold. Couzens speculates that Horn left Arizona in the early 1890s.

From the Osage Reservation to Pittsburgh

We pick up Horn's trail again around this time at an Indian girls' school, the St. Louis Academy at Pawhuska, Oklahoma, run by nuns of the Catholic order of St. Francis: "I think this must have been the time when Dad began to teach the Indian ladies painting." Although Couzens provides some fascinating references concerning the Osage Indians themselves, there is little more on how the Horn family spent their time at the school, except to say that Horn must have felt very at home among these people. He also seems to have contributed—through his old skill of bricklaying—to the region's architectural heritage by leaving some of the few permanent brick structures in the nearby town of Bigheart. As an aside, Couzens describes how in 1897 (after Horn had left) oil was discovered on the Osage reservation, making them "the richest tribe in the world." And in spite of his millionaire status, Chief Wah-she-ha, alias Bacon Rind, continued to resist any change in his way of living. Marie writes of this period, "The Indians were generous and kind to us, and I often wondered why we left."[47]

Our next sighting of Horn is in the city of Pittsburgh. Couzens' only clue to Horn's arrival there is an entry in the Pittsburgh City Directory for 1892–1893 for an Alois. Smith, described as a "laborer." This is frustrated, however, by an account from Horn himself that he was painting signs in Pawnee, Oklahoma, including one in the Sheriff's office, which would put the date that Horn was still in Oklahoma *after* 1893. In all probability Horn came to Pittsburgh looking for work, which may, according to a recollection of his grandson Sandy, have included working as a Pinkerton Detective. Couzens is continually chasing ghosts in his own relentless investigation, though never failing to follow up a lead. The "Tanny Hill Convent" where Marie seems to have received her first schooling could have been anywhere in America, yet a map of Pittsburgh identifies a Tannehill Street very close to the downtown area and, backing on to it, is a large Catholic Church called St. Benedict the Moor. "Behind the church are the remains of a large building—a convent or school."[48]

From a letter written by Amy's half-sister, May, to Amy's granddaughters, entries from May's diary, and an interview with May before she died in 1983, Couzens was able to ascertain the following information. Horn was not always with his family during their time in America, although whether this was because he had to travel to find work or was simply tramping we are not told. What May did reveal was that Amy made five trips across the Atlantic, sometimes with her children, to visit her father and stepmother Mary, with whom by this time she was reconciled. It turns out that Mary Knowles was kindness personified and was later very close to her granddaughter Marie. May reveals that when she was old enough to have her own memory of Amy's visits, she recalls Amy arriving one night with Marie and Willie, but that Amy's second daughter Annie had died from scarlet fever on the journey and been buried at sea. Amy stayed for a time in Preston and Marie described Grandma Knowles' house as "such a lovely home that I think Mamma was terribly homesick each time she went back."[49]

Eventually Amy decided to return to America, although she never got over Annie's death. As if Pittsburgh at the time was not harsh enough, 1893 was the height of the depression and also the coldest winter in the city's history. It was into this inhospitable environment and the "Tanny Hill Convent" that Amy returned. Now identified as the St. Paul's Roman Catholic Orphanage Asylum (1838–1965), Tannehill Street, in the Hill District of Pittsburgh, Amy was to leave Marie as a boarder at the orphanage while she continued to live with Horn and Willie. Marie has memories of being visited by her mother, by now showing advanced signs of tuberculosis, in the company of Horn's brother Robert who had come to take Marie back to Preston. The only surviving writing of Amy's is a letter written to Marie, by this time living with her step-grandmother in Preston. In the letter Amy says that she has "been in bed sick with phnewmonia," probably already dying of consumption in Pittsburgh, and sends love from "Dada Willie and myself." Whatever Horn himself may have related to Lewis about his wife's illness, the only surviving words are a reference that he "carried her out on the porch to see the fireworks," presumably on the Fourth of July, 1894. Couzens notes that Horn must have been living in some degree of poverty, along with 10,000 other unemployed families recorded in Pittsburgh in November of that year. Amy's death is recorded on November 28, 1894 in Williams Street in the 30th Ward of that city. The death certificate records that she was a white female of 27 years of age born in England of a father "unknown." Amy was buried in an unmarked pauper's grave two days later.

Trader Horn's Return to Africa

Such was the ignoble end to the woman of Horn's dreams and fantasies, and one of the lowest moments of Horn's own life. Small wonder then that Horn should turn his back on America and travel to Africa once again, although this time the east rather than the west coast. It would seem from Ethelreda Lewis' writings that Horn initially landed in Morocco, where she believed he had a job connected to railway construction, but his eventual destination was the island of Madagascar as is recorded in his third book *Trader Horn in Madagascar: The Waters of Africa*. Lewis concludes that Horn arrived in Madagascar "some time after the Anglo-Boer War," and the book itself places his arrival there between 1895 and 1896.

Horn described his third volume as "fiction buttressed with truth" and that the story was "Founded on as much truth as fiction would allow."[50] For the purposes of this chapter, attempts have been made to throw some light on those aspects of Horn's story that are truly autobiographical, and those embellished with fantasy. Yet predictably, given the manner in which Horn seamlessly wove fact and fiction into his first volume, in *Waters of Africa* we are again introduced to a mish-mash of real-life acquaintances presented as fictional characters, including another Nina T-like figure. The drama of *The Waters of Africa* takes place variously between the port town of Majunga (Mahajanga) in Madagascar, the Chesterfield Islands in the Mozambique Channel (although Couzens' research shows that Horn probably used this description to disguise the location of the real island behind his tale), the island of Zanzibar off the Tanzanian coast, and Cape Guardafui on the tip of the Horn of Africa in Somalia. Given the location, and that here again we have another seafaring story (in which this time Horn himself appears as a Captain Smith), it is little wonder that piracy again dominates his writings.

The heroine of *Waters of Africa* is no goddess but another strong female character in the person of whip-cracking croupier Belle Seymore, a half-breed Cherokee Indian maiden who had become the slave of his pirate villain Parker Pasha. Belle was also cousin to Buck Johnson, another leading character in the book, whose father was Ben Johnson, sheriff of Pawnee, Oklahoma. Couzens has painstakingly researched all of these American connections, cross-referencing them with real events and real characters, including Horn's accurate description of the fate of the notorious outlaw Cherokee Bill in 1896. Couzens also speculates as to whether Horn may have even witnessed an actual raid by Cherokee Bill in 1894. Horn would have been aware of the woman outlaw Belle Starr, associated with the Oklahoma Indian territory in which Horn lived and worked. Belle Seymore's description in Horn's third novel as a crack-shot, bronco-riding, lariat-wielding heroine (sometimes referred to as Cherokee Belle) does point to Starr, or a pot-pourri of Starr and others, as a possible model for Seymore in Horn's book. In any event, the fiction, described by Couzens as an "Eastern Western"—set both in Oklahoma and Madagascar—ends with Parker Pasha's demise from a bullet fired by Belle Seymore during a dramatic sea battle, following which Belle and Captain Smith marry and live happily ever after. Such are the more fictional elements of the book.

Lewis admits to finding both of Horn's later attempts at the novel tedious and "banal" in a way that the fictionalized autobiography of his first volume was not, but there were some compelling passages. One is Horn's description of the deliberate wrecking of ships for the purposes of salvaging their cargo, an occupation Horn refers to often in his writing. This episode comes from where Horn (alias Captain Smith) is employed by the British Navy for his skills as a diver and navigator to locate a sunken ship loaded with treasure off the East African coast, but also to lure the pirates to the spot where the British Navy would be waiting out of sight to capture them.

> When Baba told me he could show me by going on shore the exact spot at which the decoy ship was set up, I decided to go. We took our rifles after safely searching the coast with our glasses for any moving objects but we found nothing. We landed and Carrol took us directly to the spot. There was no mistake, he had told us the truth. There driven in the sand were three stout stakes, the dummy ships masts had been rigged too, and one of these had the bolts still in them.[51]

We can speculate as to whether Horn himself was ever a wrecker: "'twas in the way of wisdom to be friendly with those wreckers. When you're in the salvage profession round about those parts it doesn't do to have them for enemies." Horn certainly had experience of the salvage business and seemingly also as a diver, if only for sponges off the semi-fictional Chesterfields. He was also certainly in charge of a cargo such as that described below, although on that occasion he must have resisted the temptation to make off with the untold riches in his charge. In the fictional version, Horn sets out to locate the *Empress of India* (not to be confused with the 1891–1913 battleship of that name), sunk off the African coast with a cargo of gold on board and a fortune in jewels carried by the ship's passengers. In the following passage we have an example of Horn's fanciful and macabre imagination as he describes to Lewis ideas for his next chapter (all the ellipses in the following piece are from the original text representing Horn's staccato discourse):

> "Well, I'm getting along to the sensational later. That'll provide me contrast to the quietude of the Chesterfields. What do you say to finding Eastern ladies of high rank, looking their best, and fully be-jewelled, afloat in the cabins of the ill-fated Empress of India?
>
> Aye, they'd be fully caparisoned in their beautiful clothes, nearing Zanzibar as they were ... Golden slippers and silken trousers ... Emerald rings weighting down the floating hands of the dead ...
>
> Naturally they were pressed up against the cabin roof by the floating furniture ...
>
> All those fabulous scents, attar of rose etcetera, and so forth drowned in the smell of death that can't get free to the cleansing of the sea ...

> Sharks're very quick to notice tainted water. They must have been sailing their fins about the Empress of India for many a day, hoping for the best ...
>
> High class Mohamedan ladies, meant for the Sultan's harem ..."[52]

In the fictional story itself Horn describes opening a sack he had removed from the wreck and removing "the tiara of diamonds with a large pigeon blood ruby and an emerald on each side, it was a beauty, there were also four strings of black and white pearls, nicely graded and the gold work slippers."[53] But in conversation with Lewis following Horn writing the chapter, he apologizes to her for not being able to include the bit about the dead women floating below the cabin ceiling: "'Twould a' led to too much reality and other unpleasantness. No way to treat a poor dead woman to expose her bones to the public gaze."[54]

If it were not for Horn's internal censor and editor giving the reading public what he felt they wanted, his attempts at writing novels may well have been more celebrated today. Horn's "conversations" reveal just what a fantastic imagination he had, and it is a sadness that he felt he had to temper his work for public sensibilities when his own life and imagination were so rich. On reading Horn's third volume, one has to question why he needed to introduce Belle Seymore into a fiction set in the Indian Ocean, when in real life Horn was on familiar terms with the last Queen of Madagascar, Ranavalona III, and her sister Princess Betselao?

> "A dignified, gentle woman ... Why, I've seen her disrobe and bathe among the crocodiles.... 'Twas a yearly ceremony to show her royalty to her people. The crocodiles, being sacred creatures, knew better than to touch the Queen of the Malagassies."[55]

Here again we have evidence that Horn must have been in Madagascar prior to 1897, because it was in that year that the French finally exiled the queen to Réunion Island in the Indian Ocean after their four-year campaign to colonize Madagascar. Horn claims to have been occupied collecting taxes for the queen and also prospecting for gold, which he describes as being of the finest color in the world. Not surprisingly, Horn also fell foul of his old enemies the French: "Little fancy officers sitting down on a fine island full of minerals like Madagascar. Like a mistaken hen on barren eggs."'[56]

Couzens speculates that Horn may have been involved in gun-running for the Imerina rebels in their fight to resist colonization by the French. A campaign in which the British, who to Horn's disgust showed no outward interest in Madagascar themselves, may well have played a clandestine role. In any event, the French were as hostile to Horn as he was to them, resulting in him being jailed for his troubles. He berated the French for their poor administration of the jail in which he was held, as much as for their shortcomings as colonizers. He has a lot to say about certain of his fellow prisoners, including an Italian who was eventually executed for murder but from whom Horn learned the art of sausage making. Horn's incarceration in the Madagascar prison also provides us with a more accurate chronicle of his onward adventures. Horn tells us that when the French served him with his deportation order, he showed his contempt for them by lighting his pipe with it, at which the French "got somewhat over excited." Horn then describes how, in true buccaneering spirit, he rode his horse into the market, letting it feed on the vegetables and then kicking over stalls on his way out. Horn describes his last moments in Madagascar, Cervantes-style, being accompanied by the French Consul to a ship waiting to take him to the African mainland: "I could laff still when I think of Monsieur le Capitaine marching me down to that jetty. Brandishing his little sword and puffing and blowing."[57]

Horn's further Adventures in Eastern, Southern and Central Africa

Horn arrived as a deportee in Lourenço Marques (now Maputo) in Mozambique, and the Portuguese, not wanting to give domicile to a British mercenary any more than did the French, took him under escort directly to the British Consul, Roger Casement, with instructions to have Horn sent back to Britain via Swaziland—and from here we again have to rely on Horn's own testimony for details of his onward travel.

Whether or not Horn did return to Britain to visit his family between 1896 and 1897, he was soon back in southern Africa, if claims in all three of his books that he was at war with the Matabele are to be believed. At the most Horn would still have been only 35 years of age.

Horn seems to have dropped out of sight for some years, "as near becoming native as a white man could." And we next pick him up in Southern Rhodesia (Zimbabwe) working as an independent trader and store keeper. Here Horn recounts not only a meeting with the founder of the former colony, Cecil Rhodes, but also claims to have saved Rhodes' life. Horn describes how he had been making prickly-pear brandy in the back of his store in Rhodesia when Rhodes turned up on a fishing trip with a friend, insisting that they take some of the brandy with them. Horn warned them that it had not matured and would "treat 'em queer," but they "took a good lot of it" anyway. One of Horn's workers took Rhodes and his companion to a good fishing spot by a large flat rock near the river bank. Later that afternoon, Horn's worker came rushing up in a panic because Rhodes and his friend had fallen asleep on the same rock from which a woman had been snatched by a crocodile while washing clothes only a week earlier. When Horn arrived at the spot he discovered Rhodes and his companion fast asleep. "Dead drunk they both were and very red in the face. They might'a' got sunstroke lying out like that, let alone the crocodile." After being taken to Horn's store and laid out to sleep it off, Rhodes expressed some astonishment when he found out what had happened. "He wasn't a man was often caught napping."[58]

By the time the Boer War broke out in 1899, Horn says that he was in South Africa's Cape Colony working at his old occupation of bricklaying. He initially enlisted in a local regiment but then joined an irregular outfit he called Kitchener's Cattle Thieves. The role of this troop was to commandeer cattle from the Boers and drive them hundreds of miles to British army headquarters—although Horn insists that they never took the "family cow" needed to provide milk for the children. Couzens has unearthed independent evidence of Horn's role in the Boer War from a piece written by a Major George Witten for the *New York Times* in 1928. Witten, who had ridden alongside Horn for two weeks and met up with him on other occasions, was by this time president of the Writers' Club of New York. He was provoked to write in response to those who were branding Horn and Lewis as charlatans. Witten had first met Horn out on the veldt among a group of generals, and on asking who he was, Witten was told that Smith knew Africa better than any other man. Witten's own opinion was that he had no doubt of the veracity of Horn's adventures, adding that he found Horn "remarkably keen and alert." Lewis also provides evidence of Horn's involvement in the Boer War in that she helped him claim a war pension from the government of the new Union of South Africa of 50 shillings per week.

March of the Prisoners

Our next sighting of Horn comes from a former British South African policeman, F.L. Rack, who claimed to have come across Horn in the northwestern Rhodesian mining town of Wankie (now Hwange) in 1904. This appearance of Horn coincides with the tale he tells in "The March of the Prisoners," one of four chapters under the heading Odd Conversations at the back of *Waters of Africa*. In spite of Horn's diatribes against slavery, it seems he was not averse to engaging in the commerce of kidnapping, human trafficking and forced labor—he also adds an entirely new meaning to the glossary of "tramping" in the introduction. Horn had slipped over the Mozambique border and bribed a prison official to hand over three hundred prisoners (including "murderers in leg-irons") plus six armed Portuguese soldiers to guard them, and then marched them for over a fortnight (without losing a single prisoner) to a mine in Rhodesia where they were handed over as laborers at two pounds apiece, of which Horn received half. Horn justifies this enterprise by claiming that his captives enjoyed a comparative freedom (on the trek at least) to their former plight in jail, "rotting there among their dirty crusts of mouldy bread."[59] Horn describes how the prisoners grew more cheerful day by day, "mountain water and old Sol and bit o' God's freedom going far to healing any wound." Horn's conscience was further fortified by the fact that the six soldiers were also persuaded by "a bit of natural coercion" to stay and work in the mine: "No great compliment to their Government that its soldiers are as lief to work half naked in a mine as to wear froggings and epaulets in a state of repose."[60] As Horn was to hear from a friend later, the postscript to this story was that it was only after some time that the prison authorities realized they were three hundred prisoners short, for whom they had been supplying extra rations. The prison captain no doubt sold the surplus supplies and covered his back by producing a forged document from Horn: "Please give the bearer three hundred prisoners and oblige yours sincerely the governor." Horn further justified his escapade by postulating, who was going to worry about retrieving three hundred hardened criminals anyway?

On The Wandering Jew and Animal Cruelty

Whatever the morality of this episode, it is in stories such as "March of the Prisoners" that Horn as both the scoundrel tramp and delinquent storyteller are fully appreciated. It was also in Mozambique (related in Odd Conversations, "The Wandering Jew") that Horn met another archetypal tramp character. We don't know what Horn was doing inland from the coastal town of Inhambane, but it was there near the village of Panda that Horn met one of the many manifestations of the Wandering Jew. Horn describes the Jew as having:

> the look of Jesus about him ... Sandals and a long gown and so on, and carrying a tall stick in his hand ... There he was, walking down Africa like that dove seeking land after Noah's flood. A home for the Jews he said. Come all that way from Palestine receiving food and shelter, but without a coin.[61]

Horn formed a brief but profound friendship with this person, who reinforced for Horn his already developing affinity with nature. In the chapter, Horn reflects on human beings' cruelty and selfish disregard for their natural surroundings. Although in his youth Horn had shot his own share of animals, he later came to detest the unnecessary killing of wild animals, even by hunters who made a living from it. But trophy hunters were the most loathsome: "nothing but licensed murder'll satisfy their kind." Horn describes the most brutal and wanton act of cruelty he ever witnessed by "a Major Somebody ... A red-faced ignorant whatever his fancy title may be." Horn tells how this trophy tourist shot a female sable antelope before pushing its trembling baby to one side to drink the milk from the dying animal for himself. But Horn was not sentimental. In the dangerous environment in which he chose to exist, there were times when it was entirely necessary to kill animals, either for food or one's own protection. On at least two occasions Horn had to be rescued from maulings by lions by his friend Tom Connolly. On the first occasion, although the lion was shot, Horn received a bullet wound to his shoulder but was saved once again by the timely intervention of a witch-doctor. On the second occasion, Horn was sleeping off a drinking binge under a wagon when the lion struck: "I was lying in me cups one night under a wagon and Tom was asleep there by the fire. Something woke him, and he sat up just in time to see a lioness lying on her back trying to tickle me with her paws."[62]

Horn's conscience toward animals and the natural environment was surprisingly advanced for the time, further evidence of which is provided in his writings of the peoples and places of Madagascar. He talks about the so-called Madagascar cat (lemur) and the spotted seals on the south island with pelts like a leopard, worth 50 pounds each, before entering into a lengthy diatribe against the fur trade: "Aye, for decking some proud beauty in Piccadilly men've got to ransack an obscure group of Islands in the Indian Ocean. ... Vanity's the cruellest instinct in the world."[63]

Human Trafficking and Slavery

For other places in Africa that Horn might have spent time, we have only passing references, but there were clearly times when as well as working he was "Travelling on the contents of me pocket." And so as well as both legitimate and illegal employment, there is evidence that Horn must have spent many years in Africa as a tramp, albeit a very resourceful one. Of the other places he mentions visiting we can include Gwelo and Que Que in Southern Rhodesia, Tati and the Kalahari Desert in Botswana, the Lake Chad area somewhere between Somalia and northern Nigeria (see below), as well as tramping from the Persian Gulf (where he was involved in salvage work) via Mocha and Aden in Yemen, down the East African coast to the island of Zanzibar where he worked for the Sultan, collecting tithes from Arab traders: "My official duties made it necessary for me to collect the Sultan's levies on the high seas." But Horn also accepted a mission from the Sultan to escort the Sultan's daughter on her bridal voyage to the Persian Gulf to be married to "one of the Mahomedan princes there." Given the untold riches on that voyage, Horn resisted the opportunity of turning pirate and making himself extremely wealthy. "Grand loot it would a' been. The jewels alone..." The fictional description of the salvage operation from the *Empress of India* in Chapter 5 of *Waters of Africa* may well have been influenced by this voyage.

After tiring of Zanzibar and the sea, Horn traveled to the highlands of Abyssinia (Ethiopia) from where he tramped onward to Somalia and Cape Guardafui. It was this place, "notable for bloody violence," together with his Zanzibar escapades, that prompted Horn's diatribe against slavery in *The Waters of Africa*. Young boys were trafficked up to places like Muscat in Oman from Zanzibar and Madagascar and young women brought back from Turkey and Georgia on the return journey. The best example of Horn's use of the diatribe (the philosophical genre favored by the Cynics) comes in a seven-page rant to Lewis' husband and is reproduced in Horn's third book. Here Horn is venting his anger on the practice of enslaving young boys to work as eunuchs in the harems of the Persian Gulf states. "Doctor, there's suffering lads with none to put out a hand to save 'em. Where's England's manhood that can sit still and see an unnatural outrage perpetrated on helpless lads?" These boys, Horn tells us, were sold for 50 pounds apiece for work in the harems. He blames the British for turning a blind eye to this barbaric form of slavery in the very countries they had colonized. "Oh aye, cover up your face like an ostrich and pretend such things could never be, and you'll murder tender lads with every blush a Christian's proud to summon up!"

> As for Parliament, they daren't mention such a word in front of the peeresses' gallery. Better let slavery go on than disturb the ladies in their crinolines and laces. Oh, aye, and you mustn't shock the distinguished strangers either or there'll be international troubles rising. Might be a Mohamedan listening there ... Christian? What'd Christ do in the circumstances? ... Did He ever cover up His eyes from wickedness and fall back on prayer? ... Doesn't Jesus Himself forbid slavery? "Feed my sheep" and so on ... What's become of His teaching? Where are the apostles of Jesus to-day? Nothing but *homo stultus* [human stupidity] if slavery's still rife after two thousand years.[64]

It is interesting that Horn's rancor was focused specifically on the trade in young boys as eunuchs, and not the trade in young girls as concubines destined for the harems whom the eunuchs attended. Horn begins by apologizing to Dr. Lewis that he was not able to produce an essay on the subject. But the form of the diatribe can be every bit as persuasive, and often more coherent, than the conventional essay. As usual, Horn has little awareness of his own talents as a philosopher, resorting instead to self-deprecation. In fact, Horn's inside knowledge of the subject, his anger at its obscenities, and his own idiosyncratic writing style make this a very powerful treatise indeed.

The Lake Chad Road: in which Horn engages in highway robbery

We cannot be sure exactly when Horn was in the southern Sahara Desert, but one of the "Odd Conversations" from the end of *The Waters of Africa*, titled "The Lake Chad Road," describes how he spent his time there. In this 24-page memoir, Horn admits to his involvement in highway robbery and kidnapping. He says that "when the French became impossible to live with on the coast," he traveled to northern Nigeria with his own "outfit of armed natives," with the intention of opening up a trade route "right through Mahomedan country." At some point Horn then joined forces with the leader of a local brigand gang he refers to as "Mahomad Alie." Their business was taking human hostages for ransom as well as outright robbery. And yet, as is the paradox of many of Horn's adventurous affairs, he relates this episode of his life to Lewis with a strange combination of both romance and regret: "Camels! ... You've got to see a caravan in the moonlight to seize the beauty of it. The desert moon's the grandest in the world. ... But you've got to harden your heart to break up the panorama with common violence." Horn even acknowledges that his intervention in attacking the caravan brought to an end a business endeavor that some innocent entrepreneur had likely planned and worked to fulfill for over a year: "The destruction of a big enterprise'll always weigh heavy on the mind of any feller born with natural feelings. ... Some poor feller's venture that'll never come to fruit and can't be replaced."[65]

As though to justify what seems by any accounts (including Horn's own) a despicably criminal act, our hero later emphasizes the virtuous manner in which the female hostages were treated, having made an agreement with "Mahomed Alie" not to touch or molest them and give them the benefit of their protection while the ransom was being sent for. Rogue he certainly was, but whatever crimes Horn may have committed in his life, these were paltry and restrained indeed compared to those institutional atrocities committed by both state and church during the Victorian era. In terms of his personal morality, Horn was probably more of a "Christian" than many priests or missionaries, then or now. Trader he might have been, but here again Horn shows little regard for money or material possessions, his motives always driven by a thirst for adventure and a need to mine whatever experiences he could from the exotic and the novel. As Lewis remarked, whatever money Horn had, he derived pleasure from giving it away. Identifying himself as a Catholic throughout most of his writings, Horn also describes himself as a "white Mahomedan" and describes elsewhere how he both read and practiced elements of the Qur'an.

Trader Horn's Return to America and Hobo Culture

By 1905, now aged 44, Horn joined his brother who was at that time working in Jersey City. It must be assumed that up until this time, Horn's two surviving children were residing with Amy's stepmother and half-sister in Preston, England. The two brothers traveled together for a while, working in both Bayonne, New Jersey and New York for 70 cents an hour. On April 8, 1905, Robert sailed for Panama having signed up for work as a bricklayer on the canal for 72 cents an hour—as a skilled laborer he would have been paid this in gold. However, in less than a year Robert returned to England having been summoned home by his importunate wife Annie. As for Horn himself, it seems that he returned at some point to Oklahoma and also Kansas where he engaged in prize-fighting, before moving to the southern Mississippi River states, New Orleans and on to Florida. Horn may have spent time in prison in New Orleans accused of stealing fish from a net: "Half-French Creoles. Ran us in for theft." He also describes a flood: "The Arkansas rose and swept the levees and we jumped on a passenger train for safety. No need to hide in the blind baggage. With the river rising there was no one with the heart to turn us off."[66]

Bart Kennedy (Chapter 3) was born the same year as Horn in 1861 and was also in a New Orleans jail around the same time. Kennedy also describes escaping a flood, though whether this was the same flood encountered by Horn is difficult to establish. From his conversations with Lewis, Horn was certainly riding the rails as a hobo around this time:

> Oh, aye, I've walked the tracks. Like this Jack London feller they talk about. I've seen a fair lot of American society riding under the rods. All sorts o' fellers, changing their State for the good of their State.... Aye, the track's full of 'em. Blind baggage and so on.[67]

Another talent of Horn's, not yet fully acknowledged, was his ability as an artist. He was certainly talented enough to have works commissioned to adorn public buildings across America, and mischievous enough to include a small figure of himself somewhere in the picture. Couzens refers to one such commission in which Horn had included himself as a figure fishing, but when the town council reneged on the price, he altered the figure to one pissing. Couzens also claims that Horn may have visited Peru, though whether this was to look up his childhood friend we do not know. What we do know is that he spent some time in Mexico around 1913 with Pancho Villa's revolution. Lewis wrote a story on his anecdotes of this period which has unfortunately been lost.

Around the same time, and presumably unknown to Horn, his daughter Marie had married and was living in Georgetown, Guyana, with a Will Scales.

On January 8, 1913, Horn's first grandchild, William Alexander "Sandy" Scales, was born in Georgetown Hospital. There are remarkable photographs of Marie's family in Couzen's book. Marie was by this time Horn's only remaining child. Of significant interest is the fact that Couzens is later to enter this story himself, this time as a character rather than simply a source of reference. Couzens first met Sandy in 1981 when Horn's grandson would have been 68 years old. This meeting was to lead Couzens (via a lynching in 1915 in which Horn, at the time aged 54, may or may not have been involved) on a journey across America visiting people who knew Horn. Some of these even had in their possession Horn memorabilia. The meeting with Sandy, and a subsequent trip to America, places Horn as living in a settlement called Kramer, halfway between the towns of Rochelle and Abbeville in Wilcox County, Georgia, sometime between 1913 and 1914. Here Horn "took possession of an abandoned house, slept on a mat and did his own cooking, until he was eventually joined by Marie and Will Scales." This would certainly have been by 1915 when Couzens is able to provide a first-hand account of the home occupied by Horn, his daughter and her family, from a woman who (although she was only 15 at the time) remembers having to drive Will Scales to a musical program in Rochelle School. "Mrs. Hillis talks of the regal way in which the Scales family carried themselves even though they were considered refugees by the townspeople."[68]

1915 was the height of another depression in America and Will Scales had to travel to find work. Horn managed to make ends meet picking up work as a bricklayer and painter (of pictures, not buildings). Sandy related a story to Couzens of how his grandfather (by now known as Uncle Pat, as the townsfolk assumed that all Catholics were Irish) had painted a picture of a horse for the local sheriff, Ben Edwards. Couzens was later able to identify surviving paintings by Horn and also building work:

> In Nell Johnson's beautiful old house there is a painting above the mantel piece. It is about six feet high and depicts a palace, seemingly on an island. A good deal of the painting consists of a background of sky and cloud and a foreground of sea with yachts rather like dhows sailing on it. The painting is predominantly blue.[69]

Perhaps Horn's painting was influenced by his *Waters of Africa* adventures. In any event, some of Horn's time in Georgia must also have influenced that book. Horn's family seem to have been quite popular in Rochelle. Marie played the piano and gave musical performances; she also had a job as a housekeeper in a local boarding house. Horn by this time had become friendly with a local millionaire, Jonathan Walker, a character even more eccentric than Horn and whom Horn on his first meeting had mistaken for a tramp. Couzens says that Horn is remembered in Rochelle for what he did best, storytelling: "some of the stories the old cracker-barrel philosopher told there must have been practice for the books to come." But Horn, never able to put down roots for long, would soon be on his way again. Marie was to keep in touch with the Walker family for many years, and Jonathan Walker himself lived to the age of 105.

Trader Horn's Second Return to Africa and Ignominy

Early in 1916, Will Scales and his family returned to England, and Horn was to join them in May that year. But sometime later an incident occurred that was to separate Horn from his family for many years. On taking Sandy out one day on a trip around the streets of London, Horn claimed that he was watching airplanes flying overhead when the next thing he realized, Sandy was missing. The boy eventually returned about midnight safe and smiling in the company of a police officer, but Horn was severely shaken by the incident and Marie was naturally enraged. On September 19, 1916, once again Horn set out for the African continent, leaving behind a letter giving Marie legal authority over his property and affairs.

The first postcard Marie received from Horn was posted from Madagascar, asking his daughter to let Jonathan Walker know where he was. But in a letter that Marie wrote in 1921 to Walker's grandchildren, Lina and Ida Walker, enquiring after their grandfather, she told them that she had not heard from her father, by this time 60 years of age, in over four years.

We are now coming closer to the final episode of Horn's life. He was working in Pretoria in the building trade when he fell from some scaffolding, badly injuring his leg from which he contracted lead poisoning. The doctors advised Horn in hospital that they would have to amputate his leg to save his life. Horn refused to consider this but the doctors were adamant, and so Horn got word to a friend, Tom Connolly, who smuggled a rope into the hospital which Horn scaled down to his friend and two waiting mules. The pair trekked to a witch-doctor friend of Horn's who cured the poison and saved Horn's leg.

Horn was now too frail for physical labor, surviving for a while on his painting. We are told he received two pounds for a copy of Landseer's *The Stag at Bay* from the owner of a shabby café, and also a painting of lions on the side of a paraffin can that ended up in the bar of a hotel. Eventually Horn did return to trading, although now reduced to the role of a street peddler like those he had befriended while a police officer in London. There was little pleasure for Horn in his new occupation, particularly as he was now forced to live in a Salvation Army hostel in Johannesburg, having always preferred the open expanses of the outdoors. As Couzens later observes, to Horn it was the indignities of the dosshouse that represented the savage side of civilization, not the cliché of "Darkest Africa." Horn's indignation at his Icarian collapse from trading on the Ogowe with a small army at his disposal, to hawking gridirons, baskets and toasting forks around the suburbs of Johannesburg, is barely disguised in the following passage:

> Aye, when you've got to assuage the cannibal into the buying mood 'tis a more manly effort than facing a woman who doesn't want to buy. Some of 'em set the dog after you. They don't know I've faced rogue elephants. When you've heard the gorillas roar at dawn it takes away the capacity for fearing the common house dog.[70]

Trader Horn, Writer and Celebrity

And so we finally arrive at the point where Trader Horn's story began at the start of this chapter: the accidental meeting with Ethelreda Lewis that was to save Horn from an undignified slide into death and launch his new career as a writer. We have first-hand accounts from both Horn and Lewis as to what happened next, but the chapter from Couzens' book titled 'From Joss House to Doss House' (the Joss House was a symbol for the magical world of youth; the Doss House a more realistic assessment of old age) provides fascinating testimony, supported (as is the whole of Couzens' book) with numerous photographs, of the transition of Trader Horn from an unknown tramp and adventurer to entering the consciousness of an entire generation of readers, moviegoers, and critics around the globe.

But Horn's newfound wealth and fame were not to change his philosophy on life, nor his treatment of his fellow man. Not easily forgetting the fellowship of tramping, a bond and code of behavior described by other tramp writers in this book, Horn initially remained at the hostel, sharing his early royalties with those less fortunate than himself. As he told Lewis: "Ma'am, as a human being, you don't display much of the gentleman if you refuse your last cent to a starving man made in the same image as yourself."[71]

Horn's new notoriety would also reunite him with his daughter and grandchildren. Having thought by now that her father had probably died somewhere in Africa, imagine Marie's surprise to see his photographic portrait in a copy of *Illustrated London News* dated September 24, 1927. Two weeks later Horn received a letter from his daughter addressed to Ethelreda Lewis, and by the end of the year he was back in England and the Scales' new family home in Whitstable on the North Kent coast. There is a splendid photograph in Couzens' book of Horn, all dressed up in his new togs, celebrating Christmas with his daughter, son-in-law and (by now) five grandchildren. Couzens also provides a comical description of the difficulties encountered by Lewis in her efforts to get the old reprobate to adopt a wardrobe befitting his new status:

> His dress sense had always been a source of some despair to her.... Ethelreda dispatched him to Durban in April with a new outfit of clothes. He returned to Johannesburg in September, and two days later she saw him approaching her front gate. He had got rid of everything—even his socks—and was marching along in a hugely happy mood chewing tobacco and clothed in an aura of disreputable triumph.[72]

Lewis relates an interesting episode of Horn's departure to Durban where she had sent him to improve his health. As she was seeing him off from the platform, "a remarkable-looking elderly man" spied Horn in the train carriage and declared, "Why, it's Zambesi Jack!" After greeting Horn warmly, he turned to Lewis and declared, "This is Zambesi Jack, whose life beats Rider Haggard's fiction hollow. Somebody ought to write a book about him."[73] Lewis declined to tell the man—who Horn later informed her was a former British aristocratic and ex-army Major fallen on hard times—that not only was the book written, but also accepted for publication. In any event, Horn did eventually agree to take a new set of clothes to England and "be suitably caparisoned as an old Victorian gentleman with a beard ought." But at the final hour, Lewis says, he rebelled and "went off in an old suit of reach-me-downs, and old jersey and no tie. He had also smuggled ... some still older, more disreputable clothes into a kit bag." Anticipating this, Lewis gave instructions to the train steward to deal with it. And this is how the now-transformed grand old Victorian gentleman, as most photographs represent him, arrived in England. But Horn was not to stay long in England; his publishers had arranged a lecture tour of America, and in March 1928 Horn sailed for New York on the White Star liner *Olympic*.

Horn seems to have been just as at ease surrounded by adoring and sycophantic society fans in New York as he was surrounded by cannibals on the Ogowe. When asked by one of these New York ladies how he was going to spend the four or five thousand dollars a week he was allegedly to get in royalties, he simply replied through tears of laughter that all he was currently in possession of was two pounds and six pence. Couzens describes his inaugural lecture at 3:30 p.m. on Wednesday, March 28, to a packed house in the 1,500-seater town hall off Times Square. "He spoke of the skills of medicine men, rolled up his trouser leg above his knee to show the audience his scar, and threatened to take off his shirt in front of the whole Town Hall to show where a lion had carried him off and was shot only just in time."[74]

After two weeks of being driven from one publicity event and dinner party to another, smothered with platitudinous solicitations, Trader Horn must have felt relieved to be traveling back to Liverpool on the SS *Carmania* and returning to Whitstable where he would enjoy some well-deserved serenity. By the spring of 1928 Metro Goldwyn Mayer had bought the film rights of Horn's first book for $25,000 and the second two books had been accepted for publication, so Horn and Lewis would at least have no further money worries. Even so, Horn still had the Viking and the tramp running through his veins and, after a particularly long and dismal spell of British weather, instead of putting up his feet and relaxing by the fire, he came downstairs one morning and shouted to Marie, "Tell that girl to get the car out. I'm going to Africa."

Trader Horn's Round-the-World Tour and Final Journey

Marie received a postcard from Horn, dated October 7, 1928, a day's sailing from Madeira, to say that all was well and he would write again when he arrived in Cape Town. Horn had traveled third-class, not wanting to endure the "hardships" of first-class. And so one year after leaving Lewis' front porch in Johannesburg, and not having warned her of his return, Horn crept up the steps "like a dog making hastily, and he hopes unseen after unexplained absences, to his mat." Lewis had feared that money and celebrity would have harmed Horn, even warning his publishers against the American tour because of his vulnerability and partiality for drink. But she need not have worried. Horn survived the ordeal and was happy to return to his literary homeland as though he had never been away. When Lewis pushed a pile of reviews toward him he simply swept them to the floor. He then produced his own wad of letters and documents from his pocket saying, "When the doctor comes in I want to give him these. They're only a nuisance to me. ... I feel safe with the doctor. Don't have to think for myself." Horn clearly found the trappings of life as a successful author altogether burdensome and set about trying to re-engage with some of his familiar pursuits, although on this occasion based in a hotel room rather than a dosshouse, with the added luxury of a beat-up old Ford and the assistance of a chauffeur-*cum*-companion, cook and general factotum. And so it was that Horn, clutching a new German translation of his book, with his chauffeur, B. Charlie, set off to pan for gold in the Rustenburg fields midway between Johannesburg and the Botswana border. Whether or not he found any gold we do not know, but by February 1929 he had left Johannesburg and boarded the SS *Demosthenes* in Cape Town, bound for Australia.

On arrival in Australia he explained to a journalist that—following a bout of "feeling queer"—when he had asked his Harley Street physician what was wrong with him the response he got was, "'Trader, nothing's wrong except that you have about five miles of nonsense in your head. Travel, and get rid of it.' So here I am talking to you."[75]

From Australia, Horn traveled on to New Zealand where Couzens says, "he could be found in odd corners of Wellington and Auckland dispensing pearls of wisdom," and from there he boarded the *Niagara* bound for Hawaii, arriving in Honolulu on April 19. Eight days later, Horn was once again back in America and taken on a tour of the MGM studio where a short film of him was shot in conversation with Cecil B. DeMille as a prelude to the shooting of *Trader Horn* the movie. Couzens devotes a 40-page illustrated chapter of his book to the making of the film, which at the time broke records for both cost and innovation. The film, which premiered in London in April 1931, cost $3 million to make (the average cost of an MGM movie at the time being just $350,000) and had grossed $1.7 million by the end of the year, not to mention all the merchandising spin-offs. The film also represented a breakthrough in sound recording and was the first ever non-documentary movie to be shot on location in Africa. The whole family attended the premiere of the movie and Horn had to be silenced by the usherette for complaining aloud about inaccuracies in the film. Lewis also, in her unpublished autobiography, decried the fact that "in no respect" was the book represented by the film. The story now returns to Horn the inveterate vagabond and wanderer.

From Hollywood, Horn crossed America via Chicago in a regular train compartment, arriving in New York the same day that the movie party had arrived in Mombassa to shoot the film. On May 9, 1929, Horn left America for the last time on board the SS *Muenchen* bound for Southampton. Horn would not leave England again, and apart from a couple of trips down to Cornwall and tramping around the Kent countryside near Marie's home at Joy Lane in Whitstable, he spent most of his last months either in front of Marie's fire or in three of the local pubs where he continued to entertain with his stories any who would listen.

Trader Horn was moved to a nursing home only days before his death on June 26, 1931, the same year as *Trader Horn* the movie was released, and just five days after his 70th birthday. The cause of death is reported as a cancerous tumor, although as far as can be discovered it only slowed the old tramp down in his final weeks. The day before he died, a nurse found Horn wandering around with his hat on and reports the last words he spoke as, "Where's me bloody passport? I'm off to Africa." But the reader should not assume that even death marked the end of Horn's wanderlust, as the penultimate paragraph of his third book hints:

> To a feller that's always been one for liberty the railings of a cemetery're no more than the prison of the soul that's forced to witness the humiliation of the body. Whether in life or in death walls're a mistake. A man needs a getaway ...[76]

ENDNOTES

1 Horn, Alfred Aloysius. *Harold the Webbed or The Young Vykings*, New York: Simon and Schuster, 1928, p. 16

2 Lewis, Ethelreda, in Horn, Trader. *Trader Horn in Madagascar: The Waters of Africa*, London: Jonathan Cape, 1932, p. 10

3 Ibid., p. 16 (footnote)

4 McFee, William (Foreword), in *Harold the Webbed*, op. cit., pp. 12–13

5 Horn, Alfred Aloysius. *Trader Horn: A Young Man's Outstanding Adventures in 19th Century Equatorial Africa*, San Francisco: Traveler's Tales' Classics, 2002, pp. 10–11

6 *Waters of Africa*, op. cit., p. 170

7 Ibid., p. 204

8 Ibid., p. 15

9 Couzens, Tim. *Tramp Royal: The True Story of Trader Horn*, Johannesburg: Witwatersrand University Press, 1994, p. 83

10 *Harold the Webbed*, op. cit., p. 66

11 Ibid., p. 43

12 *Harold the Webbed*, op. cit., p. 223

13 *A Young Man's Outstanding Adventures*, op. cit., p. 1

14 Ibid., p. 52

15 Couzens, op. cit., pp. 81–82

16 Ibid., p. 42

17 Ibid., p. 92

18 *Waters of Africa*, op. cit., p. 135

19 *A Young Man's Outstanding Adventures*, op. cit., p. 3

20 Ibid., p. 27

21 Ibid., pp. 31–32

22 Couzens, op. cit., p. 142

23 *A Young Man's Outstanding Adventures*, op. cit., pp. 45–46

24 Couzens, op. cit., p. 155

25 *A Young Man's Outstanding Adventures*, op. cit., pp. 48–49

26 Ibid., p. 197

27 Ibid., p. 53

28 Ibid., p. 58

29 Ibid., p. 53

30 Couzens, op. cit., p. 185

31 Ibid., p. 187

32 Ibid.

33 *A Young Man's Outstanding Adventures*, op. cit., pp. 137–138

34 Ibid., p. 101

35 Couzens, op. cit., p. 163

36 *A Young Man's Outstanding Adventures*, op. cit., p. 146

37 Ibid., pp. 156–157

38 Ibid.

39 Ibid., p. 159

40 Ibid., pp. 168–169

41 Ibid., p. 164

42 Ibid., pp. 173–174

43 Couzens, op. cit., pp. 180–181

44 Ibid., p. 188

45 Ibid., p. 183

46 Couzens, op. cit., p. 217

47 Ibid., p. 247

48 Ibid., p. 258

49 Ibid., p. 259

50 *Waters of Africa*, op. cit., p. 204

51 *Waters of Africa*, op. cit., pp. 174–176

52 Ibid., pp. 172–173

53 Ibid., p. 180

54 Ibid., p. 182

55 Ibid., p. 74

56 Ibid., p. 33

57 Ibid., pp. 195 & 185

58 *Trader Horn: A Young Man's Outstanding Adventures in 19th Century Equatorial Africa*, p. 150

59 *Waters of Africa*, op. cit., p. 244

60 Ibid., p. 246

61 Ibid., p. 248

62 Horn cited in Couzens, op. cit., p. 340

63 *Waters of Africa*, op. cit., p. 65

64 Ibid., pp. 159–163

65 Ibid., pp. 230–231

66 Horn cited in Couzens, op. cit., p. 381

67 Ibid., pp. 352–353

68 Couzens, op. cit., p. 384

69 Couzens, op. cit., p. 408

70 *Harold the Webbed*, op. cit., p. 69

71 *A Young Man's Outstanding Adventures*, op. cit., p. 40

72 Couzens, op. cit., p. 469

73 Ibid., p. 469

74 Ibid., p. 495

75 Couzens, op. cit., p. 510

76 *Waters of Africa*, op. cit., p. 256

Josiah Flynt

(1869–1907)

I should expect to find the ancient Egyptian hobo ... if he could come to life and would be natural, pretty much the same kind of roadster that we know in our present American type.

Josiah Flynt, *My Life*

Preamble

Put "Josiah Flynt" into a search engine and up will pop several sites all providing the identical, unhelpful information:

> Josiah Flynt (properly Josiah Flynt Willard), Jan. 23, 1869–Jan. 20, 1907, was an American sociologist and author, born at Appleton, Wisconsin. He was educated at the University of Berlin in 1890–1895 and after several years of experience as a professional vagrant published in 1899 *Tramping with Tramps*.[1]

That Flynt attended university, attained a Ph.D., and is acknowledged variously as a sociologist and a criminologist, are probably the least remarkable facts about him. They were also, like all the other events in Flynt's life, unplanned and accidental—even if a passion for writing was a more constant aspect of his character. As his friend and fellow writer Emily Burbank describes him—and this is a singularly important fact to consider: "it must be remembered that Flynt was the tramp writing, not the literary man tramping."[2]

Burbank also describes Flynt as a gifted actor. He was as comfortable and at ease with the tramping and criminal classes as he was with philosophers, politicians and others notable in public life. "Give him a part in a play ... the disguise of a vagabond, or whisky with which to fortify himself, and the man's spirit sprang out of its prison of flesh, like an uncaged bird."[3] But Flynt's chameleon-like ability to adopt different roles to suit the company in which he found himself was confined to those who were, like himself, out of the ordinary. In between mixing it with tramps and petty criminals, Flynt the actor was equally at home with those from the opposite spectrum of society, including among his acquaintances the following random celebrities:

- Rudolf Virchow, German physician, anthropologist, statesman, champion of public health and antagonist of Bismarck
- Henrik Ibsen in Munich
- George Augustus Sala in London
- An earlier Bloomsbury set, also in London
- Horatio Brown in Venice
- Leo Tolstoy as a guest at his farm
- Prince Chilkoff, Russian Minister of Railways
- Aleksey Kuropatkin, Russian Imperial Minister of War (1898–1904)
- Apache chief Geronimo in Fort Sill, Oklahoma, to conduct an interview; but the old chief was in a bad humor and would not talk.

Flynt may well have been close to other famous persons not mentioned in his autobiography. For instance, he does not refer to his association with Gertrude Stein and her brother Leo, yet this fact is reported by Stein in her third-person parody, *An Autobiography of Alice B. Toklas*:

> They settled in lodgings in London and were not uncomfortable. They knew a number of people through the Berensons, Bertrand Russell, the Zangwills, then there was Willard (Josiah Flynt) who wrote *Tramping With Tramps*, and who knew all about London pubs, but Gertrude Stein was not very much amused.[4]

It should be acknowledged also that Flynt was the nephew of author, social reformer, and president of the Woman's Christian Temperance Union, Frances Willard. Her house on 1730 Chicago Avenue, Evanston, Illinois, remains a museum to her life and work to the present day. It is reported that the reason Flynt did not write under his real name of Willard was to avoid any embarrassment to his aunt occasioned by his tramping exploits and criminal history. Flynt's cousin, from another relative, was American film director Bannister Merwin (1873–1922).

Most of this chapter will draw from Flynt's autobiography, *My Life* (1908), published the year after his premature death from alcohol and cocaine addiction aged 38, and *Tramping with Tramps* (1899), a collection of Flynt's essays published separately by *The Century* between 1893 and 1899 (including the five years Flynt was at university). As far as can be established, Flynt's full list of books and essays (not included in *Tramping with Tramps*) is below:

What to do with the Tramp (1894)
How Men Become Tramps (1895)
Tramping with Tramps: Studies and Sketches of Vagabond Life (1899)
Tramp Boys (1899)
Railroad Slums (1899)
Tales Tramps Tell (1900)
Notes of an Itinerant Policeman (1900)
How Hobos Are Made (1900)
The Powers that Prey (with Francis Walton) (1900)
The World of Graft (1901)
The Little Brother: A Story of Tramp Life (1902)
The Rise of Ruderick Clowd (1903)
My Life (1908)
"Homosexuality Among Tramps," in *Studies in the Psychology of Sex* (Volume 2 [of 7], Appendix A) by Havelock Ellis (1908)

Early Life

Fatherless from a young age, Flynt was brought up by his mother in Evanston, Illinois, a Methodist community on the shores of Lake Michigan that later became a suburb of Chicago. A closeness to his mother throughout his life probably mitigated the worst excesses of tramping, and was certainly responsible for Flynt graduating from the University of Berlin.

Flynt's mother recalled that his first tramping expedition was at the age of five, and first time in jail also, as it was from there that he was returned to his parents. Flynt's own recollection was that he was only four at the time as he remembers still wearing dresses. In any case, his parents were in the neighboring city for the day, and Flynt had been left at home in the care of his nurse. After the nurse punished him severely for some slight misdemeanor and went to the lake for water, Flynt, much disquieted at the scolding, was overcome with a sudden impulse to run, "anywhere, it did not matter, so long as the nurse could not find me." So off he ran for the main street of the village, "my little white panties dangling along after me." It was his first conscious and determined effort to see the world in his own way, the "beginning of that long series of runaway excursions which have blessed or marred my life ever since."[5]

This was the first of many tramping adventures that even whippings from his father and pleas from his mother failed to prevent, and which Flynt credits to being "a helpless victim of the whims of wanderlust." In those early days, the person responsible, time and again, for returning Flynt to his family, was a close relative involved with the railroad and journalism. Not trusting Flynt with the money to purchase a ticket home after his various adventures, this relative furnished Flynt with a note he was to present to the train conductor reading, "This is a runaway boy. Please pass him to— and collect fare from me on his return." Flynt well understood the value of such an open endorsement to travel free on the railroads and made good use of it. He also acknowledged that he was a victim of his own personality. All he could offer by way of explanation was: "I have never met a boy or man who has been plagued [by wanderlust] to the same degree as I was."

At the age of 15, Flynt's mother and sisters moved to Berlin while he was sent as a boarder to a small college in Illinois. After losing an essay competition which both Flynt and other students felt he should have won, Flynt abandoned college and jumped a train to Buffalo. He was just short of his 17th birthday and was offered his first job as a "yard car reporter" in the railway yard in Buffalo where he had disembarked. He had already begun to calculate the amount of savings he could make by the end of the year, when he chanced to see a horse and buggy standing idle in one of the main thoroughfares. "What it was that prompted me to get into the buggy and drive blindly onward I cannot say."

But on he drove for a good hour, regardless of direction or the police. "Then the seriousness of my offence gradually began to dawn on me."[6]

To cut a long story short, Flynt ended up in Pennsylvania where he sold the horse and buggy to an acquaintance on the pretext that he had purchased them as a result of his savings. Getting away with horse-thieving once emboldened Flynt to repeat the transaction, except that on this occasion he was arrested and jailed. As would have been expected, Flynt managed to escape and his story reads like a real-life Mark Twain adventure. The escape itself, Flynt says, "began that long eight months' tramp trip," the first of what would be many subsequent tramping expeditions, ending in another jail sentence, on this occasion 30 days for being found sleeping in a boxcar. But this tramping apprenticeship also represented a turning point and coming of age in Flynt's career as a tramp. He made the decision, from that point on, that he was done with stealing. "There was no long consideration of the matter, I merely quit on the spot; and when I knew that I had quit, that I was determined to live on what was mine or on nothing, the rest of the Road experience was a comparatively easy task."[7]

To Berlin and University

Flynt's first tramping expedition ended shoveling coal and ash in the boiler room of an oceangoing liner bound for Bremerhaven in Germany, and then on to Berlin to locate his mother's lodgings in that city: "The Berlin of the late eighties was a very different city from the Berlin of to-day [circa 1905] ... there were no automobiles that I can remember having seen ... the place resembled a great overgrown village more than it did the capital of a great country."[8]

It is not difficult to appreciate how after eight months of tramping, followed by the indignities and discomfort of shoveling coal in the bowels of a ship, that Flynt, severely malnourished and otherwise physically and mentally traumatized from his adventures, would not fully succumb to the relative comforts of his mother's Berlin apartment and give himself over to being pampered and persuaded. Flynt describes how his mother did persuade him to enroll for a course of study, and observes with some surprise: "In five minutes, thanks to the rector, I had changed from a quondam coal passer to a would-be Doctor of Philosophy in the great Friedrich Wilhelm University, a royal institution." Further, he acknowledged, as a foreign student in the early 1890s, he did not even have to provide evidence of matriculation at previous learning institutions. All he needed "was to have a twenty-mark piece in your pocket to pay the matriculation fee, and perhaps fifty marks more to pay for your first semester's lectures. ... There were no examinations until the candidates for degrees were ready ... to try for their Doctor's degree. ... The examination was oral and alleged to be pretty minute."[9]

Flynt's choice of dissertation (his experiences of tramping dressed up for the university as "Political Economy") ended up crediting him as one of the first "participant ethnographers." By accident rather than design, Flynt became a major influence—through Nels Anderson and others—on the formation during the 1920s and '30s of the Chicago (or Ecological) School, the institution that pioneered ethnographic fieldwork in urban sociology and criminology.

Tramping Adventures in Europe

The several tramping excursions Flynt took while at university, one suspects, were more for pleasure and to maintain his tramping "skills" than for genuine research purposes, even though many of these trips were subsidized by a newfound occupation as a freelance reporter. The following accounts are drawn both from Flynt's autobiography, *My Life*, and from *Tramping with Tramps*, where Flynt's European adventures are described in separate essays according to the countries he visited.

Germany

Flynt made his first serious tramp around Germany after two years in that country, dressed in tramp garb and without any form of ID, something he later regretted. But he had been told by a university professor that "The only way to know the entire truth about the tramp is to live with him," advice of which Flynt was already well aware. His initial research identified that there were 200,000 arrests in Germany each year for begging, 100,000 of which represented "irreclaimable vagabonds." Flynt's plan was not to study the enforced vagrant, but "those who wander because they desire to." As with all his other tramping exploits, Flynt gave a great deal of attention to learning the German tramp slang. From his conversations with various tramps en route, Flynt had to revise his preconceptions that the primary causes of vagabondage were laziness and liquor. As a German tramp told him, "...if I should follow my trade I could earn about eighteen marks a week. ... we lads on the road seem to have more money than most laborers ... we're never sick, always happy, and perhaps we're just as well off as anybody else."[10]

Britain and Ireland

In 1893 Flynt embarked on a tramp around Britain with a fellow student from Berlin University. They took a boat from Hamburg to Grimsby and made a planned round trip of Britain and Ireland, sometimes together, other times separately, but agreeing to meet up at certain points on the way. From Grimsby, Flynt tramped to Hull, Edinburgh, Dublin, Liverpool, Chester, Shrewsbury, Hereford, Bristol, Bath and Reading, finishing up in London, describing many tramp characters and doss-houses along the way. An interesting summary of Flynt's impressions of the British tramp include that he found most of the tramps he encountered as "being a trifle insane. They are fond of philosophizing about themselves, and in a comical way."

> Most of the tramps we met were well informed, and fully half of them had been in America ... They also keep up to the times on political issues and pugilistic and police news. ... They are a very hospitable set to their own kind. ... Though they are without doubt the dirtiest and the raggedest and the poorest of men, I was everywhere treated by them with politeness, so far as they understood politeness.[11]

As regards the female tramp in Britain, Flynt comments that he noted relationships between those on the road in Britain, and that women tramps tended to ally themselves more with male tramps than with other women (see Chapter 15 concerning the 25-year tramping relationship between Jim and Kathleen Phelan). "The woman is practically the slave of the man; he is the supposed breadwinner, but the Judy does more than her share of the begging all the while."[12] This was not the case with Jim and Kathleen Phelan, who enjoyed an unusually equal relationship for a tramp couple.

Switzerland and Italy

Flynt set off the following year for a tramp around Switzerland and Italy using Mark Twain's *A Tramp Abroad* as a travel guide. Flynt and his friend climbed the Breithorn simply because they did not have sufficient funds to pay a guide to climb the Matterhorn, 30 francs as opposed to 300. But it was Venice that captured Flynt's heart:

> I thought then of the city, as I do still, more as a lovely, breathing creature, truly as a bride of the Adriatic, than as a dwelling place of man. I walked from my lodgings to the Piazza. As I turned into the Piazzetta, and the glory of that wonderful square flashed upon me in the glow of the bright

> afternoon sun, I came suddenly to a halt. Such moments mean different things to different men. I remember now what passed through my mind, as if it were yesterday: "If to come to this entrancing spot, young man, is your payment for pulling out of the slough that you once let yourself into, then your reward is indeed sweet."[13]

Flynt spent some months engaged in the new and novel experience of tramping the canals of Venice by canoe, before visiting Rome and Naples, and then back to Berlin to complete his studies.

Russia

On completing his studies, Flynt embarked on a two-year, 25,000-mile tramp around Russia, some of which was financed by an American magazine in exchange for whatever copy Flynt could provide of his adventures and meetings with Russian celebrities. Flynt spent 10 days at Leo Tolstoy's farm, discussing tramping, among other things, at which Tolstoy regretted being too old to accompany Flynt. When Flynt met Tolstoy in 1896, he described him as "a fairly well preserved old gentleman, with a white beard, sunken gray eyes, overhanging bushy eyebrows, a slight stoop in the shoulders, which were carrying, I think, pretty close to seventy years of age. He wore the simple peasant clothes about which there has been so much nonsensical talk."[14]

Flynt met up with Tolstoy and his family practically every day, even when he was not staying on the farm. He divided his time between the Tolstoys' house, where he slept in the count's library, and the home of a neighbor of the Tolstoys. At the neighbor's home he slept in a cot in the barn along with two young Russian friends of the count. "They were helping Tolstoy 're-edit' the Four Gospels, omitting in their edition such verses as Tolstoy found confusing or non-essential."[15] In the fall of 1897 Flynt set off for Central Asia, this time with an endorsement that most tramps could only dream of: three months' free transportation on the Russian State Railways by order of the tsar. Prince Chilkoff, the Minister of Railways, had also become fascinated by Flynt's exploits, and "on learning that I contemplated excursions into remote parts of Russia he kindly offered to ask the Tsar to grant me free transportation for three months 'in order that my investigations might be facilitated.' When the transportation finally reached me, it read: 'With Imperial Permission.'"[16]

But Flynt was not to let this VIP treatment go to his head. True to form, and dressed in tramp attire, he used the opportunity to further his own interests of spending time among Russia's poor and dispossessed and exploring the local vagabonds' resorts, including the notorious Dom Viazewsky, "the worst slum of the kind I have ever seen anywhere." On a particular winter's night in 1896, Flynt reported that "10,400 men, women and children slept in five two-story buildings enclosed in a space about the size of a baseball diamond. Only a hundred paces away is the Anitchkoff Palace."[17]

> What a medley of humanity that vile-smelling room contained! Old men barely able to climb out of their bunks; rough middle-aged ruffians, cowed for the moment, but plainly full of vindictiveness and crime; youngsters just beginning the city life and quaking with fear at the unannounced visitation—never before have I seen human bodies and rags so miserably entangled.[18]

The following year, and again, making much of his role as a journalist, Flynt managed to secure the perfect insurance against running into trouble, even if he also enjoyed the thrill of remaining undercover. The prefect of St. Petersburg, General Kleigels, provided Flynt with a general letter to the police that read as follows: "The bearer of this is Josiah Flynt, an American citizen. He is here, in St. Petersburg, studying local conditions. Under no circumstances is he to be arrested for vagabondish conduct." An American acquaintance of Flynt's in Russia told him that with such a letter in his possession he "could almost commit murder with impunity."[19] In the event he got arrested for a much less serious offense. The incident Flynt refers to was manhandling two special constables while out drinking with an American and an English friend in St. Petersburg, no doubt emboldened by his pass from General Kleigels. Needless to say, Flynt was let off with a handshake; his friend was later fined 25 rubles for the crime of whistling in a police station. Flynt acknowledges that although he learned a great deal from his tramping around Europe, "unconventional experiences as I never could have learned about ... had I spent all of my time in libraries and the lecture room," these were also a submission on his part, "to the all-demanding passion for wandering." Concluding: "It was also a good thing for me to be let loose every now and then into the jungle of Europe's vagabond districts and then vent such lingering Wanderlust as my temperament retained."[20]

Return to America

Flynt acknowledges that his European experiences had provided him with useful skills and contacts as a reporter, but that he was glad that Europe was now behind him and that he was free to return to America; however, his choice of work on his return is something of a surprise. His first job on returning to America was in response to being summoned by the railroad executive, Leonor F. Loree. At the time, Loree was general manager of the Pennsylvania Railroad that covered five states including the terminals of Cleveland, Chicago, Cincinnati, Wheeling, and Pittsburgh. No doubt aware of Flynt's reputation as a former hobo turned social scientist, Loree asked Flynt to write a report on the tramp problem affecting his railroad and the effectiveness of his railroad police in dealing with it. Following this experience, Flynt published an essay titled "The Tramp and the Railroads," in which he refers to his writing this time as an "investigation," rather than anecdotes of the tramp, horse thief and escaped convict of his previous American tramping adventures. On this occasion Flynt talks about "the best methods to employ in attacking the tramp problem in this country," providing Loree with much-needed propaganda that if tramps could be kept off the railroads this mode of travel would no longer be attractive to them. "No other country in the world transports its beggars from place to place free of charge, and there is no reason why this country should do so."[21]

Even though Flynt describes this episode as a "tramp trip," the shift in voice and perspective are markedly different from other chapters in *Tramping with Tramps*. It does not seem to have been in Flynt's job description as an undercover investigator that he get involved with tramps directly, yet as part of this employment Flynt also unashamedly recalls an account in his autobiography of pursuing and confronting three black tramps who had taken a free ride on a train in which Flynt was traveling, and being responsible for their arrest. Contrast this episode with one nearer the end of Flynt's life, and one is struck again by just what a complex character he was. His own peculiar morality, it seems, suited his all-too-human instincts for whatever impulses touched him at the time. This second anecdote appears in an afterword to Flynt's autobiography, written by Flynt's cousin, American film director Bannister Merwin, who describes Flynt as becoming "more accustomed to a saddle, and rode to many points of interest near Sapulpa." Merwin describes how Flynt made several trips to the home of an African American who lived near a ledge of rocks called Moccasin Tracks, five miles from Sapulpa. United States marshals had "marked" this man and "planned to 'get him' at the first opportunity," but Flynt spoke up for and protected the man.[22]

On this occasion Flynt seems to have intervened in a positive way. In any case, there seems no doubt that he was seduced by, and continually drawn to, the underworld. A clue, perhaps, to his own morality may be a certain cynicism toward any consistent code of honor among the criminal classes that so fascinated him. In the final chapter of *My Life*, "Honor Among Thieves So Called," Flynt goes into a fairly self-indulgent spree of name-dropping of New York underworld characters who are known to him, at the same time flaunting his knowledge of (just too much) criminal slang. Yet Emily Burbank describes him thus: "Flynt's ethical code was that of the Under World, and, in some respects, superior to the one in use on the Surface of Life." One conclusion is that Flynt's ethical code, if he had one at all, is too inconsistent to support any unifying assumption. Another theory is simply that Flynt was an actor, perpetually inhabiting different roles depending on what suited the occasion.

However consummate a performer Flynt might have been in the company of men, Merwin relates an anecdote that demonstrates his vulnerability and very human face, and concerns Flynt's only recorded romantic inclinations. For years Flynt had worshiped a particular young woman without making his feelings known to her. In July 1894, when Merwin had stayed for some days at Flynt's home in Berlin, Flynt told him that the girl was spending the summer at a mountain resort in Europe and that "it was time for him to go to her and declare himself." Flynt traveled many hundreds of miles to visit the young woman, "dreaming we may not guess what dreams along the way." It was several months before Merwin met up with Flynt again, and when he asked Flynt about the girl he got the reply, "Well, I went there, and I saw her, but I didn't speak to her." "Did she see you?" Merwin asked. Flynt replied "No." "Again he had been the watcher by the wayside standing in shy self-effacement while the girl of his heart passed by."[23] Merwin summarizes Flynt's character as follows:

> [F]ew men who have set out to write their own stories have been able to show themselves as truly as he has shown himself. That is because he was essentially a man of feeling—sensitive, proud, filled with sentiment—though only his close friends may have known this of him.[24]

Having completed his assignment for the Pennsylvania Railroad, Flynt then responded to his second passion, writing, and became one of the founding members of the original group of writers and hell-raisers known as the Griffou Push, so called because of their base at the Hotel Griffou in Manhattan's West Village. It is interesting to note that the emergence of the Griffou Push is popularly credited as some 20 years after Flynt writes about it, and some 11 years after Flynt's death. He refers fondly to this period of his life and of his weekly trips to the *Sun* office, Park Row, where he handed in his bill for copy and collected the money due to him. "I shall never forget how proud I was one Saturday, when, with seventeen dollars' space money in my inside pocket, I strolled back to Ninth Street, through the Bowery—or the Lane, as 'Chuck' Conners prefers to call it."[25] It should be noted here that this Chuck Conners was the famous Chinatown guide and inventor of slang, not the actor and pro baseball player famous for his role in the series *The Rifleman*. But to return to Flynt the tramp writer, the rest of this chapter covers the various themes discussed in his books and other writings.

The Child Tramp

Flynt makes much of his endogenous drive toward "foreign" experiences, his wanderlust, as the primary motivation for tramping:

> To-day I can laugh at all this, but it was a very serious matter in those days; unless I covered a certain number of miles each day or week, and saw so many different States, cities, rivers and kinds of people, I was disappointed—Hoboland was not giving me my share of her bounteous supply of fun and change. Of course, I was called "railroad crazy" by the quieter roadsters in whom the fever, as such, had long since subsided, but I did not mind. Farther, farther, farther! This was what I insisted on and got.[26]

"Jamie the Kid," in which Flynt writes about a young boy bitten by wanderlust who forms a relationship with an experienced tramp, and when close to death pleads to be returned to his mother; "Old Boston Mary," a story of a remarkable woman tramp who provides a safe house for hobos; and "The Children of the Road" make up three of the most engaging stories in *Tramping with Tramps*. But importantly, these stories also show the tender and caring side of Flynt that belie descriptions of him elsewhere as being selfish and self-serving. "Jamie the Kid" and "The Children of the Road" also provide a unique insight into Flynt as a child vagabond himself. For in discussing other child tramps, one suspects that Flynt is identifying closely with his own youthful wanderlust, free from either the actor's bravado as the seasoned hobo or that of the social scientist. Flynt's own theory about child tramps is that "they are possessed of the 'railroad fever' ... the expression in its broader sense of Wanderlust. They want to get out into the world, and at stated periods the desire is so strong and the road so handy that they simply cannot resist the temptation to explore it."[27]

Flynt emphasizes elsewhere in his writings the vulnerability of these tramp children and how they are easy prey to adult tramps, many of whom deliberately set out to seduce what Flynt describes as "slum children" with tales of adventure and money. On the road, the child tramp is referred to as a "prushun" and his adult protector (or abuser) as a "jocker." "Jamie the Kid" is the story of one such child tramp who, like Flynt, left a loving home and mother as a victim to wanderlust. Typically, there is a bond of kinship (ownership also) and mutual dependency between the adult hobo and the child, who is taught all the tricks of begging as well as surviving on the road. Not least of these dangers is being stolen by another adult, for these children were a valuable asset in the begging profession. And although one suspects other motives, Flynt gives no hint of these children being sexually exploited in either *My Life* or *Tramping with Tramps*. Neither is this aspect of "hobohemia" given any real coverage in the two main secondary texts on the subject discussed in the introduction, *The Tramp in America* and *Citizen Hobo*. It was only on discovering an obscure appendix by Flynt in the second volume of Havelock Ellis' encyclopedic *Studies in the Psychology of Sex* that the full extent of sexual exploitation of children by hobos became clear. A very explicit thesis from Flynt is provided on pedophilia (under the banner of homosexuality), one that, unintentionally perhaps, would have had the potential to reinforce a whole range of additional fears and prejudices about tramps. In his essay, Flynt claims that "every tenth man practises it, and defends his conduct. Boys are the victims of this passion."[28]

Flynt did much to publicize the vulnerability of these "children of the road" and does not give himself sufficient credit for the public attention he attracted to this particular issue. But it was a source of great regret to Flynt that his work did not do more to alleviate the plight of tramp children. "I have more than once had dreams and plans that looked to the rescue of these prematurely outcast beings. It needs skilled philanthropists and penologists, however, for such a work."[29] Flynt's categorization and sub-categorization of tramps in "The Children of the Road" alone is mind-boggling. For instance, the gypsy ("ambulanter" in tramp parlance) is one of those groups Flynt describes as "born on the road." He describes one such family, that of Cavalier John, as follows:

> A negro wife, five little mulattoes, a deformed white girl, three starved dogs, a sore-eyed cat, a blasphemous parrot, a squeaking squirrel, a bony horse, and a canvas-topped wagon, and all were headed 'Texas way.'[30]

He then goes on to describe further categories of tramp families known respectively as "the McCarthys," "the Night-Hawks," or "the Holy Frights." "They are not exactly out-and-out criminals whom the police can get hold of, but moral lepers who by public consent have been sentenced to live without the pale of civilization."[31] Creeping into Flynt's narrative, one cannot avoid noting the voice of the sociologist—not only his need to categorize, but also the generalizations (at times disdainful) he uses to describe the subjects of his "investigations." It is not surprising perhaps that Flynt the actor—his need to inhabit different roles in his life—should also extend to his writing voice. A similar paradoxical writing style is discussed in the chapters on Stephen Graham, Trader Horn and other tramp writers. Nonetheless, it is interesting to observe the manner in which Flynt is, on the one hand, able to identify warmly with vagabonds and the vagabond he is, and on the other, describe his fellow tramps with such detachment. Perhaps here Flynt is doing no more than his job: meeting the demands and agendas of those who are paying him for his writing. Such is the difficulty of reconciling these two very different aspects of the man. At any rate, intentionally or not, and whatever the motive, Flynt did contribute to the field of sociology and criminology by pioneering the role of the participant observer. But before looking more closely at Flynt the sociologist, let us return to Flynt's adventures as a tramp, all the time conscious of the different voices emerging through his writing (the tramp storytelling, the scholar discoursing, and the journalist reporting) often inseparably woven through the text.

Adult American Tramping Adventures

Flynt distinguishes between "blowed-in-the-glass-stiffs," mature hobos who supported themselves purely through begging and thievery, and "gay-cats," mainly younger tramps, who were prepared to work and hustle to make ends meet. And while acknowledging that the paths of these two species of tramp often crossed, it was also clear that "The hobo considered himself, and really was, more of a person than the Gay-Cat, and he let the latter know it."[32] A further distinction is made between the tramp who begs and the tramp who steals—both he acknowledges to be equally tough professions, and both of which he avoided unless driven by absolute necessity—"stealing in Hoboland is not a favourite business or pastime. Hoboland is the home of the discouraged criminal who has no other refuge."

In "The American Tramp Considered Geographically," Flynt describes the different characteristics of the American and Canadian tramp according to geographical definitions that would only make sense to the tramp of his day. North, South, East and West, all had unique tramping characteristics, the following being Flynt's explanation for why he was never in the company of black tramps ("shinies"), as opposed to the exclusively white tramp or hobo, while tramping in the South:

> The hobo seems to do better when traveling only with hoboes, and the shiny [shinie] lives much more comfortably in his own clan. My explanation of this fact is this: both parties have learned by experience that alms are much more generously given to a white man when alone than when in company with a negro. This, of course, does not apply anywhere but in the South, for a colored tramp is just as well treated in the East and West as a white one.[33]

In a chapter titled "The City Tramp," Flynt describes the different specializations to which tramps apply themselves, all generously illustrated, as is the whole book, although no reference is made to the artist:

> [T]o-day we have all sorts of hoboes. There are house-beggars, office-beggars, street-beggars, old-clothes beggars, and of late years still another specialization has become popular in vagabondage. It is called "land-squatting," which means that the beggar in question has chosen a particular district for his operations.[34]

Flynt goes on to describe: the "tomato-can vag ... the lowest type ... in tramp parlance" and also notes that, at the time of his writing, English cities were more populated with tramps than American cities, adding that class hatred and suspicion between groups of tramps is more noticeable in the U.K. than the USA. The chapter titled "What the Tramp Eats and Wears" is more anecdotal than philosophical and very specific to the place and time of Flynt's adventures, although, as with Graham's *The Gentle Art*, there are some helpful tips for the aspiring tramp. But it must be emphasized that those who Flynt categorizes as tramps throughout most of his writings are more accurately beggars and petty criminals than they are true tramps. Only briefly, and in a separate essay titled "How Men Become Tramps," does Flynt describe the tramp ascetic, as opposed to the vagrant as petty criminal. Here he acknowledges those on the road—easily identified elsewhere in this book—who were tramping purely and simply because they loved to tramp and could not conquer their passion for roving, "the truest type of the genuine voluntary vagrant. ... He is free from the majority of passions common among vagrants, yet he is the most earnest vagrant of all. To reform him it is necessary to kill his personality, to take away his main ambition. And this is a task almost superhuman."[35] In this single paragraph, Flynt shows significant insight into—but then abruptly dismisses—the "tramp of choice."

Dangers of Riding the Rails

Of accidents during his travels, Flynt says in his autobiography that there was very little to report. "While other men and boys were breaking legs, getting crushed under wheels and falling between cars, I went serenely on my way unharmed." And yet in *Tramping With Tramps*, Flynt reports several near-misses, such as being knocked to the ground from a moving train by a water pipe, and shot at by an angry conductor. His most amusing story is told in "One Night on the 'Q.'" Flynt and a fellow hobo traveling to Chicago look for an empty boxcar on a cattle train but they all are full of steers. They climb onto the roof in the pouring rain but the brakeman spots them and tells them they are fools. To their surprise he shows them that on the outside end of each car full of steers is a hay box. He lifts up the lid and they climb down into the comfortable bed of hay. Only later do they discover that the brakeman has locked the lid behind them, which they are unable to kick open. The only thing between them and the steers' horns below them is the fast-diminishing hay, held in place only by widely spaced wooded slats. Both are convinced they will end their lives impaled on the steers' horns but as the train slows to a stop six miles outside of Chicago, they hear other tramps outside the train and call them to unlatch the lid and free them. "There was still a fair amount of hay in the box. I rooted down to the slats for a last look at our tormentors, and there, right before me, stood those awful beasts, wild and fresh from the fields of the Lone Star State. There were nearly twenty of them, I should say, but not a single one had a horn!"[36]

Flynt the Sociologist

Flynt's theories on criminology are most eruditely expressed in the opening chapter of *Tramping With Tramps*, "The Criminal In The Open," in which he sets out his rationale for studying the vagabond in their natural habitat. Up to the time of Flynt's writing, he acknowledges that the criminal had been studied exclusively behind prison bars, and that the environment and the subject of scientists' observations and measurements could not have been further from the condition in which the criminal operated. There are volumes, he writes, "about the criminal's body, skull, and face, his whimsical and obscene writings on prison-walls, the effect of various kinds of diet on his deportment," et cetera. But that from this mass of information, gathered by prison doctors and other officials, they conclude that "the criminal is a more or less degenerate human being … that he is abnormally deficient in mental and moral aptitudes, and, in a large number of instances, should be in an insane asylum rather than in a penitentiary." Flynt suggests that the scientists were asking the wrong questions and that instead, they should start their investigations by examining the criminal's "most natural state of body and mind," not their confinement in prison. "I claim that imprisonment should be considered rather as an incident in his existence than its normal sphere … we have to-day a distorted view of the criminal and an illogical tendency in penology."[37]

There is much to be admired in Flynt's diatribe against the doctors and the criminologists of his day. But it is when Flynt starts offering his own explanations for vagabondage, and offering solutions to the "problem," that the difficulties of reconciling Flynt the tramp with Flynt the social reformer really start to emerge. His essay "How Men Become Tramps: Conclusions from Personal Experience as an Amateur Tramp" (1895), published in *The Century* when he was 26 and in the final year of his Ph.D. studies at Berlin University, does little to exploit his remarkable and authentic first-hand knowledge of tramp life. Had someone else's agenda influenced Flynt's writings? Was he simply being used by reactionary forces to reinforce common fears and preconceptions of tramping? In the essay he summarizes the principal causes of vagabondage as follows:

> There can be no doubt that the tramp is, in a certain sense, the maker and chooser of his own career. The writer's experience with these vagrants has convinced him that, though they are almost always the victims of liquor and laziness, fully four fifths of America's voluntary beggars have begun their wild and restless ways while still in their teens ... The American tramp does not want to work, as a rule; but I know that he does want to be free from liquor. And if this can be accomplished, I feel safe in saying that he will go to work. Under the influence of drink, he becomes a sort of voluntary idler; but if he were temperate, he could be made a valuable citizen."[38]

Flynt makes some progressive (even by today's standards) observations as, for instance, when he says: "The reader may wonder why it is that boys are allowed in jails, and not confined to institutions exclusively devoted to their needs." And yet in the same short essay he also advocates stiffer punishment for adult tramps, not for crimes against the person, but simply for vagrancy and begging: "During an eight months sojourn with tramps, I have seen policemen and justices time after time simply order roving vagrants 'out of town,' when there was plenty of evidence to have punished the fellows in workhouses and jails." That vagabonds are not punished more severely is a fairly constant refrain of Flynt's, but surprisingly, it also seems one shared by many tramps of his day. And this is not simply the desire to spend time being fed and sheltered by the state, a common strategy for many of Flynt's hobo friends during winter when they would calculate just what crime would secure the desired number of weeks in jail. The tramping fraternity that Flynt describes seems a conservative bunch and can be quite critical of leniency, even toward their own kind.

Ultimately, one has to accept Flynt for *all* the characters he leaves us with in his writings, and take from them what we want. And, some of the banality aside, there is much both to admire and enjoy. Flynt the visionary thinker and Flynt the ordinary yet extraordinary thrill-seeker, trying to make the best of what life threw at him, can all be summed up in his following lines:

> There were tramps thousands of years ago, and I fear that they will be on the earth, if there be an earth then, thousands of years hence. ... I should expect to find the ancient Egyptian hobo, for instance, if he could come to life and would be natural, pretty much the same kind of roadster that we know in our present American type. Laziness, loafing, Wanderlust and begging are to-day what they ever have been—qualities and habits that are passed on from generation to generation, practically intact.[39]

Flynt's Death

Flynt's short life and writings are probably richer for that fact that he never really gave up his tramp persona for that of the social scientist. That he was addicted to what he himself identified as one of the primary causes of vagabondage was a personal tragedy. Not "laziness," contrary to his own stereotype of the tramp, Flynt was a grafter.[40] Sadly Flynt remained addicted to liquor, and latterly narcotics, dying of pneumonia after two hours of unconsciousness, at 7 p.m. on January 20, 1907 (aged 38), in the opulent Kaiserhof Hotel, Clark Street, Chicago. Flynt had returned to Chicago to write an article on poolroom gambling for *Cosmopolitan* magazine, but more importantly to be near his mother with whom he had had a closeness throughout his life. The final words on Flynt are left to his friend Emily Burbank:

> Flynt often talked of his death after disease fastened upon him, but always with an inconsequence as to what lay beyond the grave—not bravado, but the philosopher's acquiescence to the inevitable, whatever it be. He had great faith in the loyalty of friends who might survive him. "So-and-so will speak a good word for me, I know!" he would say. Separation, by geographical distances, never bothered him, yet he wrote but few letters. He seemed to get satisfaction out of his belief that he and his nearest friends communicated by thought transference: "The wires are always up!" Doubtless he passed out with the conviction that this would continue.[41]

ENDNOTES

1 Composite from various web pages
2 Burbank, Emily M. "Josiah Flynt—An Impression," in *My Life*, op. cit., p. 346
3 Ibid., p. 347
4 Stein, Gertrude. *An Autobiography of Alice B. Toklas*, New York: Vintage Books, 1955, p. 83
5 Flynt, Josiah. *My Life*, New York: The Outing Publishing Company, 1908, pp. 2–4
6 Ibid., p. 75
7 Ibid., p. 98
8 *My Life*, op. cit., p. 139
9 Ibid., p. 150
10 *Tramping with Tramps*, op. cit., p. 184
11 Ibid., p. 264
12 Ibid., p. 242
13 *My Life*, ibid., p. 210
14 Ibid., p. 226
15 Ibid., p. 229
16 Ibid., p. 245
17 Ibid., p. 254
18 Ibid., p. 256
19 Ibid., pp. 257–258
20 Ibid., 262
21 *Tramping with Tramps*, op. cit., p. 302
22 Merwin, Bannister. 'A Final Word' in *My Life*, op. cit., p. 357
23 *My Life*, op. cit., pp. 354–355
24 Ibid., p. 352
25 Ibid., p. 295
26 Ibid., p. 108
27 *Tramping with Tramps*, p. 53
28 Flynt, Josiah. 'Homosexuality Among Tramps,' Appendix A in Havelock Ellis, *Studies in the Psychology of Sex, Volume 2, Sexual Inversion*, Philadelphia: F.A. Davis Company, 1927, p. 360
29 *Tramping with Tramps*, p. 29
30 Ibid., p. 31
31 Ibid., p. 34
32 *My Life*, op. cit., p. 101
33 *Tramping with Tramps*, op. cit., p. 109
34 Ibid., p. 113
35 Flynt, Josiah. "How Men Become Tramps" in *The Century Magazine*, New York, October 1, 1895, pp. 944–945
36 *Tramping with Tramps*, op. cit., p. 365
37 *Tramping with Tramps*. op. cit., pp. 1–2
38 "How Men Become Tramps," op. cit., p. 941
39 *My Life*, op. cit., pp. 115–117
40 Flynt has been credited for the introduction of the word "graft" into book English.
41 Burbank, op. cit., p. 350

Jack Black

(1871–1932)

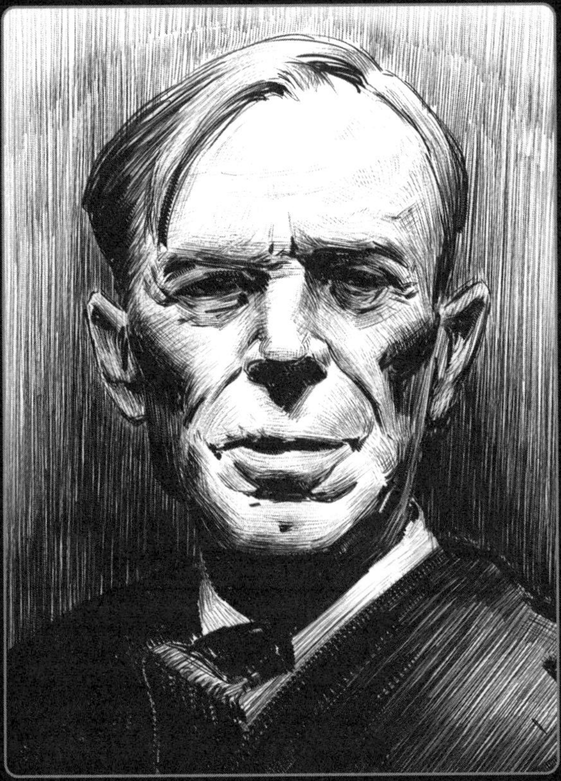

I had not spent one hour in the company of an honest person. ... I thought in terms of theft. Houses were built to be burglarized, citizens were to be robbed, police to be avoided and hated, stool pigeons to be chastised, and thieves to be cultivated and protected. That was my code; the code of my companions.

Jack Black, *You Can't Win*

Preamble

Although Jack Black shares the same credentials as the other tramp writers discussed in this volume—beating trains, sleeping in hobo jungles, familiar with starvation, jail and beatings from police—Black's principal role was that of a professional criminal, or "yegg," a term previously discussed as applying to the more feared "outlaw hobos." In Black's case, within his main activities of burglary, armed robbery and safe-cracking, he developed a strong moral code that rejected wanton violence, even bringing trouble down on his own head to protect friends and other unfortunates from harm. Like Flynt and London, Black was also addicted at various times to narcotics—in his case combined with the thrill of gambling.

Born near Vancouver, British Columbia, Black was raised in Missouri. His adventures and philosophy on life started at the age of 10 and are contained in a single volume titled *You Can't Win* (1926), published six years before his death. Black's autobiography is also the subject of a 2016 movie of the same name, starring, co-produced and co-written by Michael Pitt. As with Flynt and London also, Black's writing had a major influence on the Beat movement and its writers, particularly William Burroughs who in his first book, *Junkie* (1953), reflected much of the style and subject matter of *You Can't Win*. Burroughs wrote a foreword for the later 1988 Amok Press edition of *You Can't Win,* and commenting on the book's title, American society at the time, and Black's own philosophy on life, Burroughs acknowledges, "Well, who can? Winner take nothing. Would he have been better off having spent his life in some full-time job? I don't think so."

The most recent edition of the book, and the one used as the research for this chapter, was published by Feral House in 2013.[1] As well as Burroughs' 1988 foreword, the Feral House edition also includes a biographical essay on Black by Donald Kennison, Joe Coleman's original artwork from the 1988 Amok Press edition, and two of Black's extended articles: "What's Wrong with the Right People?" from *Harper's Magazine* (1929) and "A Burglar Looks at Laws and Codes," *Harper's Magazine* (1930). As a first-person witness, Black also wrote extensively about the Folsom Prison breakout of July 27, 1903, the penitentiary where he served an eight-year sentence and was released the year following that revolt:

> This break was a protest of helpless men against hopeless conditions. Wrought up to a frenzy by brutality, violence and fear, the men rose, cut down guards, rushed a gatling gun tower and captured it with no weapons but razors taken from the prison barber shop. They took officers of the guard as hostages and escaped with them to the woods.[2]

Black was a reformed character and professional journalist by the time he wrote *You Can't Win*, and part of his motivation for writing it was to dissuade would-be criminals from a life of crime, at the same time pointing out the inability of the courts and judiciary to deliver justice. Paradoxically, it was while working for *The San Francisco Evening Bulletin,* and during a circulation war between the *Bulletin* and Randolph Hearst's *San Francisco Call,* that Black was near fatally wounded by a stomach shot from a rival journalist. True to his code of never snitching to the police, Black later refused to identify his would-be assassin and the case was dismissed. During his writing period Black wrote essays and participated in lecture tours. As with Jim Phelan's writings on penology, Black's writings represent an important social history on many aspects of criminality and prison life during the particular period covered. Black spent about 15 years of his 30-year criminal career in various jails and penitentiaries that also included several prison breakouts.

Early Life

Black's mother died when he was 10 years old, following which, although his father was kindly, he was pretty much left to his own devices, running around the hotel where he was left alone while his father was out working until he took him off to a Catholic boarding school a hundred miles away. During his three years at the school, Black was a model student and avid reader. Among the things he read and became obsessed with were newspaper reports about the life and death of the outlaw Jesse James, following which he devoured newspaper reports of other outlaws and their activities. Aside from fantasizing about the world of crime, Black left school aged 14, acknowledging that "I was as unsophisticated as a boy could be. I knew no more of the world and its strange ways than the gentle, saintly woman who taught me my prayers in the convent." He returned to the same hotel he had left three years earlier and continued with his reading during the long hours his father was absent during the day:

> I found lots of papers lying around—some cheap novels, Police Gazettes, etc.—and I read them all, everything I could get hold of. I saw my father only at night, occasionally we would take a walk then for an hour.[3]

It was around this time, also, that the first stirrings of wanderlust got a grip of the young vagabond. He describes how he followed a man back to the hotel one day and how he became fascinated by the man's leather trunk with brass fittings that was covered all over with stickers from the many hotels he had stayed at and steamship lines he had traveled on. "I stood around and felt it, read the stickers, some of them from foreign parts of the world, and wondered what kind of man he could be that possessed such a wonderful trunk."[4] Black became restless and disturbed by the image of the trunk and its owner. "It had roused strange thoughts and longings in my mind that I did not understand then. I know now that it suggested trades, adventure by land and sea—the world."

Determined to get money to save and kit himself out like the traveler, and without telling his father, Black took his first paid job sweeping and tidying up in the hotel bar for the friendly saloon owner Cy. After his first week he was given three dollar-coins in wages, which he gave to his father for safe keeping after getting his father's blessing to hold down the job. Shortly afterwards his father announced that they were leaving for Kansas City where he had got a new job, and Black was put up in a small boarding house while his father would often be absent at work for weeks, even months, at a time. Before leaving, Black's father gave him the money he had saved up from his sweeping job and told him to find more work. And a job he soon found, minding a tobacconist's store for three dollars a week and "all the cigars you can smoke." When Black protested that he did not smoke, the tobacconist replied, "Well that's your bad luck kid." Black was soon to discover that the cigar shop was just a front for a poker and dice salon out back and that his job was to make the front of the shop look authentic, sweeping up and serving the odd customer. "The dice shakers and crap shooters showed me their favorite 'shots.' I was an apt scholar, absorbing everything like a young sponge."[5]

Next door to the cigar shop was a small milk depot, and the owner told Black that he would pay him to collect money from customers who owed him. Black figured out the best time to catch people at home. His tobacconist boss, Tex, was fine with him having two jobs and even gave him tips, advising him that the best time to catch women at home was around 5 p.m. when they were preparing the evening meal. Most of the women were kind to him and paid up with little fuss. Tex had a run of luck in the casino and raised Black's wages to four dollars a week, and the milkman paid a premium when Black collected from customers who resisted paying. Thoughts of adventure were never far from his mind but Black was not impatient and determined to save up a good stash of money before setting out traveling.

Black's first run-in with the law happened when he went to collect a milk bill from the owner of a local brothel. While he was waiting to collect, a customer of one of the girls complained that he had been frisked by her of a hundred dollars and the police were called to the scene. The captain was friends with Kate, the madam of the brothel, but had to be seen to do his job. No one was allowed to leave the premises, and Black, along with the girls and several drunks, was bundled into the police van and taken to the local station. After the initial questioning one of the cops asked the captain what he should do with the men who had been taken in: "Oh, charge them with drink." "The kid's not drunk." "Vag him then." Then, turning to Black, the officer asked him, "What were you doing in that joint anyway?" Black explained, even producing the milk bill, followed by "Why the hell didn't you say so at the start?" "I tried to, sir, but everyone kept telling me to shut up." Not that that did it either. After everyone else was let go the captain said, "Take the kid upstairs and lock him up with George. I'll find out more about him."[6]

This was Black's first lesson in the injustice of the law. Then there was George, a distinguished criminal who had stolen fortunes and spent them, killed a crooked partner, and enjoyed special privileges out of reputation and respect from crooks and cops alike. George would turn out to be a long-term friend and mentor of Black, and it was from that cell and encounter that Black's criminal career would emerge. Kate and her girls had forgotten all about Black in the excitement of the previous 24 hours, but when they did remember him there was a great deal of remorse and not a little fuss made of the young milkman's assistant. And so began a close friendship with the young girl who had pickpocketed her client. This odd couple spent a good deal of time together when they were not working. Black got to learn from Julia about another kind of imprisonment: what becoming a whore meant when young girls who were down on their luck (in Julia's case an unwanted pregnancy from a rape, only to be raped again by the doctor at the hospital where the baby died) were taken in by what appeared to be a kindly benefactor, only to become slaves to that individual from which there was no escape. But with Black and a kindly hack driver's help, Julia did escape. The plan was that she would throw her bundle of clothes out of the brothel window and then sneak out through the kitchen, without hat or street clothes so as not to arouse suspicion, into the back alley and the waiting hack. A week later Julia came to the cigar store to tell Black that she had got a job as a barmaid and a clean room of her own. No more was said about the matter and Black was not suspected the next time he collected the milk money from the brothel.

The next time Black's father came home, Black told him everything about his work, his arrest and his rescue of Julia. His father left the next day with these parting words: "Well John, you'll be what you'll be, and I cannot help or hinder you. Go back to your job in the morning if you like." They were kind words, Black recalls, "and I have always remembered them and their ring of fatality." Black would never see his father again, although he did learn much later that he "lived out his life orderly and died decently."[7]

By now Black had become "tired of Tex and his tribe and their smokey back room and cheap cheating … sick of the sight of the crabby widow at the boarding house." Black had money, the wanderlust had become an irresistible force, and so he took off walking westward until nighttime and tiredness found him in a hobo jungle. There, two bindlestiffs invited him to join them for a tin of java (coffee) if he collected up some firewood, following which one of the hobos surprised both Black and the second hobo by producing "a gump," a live chicken, from his bindle. And so began Black's hobo career with a hearty meal under a bridge where he learned the ways of existing on what nature, thieving and the detritus of the jungle provided. In response to one of the old-timers saying to him,

"If you're goin' west you'd better learn to talk west," he also started familiarizing himself with the language of the road. On offering to go up to the nearest farmhouse and buy some supplies, he was severely admonished by one of his fellow vagabonds who told him that it was green kids like Black that made it tough on seasoned tramps: "Go up to that house and tell the woman you and two other kids run away from home in the city three days ago and you ain't had nothin' but a head of cabbage that fell off a farmer's wagon."[8]

This advice, together with Black's existing winsome ways, produced the desired results and the following compliment from his companions: "You're a good connector, kid," together with sound advice about how to deal with troublesome dogs. Black also learned about "D.D.ing," carrying a note to identify to would-be targets that one is deaf and dumb, and carrying small inexpensive items such as bags of lavender in order to avoid getting done for begging—"selling" isn't begging.

Black's first attempt at beating a train nearly lost him his life. After directing him to a rail junction—his companions being too old for that game and leaving Black to proceed alone—the novice hobo jumped a car with the door open on a slow westbound freight train. The car was stacked high with sawn lumber that was six feet shorter than the end of the car, leaving space for Black to drop down in the gap. A few stops further on, a kid about his own age crawled over the top of the lumber and dropped down to join him. After a brief conversation the both of them were sleeping, but something in the evening woke Black. As the train was traveling down an incline, part of the load started creaking and shifting. Black's companion panicked and started to crawl up to get on top of the lumber. There followed a grinding and a crash that splintered the wooden end of the car:

> The boy had died instantly. His body from the waist up was flattened between the lumber and the front end of the car. His legs dangled below, down where I was imprisoned, with each movement of the car, like the legs of a scarecrow in the wind.[9]

Black was now trapped in a space half the size but safe as the weight of the lumber above meant the lumber below was unable to move. He now went to work with his pocketknife on the half-rotted timber that made up the side of the car, and after two hours, with hands badly blistered, had cut through the ends of three boards. As the train started slowing to a halt, Black finished the job by kicking out the boards from where he had cut them through at the top, leaving him enough space to squeeze out from the car. Once on the town's main street he noted that he was in Dodge City, "a town at that time largely given over to gambling, fighting and whiskey drinking"—amusements that the young Black had still to develop a taste for. Next stop Denver, where Black got his second bust. He had gone for a swim in a river alongside a camp where the local bums congregated. The alarm went up but Black did not get a chance to grab his clothes and make a run for it before he was bundled into a patrol wagon and taken downtown. The police had had orders to clean up the town and Black found himself in court for the first time charged with vagrancy. When he pleaded to the judge that he was not a vagrant because he had $20 in the jail office, the judge looked at him "coldly and impersonally as if I had been a dish of parsnips. 'Fifteen days on the chain gang. Next case.'"[10]

Black spent a night in jail where he struck up an immediate friendship with another inmate, Smiler, due for release that morning. The next morning, on being led to the wagon bound for the chain gang, Black instinctively made a dash for it to the cheers of onlookers, and the guards, fearful of losing the rest of the prisoners, did not bother to give chase. And so for the first time Black becomes a penniless fugitive from justice. Twenty miles outside of Denver he came across a hobo jungle on the outskirts of a small town: "Confidently I walked up to the fire. I was one of them. I had escaped; I was hungry; I was ready for anything; I belonged around the fire." A shout went up from the fire where he was embraced by Smiler who congratulated him on his escape and was promised fresh clothing as soon as they located a likely house to burgle. After securing a bundle of clothes, jewelry, cash and a parcel of food to eat, the pair beat the next train out. Inside the freight car Black was given further coaching into becoming a successful burglar. Smiler told him to throw out of the car door the watch and jewelry as, if caught with it, "That junk would get us five years, kid, if we got grabbed with it, and it ain't worth two dollars."[11] Black found the whole experience satisfying and justified the burglary on the basis that he had been deprived of his coat and $20 by "the law" for nothing but going for a swim, and so it seemed right to him that he should be recompensed for his lost possessions from some wealthy law-abiding citizen who was probably insured anyway.

Smiler had been a "prowler" since being run out of his hometown by the cops. The two were by now fast friends and Smiler was determined to teach Black the "real thing" as soon as they arrived in Salt Lake City. But their next burglary took place en route from Cheyenne to Salt Lake City at a junction point where they spotted a jeweler at work in his shop window. Smiler told Black to go around to the back of the store and hurl some rocks at the back door while he grabbed a tray of watches as the jeweler was distracted. Back at the train yard, Black would learn about planting loot to avoid any chance of being caught with the stuff. Smiler noted a freight train bound for Butte, Montana, bundled the watches up in a handkerchief, stowed them in a corner of a freight car which he covered in coal, and then tore the corner off the destination card so that he could identify the same car later. Then they took a different train only to reconnoiter with their booty later at Evanston—en route to Butte—and from there go with the watches to a fence Smiler knew in Pocatello, Idaho.

Salt Chunk Mary—there is no way of knowing if this was her real moniker, as no reference to anyone of that name appears outside of Black's narrative—was an infamous brothel keeper and disposer of stolen goods. She is one of the major characters of *You Can't Win* and reappears often in the book, fencing stolen property and helping spring criminals, including Black, from the jaws of justice. Police and judges were also on her payroll or received other favors at her disposal. The origin of the moniker Salt Chunk Mary was the large pot of salt pork and beans that was forever simmering on her stove, ready to give sustenance to the hungry vagabonds who continually arrived at her house as free passengers from passing freight trains. Noteworthy is that Mary's treatment of her "girls" could not have been in greater contrast to the kindness and generosity she showed toward her male visitors—who paid generously for her hospitality either directly or in the profits she made from fencing stolen contraband. In contrast, Black had a deep regard and respect for women. This rather strange Mother Teresa character, an equal mix of good and evil, is described by Black as "about forty years of age, hard-faced and heavy-handed. Her hair was the color of sunburned brick and her small blue eyes glinted like ice under a March sun. She could say 'no' quicker than any woman I ever knew, and none of them meant 'yes.'"[12]

And so when Mary gave Smiler $400 for the watches, he was satisfied that he had received a fair price in the full knowledge that they would be passed on for significantly more. With a substantial amount of money in their pockets, they beat a train to Ogden and over the Pacific Railway to Sacramento and then onwards to San Francisco to get their first glimpse of the sea. But not before being put off a car full of hay at Port Costa, where they had spent the night and appeared before the unusually humane Judge Casey. The judge fed them a meal before sentencing them to five days and locking them into a boxcar for onward transportation. Black told Smiler how he had escaped from the car full of lumber and the pair soon set to work with a knife and were out in an hour, resuming their journey to San Francisco. After spending a month on the waterfront watching the ships and sailors by day and frequenting the bars and dancehalls by night, the pair were broke and decided to return to Salt Lake City in search of more pickings.

While drinking in a small gambling house in that city, they watched a locksmith at work changing the combination of a safe for the new owners. After writing down the combination numbers on a slip of paper, the locksmith left the slip with his tools while he went to the bar for a drink, giving Smiler the opportunity to pick up and study the numbers before throwing the slip back on the floor. Not having the faintest idea how to open a safe at that time even *with* the combination, the pair set out for a penitentiary a mile out of town to visit a safecracking friend of Smiler's who was doing time there. That night they opened the safe, but instead of finding the thousands of dollars they were expecting, the safe only yielded a few hundred because the new owners had opened the place on a shoestring and as yet had no bankroll. By this time, hooked on gambling, the money was gone in a matter of days and they returned to the more familiar burglary to replenish their stash. Smiler's modus operandi was to watch rich-looking folk coming out of the theater, particularly those decked in jewels, then follow them home to check whether the house was free of children and dogs, was not overlooked, and had a reasonable chance of access. Having located a likely victim, they kept watch on the place until the early hours of the morning when everyone would be sound asleep. House burglars need to work single-handed and so Black stayed outside to keep watch while Smiler went to work.

As Smiler slowly and soundlessly raised an unlocked sash window, there was a blinding flash of light followed by the explosion of a rifle. Then came sounds of breaking glass and a woman's screams. Smiler staggered backwards from the wind clutching his throat and then sunk to his knees. After instinctively running for the gate and alleyway, and expecting to hear more shots, on a further instinct Black returned to help his friend and, with blood streaming from Smiler's mouth, he half carried him out into the alley where his friend collapsed. Unable to lift the dead weight, Black stayed with his friend briefly, but long enough to see him shudder and die. Soaked in the blood which had spurted from Smiler's wound, Black found a derelict house to hide out in until he could decide what to do next. Tired, hungry and fearing for his life, Black had time to reappraise the path he had taken and, while not having any regrets over previous events, he determined there and then to give up life on the road as an outlaw and return to his father. There he stayed until the following evening, only venturing out when he felt it was safe and made his way to a sulphur spring in the hillside to clean up. Then, with the money he had left, he bought some clothes in a store and went to a nearby restaurant for food. While eating his meal, he overheard a policeman at the next table describing the recent events, accounting for why everything went silent following the shooting and no chase had been given. The man of the house had been called out urgently and his wife, unable to sleep, had been prowling restlessly around when Smiler had appeared at the window. In a panic, the woman grabbed the gun, fired it at Smiler, and then dropped down in a faint.

Black returned to the room he had shared with Smiler and passed out on the bed from exhaustion, only to be roused some time later by loud knocking at the door. He was arrested and handcuffed by two police officers who showed him a bloodstained receipt for their room rent that they had found in a corner of Smiler's pocket—the kind of carelessness that Smiler had drummed into him which he now regretted overlooking. To cut a long story short, Black was put on remand pending his trial as an accessory to the burglary, but within an hour of arriving at the penitentiary had "made friends and incurred obligations that turned my thoughts away from home and sent me back on the road."[13]

Some of the inmates at the penitentiary knew of and respected Smiler, and on hearing Black's story took him into their circle, adopting him as one of the

"Johnson family," denoting those who are straight and to be trusted within the criminal fraternity. One such was Black's old acquaintance George. George pretty much ruled the prison from the inside, aided by his second in command known by the moniker the Sanctimonious Kid, Sanc for short. Third in the pecking order was Soldier Johnnie. Black also got close to a mature bank robber known as Shorty. "They had brains and character backed by courage and the valuable background of a reputation for doing things on the outside." All these characters make several further appearances in Black's book.

On George asking Black if he'd made any statement about the Smiler affair and being told he had not, George and his friends vowed to help Black beat the rap in no time at all with the help of a friendly judge, and no small amount of money available to them in the prison office from friends on the outside—with which they were able to buy favors. So comfortable and well-fed were they that they often did not go to the prison dining room for a week:

> Loaves of fresh, hot bread were smuggled up from the bakery, and juicy steaks from the guard's quarters. These creature comforts helped to take the curse off the place, and mitigate the prison pangs. Our light was put out, not when the nine o'clock bell rang, but when George, or Sanc or Johnnie felt like going to sleep.[14]

When the time came for Black to be put on a work detail he refused to work because Johnnie, who was something of a jail lawyer, had told him that they could not force prisoners to work who had not been convicted of a crime. When Black said this to the officer in charge of the work detail, he was marched to the office of the prison captain who ordered the "fresh kid" to be thrown in the cooler until he changed his mind. The cooler was an empty cell (apart from a bucket to piss in) without any light, its steel floor and walls making it uncomfortable and cold to sleep in, there being no option but to lie on the floor. Black was only given one slice of bread and a quart of water a day, and so began a battle of wills between our hero and the not unkindly prison guards who kept pleading with him to weaken and promise to go to work. Black just saw the whole affair as a way of increasing his reputation with the other prisoners who were all well aware of his plight and waiting for him to crack. The first morning, teeth chattering from the cold, the guard arrived with his bread and water. On biting into the bread his teeth made contact with what turned out to be a chicken quill, and inside the quill was a note which Black could just about read by lying on the floor to use the crack of light from the bottom of the cell door. The note read, "Stick, we'll feed you to-night." That evening at lock-up, Black heard a low, grinding noise above the ceiling of his cell, partly muffled by a lot of walking to and fro, presumably to disguise the noise and keep an eye out for the guards. "Before nine o'clock there was an inch hole in the floor and strips of tender meat, long strips of bread, toasted to keep them together, cigarettes and matches, were being lowered into my cell." His friends had also bribed a prison guard to give Black a blanket.[15]

In this manner, Black survived three weeks in the cooler, never missing his evening meal, and only let out because he had to appear in court on the burglary charge looking half human. His friends apologized for not getting food to him the first night due to the complications of getting the two occupants of the cell above the cooler moved out, and two members of the Johnson family moved in. On being advised by the judge to plead not guilty, a date for the hearing was set two days hence. In court, Black followed the judge's instructions, pleaded not guilty and refused to answer any other questions. The woman who shot Smiler was asked if she saw any other person at the scene, to which she replied no, and the detectives had no incriminating evidence to offer. The prosecutor argued with the judge about the lodging receipt, Black's change of clothes, his absence from the room that night, and his refusal to make a statement—all of which drew irritation from the judge and some clear instructions to the jury. But given Black's previous experience of the law, he was agitated and had no confidence of being acquitted. He strolled backwards and forwards in the courtroom, each time a little closer to the courtroom door, and then finally, the court bailiff being busy talking to another man, out of the door and down the street. From there to the rail yards where he slept in a barn waiting for the next train out. After holding out in the blind baggage of a passenger train all night, dodging the bulls at every stop, he was then arrested by a rail guard tapping away at a large pistol in his holster. In desperation and fear of being returned to the penitentiary, as the train pulled out and the last carriage was passing, Black used all his force to push the constable into a ditch and hoist himself back on the train. But just as he alighted the train, a guard came out through the end door of the car just in time to see the constable crawling out of the ditch and firing into the air, at the same time signaling to pull the cord to stop the train. Black jumped down straight into the arms of the constable, now reinforced with two locals from the depot, upon which all three set about him and gave him an "unmerciful skull dragging." It turned out that the constable was part-time, doubling as the postmaster and section boss, and "a very decent fellow." He apologized for the roughing Black got and brought him a banquet of food. To Black's surprise, he had not been arrested for fleeing the courtroom but for trespass: a bunch of hobos had burned a string of boxcars and the company had orders to arrest any suspicious characters on sight. Black also learned later from newspapers that a not guilty verdict had been pronounced *before* he walked out of the court and that the whole thing was already forgotten.

While serving his 10 days in the local jail, Black gave a lot of thought to how he could raise the money he wanted to pay back George and Shorty for the money they had used to get him free. Black had learned a great deal from others during his month in the penitentiary about various ways of relieving fat post offices and country general stores of their cash, and was already planning his next move when, on his release, he had time to notice the large and unprotected safe in the store of the town he had been staying in. He got news to Sanc, who was due out imminently, where to meet up with him, and they agreed to wait for Soldier Johnnie also, who only had another three weeks to serve. In the meantime they would survive on the money the older yeggs had available. Johnnie had no qualms about cracking the safe but was concerned that there was no obvious getaway; the night train did not stop at the town and the distance to Salt Lake was too far for horses. But Black had already anticipated this problem and come up with a foolproof plan. Sanc and Johnnie were to get themselves locked up for 10 days in the same jail that Black had just been released from after cutting a set of keys for the jail. They would crack the safe and plant the loot before locking themselves back into the jail, thereby creating the perfect alibi. Black's friends were amused by the plan and also convinced of its merits.

Being the apprentice burglar, the rough and unskilled work fell to Black for getting together the tools, dynamite, caps, etc., and planting them near the store. Johnnie and Sanc cut keys to fit the jail which they were to hide in their shoes, planting an additional set plus files in the jail itself. The store was full of arms and ammunition and the jail was empty. The only thing that could go wrong was that a couple of other bums would be thrown into the jail with them, foiling their plans to leave and return to jail unnoticed:

> Ten days later the burglary was reported in the papers. Four thousand dollars had been taken from the general store and the man hunt was on. ... The theft was not discovered until opening-up time the next morning. The thieves were evidently experts and left behind them the most complete set of safe-breaking tools seen in years ... They had escaped by taking a hand car from the section house. It was found wrecked several miles down the railroad track.[16]

The gang met up at Salt Chunk Mary's where they would be housed and fed for a month before returning to the plant to pick up the dollars. Pick it up Johnnie and Sanc did and split it into three equal shares, praising Black for his sharpness in locating the scene and planning the alibi. "But here's the main reason we gave you an even cut of the coin. From the way you stepped up in Smiler's case, and the way you took your jolt in the cooler at the 'big house' we knew you are 'right.'" No small praise for the apprentice burglar who now admits that all the thoughts he had of quitting the road when he was hiding out covered in Smiler's blood had gone. "Now I was safe, independent, the life fascinated me. No thoughts of home now."[17]

After this adventure, Black and Sanc set out for San Francisco leaving Johnnie to make his own way. On arriving in San Francisco, having learned his lesson from sharing lodgings with Smiler, Black and Sanc rented separate rooms; their dollars they put into safety deposit boxes to avoid any unnecessary bureaucracy with banks. They also purchased a couple of guns, and here Black writes a mini-thesis on how and where to purchase shooters. Sanc had to offer Black advice on what clothes to buy so as to make himself as inconspicuous as possible—people often remember what a person is wearing when they don't recall their individual features. Sanc was often out of town and on one occasion provided Black with a list of 50 names and addresses he had paid for of people who carried insurance for valuables. Black's job was to check out the addresses on the list against the criteria provided by Sanc—details like dogs, kids, servants, sick people, the layout of the house, porch, basement, yard, the alley. He was not to ask questions in the neighborhood, just walk by and look. "There was nothing of the Bill Sykes about Sanc. He ordered me to do things as a plumber would of an apprentice. I took orders and obeyed them as any apprentice should, cheerfully."[18]

The details of the robbery that followed can be read in the original text but Black continues to learn the finer arts of the burglary game and minimizing the chances of getting caught, like, for instance, not carrying away anything that would be difficult to dispose of or could be easily linked directly to the crime. Later in their room, Black tore off a piece of a newspaper to wrap the jewels in, and Sanc patiently said to him, "Wouldn't it be just as well to take the balance of that paper and throw it away, Kid? Why leave it in the room? It fits the piece you have in your pocket. And be sure to throw that junk away." The latter refers to settings from which the stones have been "unharnessed" and though having some value, were not worth a fraction of the stones themselves and could be linked directly back to the burglary. When Sanc noticed that a button was missing off Black's new suit jacket, he ordered that to be thrown away also. "Old Captain Lees (you've heard of him) would give that button to one of his smart young 'dicks' and stand him on the Richelieu corner ... He would stand there from four in the afternoon till midnight waiting for you to come along, which you do every evening."[19]

Sanc was not above silently breaking into someone's bedroom while they were asleep in the early hours of the morning, even removing their wallet from under their pillow while they were snoring. Before leaving on his next trip, Sanc left Black with the further task of renting hotel rooms for the night and registering from out of town, then cutting duplicate keys and planting them in safe locations for future use. "In a week you'll have keys to half a dozen good transient rooms in the best hotels, and I might get some real money out of them."[20] When he was not working, wearing an inconspicuous old suit and with only a small amount of silver in his pocket, Black hung out around the Barbary Coast and the waterfront where tattooed, seafaring men from around the globe spent their time drinking, fighting and singing their strange songs. He also spent time in the "wine dumps" where winos drank various concoctions and ate from large cauldrons of stew. The fascination of the latter category was that the winos where drawn from every walk of life:

> Scholars, quoting Greek and Latin poets, lawyers dissecting Blackstone, writers with greasy roles of manuscript fraternized with broken bums from the road, sailors too old for the sea, and scrapped mechanics from the factories—all under the lash of alcohol. ... This pitiful crew, gathered from the four corners of the earth ... drank themselves purple in the wine dumps and died on the floors or under the city sidewalks.[21]

Black also describes the culture and habits of the dope fiend, acknowledging that, at the time, morphine and opium cost little more than tobacco and that a day's supply could be bought for 50 cents. The "hypos" he describes as frequenting the "cook ovens" built at the back of Chinese lodging houses—warm places to sleep and take advantage of the charitable generosity of their Chinese proprietors. Black claims that the term "yegg" originated in these Chinese boarding houses, being a corruption of the way the Chinese referred to beggars as "yekk man." "In no time it had a verb hung on it, and to yegg meant to beg. ... Its meaning has since widened until now the term 'yegg' includes all criminals whose work is 'heavy.'"[22]

Black also refers to the fact—applying to him as well—that what maintained the yegg's criminal behavior was his addiction to gambling and high living, often drugs and alcohol also. "I experimented and soon laid a solid foundation for the faro-bank habit which fastened on me later and kept me broke for years." And so, no matter how great the haul from their most recent heist, it was simply not in a yegg's nature to invest their takings in buying a farm, store or other business and go straight. Few ever did, rather spending half of their lives in penitentiaries before serving out their time, linking up with old friends again, and returning to crime until they became too old to work and drifted into becoming bums or junkies. The criminal's life was habitual; no other option was considered. It was at the faro table one night, watching another player lose heavily, that Black was reacquainted with his old savior and mentor George. Only too happy to repay former debts, Black gave his friend $20 which was repaid soon afterwards.

After this latest meeting with George in Butte, Montana, which permanently cemented their friendship, Black headed out for Seattle via Spokane. He looks back with some regret that he did not stop off at one of those "spots of golden opportunity" all those years ago, buy land with his money instead of gambling it away, and become independent from the "harmful life" he subsequently embarked upon. Yet he acknowledges that "land hunger" is not a condition he inherited, that he had no more desire for it at the time he wrote his book than he did when he was at the height of his career as a criminal. "I had now become so saturated with the underworld atmosphere that no thought of any kind of honest endeavor entered my mind." Black calculates that your average journeyman mechanic will handle more money in 20 years than any first-class burglar and that at the end of that time will have a home, family, and money in the bank. In contrast, the most persistent and industrious burglar is lucky to have his liberty, and if he does he will be too old and broken to learn a new trade, and would not be offered work if he could. "He has the prison horrors, and turns to cheap larcenies and spends the balance of his life doing short term sentences in small jails."[23]

An earlier story about George—the reason behind him shooting another hobo—suggests that he might have been the brother of Salt Chunk Mary. After George was released from one of his many incarcerations, Black, George, and other friends met up at Salt Chunk Mary's in Pocatello for a reunion. After exhausting their hospitality at Mary's they all headed out for a hobo convention. Black describes, in fascinating detail, this grand get-together of vagabonds from all across the country, many of whom were carrying substantial funds from their nefarious deeds:

> Bums, thieves, beggars and yeggs appeared as if they had magic carpets. ... Cripples discarded their crutches and hopped about the camper grotesquely. "Crawlers" with cut-off legs swung themselves along on their hands drunkenly, like huge toads.[24]

Each day the bums drank more and ate less, partly because the camp cooks were too drunk to prepare food. The hobos started fighting and snarling at each other and an air of gloom soon descended on the camp. Then one day, just as able drinkers and funds for liquor had run dry, a fresh contingent of "brass peddlers" arrived with a large assortment of gold jewelry led by a yegg named Gold Tooth. It was after Gold Tooth went to Salt Chunk Mary's to offload his haul that the trouble started. George, Black, and others were seated at one of the campfires when Gold Tooth returned with his clothes in shreds, covered in blood and raving. He told how when he tried to fence his gold, Salt Chunk Mary had hit him on the back of the head with a bottle and kicked him when he fell to the ground, and that he was going back that very night to burn Mary's place to the ground. Whereupon George pulled a pistol from beneath his coat and shot Gold Tooth twice in the chest. Black tells how he could feel the slugs hitting Gold Tooth from six feet away. They then headed out for the railroad yard leaving Soldier Johnnie behind "to intimidate any of the weaker bums who might talk," but also shoo them out of Pocatello.

After successfully beating a train out of Pocatello, George and Black were picked up by the police in Butte and George charged with the murder. In spite of Soldier Johnnie's best efforts someone had ratted on George. Yet back in Pocatello the police had no hard evidence, and when they took George and Black down to the mortuary and threw back the covers on George's victim, expecting him to crack, George coolly placed a hand on the dead man's brow then held his arm out at full length, palm up, saying to the officer:

> "If I killed that man, there's the hand that held the gun, and there's the finger that pulled the trigger" (jerking his index finger back and forth), and, pulling up his coat sleeve, "there's my pulse! Do you want to feel it?"[25]

After locking the pair up and getting nothing from a further week of questioning, the town marshal, his patience exhausted and a hanging denied him, had the court sentence George and Black to six months for vagrancy. And so it was that the town fixer, Salt Chunk Mary, went to work and persuaded the judge to suspend the sentences on the promise that the miscreants would leave and stay out of town on the condition that if they ever returned they would have to serve out their full sentences.

Back in Butte, Black commenced his apprenticeship in safe-breaking under the able tutorship of George, jumping from one state to another and avoiding large cities, living on the road and in hobo jungles, occasionally playing the faro bank. "When we got a decent piece of money we quit stealing until it was almost spent, but while we were spending it we always tried to locate new spots against the day when we would be broke." George was now past 50 but had no thought of giving up the vagabond life. "He was as much attached to his trade as any carpenter or bricklayer, and went about it as methodically as any mechanic."[26] George's cold-blooded killing of Gold Tooth earned him a certain fear and wariness from the hobo fraternity, but fate was to see George end his life in similar violence.

The pair had heard about a vulnerable safe in a town 20 miles from any railroad, containing three to four thousand dollars in paper money and gold pieces. They meticulously planned out their modus operandi: all the townsfolk would be tucked up in bed by 10 o'clock, they would make their getaway on horseback and find a safe place to stash their takings. George successfully blew the door of the safe and emptied its contents, but as George led his horse out through the stable door he was confronted by a man with a shotgun who accused George of being a horse thief—even though they had hired the horses—and fired both barrels at point-blank range, nearly lifting George off his feet before he got a chance to pull out his own gun. As the shooter reloaded, Black had time to dash through a side door of the stable and hide in a cellar he knew to be below the general store. There he hid for the rest of the night and most of the following night before hunger and thirst drove him out of his hiding place. It took Black four days to get to the main line of the railway, scavenging for food in fields and gardens en route. He also had to decide where to stash the three thousand dollars of "green and greasy" worn paper money he had managed to escape with.

In spite of knowing that George could not possibly have survived the shooting, he owed it to George to protect the money he had sacrificed his life to steal. Black was to read later that the livery-stable owner who had been up early that morning to go duck shooting, knowing nothing of the robbery at the time he surprised George, found a further two thousand dollars in gold coins on George which was returned to the county.[27]

Most of the money Black kept from the robbery he spent during his later adventures in Chicago, culminating in the 1893 Chicago World's Fair. Needing additional funds to survive the coming winter, and having second thoughts about heading for New York after advice that it was "the toughest town in the United States for an outsider to get by in," Black headed west for the Dakota harvest fields. And here we are provided with an account of the tough plight of harvest hands, the working hobos who sweated for their money only to be relieved of it by the yeggs who preyed on them: "Harvest workers were called blanket stiffs or gay cats, and the process of pistoling them away from their money was known as catting them up."[28] This cruel operation found train guards and yeggs working alongside each other to relieve the harvest workers of their wages. The brakemen charged the harvest workers to ride in the train boxcars unmolested, then the yeggs took their money at gunpoint, made them jump from the open boxcar doors, then split the proceeds with the train crew. It was not an enterprise that professional yeggs like Black would have ever considered or condoned. Needless to say the process of catting was short-lived, as the harvest workers soon learned that it was more profitable to travel from the harvest fields as paying passengers.[29]

Though still only a youth of 23 years, Black's reputation soon became legendary among the yegg community as the trusted partner of George and the comrade present at his death, a story Black repeated readily. "Being young I naturally got puffed up and superior. I looked wise and mysterious, said nothing, and 'connected' only with the higher-ups among the knights of the road." With winter setting in and no money, Black headed up into Canada and west for Vancouver, arriving at one of the larger towns in British Columbia with only one dollar left in his pocket. In the town he noticed a safe of a type easily opened without the use of explosives and decided it was time to test his abilities at safe-cracking on his own. Everything went smoothly but the safe held nothing but a single roll of bills. Black got aboard a train headed for Vancouver an hour after midnight but planned to leave it earlier and head back south over the border. But his luck ran out as the train encountered a small avalanche of rocks and snow across the line. It would have been suicide to leave the train, and so Black stashed all but the change he had from one of the bills and waited for the arrival of constables from the town to learn his fate. The train guard produced the bill Black had used to purchase his ticket which was later identified as one of the bills stolen from the safe. Black was locked up in the local jail where he spent the rest of the winter with a Chinese cellmate. When spring arrived, he cut through the cell bars with saws brought in by his cellmate's cousins from Vancouver and the pair made their getaway and headed straight for that city. Black later received a letter of thanks and recommendation from that city's Chinese community for safely returning his former cellmate, a letter that would later save him from another jail sentence, though not a beating from associates of the Chinese storekeeper he tried to rob.

At this point in his narrative Black now provides his own critique of the mindset of the criminal community, acknowledging, "It's difficult to explain to a layman the pride of a professional thief." And he is not speaking here of the opportunist thief who preys on those even less fortunate than themselves; the professional yegg served a long apprenticeship in a particular line of thievery and had their own code of honor. For instance, he always bought his own clothes unless desperation forced him otherwise, he never dodged paying for his board and lodgings, and would never borrow money without thought of repaying it. In Black's case, he even took a jail sentence himself rather than incriminate a friend. Of course, his "own" money was stolen from others, but in his mind it was hard-earned and he acknowledges that he would have been better off making an honest living if he had known how to do it. He fell into the life of a criminal at a young age and knew no other trade, even though he admits throughout his book that he was always fully aware that what he was doing was wrong.

When Black first took up his trade he found it adventurous and thrilling. "Later it became an everyday, cold-blooded business." And part of being good at his business, he admits, was always to put himself in the place of his victims, the police, and the judges. Not to do so would have prevented him from doing his best work and also from opportunities to protect himself when "laid by the heels." But for all Black's philosophizing, his addiction to gambling, and later to opium, was probably the primary reason for not escaping a life of crime and jail earlier than he did. As he later acknowledges, the "gambling habit is the curse of a thief's life"; it separates the burglar from his takings as fast as he acquires it, and when he is down to his last dime and gets hungry, he is not clear-thinking and takes chances he would not take when calculating the risks of a burglary at leisure.[30]

But pickings were still rich at this time, and in Victoria, B.C. where we now encounter Black, he notes that house burglary was almost unknown. On the occasion of his next burglary, however, he had the misfortune to pick on the house of a local attorney, the even greater misfortune of being seen by the man's house-servant, and the further catastrophe that he was recognized at the local jail as the person who had escaped from the other jail in B.C. A strange twist of this particular story is that the English attorney whose money Black had stolen turned out to be a kindly soul who waived any claim to his lost money, wished Black good luck with his case, and gave him a copy of Charles Read's *It's Never Too Late to Mend*, on the promise that he would read the book—an education Black was denied until years later, as the book was taken from him en route to a new, securer jail that had been built in the town (Black avoids naming the town) from which he had escaped less than a year earlier. When it came, his sentence of two years in the local penitentiary was mild considering the charges involved both a burglary and a jailbreak, but it was stiffened with the added penalty of 30 lashes that caused Black no little amount of anxiety.

Black was determined to take his lashes when they came without crying out, and bite his tongue if necessary to suppress any outward signs of suffering. But the first blow when it came "was like a bolt of lightning; it shocked and burned." The sensation of jumping six feet in the air was invalidated by the fact he was trussed tightly to the whipping frame. Black acknowledges that Mr. Burr, who performed the lashing, was a master at his art having served his apprenticeship as a flogging master in the British Navy. By the time his punishment was over, Black describes "trembling like a helpless calf under the hot branding iron." But Black was not humbled or humiliated by the experience as was the intended outcome. Rather he walked away with "fresh confidence" and his head held high, recalling Nietzsche's maxim that what did not kill him would strengthen him.[31] Acknowledging that the whipping post is a strange place to gather new confidence, Black later uses the further analogy of steel being tempered by fire: "I give thanks that I had the metal to take the temper and hold it." Black's psychology about facing the brutalities of the penal system was particular to him but, in any event, taking the worst of the violence that the prison authorities could throw at him removed all Black's fears about the place.

But Black's prison experience and newfound confidence gained inside prison did not necessarily serve him well on the outside. On serving his sentence and returning to Vancouver, he reports that frequent house burglaries in the small hours of the night had left him a nervous wreck and that to calm his nerves he eventually gave in to smoking opium, acknowledging that eventually "every house prowler turns to booze or drugs." In Black's case, though, his strength of temperament did allow him to kick the habit with little discomfort when he became more aware of the devastating effects of long-term opium use.[32]

Black's story now moves on to an eight-year sentence he took in Folsom Prison for a jewelry heist in order to save his partner in crime from doing the time, even though it was the other fellow's fault they got caught and there was no evidence linking Black to the crime. Black describes the brutal regime in Folsom at the time under the superintendence of Warden Thomas Wilkinson. The previous warden had abused the use of straitjackets to such a degree that inmates went mad, were maimed, even killed, as a result of the abuse of this method of punishment. Under Warden Wilkinson, these brutalities were increased and added to, to such a degree that the prisoners eventually revolted in the infamous Folsom Prison breakout of July 27, 1903. The prisoners needed a leader and organizer who appeared in the person of Dick Gordon. According to Black, Gordon was a modest, kindly and intelligent 23-year-old with previous prison experience, now serving a 45-year sentence with little to lose and everything to gain by escaping.

Gordon handpicked 13 trusted accomplices and they planned to take the guards at knifepoint during their morning meeting in the captain's office. The prisoners, armed with knives made in the prison blacksmith shop, dropped out of line by the captain's office and rushed the captain, Warden Wilkinson and eight other officers. Only two officers tried to resist; the first was killed instantly and the second, the much-hated turnkey who was responsible for lacing the prisoners up in the straitjackets, was stabbed by several of the prisoners and left for dead. He survived the attack and would later brutally punish those recaptured as well as those prisoners who had nothing to do with the escape. The warden, captain and remaining six officers were marched to the prison armory where the prisoners armed themselves with guns and ammunition. They then headed for the hills with their hostages but Gordon personally prevented the warden, the captain and other guards from being murdered in spite of calls from his comrades for the warden's life. They were later all released and returned to the prison. Gordon and five of the others escaped and were never seen again, one of the escapees returned voluntarily to the prison, and six others were later captured.[33]

Needless to say, the press had a field day with the story. On the day of the breakout the *Oakland Tribune* indulged in such headlines as:

> FOURTEEN DESPERATE CONVICTS AFTER A FIERCE BATTLE
> CAPTURE WARDEN WILKINSON, CAPTAIN MURPHY AND
> GUARDS AND MAKE ESCAPE OVER HILLS THREE GUARDS
> HORRIBLY STABBED BY PRISONERS.

> When the Officers Made a Show of Resistance Then Blood Began to Flow.
> The Warden's clothing was slashed into shreds with a razor but the blade did not touch the flesh. C.J. Cochrane, turnkey of the prison, entered the office ... He rained blows upon them right and left, but he was felled by a knife through his back. It is thought he may die. William L. Cotter, a guard, was cut in the abdomen so that his entrails protruded.[34]

What the media did not question in the immediate aftermath of the breakout was, what could have led to such a desperate mutiny in the first place? Even so, Warden Wilkinson was replaced by an inexperienced warden who allowed Captain Murphy's lust for revenge to go unchecked. Black did not escape these punishments and with only three months left to serve with his two years and eight months credit for good behavior, he knew that Murphy was out to take them away. He was accused of holding opium and when he denied the charge was ordered to be examined by the doctor. Black knew this meant checking to see if he was fit for the straitjacket, and acknowledges that although he had been flogged, starved and "third degreed"—all taken with a grin—he was not confident that he could survive the straitjacket ordeal without confessing to where he had his stash of opium hidden, never mind the effects that going without the hop would have on him.

The doctor gave him the all-clear to be straitjacketed and he was taken to the prison dungeon where the turnkey, Cochrane, now recovered from his terrible wounds, was waiting with the heavy canvas jacket that had long pockets on the inside to hold the prisoner's arms to their side and eyelets down the back to take the rope that could lace up the jacket tight enough to stop a prisoner's circulation and breath. Black was thrown on the floor face down and as Cochrane proceeded to pull the laces tight, he declared, "You fellows tried to kill me; now it's my time." Black was left trussed up in this fashion for three days and Cochrane visited him hourly to ask if he was ready to give up the hop. When Black denied having it he was trussed up even tighter. The torture became so unbearable that he rolled his way to the side and tried to knock his head unconscious on the cell wall. Cochrane dragged Black back to the middle of the cell and he did not have the strength to roll back again. The guard, who had genuine sympathy for Black's situation, pleaded with him to yell or scream out, telling him that they would release him as it was no longer acceptable for prisoners to die in this fashion. But Black was determined that his fellow inmates would not hear him scream out.

On the second day the doctor ordered Black to be temporarily released from the jacket but before they returned, Black had determined to kill himself. He managed to remove a metal eyelet from one of his shoes and sharpen it on the cell floor, but try as he may, he could not cut his veins and eventually gave up and waited until morning. Under the torment of the straitjacket, Black found that he gave no thought at all to his opium habit, something which led him to the conviction that the addiction was psychological and not physical. Cochrane returned at eight the next morning, Black again denied having hop, and was again laced up in the jacket. He fell into a stupor and resolved that he would ask to speak to Captain Murphy, confess that the hop was hidden by the river bank, but then instead of revealing its hiding place, would throw his arms around the captain and pull him into the river where they could both "cease from troubling."

On the fourth morning, Cochrane returned with the jacket, telling Black that he may just as well confess where the hop was stashed as he would not last out the day. But when Black still refused to confess, the turnkey motioned to two of the trustees to carry Black back to his own cell. His three months passed quickly but he was still feeling the effects of the jacket on his release. Black swore to himself never again to make any friends or "do another decent thing." Out of revenge, he got himself a gun, some money, and returned to Folsom by stealth where he claims that he "flooded the place with hop."

Back in San Francisco, Black was arrested again by a cop who swore that he tried to shoot him and was given a 25-year sentence. The earthquake and great fire of San Francisco occurred while Black was awaiting his appeal in that case, and all his court and police records were destroyed. Now in limbo, he could not be charged or released. He went from the county jail to Alcatraz, and then to a branch jail in Ingleside where he spent six years, saying that he could have filled a whole book with stories about what took place during that stretch. He didn't. He did succeed, though, with the help of a friend on the outside, to saw through the cell bars and make his escape to Canada. There was a hue and cry over his escape, saved only by the fact that, although seriously ill, malnourished, and still hooked on opium, he made his way to Vancouver traveling first-class. "No police officer who knows his business would think of looking in a Pullman sleeper or diner for a fugitive hop-fiend yegg with a twenty-five-year sentence hanging on him."[35]

In Vancouver he paid a landlady a month's rent, telling her that he was a sick man and would not be venturing from his room. The landlady took pity on Black, saw to all his needs and helped him back to health. Black also used this time to come off the opium habit that he had been on for the previous 10 years. It took him six months to kick the habit completely before Black went back on the road, avoiding cities, and train-hopping his way through Canada. On crawling out of a boxcar in the town of Strathcona, he decided to find somewhere quiet to rest up for a few days. On entering a boarding house he was confronted by no less a person than Salt Chunk Mary, 15 years following reports that she had disappeared. Black immediately greeted her, mentioning something about the last time they were together in Pocatello, but he was met by a cold stare and the response "You are mistaken; you don't know me. My name's not Mary, and I was never in Pocatello in my life." Knowing Mary as he did, Black simply accepted that she must have taken a decision to start a new life and spend her remaining days in peace, so he went on his way, living as a highwayman, and never saw Mary again.

Inevitably, Black was eventually arrested again and, by chance, identified as a fugitive from Californian justice. The first person to visit him back in jail in San Francisco was the last attorney he had hired and who, remembering that Black had paid him the $50 he owed him before escaping from jail, decided that he owed Black the courtesy to stop by. Black was informed that his status had not changed since his escape and that his appeal was still pending. He was also visited by Fremont Older, editor of the *San Francisco Call*, who had previously befriended Black and tried to get the judge to give him an opportunity to kick his opium habit and go straight. If Black was worried that his benefactor would have been sore that he had broken out of jail, he need not have worried. Older told him that had done the right thing as, given the state Black had been in, there was a real possibility that he would have died in prison. He was pleased to note that Black was looking much healthier and told him, to Black's surprise, that the district attorney had confided to him that he believed Black had served enough time in prison. It was a big risk for the judge to reduce Black's sentence, given that his reputation would suffer if Black did not meet his side of the bargain and go straight. In the event, Black's 25-year sentence was reduced to one year, and Black read out a lengthy pre-prepared statement to the court about how he had learned the error of his ways and would endeavor to use his experience to dissuade young people from a life of crime.

Black was sent to San Quentin to serve out his final sentence. There he encountered his old friend Soldier Johnnie. They took a week to compare notes and catch up on each other's lives. Johnnie told Black that the Sanctimonious Kid had escaped from prison before finishing his five-year stretch, and had gone to Australia where he was hanged for killing a police constable. Black in turn told him the story of George's demise and Mary's disappearance to the far north. In his book, which Black acknowledges was written 13 years after being released at the end of the 10 months he eventually served in San Quentin, he says, "Johnnie finished his time first, and went back to the road, where he probably will live out his life and die unwept, unhonored and unhung."

On his release, Fremont Older offered to take Black out for a meal. Acknowledging his dislike of swanky restaurants but his liking for "quick contrasts," Black considered, "I had my breakfast in San Quentin, so why not lunch at the Palace?"[36] Following lunch, Older invited Black to join him at his ranch for a few days to get his bearings before finding his first straight job. The first of these was as cashier in a poolroom, a few months later as a salesman in the book department of The Emporium, following which, and the job he still held at the time of writing his book, he was librarian for the *Call*, courtesy of Fremont Older. During his writing period Black was also involved in journalism, writing essays and participating in lecture tours.

Black summed up his life of crime by acknowledging that he had failed as a thief but was luckier than most of them, having quit with his life and his liberty. Half of his 30 years as a criminal he had spent in prison and he calculated that around 50 thousand dollars had passed through his hands during the other 15 years—about nine dollars a day, much of which "went to lawyers, fixers, bondsmen and other places." "What price larceny, burglary, and robbery?"[37] But Black acknowledges that at 50 years old he was much healthier than many of his contemporaries. "I have no money, no wife, no auto. I have no dog. I have neither a radio set nor a rubber plant—I have no troubles."

We do not know how Black lived out the rest of his life, but it is likely that the physical and mental trauma of his former life eventually caught up with him. It is thought that he drowned himself around 10 years after writing his book, six years after its publication, after telling friends that if life got too much for him he would row out into New York Harbor and drop overboard with weights tied to his feet. In his darker moments Black described this state of mind as being "ready for the river."

ENDNOTES

1 Black, Jack. *You Can't Win*, Port Townsend, WA: Feral House, 2013
2 Ibid., p. 10
3 Ibid., p. 29
4 Ibid., p. 32
5 Ibid., p. 39
6 Ibid., pp. 41–46
7 Ibid., p. 64
8 Ibid., p. 67
9 Ibid., p. 70
10 Ibid., p. 72
11 Ibid., p. 75
12 Ibid., pp. 77–78
13 Ibid., pp. 84–91
14 Ibid., pp. 99–100
15 Ibid., p. 101
16 Ibid., p. 110
17 Ibid., pp. 112–113
18 Ibid., p. 120
19 Ibid., pp. 123–124
20 Ibid., p. 126
21 Ibid., p. 129
22 Ibid., p. 142
23 Ibid., pp. 152–153
24 Ibid., p. 159
25 Ibid., p. 163
26 Ibid., p. 165
27 Ibid., p. 170
28 Other accounts refer to 'gay cats' simply as young, inexperienced hobos.
29 *You Can't Win*, op. cit., p. 175
30 Ibid., p. 199
31 Ibid., pp. 206–208
32 Ibid., p. 227
33 Ibid., pp. 270–271
34 *Oakland Tribune*, July 27, 1903
35 *You Can't Win*, op. cit., p. 276
36 Ibid., p. 289
37 Ibid., p. 292

William Henry Davies

(1871–1940)

My impression of Americans from the beginning is of the best, and I have never since had cause to alter my mind. They are a kind, sympathetic race of people and naturally proud of their country.

W.H. Davies, *The Autobiography of a Super-Tramp*

Although W.H. Davies preferred to be known as a poet—a lifelong ambition achieved at huge sacrifice—it is for his prose memoirs of 12 years tramping in the Americas and Britain, and recorded in *The Autobiography of a Super-Tramp* (1908), that he is probably best known. For the purposes of this chapter, then, Davies' poetry will be passed over, weighed down as it is by metaphors of nature and rhyming couplets and quatrains, the most recognizable of which are probably the opening two lines of his poem "Leisure": "What is this life if, full of care / We have no time to stand and stare..." In any event, Davies was not entirely comfortable in the literary world of London at the time he quit hobo life in the Americas (minus half a leg) and decided to turn professional writer, having arrived in that company as something of a social oddity—Davies had continued to tramp in Britain with a peg leg before his writing provided an income. Davies always struggled with the strained and mannered company of literary and high-society London, rather being drawn, as he acknowledges in the opening line to his prose work, *The True Traveller* (1912), "to ill-dressed people and squalid places." And although describing himself as a writer of "natural genius," Davies was at the same time highly self-deprecating and insecure.

As with Trader Horn, Davies holds seemingly contradictory attitudes toward women. But, as already acknowledged in terms of that other tramp writer, transposing the political correctness of our present day onto those who lived in an altogether different world, leads nowhere. As the former tramp and pulp Western novelist Louis L'Amour declared, "The only way men or women can be judged is against the canvas of their own time." Davies acknowledged preferring male company and frequently discusses women in derogatory terms, yet at the same time, he demonstrated a profound tenderness and care toward women, especially those fallen on hard times—a fondness that was reciprocated by many of the women he encountered. For the most part, then, he was a gentle and vulnerable soul, but one whose passions could also be raised. He describes, for instance, in *The True Traveller*, how incensed he became with a man for refusing to pay a prostitute and that he involved himself in a fight with the man in order that she be paid.[1]

Of Davies' relationship with women, more later. But in addition to all these paradoxes in Davies' character, it would appear that Davies' reputation was not helped by some of those who later offered him patronage; neither was it helped by contemporary and more recent commentators. He is described, for instance, as marrying a 23-year-old prostitute at the age of 50, yet there is no evidence that Davies' wife Helen was ever a prostitute. In terms of his patrons, Davies does not name George Bernard Shaw in his autobiography as one of the writers to whom he sent out copies of his first volume of poetry (*The Soul's Destroyer*, 1905), but Shaw was one of the main reasons for Davies becoming a celebrity, adopting him as a project, a curiosity with which to entertain the literary world of his time. The title "Super-tramp" was Shaw's suggestion as a marketing gimmick for the book, a play on Shaw's own work *Man and Superman*, and a title that Davies came to resent. He was essentially a very modest man who, while enjoying his success, shunned and was embarrassed by the personal attention he received. The reader can judge for themselves from the preface that Shaw wrote for *The Autobiography of a Super-Tramp*; in spite of its compliments, the piece comes across as patronizing, almost an apology for it being there in the first place and barely disguising that the novelty of the book's hero outweighed any literary merit of its author. As Shaw comments, "It is a placid narrative, unexciting in matter and unvarnished in manner, of the commonplaces of a tramp's life." The reader must judge for themselves whether Davies' prose is unexciting and commonplace; his early life certainly does not fit this description.

Early Days

Following the death of his father and remarriage of his mother at the age of three, Davies was raised by his paternal grandparents who ran the Church House Inn in Newport, South Wales in the U.K. Davies was used to travel and adventure from an early age. He describes how his (frequently inebriated) grandfather, a Cornish ex-sea captain, made several trips with Davies and his brother between Newport and Bristol on a schooner named the *Welsh Prince*, a craft fondly recollected by Davies in human terms:

> On one trip we had a very stormy passage, and on that occasion the winds and the waves made such a fool of the Welsh Prince that she—to use the feminine gender, as is the custom of every true mariner, of one of whom I am a proud descendant—often threatened to dive into the bowels of the deep for peace. It was on this occasion that my grandfather assisted the captain of the Welsh Prince to such purpose that people aboard acclaimed him as the saviour of their lives, and blessed him for the safety of the ship....Alas! the Welsh Prince became childish in her old age. She would often loiter so long in the channel as to deceive the tide that expected her...What with her missing of tides, her wandering into strange courses, her sudden appearance in the river after rumours of loss, her name soon became the common talk of the town. Her erratic behaviour became at last so usual that people lost all interest as to her whereabouts...[2]

His taste for alcohol Davies credits to being raised in a pub and given porter to drink at bedtime, "in lieu of cocoa or tea, as is the custom in more domestic houses." Even after his grandparents left the pub and retired, Davies recalls these as happy times in a home consisting of: "grandfather, grandmother, an imbecile brother, a sister, myself, a maid- servant, a dog, a cat, a parrot, a dove, and a canary bird."[3]

Although an able scholar and excelling in sports and the pugilistic arts, Davies was also a frequent truant and hell-raiser. His schooling came to an abrupt end when a gang of petty thieves, of which he was the ringleader, was caught and jailed. They were returned to their homes after receiving their sentence of 12 strokes of the birch.

Davies entered the world of employment, firstly in an iron foundry and then as an apprentice picture framer, by which time he had also started reading poetry after being introduced to Byron by a friend. Unlike many other tramp writers discussed in this text, Davies was never a child tramp, traveling no further than Bristol before the death of both his grandparents. Had his grandmother agreed to his request for funds to travel to America earlier, he would have done so. In the event he had to wait until he was 21, and the death of his grandmother, before he was able to secure an advancement of 15 pounds from the family's trustee and hit the road—initially the sea on a steamer from Liverpool to New York in June 1893. It is significant to note also that Davies' arrival in America coincided with the financial "Panic" of that same year, and the subsequent depression that followed.

Tramping Debut

On his arrival in New York, Davies' first impression of Americans, one he would remain with, was that: "They are a kind, sympathetic race of people and naturally proud of their country." But he did not remain long in New York. Anxious to visit Chicago, and discovering that his remaining funds would not allow him to reach that destination, it was these circumstances, and meeting up with a seasoned tramp, Brum, that was to commence six years as an American hobo. His first tramp companion soon initiates Davies into the art of vagabondage. He described Brum as "a lazy wretch with but little inclination for work," a genuine beggar who survived on "having one day plenty and nothing on the next day." Brum would make an inventory of his needs each morning and set out to beg whatever he required. This included begging a clean handkerchief rather than washing his soiled one, and discarding an old shirt for a new one rather than sewing on a needed button, "keeping up the dignity of his profession to the extreme." Brum treated begging as a fine art in which he delighted, never failing to acquire his needs even in towns normally hostile to beggars. "In every street, he said, there lived a good Samaritan, and seeing that a good beggar knocks at every door, he must ultimately succeed."[4]

Davies was lucky to have fallen in with a professional tramp and beggar to tutor him at the start of his adventures, yet the descriptions of such individuals encountered throughout this text is also testimony to the important fact that they remain uniquely individual characters, with their own particular codes of ethics and idiosyncrasies. As Davies describes Brum: "[He was] a man of an original turn of mind and his ideas were often at variance with others." Davies' description of his initiation into riding the rails, and also the language of this vocation, will be familiar from the testimonies of other tramp writers in this text. It is also noteworthy in relationship to Davies' later catastrophe when beating a train:

> I was soon initiated into the mysteries of beating my way by train, which is so necessary in parts of that country, seeing the great distances between towns. Sometimes we were fortunate enough to get an empty car; sometimes we had to ride the bumpers; and often, when travelling through a hostile country, we rode on the roof of a car, so as not to give the brakesman an opportunity of striking us off the bumpers unawares. It is nothing unusual in some parts to find a man, always a stranger, lying dead on the track, often cut in many pieces. At the inquest they invariably bring in a verdict of accidental death, but we know different. Therefore we rode the car's top, so as to be at no disadvantage in a struggle. The brakesman, knowing well that our fall would be his own, would not be too eager to commence hostilities. Sometimes we were desperate enough to ride the narrow iron rods, which were under the car, and only a few feet from the track. ...Sometimes we were forced to jump off a moving train at the point of a revolver. At other times the brakesmen were friendly, and even offered assistance in the way of food, drink or tobacco. Again, when no firearm was in evidence, we had to threaten the brakesman with death if he interfered with us. In this way Brum and myself travelled the States of America, sleeping at night by camp fires, and taking temporary possession of empty houses.[5]

Encounters with American Justice

Davies stuck with Brum as his tramping companion for some time, descriptions of which make very entertaining and instructive reading, including an aborted summer vacation along the beaches of New Haven Sound, when the pair were arrested for vagrancy and Davies spent his first spell, a 30-day sentence, in an American jail. But eventually some friction occurred between the pair as Davies was starting to feel starved of cultural distraction, the procurement of which would entail some paid employment in a city. Brum, being ideologically opposed to employment, found Davies' need of work a source of ridicule. Davies always admired nature but could also be overdosed on it: "We often go for days without reading matter, and we know not what the world is saying; nor what the world is doing. The beauty of nature is for ever before my eyes, but I am certainly not enriching my mind, for who can contemplate Nature with any profit in the presence of others."[6]

Davies wins the argument and Brum agrees to accompany him hop picking to raise the necessary funds to provide for Davies' cultural needs. On the train ride to the hop fields they are involved in a struggle with a brakesman on the roof of the car, which could have ended in certain death for all three of them had the brakesman not seen sense and returned to the caboose, too embarrassed to alert his workmates that two tramps had got the better of him. Having reached the hop fields, in the company of a tramp named Australian Red, they completed a four-week stint with only $40 between the three of them to show for their labors. They then made for the nearest railway station with the intention of going to New York to paint that city "a forty-dollar red." But having found a vacant boxcar and settling down for the journey, their over-noisy chatter is heard by the local marshal, who puts them under arrest. What follows is an entertaining story that introduces Davies to the vagaries of Western justice.

The trio are marched not to jail, but to the local saloon where they order drinks, for the marshal too, while he summons the town judge. On the latter's arrival they occupy a room at the back of the saloon, an improvised courtroom, where the charges are read out and special mention made of the money they are carrying. The judge offers them the option of a five-dollar fine each or 30 days in jail. So indignant is Davies at losing his money, in what is clearly legalized robbery (by now aware that itinerant workers are encouraged to ride the rails free on the way *into* town, only to be relieved of half their wages on leaving), that he says he'll take the jail sentence. But this is a genial court, and the judge asks him what he would be happy to pay, whereupon Brum intervenes and agrees they'll pay three dollars each rather than face jail. On completion of the "trial" the court adjourns to the bar where the judge buys them all a drink out of the fine money. They are then put back on the next train out by the marshal without any further inconvenience.

Similar stories are related in other chapters of this book and further such anecdotes in Davies' book under the chapter "Law in America," including stories of how tramps choose the hospitality of jails over winter in preference to the harsh weather and lack of seasonal labor. Brum persuades Davies to a plan that they overwinter in a comfortable jail he knows of in Michigan and the trio head there instead of New York. There then follows a similar scam to the one reported by Jack Everson in Chapter 9 and which was rife in California at the time. When Davies inquired how they could possibly be accommodated with food, tobacco and whiskey at the state's expense, Brum informs him that the marshal gets a dollar each for every arrest he makes, the judge receives three or four dollars for every conviction, and the sheriff of the jail is paid a dollar a day for boarding each prisoner under his charge—all at the expense of the local citizenry from their taxes, and fueled by what had become America's "tramp scare." As the marshal informed them, "there is a long and severe winter before you without a break. ... Sixty days in our jail, which is considered one of the best, if not the best, in Michigan, would do you no harm, I assure you." Brum asks, "What about tobacco and a drink or two of whiskey?" The marshal gives them half a dollar for a drink and tells them that the sheriff will supply tobacco. He then tells them to proceed to Donovan's saloon where he would join them later, "when of course," he added, winking, "you will be supposed to be just a bit merry."[7]

> We were charged with being drunk and disorderly, and with disturbing the public peace. "He did not see," he said, "why peaceable citizens should be disturbed in this way by drunken strangers, and would fine us seven dollars and costs, in default of which we would be lodged in the county jail for thirty days.[8]

A reading of Davies' own book is recommended to provide a full account of how he and his companions spent their time at these various sojourns. At any rate, following this overwintering experience, they head for a fruit farm in Michigan where Davies intends to earn enough money to return to England. He arrives safely at their destination with Australian Red. Brum did not manage to jump on board the moving train and Davies never saw him again. Being averse to working, Davies assumed Brum had decided on another spell in jail instead.

Davies the Cattleman

Davies finishes fruit picking with over a hundred dollars in his pocket and very useful advice from his friend on how he can work his passage back to Liverpool and earn some extra money into the bargain. But, as seems to be the pattern of even the most careful hobos, a week after arriving in Chicago the pair are penniless once more. Nonetheless, off they set for Baltimore with the intention of securing work on a ship transporting cattle to England:

> We found the Baltimore and Ohio Railroad easy to beat, and were at the end of our journey in a very few days. When we entered the cattleman's office, from which place owners and foremen were supplied with men, it was evident to me that Red was well known in this place, hearing him make enquiries of Washington Shorty, New York Fatty, Philadelphia Slim, and others.[9]

Some of these tramp monikers do seem remarkably familiar and, allowing for the fact that there must have been many Shorties, Fatties and Slims on the road, it is tempting to cross-reference different tramp writers to see how many appear in more than one narrative. So far as can be established, none of the tramp writers featured in this book, with the exception of London and Livingstone, ever came across each other in their wanderings. In any event, while waiting to secure a passage, the two were fortunate enough to obtain work roping cattle in the transit yards. And so Davies now becomes a cowboy of sorts. A reluctant cattleman, though; Davies had a fondness for animals and did not like to see them mistreated. On his first night, the cattle were brought to the ship in a train of cars and a sloping gangway was erected spanning shore to ship; "up this incline the poor beasts were unmercifully prodded with long poles, sharpened at the end, and used by the shore cattlemen." Davies describes how the terror-stricken animals, having no notion of what was expected, "almost overleaped one another in their anxiety to get away." The whole business nearly persuaded Davies to quit the enterprise yet he stuck with it, frequently having to cross the backs of the steers to free one that was facing the wrong way. On one occasion, a steer whose back he was using to cross over the herd began to heave and toss, throwing him across the back of another which in turn reared up and was in danger of crushing him. Davies only managed to save himself by throwing the beast's rope to another cattleman who "fastened this refractory animal to the crossboards."[10]

In addition to the cattle, there were also 2,000 sheep quartered on what was known as the hurricane deck—aptly named, as during the trip, half of them were washed into the sea during a storm. Arriving in Liverpool, Davies recounts a strange story concerning these wild and lawless vagabond cattlemen, for poor as they may have been, they were also the target of every beggar in Liverpool and other port cities. Easily marked out in bars by their accents, and tough as they were, they were yet easily parted with their money, touched by the significantly worse poverty of the British vagrant and their pride of being relatively comfortably-off Americans. In a penniless state—Davies included—they boarded the same ship back to Baltimore where they were at least fed and sheltered. Davies resolved that on the very next trip out he would keep his money and return home to Newport—a plan he failed to execute, for on his next cattle trip, this time to London, he returned once more to Baltimore, and made further similar trips also, not always for want of money.

Seasoned Hobo

The characters and stories Davies tells of these adventures are rich and entertaining, alternating between paid work and begging, but also frequently having to avoid being robbed. For as well as hobos and beggars, Davies describes gangs who neither begged nor worked, the aforementioned yeggs who lived entirely on thieving from hobos. The worst of these were the gangs he encountered after quitting as a cattleman and heading out alone to Chicago to earn money working on a new canal that was then being built some distance from that city. Davies describes how men who, having been paid off and heading to Chicago to spend their earnings, were later found murdered and floating in the canal having been relieved of their wages. It then became necessary for those who had been paid off to wait for others and head for Chicago in groups, the better to avoid being attacked. Davies describes how, traveling in just such a manner with two friends, they were likewise accosted but succeeded in chasing their assailants away. A short time later, back again at work on the canal, a friend of Davies, Cockney Tom, recognized the man who tried to rob him and the two engaged in a fist fight in which Cockney was the victor. A seemingly modest outcome for someone who had likely, as Davies put it, "taken an active part in perhaps fifty or sixty murders."

His wanderlust having returned, and 50 dollars to the better, Davies now tramps to St. Louis, the city which, coincidentally at the time of Davies' arrival there, was home to Thomas Manning Page (Chapter 1). Davies reached St. Louis with 40 dollars, determined to find some sociable company. He bought a daily paper and headed for the levee to spend a few hours out of the sun, "reading, and watching the traffic on the river." On approaching a large pile of lumber to enjoy its shade, he noticed that it was already occupied by a man of middle age and "a youth of gentlemanly appearance." He sat down and began to read but was soon listening in on their conversation. The young man was discussing buying a houseboat and floating leisurely down the Mississippi to New Orleans, taking in different towns on the way. From there he intended to take a train to his home in southern Texas. The older man, with a strong Scottish accent, showed some enthusiasm for the trip. "Excuse me, gentlemen," says Davies, "I could not help but hear your conversation and, if you have no objection, would like to share expenses and enjoy your company on such a trip."[11]

Escapades in the Deep South

What started out as a promising adventure—and indeed was not short of such for some time—was curtailed when first the young Texan, and then Davies himself, contracted malaria. Having split up out of necessity, and instead of taking a train, Davies found himself walking from a nearby town in a weak and feverish state. He ended up crawling into a large swamp where he spent three days and nights unable to move.

> Wild hungry hogs were there, who approached dangerously near, but ran snorting away when my body moved. A score or more of buzzards had perched waiting on the branches above me, and I knew that the place was teeming with snakes. I suffered from a terrible thirst, and drank of the swamp-pools, stagnant water that was full of germs, and had the colours of the rainbow, one dose of which would have poisoned some men to death. When the chill was upon me, I crawled into the hot sun, and lay there shivering with the cold; and when the hot fever possessed me, I crawled back into the shade. Not a morsel to eat for four days, and very little for several days previous.[12]

From his "sick-bed" in the swamp, Davies was able to see the trains passing and knew that they were probably stopping for water or coal within a mile from where he lay, but he did not have the strength to call out. Eventually, realizing that he would die in the swamp unless he moved, he somehow managed to reach the railroad track and the next station. From there he paid to reach the next town and a cab to the hospital. "At that place my condition was considered to be very serious, but the doctor always bore me in mind, for we were both of the same nationality, and to that, I believe, I owe my speedy recovery."[13]

Davies now describes what are, for him, the peculiarities of the Southern states. Having previously given away their houseboat to a fisherman because he had no money to buy it, nor any use for it, Davies later got work in a factory producing staves but was shocked at being paid only in kind (food, clothes and other provisions). At this point of the book, he also describes the character and lives of former slaves whom he encounters on his travels, noting that there was little difference in their life before and after the abolition of slavery. They lived in the same shacks, he says, and were paid in kind only, not money, for their labors. Davies also here notes the cruelty and impoverishment of Southern prisons compared to the prisons of the North, which he likens to hotels. He describes how people would be arrested and fined 10 dollars plus costs. Then local citizens in need of cheap labor would pay the fine and take possession of the prisoner to work out his fine on their farm. They would buy the prisoner cheap work clothes for a few dollars and then charge them four times that amount. "The prisoner was not free to refuse these, and being forced to work out their price, was kept in this way twice the number of his days. I was very much afraid of all this, although a wandering white man was not in nearly so much danger as a negro."[14]

Entering a small town and seeing a group of whites congregating, all armed with guns, Davies describes his disgust at witnessing a lynching. Like a scene from a Western movie, the men head for the jail where they demand from the sheriff the keys, drag out their black victim, and summarily hang him from a tree. Unlike some other tramp writers in this book who have fond memories of New Orleans, on arrival in that city Davies is mugged and badly beaten, so he heads straight for Texas, visiting many towns along the way. In Paris, Texas, he describes, in the town saloon, the mummified heart of another lynching victim, tied in a piece of cord and displayed in a glass case. Given Davies' description, this must have been the remains of Henry Smith, who was reportedly tortured with red-hot irons for 50 minutes before being burned alive. Smith was accused of murdering the three-year-old daughter of the town marshal as a result of himself being bullied and beaten by that officer. Davies' final anecdote of the Southern states was that, on his arrival in Fort Smith, Arkansas, he witnessed the departure of a specially commissioned and heavily guarded train transporting a gang of train and bank robbers, including Bill Cook and Cherokee Bill, on their way out of that town.

There now follows, in a chapter titled "The Camp," a description of a tramp "convention" in a jungle outside Pittsburgh that has parallels with the similar gathering of tramps described elsewhere in this book. It is following this camp, and on using up his earnings from a spell at fruit picking outside Chicago, that Davies, reflecting on lost opportunities, resolves once more to return to England (he does not say Wales). We also learn how Davies recognizes the advantages he has over other tramps and paradoxically (which is a feature of the man) how this advantage has also cursed him. He had now been in America five years. "I was certainly getting some enjoyment out of life, but now and then the waste of time appalled me, for I still had a conviction that I was born to a different life." When feeling depressed, he consoled himself in the knowledge that he at least had an advantage over many others. His grandmother had left him one-third profit of a small estate which paid out 10 shillings per week, and as during his five years in America he had not drawn out a penny, he now had over a hundred pounds in his account. Neither could he use the excuse of having no money in America to return to Wales; "it could easily be done on the cattle boats." Nor could he say that he did not have the courage to return penniless after so many years abroad. "It was this knowledge that made me so idle and so indifferent to saving; and it was this small income that has been, and is in a commercial sense, the ruin of my life."[15]

First Homecoming

After a successful crossing, but not without first going on a week-long spree in Baltimore with Australian Red and diminishing his funds, Davies eventually arrives home in Newport, Wales. Somewhat lost, he is directed to his mother's new home by someone who recognizes him. He arrived in the dark yet his mother recognized him instantly by the way he knocked at the door, "just as though I had only been out for an evening's stroll." She told Davies later that the family had given him up for dead, and that she herself had had a dream in which she saw her son "beat about the head and lying bloody at the feet of strangers," uncannily recalling the exact year and month that Davies was mugged in New Orleans.

Davies vowed never to leave his native hometown again, and yet that night he experienced great difficulty in sleeping in the soft bed, tossing and turning. "The food itself did not seem so palatable coming out of clean pots and shining ovens, as that which was cooked in close contact with the embers, and in the smoke and blaze of a camp fire."[16] After two months of wandering aimlessly around his hometown and drinking, as he says, "immoderately," Davies decided to realize an ambition of his to open a bookstore in London. But with half of his stipend already spent, and little knowledge of the book trade, the project did not materialize. In any case, wanderlust having already returned, on reading a newspaper report of the Klondike gold rush Davies set off once more for the New World.

> My conception of that wonderful land, for all my travels, was childish in the extreme. I thought the rocks were of solid gold, which so dazzled the sun that he could not concentrate his glance on any particular part, and that his eye went swimming all day in a haze. I pictured men in possession of caves sitting helpless in the midst of accumulated nuggets, puzzled as to how to convey all this wealth to the marts of civilisation. What I wanted with all these riches I cannot say, for it was never a desire of mine to possess jewellery, fine raiment, yachts, castles or horses: all I desired was a small house of my own, and leisure for study.[17]

Canadian Adventure

And so once again Davies crossed the Atlantic from Liverpool (he claims to have crossed the Atlantic 18 times in total), on this occasion bound for St. John's in Newfoundland. From there he beat it tramp-style to Montréal, determined to visit two famous tramp haunts, Joe Beef's and French Marie's, that had been much talked about during his previous tramping in America. Davies spent several weeks in Montréal awaiting the arrival of spring and much enjoying his stay there with newfound companions—as his lapse here into a more poetic prose style seems to testify:

> What a glorious time of the year is this! With the warm sun travelling through serene skies, the air clear and fresh above you, which instils new blood in the body, making one defiantly tramp the earth, kicking the snows aside in the scorn of action. The cheeks glow with health, the lips smile, and there is no careworn face seen, save they come out of the house of sickness and death. And that lean spectre, called Hunger, has never been known to appear in these parts.[18]

But shortly after this idyllic sojourn, Davies' career as an American hobo was to come to an abrupt end. Jumping a train from Renfrew in the direction of Winnipeg, Davies was to join the statistics of other casualties of free rail travel. As the train pulled slowly out of the station, Davies allowed his companion to jump first owing to the fact he had a maimed hand. As the train picked up speed the other man caught the handle bar and sprang lightly on the step, then Davies grabbed the bar, running with the train, prepared to follow his example. But instead of quickly moving to the platform as expected, his friend hesitated on the step leaving Davies no room to jump. He shouted at his friend to clear the step but by the time he did it was too late. Davies' foot came short of the step and he fell, still clinging to the handle bar and being dragged several yards before he let go. He lay dazed for several minutes while the train passed swiftly on into the darkness, not realizing what had happened until he attempted to stand. It was only then he realized that something was preventing him from doing so. "Sitting down in an upright position, I then began to examine myself, and now found that the right foot was severed from the ankle."[19]

This was not the first time that Davies' consideration and kindness toward others had been his undoing, but it was certainly the most calamitous. It required two operations to save part of Davies' leg, now amputated at the knee. He became something of a minor celebrity during his stay in Renfrew, and could no doubt have led a comfortable life in that town with the amount of charity and offers of jobs bestowed on him by the kind-hearted citizens. But Davies was determined to return home. His despondency at losing his leg was lifted on the return sea-crossing by the agility and exuberance of a fellow one-legged passenger. On his return home, Davies made the following evaluation of his new situation:

> I was now more content with my lot, determined that as my body had failed, my brains should now have the chance they had longed for, when

> the spirit had been bullied into submission by the body's activity. ... A far different Klondyke had opened up before my eyes, which corresponded with the dreams of my youth.[20]

Tramp Poet

And so, at the age of 29, with a fine new artificial leg, Davies attempted to make the transition from tramp to professional poet, though he was not to find it easy. Undoubtedly, Davies did write hundreds of poems during his first few years in London, but in order to live within his budget, which had now been reduced to eight shillings a week, he had to live in boarding houses and on meals that were often decidedly more miserable than those he had enjoyed as a tramp in America. After six months' experience of a Salvation Army lodging house he had little to say in its favor. "Certainly the food was cheap, but such food as was not fit for a human being." The row of 20 beds were so close together that there was no room to undress between them. "Men were breathing and coughing in each other's faces and the stench of such a number of men in one room was abominable."[21] Davies' description of those uncharitable Christian soldiers has a resonance with Thomas Manning Page's diatribe on the sanctimonious converts of the YMCA in Chapter 1, although sadly, Davies was no satirist, only acknowledging that "The officers in charge were, according to my first opinion, hypocrites."

Davies' determination to succeed as a writer was tenacious in the extreme. He wrote to dozens of publishers without success, and when he did get the offer to publish a collection of his poetry, it was on the condition that he fund the project himself. Davies also sent out many (unsuccessful) begging letters to charitable donors, in the hope that he would find a sponsor for his publishing enterprise. So determined was he to see his work in print that he took once more to the road in order to save up the necessary amount required. He had also been advised by a fellow lodger that he should get a traditional peg leg replacement for his existing artificial leg which was by now showing signs of wear, a wooden leg being a more suitable prosthesis for tramping and also a more obvious demonstration of his disability, one which would aid him in his new career as a licensed peddler. After tramping halfway across England, and his peddler's wares having been ruined by rain, Davies once more finds himself destitute and again looks to his former tramping skills.

There then follows a description of various characters and the different types of beggars and hawkers that Davies meets in the Midland towns and cities he passes through on his trampings (including the "gridler" who sings for money, and the "downrighter" who provides no service at all, preferring honest begging) before eventually returning on foot to London, still penniless apart from his grandmother's annuity. In December of that year, Davies decides to tramp to his hometown in South Wales for Christmas. Reaching the Welsh border in less than a week, he decides to continue on to Swansea before returning back to Newport in time for Christmas Eve—an additional tramp of some 110 miles. Davies had now been tramping continuously for three months on one leg, before resting up for three weeks in Newport, and then again returning to London refreshed and in new spirits. But Davies' luck at getting his poetry published was as elusive as ever. After several more unproductive months in another hostel, he hit on the idea of getting an advance from his grandmother's trustee to pay for their publication. Strings attached to the transaction meant that Davies would have to wait six months to receive the advance and also forgo his eight shillings a week allowance. And so once more, he was forced on the road to survive—the necessary sacrifice for becoming a published writer.

In spite of the civilities of other tramps who desired company, for the most part Davies chose to travel alone, "so as to allow no strange voice to disturb my dreams." Those tramps Davies did meet thought him mad because, having served most of his tramping career in America, he had no knowledge or information to offer of the towns and villages he had passed through that same day, such as local lodging houses, "of which I was again ignorant, having slept in the open air." After tramping in this manner for two months Davies found himself in Devon en route to Plymouth. "I felt continually attracted to these large centres of commerce, owing, I suppose, to feeling the necessity of having an object in view; but was generally starved out of them in a very short time."[22]

After three further months of tramping in this fashion and the best of the autumn weather over, Davies was forced once more to secure shelter for the winter. He used his last pennies to purchase some shoelaces and peddle his way through the towns around London without entering that city. After five full months on the road and being exhausted, he returned to his former lodgings in London to spend the final month, before he could receive the advance due to him at the turn of the new year, preparing his manuscript. Davies received 250 copies of his volume of 40 poems, *The Soul's Destroyer and other Poems* (1905), directly from the printer, which he himself would have to try and sell, less the 30 copies he sent out for review. The review copies produced only two negative results, leaving Davies in despair and resolved to burn all remaining copies and return to tramping. But before he was able to make a bonfire of his poetry, he received two further reviews. One was from a Yorkshire paper saying that "the work had rhymes that were neither intricate nor original," the other from Scotland that "the work was perfect in craftsmanship rather than inspired." Further weeks went by during which time Davies started drinking heavily again. "I had come down to my last ten shillings, and had a good seven months to go before my money was again due." Once again Davies had thoughts of destroying his work.[23]

Literary Success

But Davies did not burn his books. He persevered, sending further copies out to people he thought might be interested. Some were just accepted as gifts, while others had the decency to at least send him the "half a crown" (two shillings and sixpence) cost of the book, allowing him the price of postage to send out further copies. One of those who did buy the book, indeed purchased several copies, was George Bernard Shaw who, in the Preface to *The Autobiography of a Super-Tramp*, describes receiving *The Soul's Destroyer*:

> In the year 1905 I received by post a volume of poems by one William H. Davies, whose address was the The Farm House, Kennington, S.E. I was surprised to learn that there was still a farmhouse left in Kennington; for I did not then suspect that the Farmhouse ... is, in fact, a doss-house, or hostelry where single men can have a night's lodging for, at most, a sixpence. ... The author, as far as I could guess, had walked into a printer's or stationer's shop; handed in his manuscript; and ordered his book as he might have ordered a pair of boots. It was marked "price half a crown." An accompanying letter asked me very civilly if I required a half-crown book of verses; and if so, would I please send the author the half-crown: if not, would I return the book. This was attractively simple and sensible.[24]

In his reply to Davies, Shaw gave him the names of some poetry critics he felt may be interested, urging him to use the money he had sent for his copies of the book to forward further copies to these same critics. It is not clear from Davies' account if it was Shaw's lead that produced the result (Shaw is not mentioned by name in *Super-Tramp*) or that of a *Daily Mail* journalist named A. St. John Adcock, who recognized a story in Davies. Nonetheless, Davies writes that, down to his last three shillings and about to give up altogether, he was to receive correspondence from two "well known writers ... who promised to do something through the press," following which intervention things at last started to go the would-be poet's way. Private recognition was soon followed by "a full column, in which I saw myself described, a rough sketch of the ups and downs of my life, in short telling sentences, with quotations from my work." A review in a literary paper followed the same week and then letters and offers of interviews started arriving by every post:

> It was all like a dream. In my most conceited moments I had not expected such an amount of praise, and they gathered in favour as they came, until one wave came stronger than the others and threw me breathless of all conceit, for I felt myself unworthy of it, and of the

> wonderful sea on which I had embarked. Sleep was out of the question, and new work was impossible.[25]

But Davies *was* now writing his second book of verse, still from the manager's office at the Farmhouse, and so had not escaped vagabondage entirely to realize his dream of living out his life in "a small comfortable room with a cosy fire." But a journalist and writer from the *Daily Chronicle*, Edward Thomas, was to befriend Davies and invite him to live in a place where Thomas would also write, later moving Davies to Stidulph's Cottage, Egg Pie Lane, Sevenoaks, Kent. Thomas paid the rent and other friends pitched in with money for heating, et cetera. Davies was to become close friends with Thomas, his wife and their children, and his second book, *New Poems*, published in 1907, would be dedicated to Helen and Edward Thomas. By now Davies was working on *The Autobiography of a Super-Tramp* which would be published the following year.

In spite of the help he was getting from his friends, Davies was still vulnerable and living in near-poverty. Thomas, by now also Davies' unofficial agent, along with others, would make major editing suggestions to Davies' autobiography, the most significant of which was to persuade Davies to remove all memoirs and anecdotes of a sexual nature for fear of offending his reading public and new literary friends. This is a great shame, as it removes from Davies' autobiography, focusing as it does on his intimacy with men, references to the relationships between vagabonds and women. Also lost from the original text are descriptions of the various brothels that Davies clearly frequented, not to mention the characterization of Davies himself as a Beckettian, self-imposed exile, seeking the companionship and the intimacy of others exiled from mannered society. Fortunately, however, such accounts *were* recorded by Davies in a later work, *The True Traveller* (1912), and also the autobiography of his courtship and marriage to his wife Helen, in *Young Emma*, not published until after her death in 1980, a discussion of which is included below.

Even now fully engaged as a writer, Davies still made time for tramping expeditions, both to clear his head and provide himself with inspiration for more writing. Davies wrote and published 11 works during his seven years at Stidulph's Cottage in Kent (he would publish 25 volumes of poetry and prose in his lifetime), eventually returning to the capital at the age of 43 where he embraced and shunned high-society London in equal measure. Davies' eventual residence in London was a room in Charles Dickens' former house in Bloomsbury. Those whom Davies became close to, aside from his first meeting with Bernard Shaw, included Hilaire Belloc, Walter de la Mare, W.B. Yeats, Ezra Pound, Jacob Epstein, Augustus John, and Edith Sitwell. But Davies was to turn his back on all of them in search of a simpler and, for him, more meaningful life.

We pick up Davies' story again when, at the age of 50, and after a series of live-in housekeepers-*cum*-mistresses, he decides it is time to find a wife and settle down to a more conventional, but also more private, life.

Marriage

The circumstances surrounding the publication of *Young Emma* are as strange as the story itself. In August 1924, 18 months after Davies had married Helen Payne at the East Grinstead Register Office, Davies wrote to the publisher Jonathan Cape to discuss a novel he had just finished. Six weeks later he sent the manuscript with a note that read, "I am sending *Young Emma*. It frightens me now it's done." Davies had insisted that the book be published anonymously to protect his wife and himself, avoiding any direct references that might identify them. Fearing that an autobiography of Davies' romance and marriage to a woman 27 years his junior, only thinly disguised as fiction, might damage Davies' reputation, Cape consulted Davies' former patron George Bernard Shaw. Shaw's reply is included as an appendix in the book, but while Shaw describes the book as "an amazing document," he agrees that it would do its author harm (no concern is expressed for the author's wife) if published in his lifetime, and suggests Cape leave the final decision to Davies himself. Naïvely, Davies only told his wife about the book after he had already sent it to Cape, which occasioned him to write a further letter to Cape to the effect that:

> She is very much alarmed at it ... As she is only 24 years of age and has every prospect of outliving us all I have come to the conclusion that the MS must be destroyed ... So will you please return the MS and let me have a note to say you have destroyed the two type-written copies ... Please don't try to persuade me to do anything different, as a book that is not fit to be published now can never be fit.[26]

The copies were *not* destroyed but carefully put away in a safe. They surfaced several times, but were not eventually published until the year after Helen Davies died in 1979—56 years after the book was written. Here, then, is that part of Davies' autobiography relating to his courtship and marriage. Again there is much evidence of Davies' insecurities, vulnerabilities, and paradoxical self-characterization. From the beginning of the book's introduction, Davies is on the defensive, starting with an apology to the reader that credits the abject side of his story as being redeemed by "the force of a natural genius":

> Although the book may be praised for its style and language, I would not like anyone to think or say that the matter itself is foul; and that the force of a natural genius has made common ditchwater sing like a pure spring. For had I not been convinced that the book was pure, in spite of the matter it deals with, it would never have been written or published.[27]

Davies states in his introduction to *Young Emma* that he is only tolerated by London society because of his reputation as a writer, at the same time admitting that he has tired of these acquaintances anyway, and wished to move once more to the relative anonymity and solitude of the countryside. But if there is a pattern here to Davies' attitude to high society circles, what is it? A basic insecurity: reject them before they reject you, or a genuine repudiation of a way of life that, while he craves its acceptance of his literary accomplishments, also repulses him. For he is a man modest in his tastes and needs—a tramp by nature who yearns for the freedom to indulge his natural desires without attracting attention.

> I was beginning to find society a pest, and common friendship unsatisfactory. I began to see that, although people liked me personally, their interest in me would only last as long as my power to keep my name before the public. … I decided to give them up, before their time came to sacrifice me.[28]

Davies' sense of survival is powerful. Quite determined to change his single status to that of a married man, he mentions two women from the aforementioned London society whom he claims would have been happy to marry him. His reasons for rejecting both, on the surface, appear selfish, but again, might point to an innate insecurity. The first was an actress whom Davies rejected because of his perceived conflict between "the footlights and a quiet study." The other he rejected because she was rich, "and that would not do either; for I wanted a woman who was worth working for, and would be dependent on my own loving kindness."[29]

This last admission is telling. But there is no doubt that, although Davies' approach to securing a wife is more akin to choosing furniture, again, the motivation is not entirely clear. Insecurity and fear of rejection, or some deep-seated working-class, conservative ethic? Then there is also Davies' own admission that he was drawn to the marginal and the dispossessed. But the values and ethos of tramping are about either mutual independence or mutual dependence, not the knight in shining armor rescuing the damsel in distress—so possibly Davies was an incurable romantic also?

In any event, it was with such considerations in mind that Davies embarked on his new quest, but not before he describes the last of a series of live-in lovers-*cum*-housekeepers—with the latter, it seems, being the primary need. When the need took him, he would wander the streets day or night watching, and sometimes picking up, women. Yet his self-confessed shyness, or, paradoxically (considering his pastime) good manners, meant he would only approach a woman who first approached him. In spite of his predatory behavior, he was both naïve and vulnerable. One of his "housekeepers" stole from him mercilessly, even scolding him when he accused her of buying inferior soap when he had clearly given her sufficient money for a superior product. Another was unfaithful to him, and yet a third was a drunkard. Davies had calculated that his wife should be honest, abstinent, not object to him smoking or spending time in the company of men, and, as already noted, dependent on him in every way. Quite a tall order, particularly as Davies also described himself as "lacking the charms that please a woman ... I don't think it possible that any woman could fall in love with me at first sight."[30]

But perhaps Davies was just too hard on himself. Because in spite of his odd behavior, including his feigned selfishness, boorishness and misogyny, he was by all accounts a compassionate and kind-hearted man—even if he did not always express it outwardly. Socially awkward, certainly, but more vulnerable than abusive: all this is borne out in *Young Emma*, which due to Davies' extreme candidness (there is nothing to suggest that this is merely a literary ploy—and remember that Davies believed the book would be published anonymously) leaves little doubt as to the true nature of the man, as the following lines suggest: "what am I to do with this foolish face of mine: why does it look so kind and honest that everyone takes advantage of it"[31]

Remarkable then, if not also aberrant, that at the age of 50, strolling at night along the Edgware Road, Davies sees a young woman (she is 23 but, as Davies admits, looks more like 15) who smiles at him, and within minutes is walking arm in arm with him back to his flat in Holborn. Davies admits to taking back streets to his flat for fear of being accosted by the police who, he says, would ask what a poorly dressed young woman was doing with a smartly dressed gentleman old enough to be her father. Helen (Emma) spends the night with Davies and tells him that she is up from the country and about to give notice to her employer who is treating her badly. Davies offers her work as his companion and housekeeper and she accepts, telling him that she will return to take up her post the following Saturday after working out her week's notice.

There then follows a pitiable scenario where Davies, realizing he has not asked for the woman's address, and also his stupidity for not suggesting she walk out of the job immediately, goes through all kinds of mental torment that he will never see her again. He can't sleep, and walks the streets and park around Marble Arch for a week hoping to catch sight of her. Hopelessly besotted, and convincing himself he has lost her forever, he is astounded when Saturday arrives and she knocks and walks into his apartment, the more so when she admits to having walked several times past his house hoping to catch sight of him. But there is also a disagreeable side to this love story, for Davies notes he has been infected with the early symptoms of syphilis and, convinced that Helen was the source of the infection, confronts her and persuades her to take a letter (that he writes) to his doctor. Not fully understanding the significance of what Davies is implying, Helen complies but with inconclusive results. Davies' obsession with the disease, and his harsh treatment of Helen as a result, forms a significant portion of the book. It is many months later, after their marriage, that Davies discovers from his doctor that, on examination, Helen showed no signs of ever having had the disease. Realizing that he had acquired his disease from a previous lover, Davies was not only mortified at having wronged Helen, but, given such highly personal and candid accounts of his wife's medical examinations, and his own callous stupidity, little wonder, then, that he had reservations about the book being published.

Furthermore, Davies was unaware at the time of meeting Helen that she was pregnant as the result of a rape by a friend's brother. And, as already noted, suggestions that Helen was a prostitute are completely unfounded, based only on comments that she *might* have become a prostitute if Davies had not married her. The story of how Helen nearly died in childbirth (the baby did not survive) and how Davies, himself nearly dying from an infected foot (there is no mention in the book that he has only one), drags himself to the hospital to visit her, is extremely moving and tender. As fanciful as the story is, this is the manner in which Davies met his future wife. An odd couple they certainly were, but clearly in love with one another, and in spite of the usual domestic disagreements, lived happily together for 18 years until Davies' death in 1940 following a stroke and series of heart attacks.

The final words of this saga are left to Davies in this summing-up of his tramp life from the end of the penultimate chapter of *The Autobiography of a Super-Tramp*:

> Certainly I have led a worthless, wandering and lazy life, with, in my early days, a strong dislike to continued labour, and incapacitated from the same in later years. No person seemed inclined to start me on the road to fame, but, as soon as I had made an audacious step or two, I was taken up, passed quickly on from stage to stage, and given free rides farther than I expected.[32]

As some final observations: Davies was a distant cousin of the actor Sir Henry Irving; he was awarded an honorary degree from the University of Wales in 1926; as well as Augustus John's painting of him, there were many other portraits made of Davies in his lifetime; there are to date at least five biographies of Davies, as well as references to him in countless other volumes; and lastly, Davies can take credit for the names of the rock band Supertramp and the Bristol-based soul combo The Soul Destroyers.

ENDNOTES

1 Davies, W.H. *The True Traveller*, London: Duckworth & Co., 2012, pp. 96–99
2 Davies, W.H. *The Autobiography of a Super-Tramp*, New York: Alfred A. Knopf, 1917, pp. 2–3
3 Ibid., p. 5
4 Ibid., pp. 27–28
5 Ibid., pp. 29–30
6 Ibid., pp. 46–47
7 Ibid., pp. 67–68
8 Ibid., pp. 70–71
9 Ibid., p. 87
10 Ibid., pp. 90–91
11 Ibid., pp. 127–128
12 Ibid., p. 136
13 Ibid., p. 137
14 Ibid., p. 139
15 Ibid., pp. 157–158
16 Ibid., pp. 166–168
17 Ibid., p, 171
18 Ibid., p. 178
19 Ibid., p. 189
20 Ibid., p. 198
21 Ibid., p. 214
22 Ibid., pp. 283–284
23 Ibid., pp. 319–320
24 Shaw, George Bernard, in "Preface," *Autobiography of a Super-Tramp*, op. cit., pp. viii–x
25 *Autobiography of a Super-Tramp*, op. cit., pp. 327–330
26 Davies, W.H. "Foreword," *Young Emma*, London: Sceptre, 1987, p. 12
27 *Young Emma*, op. cit., p. 17
28 Ibid., p. 18
29 Ibid.
30 Ibid., p. 49
31 Ibid., p. 77
32 *Autobiography of a Super-Tramp*, op. cit., p. 336

Leon Ray Livingston

(1872–1944)

"Wanderlust"! Ask any other victim of this strange malady—tramp, commercial traveler, railroad man, circus follower, etc., and all these will attest to the very same inability to shake off the desire to wander.

Leon Ray Livingston, *Life and Adventures of A-No. 1*

To Every Young Man and Boy

Who Reads this Book, the Author, who Has Led for Over a Quarter of a Century the Pitiful and Dangerous Life of a Tramp, gives this Well-meant Advice:

DO NOT

Jump on Moving Trains or Street Cars, even if only to ride to the next street crossing, because this might arouse the "Wanderlust," besides endangering needlessly your life and limbs.

Wandering, once it becomes a habit, is almost incurable, so NEVER RUN AWAY, but STAY AT HOME, as a roving lad usually ends in becoming a confirmed tramp.

There is a dark side to a tramp's life:—for every mile stolen on trains, there is one escape from a horrible death; for each mile of beautiful scenery and food in plenty, there are many weary miles of hard walking with no food or even water—through mountain gorges and over parched deserts; for each warm summer night, there are ten bitter-cold, long winter nights; for every kindness, there are a score of unfriendly acts.

A tramp is constantly hounded by the minions of the law; is shunned by all humanity, and never knows the meaning of home and friends.

To tell the truth, it is a pitiful existence all the way through, and what is the end?

It is an even ninety-nine chances out of a hundred that the end will be a miserable one—an accident, an alms-house, but surely an unmarked pauper's grave.

Preamble

Unlike most of the other tramp writers discussed in this book—those who celebrated their anonymity and life in the margins of society, with no thought of competing against fellow vagabonds for publicity—Leon Ray Livingston seems to have openly courted celebrity. Livingston unashamedly embraced the practice of branding, so ubiquitous today, as is evident from the logos and tag lines on the covers of his 12 self-published books: "America's Most Famous Tramp who travelled 500,000 miles on $7.61," adopting the moniker "A-No.1," and crowning himself "King of the Hoboes." Yet in spite of these accolades, none of the other tramp writers featured in this volume, bar Jack London, seems to have been aware of Livingston or even mentions him. Yet regardless of this apparent arrogance and self-promotion, Livingston's is a story as remarkable as most in this collection of tramp biographies, and (as with Jack Everson) his exploits as a child tramp from age 11 are second to none. Another facet of Livingston's writing that jars with the tramping spirit is that having enjoyed and promoted his own adventures, he then not only adopts the role of the social reformer (as did Josiah Flynt, born three years before Livingston), but establishes his reputation as a campaigner *against* tramping. One possible motive for this stance may be purely entrepreneurial: to endear himself to the general reading public. The preceding "warning" appears in the facing page of the preface in most of Livingston's books.

Let us presume then that Livingston was just an astute publicist rather than an apologist for tramping. If he lacked the integrity of the true Cynic (in the positive meaning of the term), he was not averse to using *cynicism* (in its negative context) to enhance his reputation with mainstream American society—and also increase the sales of his published works:

Life and Adventures of A-No. 1: America's Most Celebrated Tramp (1910)
Hobo Camp Fire Tales (1911)
The Curse of Tramp Life (1912)
The Trail of the Tramp (1913)
The Adventures of a Female Tramp (1914)
The Ways of the Hobo (1914)
The Snare of the Road (1916)
*From Coast to Coast with Jack London** (1917)
Mother Delcassee of the Hoboes: And Other Stories (1918)
The Wife I Won (1919)
Traveling with Tramps (1920)
Here and There with A-No. 1, America's Most Famous Tramp (1921)

**From Coast to Coast with Jack London* also inspired the movie *Emperor of the North* (1973), directed by Robert Aldrich and starring Lee Marvin as A-No. 1, Ernest

Borgnine as the sadistic train conductor, and David Carradine's character loosely based on Jack London, using the moniker "Cigaret" (previously employed by Josiah Flynt).

The Child Tramp

Livingston was born to a well-to-do family in San Francisco on August 24, 1872. His father was French, his mother German, and Livingston claims that by the age of eight he could speak both these languages fluently in addition to English, to which he later added Spanish also. At the age of 11 a minor incident at school led to Livingston running away from home to join hundreds of other homeless children and hobos roaming across America. Sent home for bad behavior with a note from his teacher requiring his father's signature, Livingston ran away rather than face disgrace—only the day after his birthday on which he had been lavished with presents. And so another hobo career started with a 100-franc note from his uncle in Paris, $28 he took from his mother's purse, and Livingston's .22-caliber rifle.

Livingston boarded a river steamboat from San Francisco to Sacramento where he booked into (unbeknownst to him) the most expensive hotel in the city where a four-night stay depleted his resources by 20 dollars. The 100-franc note he left with a bank cashier without changing it because the teller had asked where he got it. So with his rifle and his remaining few dollars Livingston walked to a water stop along a railway track where he gave his rifle to a brakeman in return for a ticketless ride to Truckee. He was eventually put off the train by another brakeman at Winnemucca in the Nevada desert, 450 miles from his home in San Francisco. With clearly much to learn about survival and beating trains, Livingston's career as a hobo had begun.

A woman in Winnemucca spotted the young boy crying on some steps and took him inside to give him a meal. Livingston was on the point of telling the woman the truth but, fortified with food, he repeated the tale that he was recently orphaned and trying to reach his uncle in Chicago. So moved were the townsfolk that they made a collection and gave Livingston a ticket to Omaha and five dollars in change. Livingston was a fast learner; after failing to find work in Omaha due to his young age, he resolved to hustle for a living. He beat his way to Chicago hidden among sheep in a stock car. There he lived on free food in saloons, bedding down at night with other waifs and strays under the bushes in a local park until the cold weather arrived. Having heard stories about the warm and sunny South, Livingston then struck out for New Orleans, on which journey, he says, he turned down four offers of adoption along the way.

Arriving in New Orleans on Christmas Day, 1883, he must have been a sight to behold. "I was dirty and ragged to the last degree, with toes sticking out of my shoes." But the warm climate and easy availability of appetizing food soon put him in good spirits.[1] Livingston survived by stealing bread, milk and cream pitchers from houses, left by the tradesmen in early morning, and then dipping this bread into the molasses leaking from syrup barrels piled on the wharves. "For lodging at night I crawled under the tarpaulins covering the cotton bales stored on the wharves."[2]

Only one week later, on New Year's Day, an incident on the wharf led to Livingston being offered a job as a cabin boy on board a British schooner plying trade among the ports of Central America at $5 a day plus board. Dressed up in his sailor's outfit and cap, and being told that all he had to do was watch the seagulls and flying fishes as the schooner sailed out into the blue of the Gulf of Mexico, must have seemed like a boyhood fantasy come true. But the fantasy was short-lived and soon Livingston found himself peeling potatoes, scrubbing the decks and forced into all manner of hard labor, amid beatings from the crew who, for most of the time, were drunk on mescal.

In British Honduras

Livingston had his chance to escape when the ship landed in Belize City in (then) British Honduras where he had to row the chef ashore for some supplies. He hid out on the edge of the jungle in view of the ship until he was sure it had sailed before exploring his new home. Again he was taken in by a kindly woman who fed and clothed him, and for the first time since running away from his parents' home, he penned a letter to let them know where he was and beg their forgiveness. One can only imagine their surprise at receiving news of their 11-year-old son from Belize.

As he was able to read and write, Livingston then persuaded the husband of the woman who had taken him in to give him work as a bookkeeper in a lumber camp several days' journey inland. Livingston describes the mahogany trade of British Honduras, worked principally by African Americans who, he says, made up 95% of Belize City's population. Livingston was given three months' pay of $24 in advance to equip him for the trip inland, and, had he been allowed to board a steamer in the bay bound for New Orleans, he would have deserted his employment for a second time. In the event, the ship had been quarantined due to a death from yellow fever in Belize and no one was allowed to board. Livingston had no choice but to return to his employer and fulfill his contract at the lumber camp. His description of the socio-economic life of the camps makes fascinating reading, not least his diet: "I became acquainted with roasted baboons, fried parrots, turtle and armadillo stews, tapir steak, iguana (an enormous and ugly tree lizard), monkey soup, etc." Below

Livingston describes the beginning of his nine-day journey upriver, with its clear parallels to the first journey made by Trader Horn up Gabon's Ogowe River:

> We embarked in dugouts—men, women, children, dogs, household effects, provisions, etc., and paddled up the Rio Hondo. After several hours passing through mangrove swamp we came to higher ground, and then we only could use poles as the river became crooked, shallow and full of rapids. Alligators and enormous turtles slid from the banks as we approached them, and at night, when we camped on the river bank around the fires, we could hear the cries of panthers, mountain lions, wild cats, monkeys and coyotes in the dark jungle.[3]

It was while in the lumber camp that Livingston received his first letter from home, his parents telling him how delighted they were to have heard from him, having given him up for dead after a long search. Livingston replied asking for money to pay his way home, but admitting that by this time he was having the time of his life, "fishing, hunting, eating new kinds of fruit, guavas, breadfruit, etc. I saw butterflies of gorgeous colors; birds more strange and beautiful than I ever imagined could exist, some of them with bills larger than their entire bodies." His employer, Captain Jones, could not have been kinder to him, as were the camp laborers; Livingston had made himself popular with them by giving them overweight rations from the camp store and charging them less on their accounts. "They in turn presented me with many pretty souvenirs."[4]

From Belize to Guatemala

But once again fate intervened. Livingston was struck down by a paralyzing tropical disease he calls Black Swamp fever. He was put into a canoe and rowed back to Belize City in 24 hours, the same journey upstream having taken nine days. Livingston received excellent care in the hospital and made a full recovery. He received a letter from his parents containing one hundred pesos to pay for his trip home. But by now, the yellow fever outbreak had become an epidemic and, as no ships could sail from Belize, passage was arranged in a one-man, 25-foot, dugout sailing canoe bound for Guatemala 250 miles to the south, and from where onward passage could be arranged. Livingston describes a horrendous trip in which slashing the sail and frantically bailing out water only just saved the pair from being drowned by a hurricane at sea. They eventually reached the coastal port of Livingston in Guatemala, at the time no more than a military outpost. On later visiting the barracks, Livingston discovered that the entire force consisted of only six soldiers, each an ex-convict, pardoned to join the army. "Their uniforms were made up of sandals with strings between the big toes to hold them, a pair of dark blue pants, a helmet and a white cotton shirt. Each man, however, was equipped like an arsenal, with a long sword, a gun, a bayonet and a big pistol."[5]

And it was here that Livingston equipped himself with books and started learning Spanish in earnest, setting off sometime later to tramp the 220-mile journey to Guatemala City and onward to the Pacific coast. He describes how on the first part of the journey he was followed by a mountain lion all the way to the first hacienda en route, and so spent most of the journey looking backwards rather than in the direction he was traveling. Livingston received such a warm welcome at each hacienda he encountered that he ended up making most of the trip on horseback; his hosts insisting on escorting him from one settlement to the next. He also describes the spectacular scenery encountered en route:

> It was just at break of day, and there in front of me in all their majesty rose two black volcanoes, Mount Agua and Mount Fuego, each nineteen thousand feet high [actually c. 12,350 feet]. They were capped with snow and cut as clearly as two pyramids. Smoke and steam were rising from their cones. Behind me was a sky of fire-red hue; but behind the volcanoes was the blackness of the night, studded with twinkling stars. The eternal snow at the summit of the gigantic mounds was aglow with the splendor of the reflection of the sun's rays. Below in a distance were white houses scattered among the trees, and softly I could hear the rhythmic sound of church bells, calling worshipers to early prayers. Over and around it all was a bluish haze, which made me recall the descriptions of the fairyland that I had read about in books at home.[6]

Onward to Mexico

But Livingston was disappointed on his arrival at Guatemala City, the more so to discover that the spread of the yellow fever epidemic had now reached the Pacific coast also, and what would have been a 20-dollar, six-day passage by steamer to San Francisco now turned into a four-month, 1,200-mile overland trek to Mexico City alone—adding further to Livingston's tramping apprenticeship. Livingston, by now a seasoned hustler, crossed the border into Mexico dressed "much like a Mexican dandy—skin-tight pants, open blouse, a sombrero nearly as big as a basket and sandals." It was the eve of the presidential elections and feeling was running high between Catholics and Protestants. Livingston presented himself as a son of either camp depending on the presence or absence of pictures of saints on the walls of the houses where he sought shelter. Receiving considerable hospitality along the way, he arrived in Mexico City with money to spare.

In order to acquire a set of European clothing for his onward journey to the States, Livingston identified the names of German, French and English residents and presented himself as in need of clothing. On arriving at the railway depot to change into his newly acquired attire, he befriended a Mexican railway guard who persuaded Livingston to continue procuring clothing in the same manner, which he in turn would sell and share the proceeds. From the significant proceeds of this enterprise, Livingston was soon living in a comfortable boarding house, bumming clothes from 10 a.m. until 2 p.m., "and in the evening attired in an up-to-date suit, I spent my time most pleasantly at theatres. After I had 'done' the city I left on a 'hobo-ticket' via the Mexican Central for El Paso, Texas."[7]

Return to America and Further Tramping Adventures

But Livingston had not completed his apprenticeship yet. On arriving in Socorro, New Mexico, with 60 dollars still remaining, he became acquainted with the roulette wheel and, fooled into thinking this was an easy way to augment his funds, was soon relieved not only of his remaining money, but his suit of clothes also. In Albuquerque, Livingston he was arrested for vagrancy and locked up "in a dark and filthy cell" until eventually released by a charitable store owner on payment to the arresting detective to cover the fee he would have been paid by the judge for arresting vagrants, a common practice described elsewhere in this book.

Livingston arrived in the town of Lathrop, California, via Salt Lake City, exactly one year after he had run away from his parents' home, and only 97 miles from his destination, San Francisco. One can only wonder at the distance and variety of experiences and adventures that the 12-year-old had covered in only his first year as a tramp, including adding Spanish to the three European languages he already spoke. But, so close to returning home to his folks, Livingston would meet up with a 27-year-old ex-con, just released from San Quentin prison following a five-year sentence for holding up a stagecoach.

Surprisingly, this seems to have been the first occasion that Livingston was shown any interest by an adult tramp. In Josiah Flynt's writing, there are extended accounts of the relationship between children groomed for begging and stealing and their adult protectors or abusers. Just as in Flynt's accounts, Livingston was seduced by tales of easy living and adventure. In the case of his new tramping partner, Frenchy, this was reinforced by the latter's reputation as a hardened criminal and the fear and respect shown to him by others on the road. And so, at the moment that Livingston was within 20 miles of his parents' home, he chose instead to throw in his lot with Frenchy and embrace the life of a hobo.

The rest of the pair's trip included the usual hobo adventures, riding the rails, begging, stealing and hustling their way across America until they arrived at the port of Pensacola in the westernmost part of Florida. Here Frenchy took a job as a cook on board a ship bound for South America and took his leave of Livingston. But before parting, Livingston relates the story of how he got his hobo moniker: "'Listen, Kid,' said he, 'Every tramp gives his kid a nickname, a name that will distinguish him from all other members of the craft. You have been a good lad while you have been with me, in fact been always 'A-No. 1' in everything you had to do.'"[8]

Frenchy also instructed Livingston, as was common tramp practice, to carve his moniker on the water tanks and mileposts along the railway tracks, with the date and an arrow indicating his direction of travel. In this way, he said, he would be able to find Livingston again when he returned from his trip. A short while later, Livingston came across a "wanted" poster for Frenchy offering a $1,000 reward for his capture for "dosing crew and captain on New Year's Eve, 1885, with knock-out drops, and robbing the captain's safe of 3,000 pesos, Mexican currency." And although Livingston would never meet Frenchy again, he kept up the practice of leaving his moniker and date wherever he traveled.

A Trip to Germany

On Livingston's arrival in Jackson, he found mail waiting from his father telling him that his mother was brokenhearted and begging him to return home. He replied that he would return in the summer and continued with his travels and adventures. Then in Charleston, South Carolina via Atlanta and Savannah, Georgia, and narrowly avoiding another jail sentence, the 13-year-old Livingston was offered a job as a waiter by the steward from a German steamer bound for Hamburg. Shortly after sailing, Livingston was put to work passing coal for 14 hours a day in the hot, dark boiler room, and on arriving in Hamburg, all he got for his labors was a 10-mark bill (two dollars and fifty cents) with the threat that if he reported the captain, he'd be arrested as a stowaway and sentenced to jail for a couple of years.[9]

But Livingston learned quickly from this and the other occasions when he fell victim to trickery and injurious experiences. Unlike many of the other tramp writers discussed in this volume, Livingston was to spend his life avoiding smoking, drinking and gambling. When the young tramp tried to rent a room in a hostel, he was told he would have to register first with the police to obtain papers or the hostel manager risked being fined. These papers entitled the bearer to stay for 24 hours in any one place, but no more unless actively seeking work. They also conferred the right to room and board for a night and permission to beg. As Livingston spoke German, and was by now an accomplished storyteller, he had no difficulty in getting the necessary papers, nor in making friends with other tramps at the hostel who related tales about tramping in Germany. Soon after arriving in Hamburg, Livingston set out on foot for Berlin with a tramp he had befriended at the hostel who educated him in the art of tramping in Germany. For starters, German tramps rarely beat trains, the penalty for which was life imprisonment—they got a year's hard labor just for walking on the tracks. Instead they walked the old toll roads where they were kindly received. Yet Livingston acknowledges that German tramps were "about the meanest piece of humanity I ever met. ... There is no honor or kindness among them—everybody for himself."[10]

Livingston reached Berlin after what he described as "more than two weeks of tiresome walking," only to be arrested on arrival in that city for "too much loafing." However, the 48-hour prison sentence turned out to be a welcome respite, being "more like a home than a jail," receiving five meals a day and a further 24 hours to find work. But work was not needed. On running into a couple of American tourists in a park, Livingston spun his tale of woe, received 10 dollars for his trouble, and headed to the train station. There he purchased a fourth-class ticket straight back to Hamburg where he loafed around until the middle of June, getting plenty to eat and small sums of money from crews of English, French and American steamers and sailing ships. "I saved every cent possible, so as to have enough money to pay my way back to the States."[11]

In the event, Livingston kept his savings and managed to get work as a waiter on a ship bound for Boston by promising the steward half of his wages on arrival. But once at sea he pulled a scam he had learned from Frenchy and spent the rest of the voyage in bed in a clean cabin having drunk soap and water to make himself ill. Livingston was taken straight to hospital on arrival in Boston with his full pay of $7.50 (the steward not having the opportunity to claim his share), plus the 23 dollars he had saved up in Hamburg.

Brief Homecoming and Alienation from Family

Livingston's first homecoming to his parents is dismissed in a single paragraph of his autobiography. After only two weeks back in San Francisco, the wanderlust becomes irresistible and he hits the road again, this time for Victoria in British Columbia. By now, Livingston had become an accomplished beggar, but made the mistake—he calls it "boyish foolishness"—of lying to acquaintances of his father and a family relative on his trip north that he was destitute and needed money to return home. On each occasion, receiving food and kindness, he simply took the money before finding another victim for his deceit. News of his exploits got back to his family. Well-to-do and locally respected, their son's behavior brought shame on the family and, after a monumental row with his father, he was kicked out of the family home and told never to return.

"Thus I was turned from my father's door, my future ruined through wild and heartless pranks. They are still residents of San Francisco, respected and wealthy; I, their only son, am an outcast, homeless and nameless tramp."[12] Livingston writes more regrets in these passages, penned 25 years after the event, including letters returned to him unopened, but the degree of unresolved bitterness he still nurtures at his plight in becoming a tramp is difficult to reconcile with his self-promotion as "King of the Hoboes." The question must be posed that if Livingston had really regretted becoming a tramp and had wanted a reconciliation with his family, given his resourcefulness and the fact he spoke four languages, it would have been a simple matter for him to achieve conventional success and respectability in a different line of business—in the same manner as did the tramp Frederick Palmer in Livingston's novel *The Adventures of a Female Tramp.*

Professional Tramp and Some Attempts at Employment

Let us now return to the 14-year-old Livingston, forced to abandon his tramping apprenticeship and become a "professional" hobo. If his situation was not dire enough, on beating a train to San Francisco he was robbed of his money and clothes by the first two hobos he encountered. A train guard found him tied up and gagged in a boxcar and advised him to hand himself in to the sheriff at Bakersfield. After receiving breakfast and a visit to the judge where he received a 30-day sentence, the sheriff bought Livingston a pair of shoes, gave him a dollar, and sent him on his way. A tramp explains to the bemused Livingston the details of the scam:

> They fined you thirty dollars and thirty days; you can't pay the thirty dollars, but the sheriff gets one dollar a day for every day you are supposed to be locked up; the judge, five dollars for your sentence; the lawyer, five dollars for your conviction; the clerk, five dollars for your commitment, and the deputy sheriff five dollars for arresting you, so you see it is all graft. None of them receive a regular salary, so an officer has to steal all the fees he can to make a living.[13]

This same tramp acquaintance now delivers a lecture to Livingston on the corruption and hypocrisy of criminal reform measures and how he would deal with the tramp problem—something Livingston later takes on as a campaign theme in his own role as a tramp reformer. This sermon includes yet another categorization of tramps: "child tramps" (runaways or abandoned), "distillery tramps" (drunks), and "scenery tramps"—the latter describing those who tramp and avoid paid employment out of a lifestyle choice. This 11-page chapter titled "Why Permit Men to Become Tramps?" jars somewhat with what is otherwise a straightforward autobiography of Livingston's early tramping career.

For a while, Livingston did attempt to reform himself. Arriving in Los Angeles, he encounters a Salvation Army captain who kits him out with a new suit of clothes, and Livingston tries to engage in a series of jobs (bellboy, factory hand, fruit picker, ranch hand), all exploitative and abusive in different ways and so he did not stick to any for more than a week. Livingston also worked for a while at one of the many charitable institutions set up to alleviate poverty—also condemned by other tramp writers in this book. Praying on wealthy, God-fearing sponsors, Livingston calculated that the fraudulent proprietor of this particular establishment must have received around $100 in donations per week, dispensing only $10 for charitable purposes, most of which (such as the stale bread he received from a bakery) had been donated free.

Return to Latin America

By this time Livingston had concluded that honest tramping was preferable to dishonest employment and, reading in a newspaper about the fortunes being made in Brazilian diamond mines, resolved to tramp to that country to try his luck. On reaching Tampa, Florida, Livingston begged transportation on a steamer bound for Havana. From there he worked his passage on a lumber schooner to Santiago de Cuba on the south coast, only to find that there was no possibility of sailing further south from that port. After tramping the nearly five hundred miles back to Havana, for the third time Livingston would find himself stranded by the quarantine rules of a yellow fever outbreak. Having no choice but to find food and shelter in Cuba, Livingston threw himself first on the mercy of the American consul, who ignored his pleas, then on the German consul—with the tale that he was a shipwrecked German cabin boy—who gave him an order for a few weeks' board and room. When that was up, he tried a similar scam on the Austrian consul, telling him that he had come from Vienna and had lost all in a shipwreck. The consul swallowed Livingston's yarn and gave him a ticket to New York, an order for a ticket from New York to Vienna, and 20 dollars in money for expenses. Three days later Livingston was aboard the

Niagara steamer headed for New York where he sold his voucher for a ticket to Austria for $40. "It thus happened that even the Imperial Austrian government paid for some of my travels."[14]

Determined to continue with his Brazilian adventure, and this time better prepared and resourced, Livingston successfully beat it by rail all the way to the town of San Luis Potosí in central Mexico, where, collapsing exhausted in a boxcar, he was woken by a railway guard only to discover that it was the same guard he had procured second-hand clothes for in Mexico City two years previously. Livingston enjoyed a happy reunion and hospitality at the guard's home for a few days before setting off for the port of Vera Cruz. There he secured passage as a cabin boy on a German schooner loaded with lumber bound for Venezuela, saving himself the 2,000-mile overland trip through Central America and over the Isthmus of Panama.

On arrival at the port of La Guaira in Venezuela, the lumber was unloaded and the schooner continued to Maracaibo to pick up a load of coffee. Here Livingston jumped ship to continue his journey to Brazil. It is also the first time, Livingston says, that he was offered work on account of his ability to speak several languages, but he had other plans. In Maracaibo he met another American boy of his own age. Tom Hanrahan from Pennsylvania had also jumped ship in Maracaibo but, unable to speak Spanish or get a passage back to North America, he was near starvation when encountered by Livingston. The latter, by now well-schooled in the art of begging, soon collected the equivalent of $48 and persuaded Hanrahan to join him on his expedition south. Now assisted by the purchase of two donkeys, the new friends set out for Bogotá, the capital of Colombia, 475 miles inland to the south. Their plan was to follow the single telegraph wire strung from tree to tree all the way between Maracaibo and Bogotá. With ropes for bridles and empty coffee bags for saddles, they set out, camping at night and amply provided with provisions from friendly locals during the day. Livingston's Spanish opened doors and his story of "our uncle in Rio" touched the hearts of all those they encountered.

Their burros were used to carrying loads nearly their own weight but seemed to enjoy the company of their new owners, the more so because they were treated more kindly than they had been by their previous owners. Good progress was made, even when crossing the high mountain ranges. "We received letters of recommendation from one hacienda to another, the same as I had in Central America, and everybody was anxious to provide us with the best and help us on our journey."[15]

It took one month for the pair to reach Bogotá in this fashion, and then onward to Quito, in Ecuador, 450 miles further to the south, this time without the aid of the telegraph wires to guide them: "The country became more and more desolate, with dangerous trails up and down steep mountain sides; wire bridges swinging in the wind over gorges and chasms, we crossed often." It took

Livingston and Hanrahan two months to reach Quito, this time encountering not only Spanish settlers but indigenous Indians also. In Quito, Livingston claims to have had the greatest success in begging so far. He targeted German settlers while Hanrahan approached Americans, netting the equivalent of $155 between them in just one day. The pair rested up in Quito for three weeks after the grueling but adventurous nine-hundred-mile trek by donkey, and also kitted themselves out with much-needed supplies, not least new footwear and a pistol. They were about to enter hazardous territory.

Amazon Adventure

After crossing through the snow and ice of Andean mountain peaks, and receiving food and shelter mainly from monks, the pair eventually reached the navigable source of the Amazon tributary, the Rio Napo. And here, after having carried them for 1,250 miles, they exchanged their burros for a large ironwood canoe to continue to their destination in Brazil, according to Livingston, a further 5,000 miles downriver. The change from riding the slow jolting burros to floating down a crystal current in a canoe was a welcome change. At an altitude of nearly 6,000 feet they could enjoy stunning tropical scenery along with cool and pleasant nights. The Rio Napo had many falls and rapids where it was necessary to carry the canoes and their cargo down steep slopes and reload them before setting off again. "Some days we had to make three portages thus, and it was this very unpleasant job that prevented us making rapid progress."[16]

It took them three months in this fashion to reach the Marañón river in Peru, from where they would enter the Madeira river and then the Amazon proper. By now, there were no more portages to navigate and as the rainy season had just ended, they were moved downstream by a rapid but steady flow of water, making the journey more peaceful. Here also they met other much larger craft, not to mention a dazzling display of wildlife:

> Parrots, monkeys and gaily plumed birds we encountered by the millions. Every little hut along the banks had them for pets. To try and buy them only seemed to amuse the natives, and when we explained to them that each parrot would be worth $10.00 in the States, they seemed to think we were telling them yarns.[17]

On reaching the Peru/Brazil border at Tabatinga, the pair went through customs procedures before continuing downstream. From here on, neither speaking Portuguese, communication would present some difficulty. A further disadvantage was provided by the tropical heat and relentless sun, not to mention constantly having to dodge tree stumps and the ever-waiting crocodiles. Now they also had to keep watch at night from preying animals and indigenous bandits who stole their paddles and would have taken their canoe also had they not been vigilant. Their only source of hospitality now were the few Catholic fathers and monks they encountered along the river. But on the night of July 1, 1887, while camping on a slight rise on the confluence of the Amazon with the Rio Negro, tragedy struck. Hanrahan woke to put a few more dry branches on the fire. Suddenly he screamed out and Livingston saw him stagger to the fire and then fall to the ground. Hanrahan was able to tell him that a venomous snake had struck him. Livingston ripped open the leg of Hanrahan's pants with his knife and cut into the flesh where two small spots marked the place the fangs had entered. But in less than 10 minutes, following frightful convulsions, Hanrahan turned purple-black and died. "His last words were to tell his mother that he thought of her, and to give her his rosary and prayer book."[18]

Livingston was dazed and distraught by the loss of his friend to whom, after all the adventures the pair had shared together, he had naturally formed a very close bond. It was a further two months before Livingston reached the settlement of Santarém at the confluence with the river Tapajós. At the time he left his friend at their last camp he had been strong and healthy. On reaching Santarém he was worn out by sorrow, hardship and malaria. French merchants at the settlement took Livingston to a small hospital run by the Sisters of Mercy. There he stayed until May, 1888, taking nine months to recover. "I tipped the scales at 37 pounds heavier than when I entered, thus giving a vivid idea of what a condition I must have been in. I was dark yellow, only skin and bone, and nearly dead."[19]

On his discharge from the hospital, having learned that the diamond mines were a further 1,700-mile overland trek and all claims had, in any case, been bought up by syndicates, Livingston abandoned his original quest and gladly accepted passage on a German steamboat to the coast in return for working his passage. In two months the boat reached the harbor of "Para" (Belem), the main port serving the Amazon basin where, on account of his adventure being published by the local newspaper, he made many friends, eventually securing employment as a steward on a coastal steamer plying trade between the Guyanas (French, Dutch and British). While in the capital of Dutch Guyana, Livingston was offered a job on an oceangoing liner bound for Rio de Janeiro. Having received his discharge pay of $5 on arrival in Rio, Livingston spent time enjoying the sights of what he described as "a European metropolis" with opera houses, banks, military warships in the harbor, and fine parks. There he also encountered many American, German, Spanish and English residents, not to mention several genuine American tramps with whom he met up again later in the States. He was offered several jobs but, already restless to move on, was then thwarted in his travel plans on Christmas Day after being rushed to the hospital by ambulance with the very illness he had escaped on so many previous occasions—yellow fever. "It took only three weeks to be discharged, but three months to get over the after-effects, showing how dangerously near I came to dying. People, Europeans especially, were dying like flies, there being over 2,000 funerals from September till May."[20]

Return to America via London

On May 1, 1890, still only 18 years of age, Livingston stowed away in an Italian tramp steamer bound for Montevideo in Uruguay. Lucky to escape with his life on being discovered, having breached quarantine regulations, and saved only by the discovery on his person of Tom's rosary and prayer book, Livingston was put ashore 80 miles from Montevideo with dire threats against revealing the name of the vessel that had taken him there, having to tramp the last few miles on foot. From Montevideo, Livingston then made the six-hundred-mile trek to Buenos Aires in Argentina and, after enjoying the delights of that capital, signed on as a crew member on a ship carrying cattle to London, England, for 10 dollars' wages. Following the three-week trip to London, Livingston signed on to work his passage back to New York, finally returning to America after a four-year absence.

Livingston's first assignment on his arrival back on American soil was, as promised, to deliver Tom's rosary and Bible to his mother in Pennsylvania, but on meeting Mrs. Hanrahan, and she being overcome by the news that Livingston had met and spent time with her son, he did not have the courage to inform her of his death. After relating some of their adventures, and how Tom had spoken often and fondly of his mother, he left the woman with her hopes and dreams and went on his way, still in possession of the rosary and Bible. Sometime later, Livingston told the tale of Tom's death to a police officer and entrusted him with the task of informing Tom's mother of his death and returning his possessions.

How the Mature Tramp Became a Writer

Livingston does not say how he spent the intervening seven years, other than referring to not having given up the tramping life, but by the summer of 1897, with America in the grip of gold fever, he had left Oregon to beat his way by train, steamer and dogsled to the Klondike goldfields in Alaska, there to seek his fortune and make good his vow to his mother to settle to a more conventional life. A year later, due to a series of accidents, harsh weather, and illness requiring further convalescence, Livingston had returned from the goldfields without his intended fortune. However, through his bravery and skills at survival, he had saved the lives of a party of rich adventurers stranded in the Alaskan wilderness, forging some lasting friendships that would serve him well into the future. In this regard, he acknowledges that the hardships and dangers he had suffered as a child had been providential: "It showed me a way, not alone to save money, but by doing so, to gain the estimation of my fellow beings, something that I had, up to that moment, thought to be impossible to attain for those who follow the road of 'The Restless,' and made it possible for me to be proud of my record, even when I am called in disdain—'a tramp.'"[21]

Following this final chapter of Livingston's first book, *Life and Adventures of A-No. 1*, he provides a "conclusion" that dismisses his further adventures—including six different trips to Europe and one each to Japan, the Caribbean, China, and New Zealand—as being repetitious and "tempting the patience of my readers to do so." However, various of his further adventures are recounted in his later volumes, including graphic descriptions of how he was himself abused by older tramps, not acknowledged in his first book. Turning to writing at the age of 35, aided by the journals in which he meticulously chronicled his adventures, *Life and Adventures of A-No. 1* was published three years later, followed by 11 further books in the same number of years: "I have kept an exact account of every mile I have tramped from the first day I 'hit' the road on the 24th of August, 1883, and the total mileage on the 1st of May, 1910, was 471,215 miles, and my cash expenditures for transportation, exclusive of unavoidable streetcar and ferryboat charges were $7.61."[22]

Livingston's Further Writings

Hobo Camp Fire Tales

Livingston's second book, *Hobo Camp Fire Tales*, relates a series of yarns spun between three tramps, of whom Livingston is one of the company. The tales are related around a campfire on a single night to stave off the pangs of hunger after being thrown from a boxcar by an irate brakeman at a desolate water tank in West Virginia, and with no hope of either food or onward passage. The book opens with the same warning against the perils of tramping, titled "To Every Young Man and Boy," a campaign Livingston continues in his subsequent volumes. Livingston's manifesto against tramping is further promoted in the following one-page preface from *Camp Fire Tales*—in the same breath as he bemoans a lost romantic age of tramping:

◊ *PREFACE* ◊

BY FAR a majority of the present day tramp army were boys or young men when they commenced their roving. The aim of this book is to warn others (showing what a miserable life even the best of tramps have to lead), by relating how an innocent boy, who had left his good home, urged on by a longing to see the world, while listening to stories of actual tramp life told by "Old-Timers" around a campfire, gradually realized the truth of a tramp's existence, and repenting, escaped the clutches of his older companion and returned home.

This booklet will be especially entertaining to the adult reader because it gives a vivid insight into the daily life and character of the average tramp, of whom an army of more than one hundred thousand is aimlessly wandering about the United States.

The tramp, tramping and everything pertaining to tramp life in the United States at the present time, is not what it used to be in the past.

Vividly do I recall the days before 1900, when it was more often the rule than the exception, to see from ten to fifty tramps riding upon a single freight train. Hordes of tramps could be met with migrating to and from all points of the compass, while after nightfall their campfires lit the woodlands from Maine to California.

The general prosperity; the strict enforcement of the vagrancy statutes; the encroachments of "Prohibition"; but chief of all the detective bureaus, maintained by every railroad, whose officers harass him every moment of the twenty-four hours, are the principal causes for the gradual disappearance of the tramp.

Of the "Old-Timers," those who have been victims of the "Wanderlust" for more than twenty years, few are left, and while these are few in number, fewer are those who have recorded their singular adventures as they occurred.

I believe by relating a few actual tramp experiences in the shape of this story, the reading public will find something novel and interesting concerning the bright, as well as the dark ways of the "Underworld"—the more, as no stale jokes or love affairs are repeated.

I sincerely hope that these "Hobo-Camp-Fire-Tales" will meet with as good a reception as my first literary effort —"The Life and Adventures of A-No. 1."

I beg the reader to remember that, while these tales are strictly moral ones, no person can be a tramp and a saint at the same time.

—THE AUTHOR.[23]

The second chapter of *Camp Fire Tales* places tramps into two categories: "the insolent, begging drunkard commonly called 'tramp' by the press, and the inveterate wanderer ... a victim of an irresistible urging to keep constantly on the move—a malady so well designated in the German language as the 'Wanderlust.'"[24]

This broad division between the tramp-of-circumstances and the tramp-of-choice is referred to by most of the other tramp writers in this book, except that, in Livingston's case, he chooses to pathologize the tramp-of-choice by referring to wanderlust as a malady, and its advocate as a victim. But then Livingston is not a helpful reference when it comes to the "science" of tramping. For those who appreciate understanding human behavior by forcing it into categories, tramp sociologists from the early 1900s such as Ben Reitman and Nels Anderson (see introduction) have provided over 30 classifications of tramps. What Livingston *did* helpfully catalogue in *Camp Fire Tales*, and discuss more formally than other tramp writers have done, is the parlance, codes, and symbols that American hobos used to communicate with each other concerning themselves and their environment (see Livingston's descriptions and diagrams on the following page). We are particularly indebted to Livingston for preserving, though not, as some have claimed, "inventing," the information system of symbols carved by hobos into water tanks and mileposts, and described by him as "The Code of the Road."

This sharing of intelligence about whom to trust, what towns and sheriffs to avoid, the best places to hustle and find shelter, et cetera, are well documented by other tramp writers such as Josiah Flynt, Jack Everson, Bart Kennedy and Jack London, so no need to dwell further on Livingston's more instructional accounts. But Livingston's *Camp Fire Tales* are entertaining and add further to the cultural legacy of tramping, including descriptions of some of hobohemia's more colorful characters. Here also is further evidence of the vagaries of the American legal system: Livingston and his companions either get away with daylight robbery or get thrown into jail having committed no crime at all.

The moralizing in this book focuses on the evils of tramps who entice youngsters into the hobo lifestyle, ending with the sentimental tale of a reformed tramp who, in his earlier life, had lured a young boy away from his parents to become his "prushun," and then, on the birth of his own son, suffers remorse on account of his former actions. Although many of the tales told by Livingston and his companions relate the harsher aspects of tramping, they do also contain some lighter moments, such as the feast that five starving tramps enjoy on discovering that a chef has forgotten to padlock the ice-box beneath a Pullman dining car: "a hind quarter of veal, an assortment of veal, mutton and pork chops, four fat pullets and two dozen cans of fresh oysters which were labeled 'Selected Oysters For Fine Trade Only.'"[25] A grand barbecue was held out in the jungle by the river that night to be sure.

A "Key" to the Chart of Signs used by Tramps.

1. A tramp's complete "monicker" showing his road-name, the date and direction of his travel.

2.
3. Arrows pointing and indicating the route and the direction the tramp is rambling.
4.
5.

6. The tramp indicates that he intends to go across the country upon a county road.
7. The tramp indicates that he is still in town waiting for the party whose name is written below this sign.
8. The police in this place are "dead easy."
9. The police in this place are "strictly hostile."
10. There is a railroad detective here, but he is a "good fellow."
11. There is a "strictly hostile" railroad detective here. Look out!
12. This sign on a fence, post, door, etc., means "good people" reside here.
13. This sign means: "People residing here do not give."
14. This sign means: "There is a cranky woman or bad bulldog here."
15. This sign means: "There is a cross man or bad dog here.
16. The Jail here is sanitary and prisoners are well fed.
17. The Jail here is sanitary, but they starve their prisoners.
18. The Jail here is vermin infested.
19. The Jail here is unsanitary, and from it contagious diseases are spread all over the United States.
20. This town has a rock pile.
21. This town has a workhouse.
22. This town has saloons.
23. This is a "prohibition" town.
24. This is a "church" town.
25. This is a tough place. Look out for the hoodlums!
26. This town's main street is all right for soliciting.
27. This town's main street is no account for collecting alms.
28. This town is "strictly hostile". Get out as quickly as possible!
29. These "Diamonds" used in connection with any of the other signs mean next town, east, west, north or south.
30. There is a city detective here.
31. The City jail here is all right for a warm night's lodging.
32. Hostile police judge in this town. Look out!

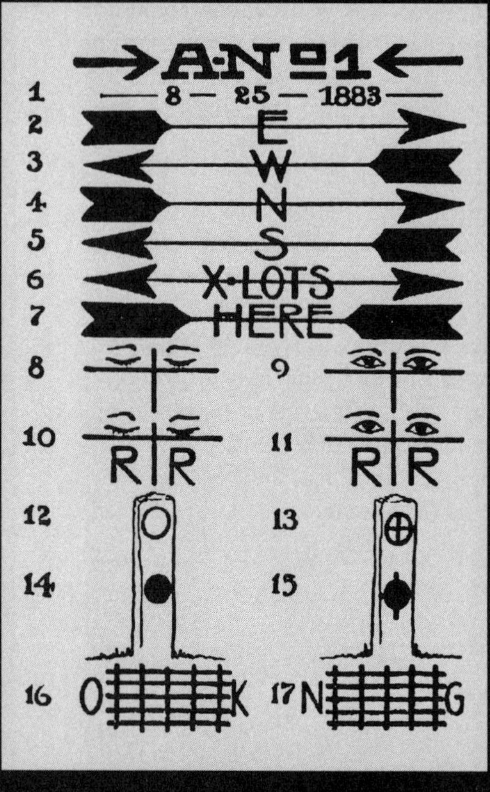

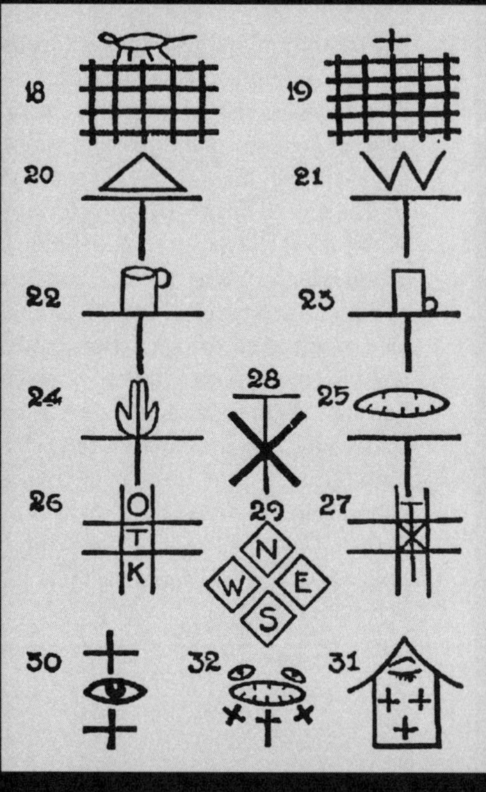

The Curse of Tramp Life

The reader will have to decide for themselves which elements of Livingston's third book, *The Curse of Tramp Life*—paradoxically, containing both the best and the worst of his writing—are based on actual experience, and which are fiction. Here again, Livingston expounds on the dangerous effects of wanderlust on young boys, this time turning to the form of the Victorian sentimental novel—full of mawkish, clichéd descriptions of aristocrats and their slaves—to tell the tale of the runaway son of a Southern land-owning family. The following passage from the opening of the book provides an example of Livingston's newly adopted writing style:

> Off to one side, some distance from the manor are the "Negro quarters," that section set apart on every large southern estate, for the humble homes of the colored house servants and farm laborers. The most pretentious one of these was the home of the manor's expert cook, "Old Aunt Dinah," as "her folks up the hill" affectionately called the trusty old-timer who was considered part and parcel of the Braxton family.[26]

The plot continues with good old Aunt Dinah joining in the general misery of the lady of the manor, occasioned by the disappearance of her 17-year-old son. "'My pore Missus! How sorrow is eating out her pore heart evah since her boy ran away.' Then she wiped a tear away that had strayed down her ebony cheek." Any authenticity that Livingston may have achieved in his first two books is now abandoned for the naked self-consciousness of the sensation-seeking Victorian novel. But the book has some original touches, such as the appearance of the author in the second chapter (describing himself in the third person) as one of the book's characters:

> In the midst of this human whirlpool, leaning against a lamp-post, stood the Author of this book, whose general appearance, dressed as he was in a natty business suit, would never have revealed to the casual observer that the wearer followed the dangerous life of a professional tramp.[27]

Livingston then shifts to the form of the soliloquy before eventually reverting to the first person and some clearly autobiographical references about the grip of wanderlust from whose addictive power it is impossible to shake oneself free: "the mighty City of Cleveland had suddenly became [sic] too small to hold me, so small indeed, that I could hardly breathe, and then some one seemed to push me away from the lamp-post and the next moment, with a bound, I was racing down the street, as if hounded by a fiend." Livingston retrieves his hidden overalls—required attire for beating trains to protect one's better clothing—and then headed for the local rail terminal. "I gave vent to a loud sigh, the sign of relief from the oppressive feeling, which only now, that I obeyed the 'Call of Wanderlust,' left me."[28] For the rest of this chapter and the next, we have Livingston at his authentic and poetic best, here describing the very life force of the true tramp adventurer as he clings to the rods beneath the train with the gravel inches from his face as he speeds through the night:

> Yes, here in the darkness, hanging under the Pullman betwixt life and death, at last I found what only seemed to satisfy that devilish something. There, so close to death, that a mere slip would have put a sudden, horrible finish to my career, at least the "Wanderlust" seemed not to prod me, and as I watched those wheels ahead and in the rear of me slowly revolve, squeaking as they passed the many cross-overs and switches, I at last felt that I had given up everything but life itself, to please that bane of my existence. The faster those wheels revolved, the easier I felt, and as we passed beyond the electric lights of the City and the train gathered speed from a soft purring and murmuring, they began to sing, and when top speed of a mile a minute and over was attained, they fairly screamed with joy. There, hanging on with only those weak, human hands, out of reach of any possible succor, speeding through the night, I felt at peace with all the world.[29]

Supported by his intimate knowledge of tramp life, Livingston now successfully merges his real-life experiences with the fanciful plot of the Victorian melodrama introduced in the first chapter, combining both genres for the purposes of a social campaign to affect a change in the law compelling judges to reunite runaway boys with their parents before resorting to custodial sentences—no small feat. In the chapters that follow, the book settles into an agreeable yarn in which Livingston, as the first-person hero, having found and returned a missing diamond bracelet to its owner—Mrs. Braxton, lady of the aforementioned manor—is then freed from the horrors of a chain gang to exploit the lady's loss of her son in his avowed mission to change the law concerning the treatment of child tramps. The rest of the book recounts Livingston's mission to rescue the runaway boy from his "jocker" and return him to his grieving mother. Tellingly, Livingston admits to this story being provoked by feelings of guilt toward the sorrow he caused his own mother.

The Trail of the Tramp

Livingston's fourth book, *The Trail of the Tramp*, once again concerns the author's obsession with child tramps or "road kids"—opening thus: "I shall relate to you a rarely strange story that will stir your hearts to their innermost depths and will cause you to shudder at the villainy of certain human beings, who, like vultures seeking carrion, hunt for other people's sons with the intention of turning them into tramps, beggars, drunkards and criminals."[30] In this version of the plight of the road kid, Livingston tells the tale of twin boys who run away from home following the death of their father. They are robbed and then befriended by two villains, one a confirmed tramp beggar and the other an armed criminal, only to then be separated for the first time since their birth. The twin who is conned into accompanying the tramp ends up in a Denver camp full of other beggars and their road kids. Here Livingston again repeats his familiar refrain concerning the fate of those tricked into this form of tramping apprenticeship, and also the means by which the victim's allegiance is secured: "One of the road kids in the den of the plingers, who was known by the name of "Danny" ... his present jocker ... had taught him first to drink, then to like and last to crave strong liquor ... which caused his young victim to quickly forget all desire to return to his home and his parents as there he could not secure the dram he yearned."[31]

Brutality is piled on brutality in Livingston's further composition on the evils of tramping, including graphic descriptions of the practice he refers to as "busting a bronco," in which a newly recruited road kid who attempts to escape is first beaten unconscious and then lavished with attention by his jocker, as part of the dehumanizing process of eliciting total obedience. At this point of his story, Livingston departs from his fiction to admit: "The actual experiences of the Author, who when a young boy was at one time a plinger's road kid, are embodied into this chapter and have been even far more revolting than herein described."[32] Unlike Flynt, Livingston does not refer to the frequent sexual abuse of road kids. He uses the term "plinger" to distinguish tramps who choose hustling and begging from "yeggs" (out-and-out criminals—see Chapter 6, Jack Black), often with the assistance of a child tramp sporting sores ("jiggers") or fake disabilities to elicit sympathy from their victims. In this book, plingers also abuse alcohol both for their own use and to develop a dependence among their young charges. Livingston's campaigning motives are never far from the surface of his storytelling, as when he breaks with his fiction to propose a solution to the road kid problem, emphasizing that it was not just kids fleeing abuse but also those from loving families who succumbed to the guile and trickery of the jocker. Livingston's proposed changes to the law include offering aid instead of custodial sentences to young boys caught begging, rather penalizing the adults who exploit them:

> Should any minor be found beyond the limits of his legal residence tramping, peddling, begging or stealing at the command or for the benefit of an adult person, who cannot prove that he had the legal consent of the minor's guardian, then this adult person shall be sentenced to a long term at hard labor in the state penitentiary.[33]

The remainder of the book involves the quest of the twin who had been duped by the yegg, in tracking down his brother who had been led astray by the plinger. The latter only escaped the fate of less fortunate road kids by being arrested while carrying out his jocker's dirty work and serving a prison sentence for his trouble. Livingston has by this time perfected the art of writing the plot- and character-driven suspense novel, embellished as they are by his intimate knowledge of tramping, especially his experience of having lived the life of a road kid himself from the age of 11.

The Adventures of a Female Tramp

Livingston opens his fifth book, *The Adventures of a Female Tramp*, with a brief history of the American hobo pre- and post the American Civil War and the financial crash of 1869 (Black Friday); as these events are already covered in the introduction they will not be repeated here. Livingston is now in full swing as a novelist with a tried and tested formula that piles tragedy upon tragedy before concluding his book with the most unlikely of reunions and happy endings. The underlying message of this tale, as with others, is the folly of tramping and the inhuman and heartless treatment of child tramps, of which the heroine of this story is just a further example—starting her tramping career disguised as a boy. After a successful business venture and marriage to an ex-hobo, he suffers a resurgence of wanderlust and drags his new wife along with him to certain disaster. But, other than the entertaining twists and turns of the romantic thriller-*cum*-bildungsroman, this volume adds nothing more of particular substance regarding women tramps than discussed elsewhere in this book.

The Ways of the Hobo

The subtitle of Livingston's sixth book, *The Ways of the Hobo*, reads *A Book of Educational Worth in Connection with the National Demand for a Solving of the Tramp Problem*. Livingston is now well into his campaigning stride even if his refrain has now become repetitive, as the opening passages of the preface to this volume indicate:

> The Road took thirty of the best years of my life ere I broke its bonds as if by a miracle. While I traveled with tramps I did missionary work among them, but failed to induce even one of the three hundred thousand chronic hoboes who ceaselessly and at will range over this continent, to forsake his unnatural existence. ... I set to the task of saving penny upon

> penny, at the same time studying (at the age of thirty-five) the "First Reader" and other literature of primary learning. Thus, but insufficiently equipped, I attacked the Road by writing and publishing books which exposed its foremost curse —the boy tramp shame.[34]

Apart from the appearance of Livingston's manifesto on the tramping problem halfway through the book, *The Ways of the Hobo* is another collection of hobo stories similar to those narrated in *Camp Fire Tales*, only this time related by a group of hobos to the landlady of a boarding house. Livingston's tramping anecdotes are lively and entertaining, but the obvious fondness and pride in the manner he relates his tramping career is difficult to reconcile with the political posturing on the evils of tramping that preface his books.

The Snare of the Road

The Snare of the Road is yet another treatise on the dangers facing child tramps, part anecdotal, part autobiographical fact and fiction; there seems no end to the tramping tales collected or experienced by Livingston, and the book contains yet another version of the classification of American tramps referred to elsewhere: "tramps are classed in three grand divisions: 'Pikers' they are called who walk; 'Rattlers,' who ride freight cars, and 'Ramblers,' who hobo passenger trains. The ramblers are further subdivided into two classes: 'Foxes' are termed those who ride within the coaches by kiting hat checks ... and 'Wolves,' tramps who depend on brute strength to accomplish their ends. The wolves in their turn are graded into three distinct ratings ..."[35] And so the description continues at some length including references to Livingston's own preferred modes of tramping.

Mother Delcassee of the Hoboes

As with *Camp Fire Tales* and *Ways of the Hobo*, Livingston's ninth book, *Mother Delcassee of the Hoboes*, provides another collection of hobo yarns, this time oddly narrated to a bunch of railroad employees in a train depot for their entertainment and enlightenment. As usual, the tales share amusing anecdotes concerning individual hobo characters, their adversaries, their benefactors, and the sundry scams and swindles they employ to survive. Of particular interest on pages 43 and 44 of *Mother Delcassee* is a further glossary of tramp classifications—excluding some of those referred to in the previous volume—yet some of which are mentioned elsewhere in this book. Livingston's glossary from *Mother Delcassee* is reproduced on the following page for ease of reference.

THE RATING OF THE TRAMPS.

1	Plinger	solicited alms at stores, offices and residences
2	Moocher	accosted passers-by in the street
3	Flopper	squatted on sidewalk in business thoroughfares
4	Stiffy	simulated paralysis
5	Dummy	pretended to be deaf and dumb
6	Wires	peddled articles made of stolen telegraph wire
7	Mush Faker	umbrella mender who learned trade in penal institution
8	Mush Rigger	umbrella mender who learned trade in penal institution
9	Wangy	disguised begging by selling shoestrings
10	Stickers	disguised begging by selling court plaster
11	Timbers	disguised begging by selling pencils
12	Sticks	train rider who lost a leg
13	Peg	train rider who lost a foot
14	Fingy or Fingers	train rider who lost one or more fingers
15	Blinky	train rider who lost one or both eyes
16	Wingy	train rider who lost one or both arms
17	Mitts	train rider who lost one or both hands
18	Righty	train rider who lost right arm and leg
19	Lefty	train rider who lost left arm and leg
20	Halfy	train rider who losts both legs above knee
21	Straight Crip	actually crippled or otherwise afflicted
22	Phoney Crip	self-mutilated or simulating a deformity
23	Pokey Stiff	subsisted on handouts solely
24	Phoney Stiff	disposed of fraudulent jewelry
25	Proper Stiff	considered manual toil the acme of disgrace
26	Gink or Gandy Stiff	occasionally labored, a day or two at the most
27	Alkee Stiff	confirmed consumers of alcohol
28	White Line Stiff	confirmed consumers of alcohol
29	Rummy Stiff	deranged intellect by habitual use of raw rum
30	Bindle Stiff	carried bedding
31	Blanket Stiff	carried bedding
32	Chronicker	hoboed with cooking utensils
33	Stew Bum	the dregs of vagrantdom
34	Ding Bat	the dregs of vagrantdom
35	Fuzzy Tail	the dregs of vagrantdom
36	Grease Ball	the dregs of vagrantdom
37	Jungle Buzzard	the dregs of vagrantdom
38	Shine or Dingy	colored vagabond
39	Gay Cat	employed as scout by criminal tramps
40	Dino or Dynamiter	sponged food of fellow-hoboes
41	Yegg	roving desperado
42	Gun Moll	dangerous woman tramp
43	Hay Bag	female stew bum
44	Jocker	taught minors to beg and crook
45	Road Kid or Prushun	boy held in bondage by jocker
46	Punk	lad discarded by jocker
47	Gonsil	youth not yet adopted by jocker

Coast to Coast with Jack London

The opening of Livingston's eighth book, *Coast to Coast with Jack London*, presents the author as already something of a minor celebrity. To prove his credentials to doubters (likely including himself) he describes a catalogue of supporting evidence of his deeds and achievements, including: "autographic commendations by a long line of national notables, such as Burbank, Edison, Admiral Dewey, three of the presidents of the United States, a governor general of Canada and others too many to enumerate in limited space."[36]

Livingston's success at self-promotion included newspaper and magazine interviews, and it was one of these that he claims inadvertently led to his meeting with (the as yet unknown) Jack London. Livingston had bet the editor of the *Sunday World Magazine* that the average citizen was so ignorant of the dangers of tramping that he would have no trouble in getting a response to a request for a companion to join him on a tramp from the East to the West Coast. To test the proposal, the editor agreed to publish an ad in the Help Wanted column: "Wanted—travelmate by hobo contemplating roughing trip to California." The response Livingston received was overwhelming, but as his ad was a hoax to prove a point, he ignored the letters and would have made his departure the next day had he not been accosted in person by a confident youth of 18 wanting to know when they could set off on their trip.

There are some inconsistencies in the telling of the tale. London's first book was published in 1900 at the age of 24, 10 years before Livingston published his first book. Livingston says that London was four years younger than him when they met, and that London was "a youth of perhaps eighteen years" (which concurs with Livingston also saying that they made the trip in 1894). So Livingston could himself only have been around 22—surely too young to have come to the attention of three U.S. presidents? As *Coast to Coast* was published in 1917, this would have been 23 years after Livingston's first meeting with London. Was Livingston, now aged 45 and a minor celebrity who had settled down to married life, confusing the trip with the date of publication of the book?

Be that as it may, to add to the authenticity of his tale Livingston reproduces some very touching letters from London (by this time very much the established author) to himself in the opening pages of *Coast to Coast*, both endorsing and encouraging his telling of their adventures, and in which London also refers to Livingston's wife. So one must simply ignore the aforementioned inconsistencies and discuss the trip itself, assuming that at the time of their travels together they were first and foremost tramps, not yet writers. Indeed when they embarked upon their trip in 1894 they had not a cent between them. Though only 18, London himself already had a respectable tramping career behind him, and experience as a sailor also. And although he had responded to Livingston's ad as a companion for a trip from coast to coast, he acknowledged himself to be "out looking for a comrade with whom to hobo-cruise around the globe." But no need to comment further on London's own tramping career here (the best known of all these tramp writers) as it is fully described in Chapter 10.

This legendary trip did not get off to a great start. Without the six cents between them required to board the ferry to cross the Hudson River, the pair were ejected from Grand Central Station and then made their way to the New York Central freight yard from which they were also chased. After sharing a loaf of stale bread with a third tramp, during the sleep that followed the pair were robbed of their shoes and coats by the ungrateful hobo. They managed to beat a train for 70 miles before being discovered by a railroad sleuth and locked up for their trouble. In the event, the beginning of the coast-to-coast trip proved even less agreeable than many of the tramp stories already narrated. What followed were the usual narrow escapes and near-death experiences both with railway employees and brigands who prey on hobos. This included several arrests and being dislodged from the rods beneath a speeding train by a brakeman playing out a line with a steel spike attached under the train, a common but deadly practice also referred to by Jim Tully in Chapter 12, as the heavy pin ricochets at high velocity between the railway sleepers and train undercarriage, splintering anything not also solid steel on its way.

Partway through their coast-to-coast tramp, due to the relentless vigilance of railroad police, the pair were forced to spend some time in what Livingston describes as Chicago's hobo "abyss." The introduction provides a description of the significantly expanded Chicago abyss, or "main stem," some 30 years later, when its vagrant population had reached up to 75,000. Livingston's account of his and London's visit to what would become the largest hobo mecca in the USA is provided in the following description:

> In 1894 the abyss of Chicago reached northward on South Clark Street from the intersection of this thoroughfare with La Salle Street. There the distance of several city squares was lined with buildings the owners or renters of which exclusively catered to the trade brought to town or created there by the transient wanderers of hobodom and peculiar to them only. Other districts scattered over the city held the hangouts of the local vagrant elements and the various subdivisions of the underworld.
>
> Bounding the Chicago abyss within narrow confines, actually it was the east side of the street only which held the "cafes," the dime flopping dumps, the nickel restaurants and barber shops and the "missions" patronized by the uncouth hoboes. Across the roadway, on the west side of South Clark, were "cheap" stores, the basement dens of vice of various degrees of viciousness presided over by slant-eyed Orientals and the boarding houses and booze resorts of low-caste Greeks, Sicilians and other human castaways of the nations of the universe.[37]

There follows a graphic description of the mean drinking dens and pseudo-religious missions of the Chicago abyss as our heroes unsuccessfully attempt to find food and shelter for the night. Their onward journey from that city resulted in the usual tramping adventures including a novel stay in the small town of Fairfax, Iowa, where the whole town ended up betting against each other on whether the pair would successfully board a train out of town. Naturally, those who had bet in their favor kept them supplied with food and encouragement, and in spite of the odds that half the townsfolk, including police and railroad officials, made it their business to prevent the hobos boarding a train, their tramping skills won out. The whole of *Coast to Coast* is in fact a catalogue of cat-and-mouse yarns concerning the two future tramp writers and a host of infamous sadist policemen, such as the chain-wielding Old Strikes and Bad Bill of Boone.

Accounts of the journey through Wyoming, Utah and Nevada, as it relates to rail travel by hobos and the various settlements and local history (e.g., the Milk and Honey routes through Mormon country and the Reno divorce colony of women), are uniquely informative for those interested in the subject. The pair made part of the final leg of their trip, to London's family home in Oakland, down the Sacramento River by rowboat, before abandoning this mode of transport having been eaten alive by mosquitoes and delirious with malaria.

Any onward round-the-world trip was curtailed, as following a sumptuous meal prepared by Mrs. London on the pair's arrival in Oakland, they were forced to take to separate sick beds to recover from malaria. When Livingston returned from his San Francisco convalescence to look for London, the latter's mother refused to provide his forwarding address—paradoxically, given Livingston's obsession with protecting road kids, suspecting the older tramp might rekindle her son's wanderlust, he having since given up the road for work in an upstate laundry.

But, as we shall learn when that writer is discussed later, London did not abandon his round-the-world tramping ambitions. Livingston received a letter from London 12 years later when the latter was recovering in Tahiti from another tropical disease, having this time persuaded his now-wife and a friend to accompany him on a seagoing tramp in the 45-foot sailing boat, the *Snark*.

The Wife I Won

The Wife I Won, unless a work of fiction, would have presumably covered that period of Livingston's life in which he decided to settle down to a more conventional life and, given his literary accomplishments, a more prosperous and comfortable existence. Tantalizingly, London had referred to Livingston's wife in the opening line of a letter he wrote to his old tramping companion dated March 1, 1917 (the year *Coast to Coast* was published) but no further mention of her is made:

> Dear A. No. 1:
>
> I can't seem to say "Dear Mr Livingston." And, as your wife is undoubtably proud of your remarkable career, she won't mind![38]

This is the only reference noted to Livingston's wife in the nine other books reviewed for this chapter. The book is every bit as strange as the title, being another odd collection of hobo stories, anecdotes and opinions (from employment and unemployment to politics and war), including a yarn on Livingston's only encounter with a Jewish tramp. One has to wait until the last chapter, "The Wife I Won," to get any sense at all of the manner in which Livingston gave up tramping for domestic life.

Livingston recalls how, alone one day in a boxcar, he ended up in Erie, Pennsylvania, jumping from the car just as a train inspector was passing. Instead of the rough treatment he had come to expect, the railroad employee invited Livingston to sit in his office by a fire and share a meal. So grateful was Livingston for the hospitality he received that he promised to return one day, and the following year sent the man a box of oranges from Florida by way of thanks, a welcome gift indeed in the bleak and cold northern town. Then, in midsummer, Livingston made good his pledge to return to Erie where he received another warm welcome and was invited to stay with the man, his wife and family, comprising four daughters and a son.

The rest of the tale is predictable enough. Having been exposed to the vocal talents of the daughters and overcome by the moment (for reasons Livingston admits that, "to this day I cannot explain how I came to express such a singular desire") he requested that they sing "Home, Sweet Home." Livingston continues:

> But it was too late for a retraction of my request, as presently Miss Mayme, the eldest, and of course, most comely of the interesting quartette of charming sisters, performed the song. When her pure soprano rang full through the room, I, who heretofore had always rated myself as being a most unemotional sort of chap, felt tears welling in my eyes—a first instance that on my long career of roving I had become conscience-stricken.[39]

Livingston is seated opposite the 19-year-old Mayme at dinner, furtive glances are exchanged, and, emotion now giving way to more practical concerns, Livingston dryly observes: "All this occurred in just a brief moment, yet proved of a duration sufficient to have me instinctively realize that the time for my mating was at hand."

Livingston was at this time a confirmed bachelor in his early forties and had already published four books. Neither was his arrival at Erie a total coincidence. He had already set up his literary headquarters in Cambridge Springs, only 25 miles from Erie. In any case, following the usual inhibited courtship worthy of the Victorian romance (whose style Livingston was imitating in his fictions), the couple marry and settle down to family life. We know from earlier chapters of the book that in 1918, at the end of World War I, Livingston, now nearing his 50th year, was living in Erie with his wife and children in their own home. Livingston continued living in Erie with his wife, whose real name was Mary Trohoske, until his death, aged 70, from heart failure in 1944. He is buried in Laurel Hill Cemetery outside of Erie.

Afterword

Livingston's wanderlust continued to haunt him even after he started his career as a writer. Just as with the trip that brought him to Erie and the subsequent trip to Florida, Livingston continued to make tramping excursions whenever the craving took him. A newspaper reporter, George B. Love, writes of several meetings with Livingston. The first was in Atlantic City in the summer of 1907, the second two years later in the office of the *Los Angeles Times*. On his third meeting with Livingston in Jacksonville in the spring of 1912, Livingston had just published his first two books and gained in prosperity. On this occasion, Love reports that Livingston was carrying two $50 bills in his pocket, copies of his books, clippings from newspapers from across the country of his life history, and was staying at "a posh room at the Seminole Hotel." "The Rambler said ... 'Simply write of me as a man who wants to save young boys, and warns the women of Jacksonville not to harbor and feed boys who run away from home. It is these same boys that become the men you drive away from your back porches as worthless vagabonds.'"[40]

But, as Love further notes, "not even fame and prosperity could dissuade the Rambler from his endless, aimless travel." In an often-quoted remark that sums up Livingston's tramping lifestyle, he confided to Love: "When I started out the wanderlust was upon me and I enjoyed the zest of adventure. Later I traveled because it became a habit with me, and now, although I hate the life, I travel because I cannot stop."[41]

Putting his overt campaign against the perils of tramping and the blatant promotion of his self-published books to one side, the formidable range and magnitude of Livingston's tramping experiences—not least his remarkable adventures as a child tramp from age 11—leaves no doubt that Livingston is a strong contender for the title "King of the Hoboes." But such accolades go strictly against the individual and egalitarian concept of tramping, and this side of Livingston's character belies the honest and often self-deprecating portraits of himself in many of his stories. There is also the paradox of his public diatribes against tramping versus the obvious fondness and passion he relates in his narratives as a practitioner of the vagabond art. And so perhaps we must just accept that Livingston was a complex and contradictory character. To speculate on the psychological effects of leaving home at 11 and never reconciling with his mother (maybe also carrying guilt occasioned by indirect suffering to other mothers) is a futile enterprise. The consequent campaign adopted by Livingston to dissuade other young men from following in his footsteps provides its own indicators. But as Livingston's own accounts of being a child tramp are limited to his (albeit fascinating) adventures,[42] giving only clues to the traumas and abuses he must have suffered, we are left to speculate on the psychology behind this strange and unique body of work.

An aspect of Livingston's writing that is of particular interest are the distinctions made between the tramp-of-circumstances and the tramp-of-choice and, in respect to the latter, the powerful allure of that phenomenon described as "wanderlust." Even in the case of the child tramp, wanderlust cannot simply be explained away by the pull of fortune and adventure. There is no allure for the true tramp in pursuing riches. The raison d'être of tramping, in the timeless, metaphysical pull it has on the human psyche, is precisely to *free* oneself from such material preoccupations. Sadly, in the case of Livingston's writing, we have only glimpses of his true tramping spirit, preoccupied as he became with his own celebrity and the approval of conventional society. Nevertheless, for those with the patience to probe Livingston's work, these glimpses are there to be found, hidden away between the storytelling and the lectures on the evils of tramping.

ENDNOTES

1 See also Jack Everson's account of the culinary pleasures of New Orleans in Chapter 9.

2 Livingston, Leon Ray. *Life and Adventures of A-No. 1: America's Most Celebrated Tramp*, Cambridge Springs, PA: A-No. 1 Pub. Co., 1910, p. 12

3 Ibid., p. 21

4 Ibid., p. 23

5 Ibid., p. 26

6 Ibid., p. 28

7 Ibid., p. 30

8 Ibid., pp. 44–46

9 Ibid., pp. 50–51

10 Ibid., pp. 52–53

11 Ibid., pp. 54–55

12 Ibid., pp. 58–59

13 Ibid., p. 62

14 Ibid., p. 95

15 Ibid., pp. 98–99

16 Ibid., p. 106

17 Ibid., pp. 106–107

18 Ibid., p. 109

19 Ibid., pp. 110–111

20 Ibid., p. 113

21 Ibid., p. 135

22 Ibid., pp. 135–137

23 Livingston. *Hobo Camp Fire Tales*, Cambridge Springs, PA: A-No. 1 Pub. Co., 1911, p.3

24 Ibid., p. 9

25 Ibid., p. 90

26 Livingston, Leon Ray. *The Curse of Tramp Life,* Cambridge Springs, PA: A-No. 1 Pub. Co., 1912, p. 5

27 Ibid., p. 15

28 Ibid., p. 17

29 Ibid., p. 22

30 Livingston, Leon Ray. *The Trail of the Tramp*, Cambridge Springs, PA: A-No. 1 Pub. Co., 1913, p. 3

31 Ibid., pp. 61–62

32 Ibid., p. 67

33 Ibid.

34 Livingston, Leon Ray. *The Ways of the Hobo*, Erie, PA: A-No. 1 Pub. Co., 1914, p. 3

35 Livingston, Leon Ray. *The Snare of the Road*, Erie, PA: A-No. 1 Pub. Co., 1916, p. 32

36 Livingston, Leon Ray. *Coast to Coast with Jack London*, Erie, PA: A-No. 1 Pub. Co., 1917, p. 8

37 Ibid., p. 78

38 Ibid., facing pages

39 Livingston, Leon Ray. *The Wife I Won*, Erie, PA: A-No. 1 Pub. Co., 1919, p. 126

40 Website on Livingston: www.angelfire.com/folk/famoustramp/livingston.html

41 Ibid.

42 Although human brutality abounds in Livingston's books, severe self-censorship—to meet what he clearly believes to be Victorian sensibilities and literary appetites, e.g., his note that "The author has carefully avoided the least mention of anything that would be unfit reading for ladies or children"—means that today's readers are denied many valuable insights into some significant realities of hoboism, and in particular the life of the "prushun" or "road kid."

Jack Everson

(1873–1945)

Practically every county and town in the state ... had passed laws allotting a fee of two dollars each to the Justice of the Peace for every tramp convicted of vagrancy.

Jack Everson, *The Autobiography of a Tramp*

Preamble

John Lewis (Jack) Everson may not have been as poetic a writer as Stephen Graham or W.H. Davies, nor as scholarly as Josiah Flynt, but his authentic and unselfconscious contribution to the obscure genre of tramp literature should not be overlooked. Not only does his work help validate the minutiae of other descriptions of tramp life in late 19th/early 20th-century America, including being a child tramp, but it is also a great yarn and is written here as a strict chronology of events. Everson's writing should stand alongside the finest fiction of the period, both for the richness of the narrative and the sensitivity of the telling, yet this writer is little known and out of print.

It is worth noting also that like many other tramps turned writers, Everson's early childhood was comfortable and middle-class. This helps to inform an important premise of this book: a view (espoused by some tramp writers themselves) that the primary cause of tramping cannot simply be attributed to a combination of economic depressions and alcohol abuse. In Everson's case, as also with Livingston, he came from a comfortably-off and caring family and had no taste for alcohol—occasionally sipping it in order not to offend. And while not suggesting that the middle classes were not also affected by the depressions and heavy drinking, the condition described in this book as "wanderlust" appears to be a far more convincing explanation.

Everson was born four years after fellow Chicagoan tramp Josiah Flynt. Like Flynt also, Everson surrendered to the lure of wanderlust, became a child tramp, and served part of his vagabond apprenticeship in a penal reform school. Having read both writers' accounts of tramping, it is surprising that the two men's paths never crossed, and that they did not share other tramp acquaintances in common. Even so, Everson was aware of Flynt through the latter's writings and reputation, and refers to Flynt's writings in the final chapter of his book. Bedridden and dying from cancer, Everson's memoir and single publication, *The Autobiography of a Tramp*, was not completed until the last year of his life at the age of 72. Everson's autobiography was eventually typed up and published by his older son, W.L. Everson, in 1992 (when W.L. Everson was himself already 86). The book is only available in a single electronic form without page numbers and contains no publication or copyright information.[1] In his preface to the book, Everson junior describes his father's basic nature and character as follows:

> He certainly, and admittedly, fell a good ways short of moral perfection. Still, I must marvel at the variety of experience he managed to crowd into his 72 years. My personal recollections are of a highly intelligent and affectionate man who, despite his faults, was a kind and loving parent who taught me much and shared with me music, baseball games,

> mushroom hunts, fishing trips, and a considerable degree of intellectual comraderie [sic]. I'm willing to settle for that.

Everson's daughter from a previous marriage, Alice Weiss Everson, was clearly not as generous about her father. This can be evidenced by some of her disparaging comments in hypertext throughout the digital version of the book. But it is too easy to impose the values of a modern-day feminist on a man (albeit her father) who survived a very different age, culture and circumstances than her own. As was acknowledged in an earlier chapter, Louis L'Amour, a later generation of tramp turned writer (of primarily pulp Westerns with some 105 publications to his credit), made just such an observation in his own autobiography when he suggested: "A mistake constantly made by those who should know better is to judge people of the past by our standards rather than their own. The only way men or women can be judged is against the canvas of their own time."[2] Perhaps L'Amour had the foresight to pen such advice as an insurance against his own reputation for upholding traditional family values and casting women as homemakers. In any event, given the times in which Everson lived, he shows some surprisingly humanistic attributes, in addition to the more macho behavior that clearly irritated his daughter. Weiss Everson initially observes that there may have been fictional and exaggerated elements to the work, but after completing her reading of the book, comments: "My apologies for questioning where fact left off and fiction began. While much was omitted, I believe all that was contained was factual."

But then what memoirs, memories even, do not contain fiction? And given that the autobiography was written in the final year of Everson's life, his work is remarkably lucid. Although not writing his autobiography until approaching his death, Everson's literary beginnings have an interesting twist. His mother, Rebecca (Carrie) Jane Billings Everson (pioneer inventor of the oil flotation separation process in the mining industry), had started to teach him to read when he was three and, by lying about his age, was able to get him into the Scammon School in West Madison Street, Chicago, at the age of five. At the time Everson attended school, West Madison Street was fast becoming the epicenter of the hobo capital of America. A city within a city, Chicago's "main stem" spread for half a mile in every direction around West Madison Street, reaching tramp populations of up to 75,000 well into the 1930s. Everson describes himself as an unruly child, constantly being punished for his unauthorized absences from home and school, "a disgrace to my parents and teachers who seemed unable to either wheedle or beat into me any of their curriculum other than reading, spelling, and arithmetic; these subjects I seemed to acquire a knowledge of instinctively." Everson's adventures went unrestrained; he roamed the streets by day and night and was a member of the notorious Carey's Patch Gang of 8- to 14-year-olds who terrorized the neighborhood with acts of vandalism and petty theft.

Everson's first arrest, aged 10, was for undertaking a mile-long swim to Government Pier, Chicago, in the nude. This also earned him a beating from his father who had to pay the $10 fine. In spite of his father's belief that flogging was a sound form of discipline, Everson maintains that he was "a most kind and affectionate man," more often cradling his son in his arms and, with tears in his eyes, pleading with him to "be a better boy." But Everson's wild and unruly behavior could not be curtailed. As well as being an experienced petty criminal, by the age of 11, Everson was also experienced in the sexual arts after being befriended by a prostitute who offered him her services for free. His parents were pleased that they had secured him work as a messenger boy for a telegraph company, though unaware that many of the packages and flowers he was delivering were to Chicago's red-light district.

On the Road

Still aged 11, and after a particularly vicious beating from his father for being accused (falsely, he claims) of stealing a penknife from another boy, Everson resolved to leave home and jumped a train heading for New York with an older boy. Getting off the train when it stopped after some 40 miles, the pair were persuaded by two seasoned tramps to split up and accompany them separately, the one pair to California, with Everson and the other tramp going to New York. There is lengthy discussion in the chapters on Flynt and Livingstone concerning older tramps bribing and cajoling child tramps (or even slum kids in the towns they passed through) with promises of money and adventure, and to become indentured to them for the purpose of begging, and occasionally also as sexual partners. The child apprentice in this relationship was referred to as a "punk" or "prushun," the older mentor being their "jocker." As luck would have it, Everson's jocker, "Michigan Curly," turned out to be kindness personified and the two became close friends for many years. Undoubtedly Curly gained from the relationship but, from Everson's accounts at least, did not abuse Everson or exploit him financially; indeed, Everson seems to have profited greatly from this relationship. The jocker's role (at least for those who did not mistreat them) was to offer the child protection from other tramps and train them in the arts of tramping and survival on the road.

Amongst these was "chronicking" (begging from private homes) with the story that his parents had died and he was making his way to stay with an aunt. If asked to share a meal, he should accept but ask to have some food put in a bag to share with another boy who was accompanying him. If begging on city streets, he should tell pedestrians, to the accompaniment of tears, that he had just dropped a quarter down a crack in the sidewalk (nearly all sidewalks were wooden at the time) and ask for help to find it, that his father had sent him to buy food and that he would get a whipping if he returned home without it. Curly also advised Everson not to have any money in his pockets when begging because if arrested and found with money he would be considered a professional beggar and given 10 or more days in jail. "On the other hand, if I had no money on me, I could expect to be given a twenty-four-hour 'floater' to get out of town."

As if to answer Everson's daughter's criticism of the accuracy of her father's text, there now follows in the book one of Everson's rare insights into the writing process itself:

> I often marvel at the faculty of memory in man. As I sit at my desk, retrospectively recalling incidents of my earlier years, it seems that no moving picture of those incidents could portray them more clearly than does my mental vision. Each incident recalled seems to forge a link in an unending chain of other incidents whereby they all become so interrelated that the picture as a whole becomes merely the past. Of conversations I remember little or nothing, but every trivial act of my life up to the time I was thirty-five stands out as clearly as the sun to an astronomer, once I mentally envision the locality in which it occurred.

There is no sense in the text that Everson has fabricated his story for dramatic effect. On the contrary, his writing is unselfconscious and at times even self-deprecating. The tenderness and domesticity of his writing negate any sense that here is a writer attempting to sensationalize his life story. The passage immediately following in the book would seem to illustrate this point:

> About the third day that I was there, I began to itch in my crotch and along the insides of my legs. Curly noticed me scratching and made me remove my short pants, which he turned inside out. He found what he expected—several large lice, or "crumbs," and a number of small white bodies in the seams which he called "nits." He told me we would have to boil our clothing, and sent me up town for a couple bars of soap.

Another episode from the pair's adventures illustrates that, in his own way, Curly was as dependent on Everson as the child was on him. Unlike Everson, Curly needed alcohol in his life, and although he had developed strategies to protect him from habitual drinking, he did occasionally embark on a drinking spree that, without Everson's help, would have left him very vulnerable indeed. One night, Curly started a drinking spree. "He came to the room about ten o'clock carrying a gallon jug and two quart-bottles of whisky." After taking a few drinks, Curly was still sober enough to instruct Everson how to care for him during his binge and not to leave him alone when awake. He handed Everson a large roll of bills to hide in a safe place and was told to keep some of the whiskey back for him to sober up on after he had consumed the contents of the jug, by administering it in ever decreasing doses diluted with water. Everson was also to refuse to go out and purchase more alcohol no matter how much Curly pleaded—significant responsibility for an 11-year-old boy.

By midnight the whiskey was two-thirds gone and Curly in a stupor. "I turned the gas light down low and lay down beside him, but I couldn't go to sleep. I was frightened for fear of what might happen to him if I failed him in any way, and lay there sobbing my heart out." Curly awoke around daybreak asking for a drink and Everson carried out his instructions, a routine that went on for several days during which time Curly was too weak to move or speak and Everson nearly called for a doctor, believing Curly was dying. "I lay beside him on the bed, crying bitterly, and when he finally awoke the sound of his voice as he stroked my head was a never-to-be-forgotten joy. I cried now with happiness."

Prison and a Trip to Australia

Curly would buy shipments of costume jewelry by mail order, before most people were aware that there was fake stuff that looked as good as the real thing, and had it delivered to various towns on their travels. Everson improved and semi-legitimized their trade (they did not have a license to peddle) by brazenly admitting in bars and brothels that their goods were imitation, and yet selling them for considerably more than they were purchased. Nevertheless, the pair were eventually arrested. Curly received 30 days in jail but Everson was sent to a reform school in Plainfield, Indiana, until he should reach the age of 21. The strict regime at the reform school did not seem to have done Everson any harm, and he resumed some of his schooling with enthusiasm.

About two months into his stay there, Everson was summoned to the governor's office with some trepidation, only to be met by his parents and Curly. The latter had thought better of springing Everson from the reformatory to resume their tramping exploits, and instead had gone to find his parents to alert them to his predicament. Curly had clearly impressed them enough for them to agree to him being introduced as Everson's uncle. Everson's father had subsequently found out that a friend of his son's had lied about the penknife. "I sat on his lap and forgave him and, with his arms about me, I cried some more when he slipped into my hand a brand-new copper-handled knife. That act of contrition endeared him to me more than anything he had ever done before."

In spite of a letter from the Governor of Illinois to the Governor of Indiana seeking clemency, Everson's parents were unable to secure his release from

Plainfield. Everson threw himself back into his studies and stayed in contact by letter with both his parents and Curly until he was eligible for parole. Following his release from the reform school, Everson describes an emotional reunion with his family, including, for the first time, a mention of his brother George who was three years his junior: "George was the good boy of the family and fulfilled the saying that 'the good die young'; typhoid fever claimed him in Denver about two years later." Everson's father had moved with George to Denver in 1887 after a failed business venture in Chicago. From this time onward the family were to live in near poverty and Everson and his mother joined the rest of the family in Denver. Later that same year, still only 14, Everson was jailed again, this time for possession of a stolen Colt .45 revolver. The handgun had been among some other items that Everson agreed to peddle for a tramp, who failed to tell him the gun had been stolen.

Everson's father died from a ruptured aneurysm while Everson was awaiting trial, following which Everson was sent to the reformatory at Golden, near Denver. In just under a year, Everson was paroled to his mother but ignoring her pleas to return to school, in January 1889 and now aged 16, he hit the road again and boarded a ship to work his passage to Australia via Honolulu. His intention was to desert the ship at Sydney and tour the country, but quickly gave up the idea on discovering that railroads in Australia were few and far between and, in any case, went nowhere in particular. Australia also had an answer to the tramp problem: hard labor. As that didn't appeal to him either he returned to San Francisco.

Reunion with Curly and Final Parting

On Everson's return to America he immediately set out in search of his friend. Here follows a further discussion on the tramp custom of carving monikers on posts and water tanks (having parallels with "tagging" today) as previously discussed by Livingston. When tramps traveled by rail, the usual embarkation point was the huge wooden water tank where the trains stopped to take on water. It was the practice of tramps at the time to carve their adopted moniker in the side of such tanks as a way of introducing themselves but also letting other tramps know they had passed on a certain date and the direction they were bound. Everson got his own moniker when Curly had carved his name in such a fashion, adding "Chi (Chicago) Curly" alongside his own. Everson bummed around San Francisco for a couple of weeks before setting out for Denver in search of Curly. At Truckee he went to the Central Pacific Railroad water tank to carve his moniker and intended directions. There he met three other tramps and in line with hobo convention introduced himself. The others introduced themselves in turn as "Sardines," Michael J. Gorman, and Liverpool Tony. Sardines told Everson that Curly had been in Truckee the day before and had headed east, showing him Curly's moniker carved on the other side of the tank.

Everson set out in hot pursuit and, after an emotional reunion, the two of them resumed peddling jewelry that Curly was by this time importing from Europe. They were now partners, Curly insisting that the jocker/punk relationship was no longer appropriate. The two visited most of the states in America and made enough money peddling jewelry to enjoy luxuries like boarding houses, restaurant meals, new clothes and occasionally paying their way on the railroads and paddle steamers. After looking up Everson's mother in Denver and taking her out for a meal and to the opera house, a conference between the three of them concluded with Curly, having already given up drinking altogether, deciding to give up tramping also and return to his wife (who he claimed still loved him) and children to try and make a go of his marriage. Everson, for the first time asking his mother's consent, agreed that if he could make one last trip with Curly he would return to Denver and resume his schooling.

Curly wanted Everson to make the trip with him to Detroit to visit his family but Everson declined, thinking that he would only be a hindrance to Curly's plans. Everson determined instead to take the river trip he had always planned to make by steamer and describes their emotional farewell as follows:

> I shall never forget that parting. It was a miserable day, with cold rain falling as we stood on the levee under a large tarpaulin, stretched on ropes to shelter some merchandise stored there. I had wanted to ride on one of the river stern-wheelers, and had bought second-class passage to Cairo [Illinois] on the one being loaded below us. We stood there hand in hand, not saying a word. I was on the verge of tears, and I think that he was as well, though he was not as emotional as I.

When the boat's bell and whistle sounded the all-aboard warning, the pair embraced and without saying goodbye, Everson ran down the levee and boarded the boat. Standing near the paddlewheel with tears streaming from his eyes, he waved farewell until Curly was out of sight. Although they wrote to each other occasionally for 10 or 12 years, Everson would never see Curly again. Curly did reconcile with his family, and several times offered Everson a job in the fur industry, which he succeeded to on the death of his father.

After returning to Denver, Everson persuaded his mother that he should not return to school but learn a trade. After training as a barber, he took a job as a quarryman, then joined a troupe of acrobats where he claims he worked with the future Douglas Fairbanks. But time in gainful employment was to be short-lived and Everson's wanderlust returned. This time, still peddling phony jewelry, he headed west for California, it being a tramp mecca at that time and because of the local vagrancy laws in which law enforcement officers and tramps colluded with each other for mutual benefit. The scam went like this: every county and town in the state, the larger cities excepted, passed laws allowing a fee of two dollars a head to the Justice of the Peace for every tramp convicted of vagrancy. And so constables would visit the jungles daily to round up any tramps they could find. They did not arrest them, simply asked them to come to the court house and plead guilty to the charge of vagrancy. The tramps would receive a sentence of 24 hours to get out of town and 50 cents each to speed them on their way—the judge clearing a dollar and a half for each conviction. At one such round-up in southern California, a Swede, unfamiliar with the procedure, refused to plead guilty and defied the judge, saying he was not a vagrant as he had five dollars in his pocket. "The Judge, an Irishman, defied in his own court, arose in righteous wrath and said, 'OH! So I can't find yez guilty, can I? Well, yez are fined five dollars for contimpt of court and yez kin take tin days in jail for yersilf'—and then added triumphantly, 'Now, can I find yez guilty?'"

First Marriage, Further Prison Sentences, and Chain Gang

Still only 17, Everson now spent six weeks tramping the West Coast from San Diego to Seattle with another tramp he had befriended, all the while peddling jewelry to make ends meet. He enhanced his reputation with other tramps by contributing generously to those worse off than himself. And at this point in the book, we again get one of Everson's rare reflections into the writing process:

> Until now I have endeavored to record events in their true chronological order. This has taxed my memory, and while the events themselves are as clear to my mind as though they had happened an hour ago, the placing of them in their true relationship in time has become so bothersome that, from here on, I shall try only to approximate the time of their occurrence. For example, I am not at all sure whether it was the winter of 1890–1891 or the following winter that I got married.

Up until now Everson seems to have been very specific about dates, often pinning events down to the actual month as well as year. But it is perhaps excusable that Everson should be vague about the date of his first marriage, as this was a very short-lived affair. He reports that he had only known the girl a week or two when he was "caught in flagrante delicto by her father," and forced to marry her or be returned to reform school. Unlike the girl and her father, Everson was not aware that the girl was already pregnant and that the forced marriage was a desperate act. "I should have suspected it," he says, "because she was unusually plump about the waist." A short time after they moved into a rented apartment, Everson, with the help of two friends, caught the girl in bed with another man, whereupon he promptly took the girl and her belongings back to her parents. The baby was born four months later but lived only a few weeks. The end of this sorry saga was that two years later, Everson received a letter from the madam of a brothel in a Colorado mining town, informing him that his wife had committed suicide after being abandoned by her pimp, and could he pay the funeral expenses. To the indignation of Everson's daughter (from his second marriage) as revealed in her notes to the book, he declined.

During this time, Everson had trained as a bookkeeper, a trade he worked at for a while. Next he took up boxing, at which he was successful but eventually abandoned due to having a "glass jaw." Everson hit the road again, this time returning to begging, using the scam of a self-applied plaster of Paris cast and a sorry tale to elicit sympathy as his modus operandi. On this tramp he received 10 days in jail for trespassing on railroad property, and later, in Jefferson City, Missouri, a further 30 days for begging from a plainclothes police officer. This time Everson was fitted with a ball and chain shackled to his ankles and his first taste of a chain gang. After being driven 10 or 15 miles into the country, they arrived at a large ramshackle frame building with about a hundred dirty straw-filled pallets on the floor. Each was given a tin cup and plate, and a fork, but no knife. Two-by-four rails of unplaned lumber served as seats and at the head of each was a galvanized pail for use as a urinal. As it was mid-afternoon, they were not required to work that day. When the road gang came in shortly after six o'clock, they were all fed a plateful of watery hash and a cup of chicory coffee.

At six the next morning they were all herded out to wash at the well, without soap, and breakfasted on oatmeal mush and more chicory coffee. Everson was given a pick and shovel and waited for the wagons to arrive to take them to work. The chain gang consisted of 60 prisoners, "two-thirds of whom were negroes." They were then divided into three road crews and set to work grading and leveling behind several mule-drawn plows and scrapers. "At noon, a wagon brought us dry bread—half a loaf per man—while the waterboy filled our cups from a large barrel rigged to a two-wheeled cart. We were allowed about half an hour to eat and then worked until six o'clock, when we were returned to our dormitory."

Two Narrow Escapes

After completing his sentence, Everson tramped through a further three states before meeting up with two other tramps who persuaded him to join them in collecting some stash they neglected to tell him was stolen, something Everson should have been wary of given previous experience. That night, after walking two or three miles to a field and pulling hay from the side of a stack where the stuff had been hidden, "suddenly came a shout of 'Hands up!'" Everson bolted immediately in spite of shots being fired and commands to stop. He kept going until running smack into a barbed-wire fence that bounced him back about five feet. After crawling under it, he ran until coming to a road that eventually crossed some railroad tracks. These he followed toward the lights of a town in the distance. When he could run no more he sat down beside the tracks, only to discover that he had been wounded by a revolver bullet now buried an inch into the calf of his leg. When rested, he got up and continued at a dogtrot until reaching the town which turned out to be Streator, in Illinois. As luck would have it, a freight train was waiting on a siding and Everson was able to ride it as far as Galesburg. Even though his leg was by now causing him pain, he was afraid the alarm was out for him and so hid near the depot until a passenger train, bound for St. Louis, came in. "I boarded it from the dark side and went into the smoking car, and when the conductor came through I bought a ticket to St. Louis. There I dug out the bullet, which was about ready to fall out, and sterilized and bandaged the wound."

Everson met up with the other two hobos some six or seven years later to learn that they had been given a five-year sentence. The farmer who owned the haystack tipped off the police after noticing that the stack had been disturbed and discovering the loot. Everson seemed to have hit a run of bad luck around this time, and even when paying for a cabin on the Mississippi cotton-carrying steamer *Oliver Beirne*, only narrowly survived the fire and sinking of that vessel in which 12 people reportedly lost their lives. Comparing Everson's account of the disaster with the actual report provides the first clue to what might be Everson's propensity for exaggeration. Although, to be fair to the man, having been burned in his own escape and looking back on such a grisly scene may well account for the impression it left on him:

> It was a terrible disaster. There must have been at least a hundred people on the boat, mostly passengers, and I believe that more than half of them were either burned to death or drowned. I sicken whenever I think of it, for there were women and children among them, and somehow the thought of women and children dying like that disturbs me much more than the thought of men dying en masse. I was too numbed by the sight of people burning to death before my eyes to think of attempting to rescue those in the water. I might have saved at least one life, but I seemed to be able only to stand and stare as the vessel burned to the waterline.

Tramping in New Orleans and Pitching as a Snake Oil Salesman

Completing the rest of his trip to New Orleans by another vessel, there follows a fascinating description of tramp life in that city, which Everson admits to liking more than any other except for San Francisco. And although he says that begging was very unrewarding, the following description of how well one could live on very little money more than compensated for this deficiency:

> The principal tramps' hangout was at the Three Brothers saloon north of Canal Street. For five cents one could get a "Cincinnati scoop" of beer, holding about a quart, and all the potato pancakes one could eat. In addition, there was a free lunch on the bar, consisting of pretzels, rye bread, sausage, and cheese. There was a small Chinese restaurant nearby that served a substantial five-course dinner for twenty cents without wine, or twenty-five cents with a half-pint bottle. By walking for several blocks to the Conti basin where the oyster smacks unloaded, fifteen cents would get one a peck basket heaping-full of freshly dredged oysters, an oyster knife, a fork, a bottle of either catsup or pepper sauce, and a large bowl of oyster crackers. ... The oysters served there were outsize, being too large for canning or shipping, but were tender and fine-flavored. There were a number of French restaurants where one could get a six-course dinner with wine for thirty-five cents, while in the French and Poydres markets south of Canal Street food was equally cheap.

After a very eventful stay in New Orleans, including working on a sugar plantation, again being shot at, and playing an extra in a blacked-up role at the opera house (not failing to comment on the absurdity of blacked-up actors in a city generously populated with the real thing), Everson headed out once more for California, but, on being nursed by a friendly boarding-house keeper for 10 days en route after coming down with malaria, decided to return to Denver to spend the winter with his mother. Because the phony jewelry racket had played out, Everson tried his hand as a quack doctor, seemingly making a success of it and cementing his post-tramping career as an insurance salesman. His first scam at his new profession involved filling and labeling two dozen bottles and crossing the river to Kansas City where he sold them all in about five hours at 50 cents each for a few and 25 cents each for the rest. "I was glad to have found a promising racket again, and stuck around Kansas City for two weeks. No one bothered me, and I even sold some of my stuff to policemen." At that time, there were few regulations for peddling, and the Pure Food and Drugs Act was unheard of. After this initial success, Everson kitted himself out in some smart duds and a "handsome leather case" that would hold six or seven dozen of his bottles, after which he confined his operations to the larger towns.

That summer Everson worked the Midwestern states before heading south again. In Cairo he sold nearly a hundred bottles in a day. He describes how "the people of Memphis, Nashville, Vicksburg, and Mobile, both white and black, bought freely," so that by the time he reached New Orleans he had saved nearly $1,000, "most of which I sent to mother." After covering all the larger towns in Texas, Everson tried his luck in Mexico, but it seems the Mexicans were more savvy than customers north of the border and he was unable to repeat his previous success.

Gold Prospecting and Another Aborted Marriage

Tramping being in his blood, and not having use for more money than required to survive (any surplus being given to other tramps or his mother), Everson was still traveling on the railroads for free, risking life and limb, including once again being shot at. It was after this incident (which he would probably not have survived but for being found and nursed by the wife of a Mexican shepherd), and having lost his medicine chest and supplies, that Everson threw in his lot with two gold prospectors and tried his luck at dry gulch panning. By the end of the summer he calculated that his share of the gold had only averaged him the equivalent of three dollars a day, "but I was not disappointed; I had enjoyed the life in the open, and I resolved to return there the following summer." In August of that year, 1893, Everson returned to Denver and his mother. The date is not provided by Everson in his narrative, but as he mentions visiting the Chicago World Fair later that year, it is simple to establish, making Everson still only 19 or 20 years of age.

The following summer Everson bought two mules, tools for gold prospecting, and set out to prove a theory he had developed the previous summer that there were richer takings to be had the further one dug from the river. He proved his theory by the end of the summer, returning to Denver $600 the better. By now Everson had resolved to quit tramping, engaging in a series of jobs over the next four years, including being motorman and conductor on the Montclair branch of the Denver Tramway Company. But a failed love affair was to thwart his plans of settling to a more conventional life.

Everson tells how in 1898 he fell in love with "the daughter of a railroad man" whom he planned to marry in June of that year. Everything was going according to plan until, for a second time, Everson was to come across his woman in bed with another man. He clearly took this infidelity harder, besotted in a way he had not been with his first wife. After struggling with himself whether or not to reconcile her indiscretion, even admitting to contemplating suicide over the affair, Everson embarked once more on a tramping spree that was to last five years. Initially he gave up peddling and resorted to the more usual, but less profitable, tramp practice of mooching. Nonetheless, Everson seems to have been able to utilize his salesman's patter to maximize the effect of simple begging. After many further adventures, including a spell at sea, Everson again resolved to quit tramping for good. He had involved himself in getting a tramp friend off an attempted murder charge. This included him kidnapping the prosecution witness, the hobo whom his friend had almost killed when he found him frisking a sleeping friend. The whole episode proved one adventure too many for Everson, who, while enjoying life on the edge, had no desire to run afoul of the law on a major charge.

Two Further Marriages but Still Tramping

After another emotional reunion with his mother, Everson set out to find work in Chicago, though still riding the train to that city for free. It was now 1900, which makes Everson around 27. Having learned to play guitar and mandolin in Denver, Everson tried his hand as a lyricist, but a series of failed and dodgy deals put an end to his songwriting ambitions. He would fall in love and marry for the second time, returning to Denver where he admitted to being "very happy," but only until the spring of 1902 when his wanderlust was once again spiked by reports of a gold strike in Idaho. The trip was a dismal failure, and by the summer of 1905 Everson had been divorced by his second wife Mary after she gave birth to his daughter, the aforementioned Alice. He then returned to Chicago where he fell in love with another woman he refers to as Louise, and to whom he proposed but was rejected after he told her about his previous failed marriages. Whatever tramping credentials Everson may have possessed, as a lover and husband he appears to have been a dismal failure at worst, a late developer at best. At any rate, he declared that he could not bear to live in the same city (Chicago) as Louise without her being his wife, and would have to return to California unless she agreed to marry him. She called his bluff, telling him that this would probably be the best thing. So off he tramped once again to the Coast.

If the reader believes that Everson's romantic exploits have been given too brief a mention, it should be noted here, and was commented on by his daughter Alice, that the accounts in Everson's autobiography concerning his marriages were typically dismissed in one or two sentences, whereas his exploits as a single man are verbose in the extreme. In contrast, given the amount of space accorded to Everson's mother in his book, one could be forgiven for thinking that she was the principal woman in his life. But then again, this is his "autobiography of a tramp," not his life story. After another failed trip and near-death experience, this time when the hotel he was sleeping in burned down during an earthquake, and a separate accident in which he lost a toe, Everson returned again to Chicago where he did finally persuade Louise to marry him. He had kept in correspondence with her by letter throughout his latest expedition, and she finally relented to his persistence. Maybe he had at last developed some skills in the art of romance. In the meantime, Louise had maintained a relationship with Everson's mother, and also his second wife Mary and daughter Alice.

Everson Finally Quits Tramping

After honeymooning in California, the couple settled and built a home in San Anselmo, Marin County, outside of San Francisco (Everson's favorite city as a tramp) to which he commuted daily for work. His first son was born in 1909, and his mother, daughter, and first wife, Mary, also moved to San Francisco that same year. Everson's mother moved into his house to live with the family in 1913 where she remained until her death. A second son was born in 1915. Again, mentions of the birth of his sons are given but a sentence in his book, without even giving their names. Everson had finally given up tramping forever, although he did go to sea until 1920, having obtained a Marine Engineer's license during the First World War. As reported in the final paragraph of the penultimate chapter of his book, the credit for his transmutation from tramping to regular employment and married life Everson gives to his third and permanent spouse, Emilie Louise Krueger Everson:

> So far as my own life is concerned, there is little more to be said. I am not proud of it; neither am I ashamed of it. I have lived it according to my lights, and if they have been dimmed by environment, heredity, mental or glandular unbalance or whatnot, there has not been much I could do about it. I shall make no attempt to explain my many so-called vices or the few virtues I may possess. I leave such explanation to the sociologists and psychiatrists. To myself I have always been an enigma; and like Popeye the Sailor Man, I can only say "I yam what I yam." That the last thirty-five years of my life have been what is termed respectable, I attribute to the beneficent influence of that paragon of all the wifely virtues, Louise. She deserves all the credit for my reformation.

Last Words

The final chapter of Everson's book, "Reflections on the Wondrous World of Trampdom," is a disappointment. There are no reflections on tramping in general; for the most part, the chapter criticizes other tramp writers for inaccurately representing tramping. Everson only credits Flynt's accounts as in any way authentic, and even then commented that Flynt "was unable to get far below the surface of Trampdom, principally because he was motivated by the sole desire to gain information from which to compile sociological data." Everson's comments here, while true in part, seem a bit harsh considering that Flynt was, like Everson, a tramp first and foremost, whatever he may have decided to take up as a profession later in life. Both shared many identical experiences, and from reading both autobiographies, one could easily imagine that they may have become close friends had their paths ever crossed.

In spite of his criticism that Flynt sociologized the tramp, Everson also cannot resist here categorizing types of vagabonds as others have done, putting himself in the more honorable classification "tramp," those who steal only to maintain life's essentials, as opposed to robbers and thieves. He further distances himself from the "hobo" whom he classifies as a migratory worker. Yet from his own autobiography, and the categorizations he uses below, Everson was, depending on circumstances, clearly involved in all of these types of vagrancy at one time or another—tramp, petty criminal, and migratory worker. This begs the question posed in the introduction as to just how useful or valid such categorizations are:

> Where I have used the word "tramp" in this narrative, it is to designate those who depend solely upon begging, peddling, and the theft of food and clothing for a livelihood. Burglars, robbers and other thieves who infrequently associate with tramps are a class about which I know but little. As a rule, they only take to tramping as a means of hiding out temporarily, and though if known they are accepted as members of the clan, the wiser tramps shun their society as much as possible.
>
> Hoboes and gaycats are definitely not tramps. The hobo is a migratory worker who makes use of the same means of transportation as the tramp, as does the gaycat. Gaycats [not to be confused with the current use of the term gay] are migratory thieves and beggars who seldom share their spoils with anybody. They are the ones who commit practically all the petty thefts attributed to tramps in the smaller towns and cities, and real tramps despise them.

The remainder of the chapter contains some references to tramp law and etiquette, and exposes some of Everson's own prejudices. Any hope of further insights into what induced young men to wanderlust, or older tramps to maintain tramping as a way of life, cannot be elicited from this book. Nevertheless, this first-hand account, concerning a primarily child tramp, does provide much valued testimony to add to that reported by others in this book. Thanks are due to Everson then for sharing his story and the enjoyment that can be obtained from reading large parts of it—and no need to insult him further by attempting an analysis of the man or his life in a manner he himself clearly wanted to avoid.

ENDNOTES

1 There are no available hard copies of this book and the only digital copy (now no longer available) has no page numbers or information about copyright.

2 L'Amour, Louis. *Education of a Wandering Man*, New York: Bantam Books, 1990, p. 24

Jack London

(1876–1916)

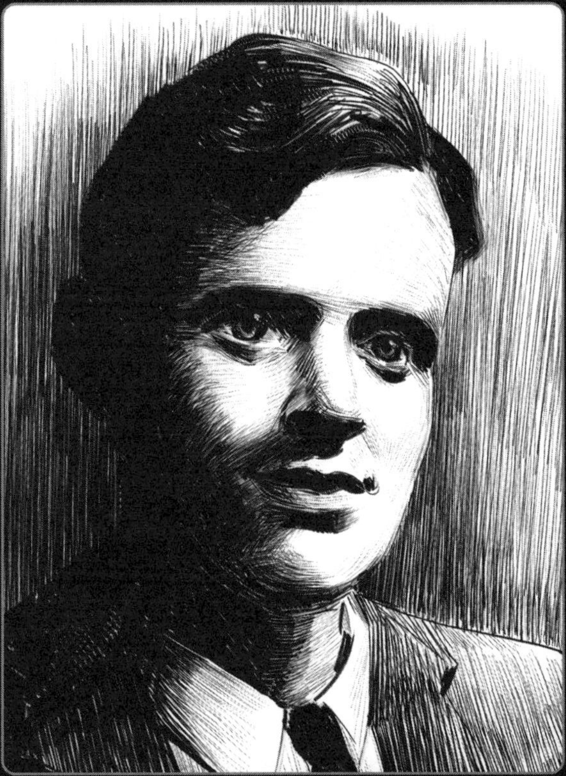

Perhaps the greatest charm of tramp-life is the absence of monotony. In Hobo Land the face of life is protean—an ever changing phantasmagoria, where the impossible happens and the unexpected jumps out of the bushes at every turn of the road. The hobo never knows what is going to happen the next moment; hence, he lives only in the present moment. He has learned the futility of telic endeavor, and knows the delight of drifting along with the whimsicalities of Chance.

Preamble

Unlike most of the other tramp writers discussed in this book, London's life history will only be referred to briefly. London was an international celebrity and so there is no shortage of very detailed accounts of his life already written, including three books by London's second wife Charmain, *Jack London: The Log of the Snark* (1915), *Our Hawaii* (1917), and *The Book of Jack London* (1921), as well as his daughter Joan's biography, *Jack London and His Times: An Unconventional Biography* (1939). This chapter is more concerned with significant vagabonding events as they illuminate London's attitude toward life in general, and his wanderlust in particular.

London was also a political animal, active in revolutionary socialist causes and the class struggle, even running (unsuccessfully) for mayor of Oakland in 1901 and 1905, though more as a political statement than a serious attempt to enter politics. In any case, such associations should not define the man, as like most with the tramping spirit in their veins, London was first and foremost an *individual*, with views often at odds with the stock political credos of the time. Indeed, in London's writing, a unique blend of "individualism" (partly influenced by Nietzsche's notions of *übermenschen*) and socialist idealism—doctrines normally taken as antithetical—seem to coalesce as a unified philosophy. But, as with Nietzsche also, instead of looking beyond the headlines and acquainting oneself with a deeper understanding of London's philosophy, many have taken London's words literally and made mischief of them. As London's daughter Joan acknowledges in the introduction of her book, "On the one hand he was assailed for his socialist beliefs, and on the other, for his racial prejudice and glorification of the Anglo Saxon 'blond beast.'"[1]

Rather than being active in any organization or "movement," London's main contribution to political ideology was through his writing. One of these works, *The People of the Abyss* (1903), a travelogue-*cum*-social critique of the poor and dispossessed of the East End of London, is discussed toward the end of this chapter. But it is in the chapter titled "How I Became A Socialist," from another political treatise, *War of the Classes* (1905), that London reveals his coming to politics:

> It is quite fair to say that I became a Socialist in a fashion somewhat similar to the way in which the Teutonic pagans became Christians—it was hammered into me. Not only was I not looking for Socialism at the time of my conversion, but I was fighting it. I was very young and callow, did not know much of anything, and though I had never even heard of a school called "Individualism," I sang the paean of the strong with all my heart.[2]

Of London's prolific writings (including 120 short stories, 26 full-length prose works, 22 essays, 45 poems, and six plays)[3] only three works are described as autobiographical: *The Road*, *The Cruise of the Snark*, and *John Barleycorn*, although, as already discussed in respect to other tramp writers, these categorizations are not always helpful as London's autobiographies contain elements of fiction, and his novels elements of autobiography. Nonetheless, for the purposes of this chapter the primary sources will be *The Road* (1907) and *John Barleycorn* (1913), a reading of which puts the lie to the popularly held misconception that (as it was with Josiah Flynt also) London was a sociologist first and a tramp second:

> Every once in a while, in newspapers, magazines, and biographical dictionaries, I run upon sketches of my life, wherein, delicately phrased, I learn that it was in order to study sociology that I became a tramp. This is very nice and thoughtful of the biographers, but it is inaccurate. I became a tramp—well, because of the life that was in me, of the wanderlust in my blood that would not let me rest. Sociology was merely incidental; it came afterward, in the same manner that a wet skin follows a ducking. I went on "The Road" because I couldn't keep away from it; because I hadn't the price of the railroad fare in my jeans; because I was so made that I couldn't work all my life on "one same shift"; because—well, just because it was easier to than not to.[4]

Early Life and Alcohol

In order to try to establish a chronology of London's tramping exploits and influences (he was a sailor tramp before he became a road tramp) it is necessary to jump between *The Road* and *John Barleycorn*,[5] the latter being London's exposition on his love-hate relationship with alcohol, and possibly the best philosophical treatise on the subject ever written. It is impossible, however, to follow an exact chronology of events from London's own books, and so those who are interested should obtain one of the many biographies of London; his daughter Joan's has the advantage of being thoroughly researched as well as her having known her father intimately.

London first got drunk at the age of five after being asked, one hot summer day, to carry a pail of beer to his father who was plowing a field half a mile away. But he did not enjoy the taste. The second occasion, at the age of seven, London got drunk on red wine in the company of some older children and adults. He was bullied into drinking a glass of wine, only to shock those around him by downing several more without showing any ill effects, at least until on his way home he collapsed unconscious into a ditch. By the time he came to, it was dark. He had been carried unconscious the four miles to his home and put to bed. "I was a sick child, and, despite the terrible strain on my heart and tissues, I continually relapsed into the madness of delirium." For several days London experienced the most terrible nightmares—he screamed, raved and fought, experiencing visions of murders, of being pursued by murderers and incarcerated in madhouses where he was beaten by the keepers and "surrounded by screeching lunatics." On emerging from his delirium he recalled his mother's voice declaring, "But the child's brain. He will lose his reason."[6]

Initially he found both beer and wine unpleasant, both in their taste and effect: "very clear was my resolution never to touch liquor again. No mad dog was ever more afraid of water than was I of alcohol." But the reaction from those around him did not help reinforce his abstinence. With the exception of his mother, whose views he says were extreme in all things, London achieved some notoriety from the event: "I felt that I had done something heroic." And in spite of his declared loathing of strong drink, London acknowledges, "the brightest spots in my child life were the saloons. ... Here was a child, forming its first judgments of the world, finding the saloon a delightful and desirable place." This was helped, as London admits, by all of the exotic free food offerings put out to entice the paying drinkers. He tells us it would be a further 20 years before he actually acquired a taste for alcohol, and even then, remained repelled by it until after he had imbibed his first drink of the day.

London describes his ambivalent relationship with alcohol thus: "This physical loathing for alcohol I have never got over. But I have conquered it. To this day I conquer it every time I take a drink." London does not buy the theory that people have a constitutional predisposition to developing a dependency on alcohol; he worked hard at it, enjoying and suffering drink in equal measure until it killed him three years after *John Barleycorn* was published. But back to the 10-year-old London and the enchantment that bars held for him, a daily tableau of danger and adventure that would sow the seeds of the young vagabond's eventual wanderlust.

Life in the saloons was different from the common everyday where nothing much happened. "Men talked with great voices, laughed great laughs, and there was an atmosphere of greatness." London describes the fights and bloodshed: "Great moments, these, for me, my head filled with all the wild and valiant fighting of the gallant adventurers on sea and land." But he also noted the pathetic side of life in the saloons, "the sots, stupefied, sprawling across the tables or in the sawdust," even though at the time they seemed to London, "objects of mystery and wonder." What is more, he was also aware that these establishments were sanctioned and licensed by the "city fathers," and frequented by reporters, editors, lawyers, and judges, whom he knew by name and reputation. And so, terrible as the saloons were, "in the same way pirates, and shipwrecks, and battles were terrible," they also represented the legitimate world of adulthood. He had not yet fathomed out what it was about these places on which "men focused like buzzing flies about a honey pot." It would be some time before he discovered that they represented no more than an escape from the "jaded toil and stale grief" of their otherwise humdrum lives.[7]

Four years later, early signs of London's wanderlust are becoming evident both in his insatiable appetite for reading and his first tentative sailings aboard his skiff in San Francisco Bay:

> When I was fourteen, my head filled with the tales of the old voyagers, my vision with tropic isles and far sea-rims, I was sailing a small centerboard skiff around San Francisco Bay and on the Oakland Estuary. I wanted to go to sea. I wanted to get away from monotony and the commonplace. I was in the flower of my adolescence, a-thrill with romance and adventure, dreaming of wild life in the wild man-world.[8]

And it was on such a sailing trip at the age of 14 that London encountered a pair of teenage sailor tramps in a sloop in the bay and got drunk for the third time. It was in the cabin of the *Idler* that London first heard and sang sea shanties such as "Blow the Man Down," "Flying Cloud," and "Whisky, Johnny, Whisky." London was also to discover that, even at 14, he could carry his drink better than most others—something he would later regard as a curse. He drank his two companions under the table and was still on his feet making his way up on deck for some air. "All the world was mine, all its paths were under my feet, and John Barleycorn, tricking my fancy, enabled me to anticipate the life of adventure for which I yearned."[9]

At the age of 15, London bought his first sloop *Razzle Dazzle* and gave up his work in the canning factory to become an oyster pirate. Drinking in the saloons along the waterfront—and learning the rules of drinking—became a necessary initiation into the world of pirates. It was also the moment that London realized that the only use of money, to those who espouse vagabondage as a lifestyle, was to buy comradeship and the respect of his fellow pirates by standing several rounds of drinks at the bar. Up to this point of his life, London had been a shrewd trader and careful with his money. But, as with all those who join the ranks of the ancient Cynics by abandoning their worldly goods and throwing their money into the sea, so London now abandoned all of his childhood possessions to cast his fate in with the hard-living, hard-drinking fraternity of the Oakland waterfront. By the age of 15, London had won his "manhood's spurs." His status on the waterfront and with the oyster pirates was already riding high. So confident was he with his newfound calling in life, and anxious to break with his past, that he sent word to his mother to call in his old neighborhood friends and give away all his childhood possessions. "I was a man now, and I made a clean sweep of everything that bound me to my boyhood." His reputation was even further enhanced when a seasoned oyster pirate, French Frank, tried to run him down with his schooner. London, standing coolly on the deck of *Razzle Dazzle*, a cocked double-barreled shotgun in his hands and holding his sloop on course with his feet, forced French Frank to alter course to avoid a collision.[10]

The Road, the Saloon and the Sea

Having already established his reputation as a tough and respected oyster pirate, it was not until the age of 16 that London first took to the road. Oyster pickings had been lean that year and London and a friend embarked on a 40-mile boat ride north to Port Costa to rescue another friend's boat that had been impounded by the police. After snatching the boat from under the constable's nose and waiting for the tide and wind to favor their return to London's home in Oakland, the weather favored a different direction and the pair set sail instead upriver for Sacramento. In the river harbor of that city, London met a group of road kids who captivated him with stories of their tramping adventures, and so, with the predictable moniker of Sailor Kid, London's hoboing career commenced:

> These wanderers made my oyster-piracy look like thirty cents. A new world was calling to me in every word that was spoken—a world of rods and gunnels, blind baggages and "side-door Pullmans," "bulls" and "shacks," "floppings" and "chewin's," "pinches" and "get-aways," "strong arms" and "bindle-stiffs," "punks" and "profesh." And it all spelled Adventure. Very well; I would tackle this new world. I "lined" myself up alongside those road-kids. I was just as strong as any of them, just as quick, just as nervy, and my brain was just as good.[11]

London recalls that on his maiden voyage beating a train, he was one of a group of a dozen road kids heading out of Sacramento to cross the Rocky Mountains on a Central Pacific overland train—a kind of initiation ceremony for new tramps. There was only one other first-timer attempting to board the train with London, with the moniker French Kid, but he never made it. He stumbled on boarding the train and both his legs were amputated by the wheels. London recalls being shown his stumps when meeting up with him two years later.

London's daughter Joan recalls that shortly before this episode, and described by London in *John Barleycorn,* that liquor might have killed him and ended his tramping career at the age of 16 before he ever started beating trains. After a particularly bad bout of drinking and a failed suicide attempt at sea, London all but gave up working for oysters and slid into becoming a barroom stiff. "They were the poor-man's clubs, and they were the only clubs to which I had access. ... I was no longer a stranger in any town the moment I had entered a saloon."[12]

On January 20, 1893, a few days after his 17th birthday, London decided to dry himself out by signing on for a 51-day voyage on the three-masted schooner the *Sophie Sutherland*, bound for a seal hunt in the isolated Bonin Islands south of Japan. After more alcoholic binges, London returned to America determined to settle down to a steady job and be done with both drinking and tramping. He slaved for several months, first at a jute mill, and then working a 12- to 13-hour day shoveling coal (damaging the tendons in his wrists), having been conned into believing that he had embarked on the bottom rung of the ladder to a respectable career as an electrician (London was on apprentice wages, enabling his employer to lay off two adult men on full wages). After coming to the realization that honest work was a mug's game, London tramped east to New York, renewing his relationship with John Barleycorn along the way.

London puts the year of his trip east at 1894, which coincides with Leon Ray Livingston's account in his book *Coast to Coast with Jack London*. Livingston was already a minor celebrity at this time and London responded to an ad Livingston had placed in the help-wanted column of the *Sunday World Magazine* stating, "Wanted—travelmate by hobo contemplating roughing trip to California." In his own account, Livingston describes London as "a youth of about eighteen," which he would have been in that year; London does not mention Livingston in any of *his* autobiographies. Neither does Joan London in her biography of her father, rather describing the trip east in terms of London's escapades in Kelly's Army (of more below). Whatever the chronology, London must have certainly packed a lot of diverse tramping into his 18th year and, apart from his year-long trek to the Klondike in search of gold after giving up university at the age of 21, he pretty much exchanged tramping for writing.

By the end of the trip with Livingston, both tramps had pledged to continue on from San Francisco on a round-the-world tramp by land and sea. Sadly, by the time the pair reached London's home in Oakland, they were severely incapacitated by malaria. London convalesced at his mother's house, and Livingston in San Francisco. When Livingston had recovered he tells how he went in search of London, but that London's mother would not give the older tramp London's whereabouts, fearing correctly that Livingston would persuade her son back on the road. All she would tell Livingston was that London had gone to work in an upstate laundry. Livingston writes that London never gave up his plan to tramp around the globe, receiving a letter from London in Tahiti 12 years later. The letter is dated February 15, 1908 and opens, "Dear A.No.1: - In reply to yours of Dec. 12. 1907, which has just reached me down here in the South Seas." London was at the time recovering in Tahiti from a tropical disease after persuading his wife and a friend to accompany him on his seagoing tramp on board the 45-foot sailing boat, *Snark*. London's autobiography, *The Cruise of the Snark*, is a remarkable travelogue and adventure tale but, with the exception of Chapter III, throws little additional light on London's philosophy of tramping. Chapter III is given up entirely to a description of the "qualifications" and motives of the hundreds of those who answered London's call for crew members to join his round-the-world voyage:

> The possession of a "passionate fondness for geography," was the way one applicant expressed the wander-lust that was in him; while another wrote, "I am cursed with an eternal yearning to be always on the move, consequently this letter to you." But best of all was the fellow who said he wanted to come because his feet itched.[13]

But for now, let us pick up London's earlier tramping adventures as cataloged in his first autobiography, *The Road*.

Seasoned Tramp

The Road is one of the most frequently quoted works of tramp literature, inspiring other tramp narratives, not least Jack Kerouac's *On The Road*. But *The Road*, in turn, was inspired by the earlier writings of Josiah Flynt (seven years older than London) whom London acknowledges with the following dedication in the front of his book: "TO JOSIAH FLYNT, The Real Thing, Blowed in the Glass." In his own writing, Flynt defines "blowed-in-the-glass stiffs" as mature hobos who supported themselves purely through begging and thievery, as distinct from "gay-cats," mainly younger tramps, who were prepared to work and hustle to make ends meet.

Much of *The Road* repeats anecdotes about tramping and beating trains that are well described elsewhere in this book, but it is London's manner of telling that makes him stand out as a writer of note. In the chapter "Holding Her Down" London tells of a particular journey on the Canadian-Pacific where 20 tramps jump the train at the start of its journey but all are eventually outfoxed by the train's crew until only London remains. A cat-and-mouse game ensues between London and the crew comprising two "shacks" (brakemen), a conductor, fireman, and an engineer. The first three carriages had blind platforms at the ends of the cars, that is, they had either no doors or locked doors into the carriage, leaving London safe from molestation so long as the train was moving at speed. Each time this particular train stopped at a station, London would have to drop smartly from the train, race ahead, and wait until the train gathered speed before again jumping on to one of the blind platforms. Every possible strategy was exploited on this trip by both London and the crew, with London time and again outsmarting his would-be assailants. The crew would occupy one or more of the blind platforms to prevent London jumping on board the train, wait for London to alight, then leap on the platform from the other side of the train, hide on the roof of a carriage to jump down on him, or even stop the train between stations:

> As I wait in the darkness I am conscious of a big thrill of pride. The overland has stopped twice for me—for me, a poor hobo on the bum. I alone have twice stopped the overland with its many passengers and coaches, its government mail, and its two thousand steam horses straining in the engine. And I weigh only one hundred and sixty pounds, and I haven't a five-cent piece in my pocket![14]

On each occasion, exhilarated by the chase, London outsmarted them. At night they carried lanterns but would douse or hide them to trick him. When they learned his strategy and the blind platforms were no longer viable boarding places, London took to the carriage roofs; when he was doused with water by the engineer or hit by lumps of coal by the fireman, he took to riding the rods beneath the carriages. Eventually he was caught, but instead of the usual merciless beating, having gained the crew's respect, they took him to the rear of the train where they planned to wait until the train had gathered sufficient speed to make it impossible for London to board the train again. The shack was holding London by the collar, giving the train time to move on before he jumped back on board; even so he was starting to look apprehensive as the train gathered speed. "Think you can make it?" London asked him sincerely. The shack released London's collar, made a quick run, and swung aboard.

There were still a number of coaches to pass but the shack remained on the step with his head out to make sure that London did not jump back on board. For the benefit of the shack, London then deliberately feigned dejection at being put off the train. As soon as the shack was satisfied that the train was now traveling too fast for London to make the last car, he withdrew inside. London then made a heroic dash to board the speeding train even though it was by now traveling faster than London could run. "In the fleeting instant of darkness I do not see the iron hand-rail of the last platform; nor is there time for me to locate it. I reach for where I think it ought to be, and at the same instant my feet leave the ground. It is all in the toss." But London's fingers *did* find the hand-hold. There was a jerk on his arms, his body pivoted, and his feet landed violently on the steps. He sat down feeling proud of his achievement. "In all my hoboing it is the best bit of train-jumping I have done." Late at night he was safe on the last platform for several stations, but he did not want to risk being spotted on the rear of the train and so at the first stop he ran forward on the far side of the train and lay on the rods under a coach.

Although now relatively safe, and the shacks convinced they had ditched him, the danger now presenting itself was that he was tired from the previous night's exertions and in danger of dozing off on the rods, something that would have resulted in certain death. At the next station, London went forward to the second blind carriage where he was able to lie down and sleep on the platform. And sleep he did until woken by a lantern thrust in his face. The two shacks were staring at him and he waited for the blows to fall, but giving him a drubbing was not on their minds. "Well, I guess you can ride, Bo. There's no use trying to keep you off." And so it was that London finished his journey as an unmolested passenger.[15]

Still aged only 18, and now bearing the moniker Sailor Jack, London tells how he had a 3,000-mile race beating trains across Canada from the east coast to the west with another tramp named Skysail Jack. The tramp signs carved by the pair on water tanks along the way told their own story—starting with Skysail Jack's first inscription in Montréal dated October 15, 1894. Sometimes London was ahead, sometimes Skysail Jack, but to London's disappointment the pair never met; Skysail Jack reached Vancouver first:

> I hurried on into Vancouver. But he was gone. He had taken ship immediately and was still flying west on his world-adventure. Truly, Skysail Jack, you were a tramp-royal, and your mate was the "wind that tramps the world." I take off my hat to you. You were "blowed-in-the-glass" all right. A week later I, too, got my ship, and on board the steamship Umatilla, in the forecastle, was working my way down the coast to San Francisco. Skysail Jack and Sailor Jack—gee! if we'd ever got together.[16]

London also provides an account of marching with Kelly's Army, part of the 1894 march of hobos and unemployed from California to Washington, D.C. (further discussed in Chapter 13). London's account is notable for his descriptions of how the protestors commandeered a train, sought or tricked citizens on the way to feed the army, and in particular, the scam he and a small group of nine others pulled on the 2,000 other marchers. Although popularly identified as a political activist, London was never an adherent to any cause but his own, rather, a resourceful individual with his own moral code and his eye on the main chance, a rogue even among vagabonds.

For much of the three hundred miles, London and his comrades were a day or so in advance of the main army. They would approach a small town or group of farmers and run up their flags, announcing that they were the "advance boat," demanding to know what provisions had been collected for the army. They would then collect several dollars' worth of tobacco, butter, sugar, coffee and canned goods. When offered sacks of beans and flour, or slaughtered animals—being too awkward to carry—they left these for the commissary boats who had the genuine role of collecting provisions. In any event, London describes this gang of 10 vagabonds as living on "the fat of the land." All attempts by General Kelly to head off London and his friends were thwarted. "He sent two rowers, in a light, round-bottomed boat, to overtake us and put a stop to our piratical careers." But, even though empowered by General Kelly to make prisoners of them, what could two do against 10? The two men hurried to the next town to ask help from the authorities, only for London and company to bypass the town by dark after enjoying an early supper.

> I kept a diary on part of the trip, and as I read it over now I note one persistently recurring phrase, namely, "Living fine." We did live fine. ... This was hard on the Army, I'll allow; but then, the ten of us were individualists. We had initiative and enterprise. We ardently believed that the grub was to the man who got there first ...[17]

Following London's adventures with Kelly's Army and his East-to-West-Coast tramp with Leon Ray Livingston, he was becoming tired of both tramping and hard labor. To escape the pointless toil of the latter and further his ambition to become a writer, London now threw himself into two years of preparation for matriculating to enroll in university. Having completed the first half of freshman year and enrolled for further courses, due to lack of money and a realization that the university was not the life he needed at the time, London then quit the course. He was satisfied that at least he had studied for the previous two years and achieved "a prodigious amount of reading."[18] In Joan London's book, she comments that her father "was not learning anything that he could not dig out of the books himself, and more quickly."[19]

After quitting university, London spent a year traveling to the Klondike with his brother-in-law, which, although having to be abandoned due to contracting scurvy, did provide some of his best writing material. On his return, London took up his career as a writer in earnest, forgoing the hobo life for the most part, but not his relationship with drinking. One of the first things that London would learn about writing was that, to succeed in the game, he would have to first "unlearn about everything the teachers and professors of literature of the high school and university had taught me." A lesson as true today as it was then because, as Joan London identified, most professors of literature are stuck in the past with dead writers.

The People of the Abyss (1903)

We now turn to one of London's political treatises to try and make sense of the following paradox. On the one hand, London feels pity for the metaphysically innocent (Nietzsche's "human herd," described by London in *The Abyss* as "dull animal happiness ... stupid and heavy, without imagination"), and yet London, as did Nietzsche also, feels envy for the freedom that "simple minded" people have from the intellectual preoccupations that expose "thinkers" to the world's limits and imperfections. There is the further anomaly in *The People of the Abyss* that, although London takes on the role of the social researcher, he at the same time identifies with the objects of his study, reverting time and again to the hobo he was, and to some extent at the time, still is.

In 1902, already a successful writer, and setting a precedent never previously undertaken by a social researcher, London spent several months living among the poor of the East End of London, including sleeping rough on the streets and in workhouses. *The Abyss* is a unique and remarkable investigation into the lives of the dispossessed of that city, witnessed mainly through the individual stories of the characters whom London befriended. The book is also a savage critique on capitalism. Initially London was warned by friends against such an enterprise: "You don't want to live down there! ... Why, it is said there are places where a man's life isn't worth tu'pence." To which London responded, "The very places I wish to see."[20]

Bizarrely, London also describes how on approaching the travel agent Thomas Cook & Son, who would have had no difficulty in organizing a trip to darkest Africa or innermost Tibet, they yet were unable to advise him on traveling to a part of that city a stone's throw from their office: "We are not accustomed to taking travelers to the East End; we receive no call to take them there, and we know nothing whatsoever about the place at all." To which London replied that the agent might at least help him by noting his plans in advance, "so that in case of trouble you may be able to identify me." This brought the response: "Ah, I see! should you be murdered, we would be in position to identify the corpse."[21]

What London had actually intended was that the Thomas Cook employee would be able to vouch for him should, during his sojourn in the East End, he get into difficulty with the police. After eventually persuading a cab driver to drive him into that part of London, he describes his first impressions on entering the East End—although surprisingly at this point of his adventure, still in the voice of the detached observer rather than someone who had himself experienced the vagabond life:

> Nowhere in the streets of London may one escape the sight of abject poverty, while five minutes' walk from almost any point will bring one to a slum; but the region my hansom was now penetrating was one unending

> slum. The streets were filled with a new and different race of people, short of stature, and of wretched or beer-sodden appearance. We rolled along through miles of bricks and squalor, and from each cross street and alley flashed long vistas of bricks and misery. Here and there lurched a drunken man or woman, and the air was obscene with sounds of jangling and squabbling. At a market, tottery old men and women were searching in the garbage thrown in the mud for rotten potatoes, beans, and vegetables, while little children clustered like flies around a festering mass of fruit, thrusting their arms to the shoulders into the liquid corruption, and drawing forth morsels but partially decayed, which they devoured on the spot.[22]

London soon discovered some of the harsh realities of living in the East End of London for himself. Renting a room, never mind two rooms, was nigh on impossible. Several families shared a single house, and single men were bunked three to a room. That was the economic reality from the landlord's point of view. The philosophy of many of the single men London encountered was to earn enough money in the city or at sea in order to find and pay for board, lodging and alcohol. The idea of settling down to married life they found laughable. They could not support themselves, never mind a family. London describes that the best the people he encounters can hope for "is a dull, animal happiness, the content of the full belly. … The Abyss seems to exude a stupefying atmosphere of torpor, which wraps about them and deadens them."

A graphic example of the abject poverty of the East End is described by London when he was walking down the Mile End Road one evening between two men who had fallen on hard times, no longer able to compete for work with younger, fitter men. The trio were headed for the workhouse in Poplar to try and secure a night's lodging. London noticed the way the other two men had their eyes peeled to the ground and kept bending down, retrieving what London at first assumed were cigarette or cigar butts, but soon became aware that their labor was of an altogether more desperate kind:

> From the slimy, spittle-drenched sidewalk, they were picking up bits of orange peel, apple skin, and grape stems, and, they were eating them. … They picked up stray bits of bread the size of peas, apple cores so black and dirty one would not take them to be apple cores, and these things these two men took into their mouths, and chewed them, and swallowed them; and this, between six and seven o'clock in the evening of August 20, year of our Lord 1902, in the heart of the greatest, wealthiest, and most powerful empire the world has ever seen.

London also described the practice the police had in the West End of the city of moving vagrants on all night long, from doorways, benches, anywhere they tried to grab a few minutes' sleep. In Green Park the following afternoon, London counted "scores of the ragged wretches asleep in the grass." It was a sunny Sunday afternoon and the well-dressed West Enders were out in their thousands, taking the air. "It was not a pleasant sight for them, those horrible, unkempt, sleeping vagabonds; while the vagabonds themselves, I know, would rather have done their sleeping the night before." And so London appeals to his readers that if they should ever find themselves in the West End and witness such a sight, they should be aware that these vagabonds are not "lazy creatures" but victims of "the powers that be" having kept them walking all night to deprive them of sleep.

In Chapter XII of *The Abyss*, titled "Coronation Day," London witnessed the coronation of King Edward VII from a vantage point in Trafalgar Square on August 9, 1902. He provides a uniquely fascinating account of the procession and celebrations that followed, a detailed and accurate description interspersed with satirical observations of the event—his own and others. Observing a man and a woman vagrant sitting on a bench later in the evening, London became incensed at the thousands of passing revelers who mocked the pair, and that not one had the humanity in the midst of their celebrations to say, "Here's sixpence; go and get a bed."

It is not surprising, given the scenes of injustice that London witnessed daily, that *The Abyss* produces harsh criticism of the kind of society that tolerates such inhumanities:

> In a civilisation frankly materialistic and based upon property, not soul, it is inevitable that property shall be exalted over soul, that crimes against property shall be considered far more serious than crimes against the person. To pound one's wife to a jelly and break a few of her ribs is a trivial offence compared with sleeping out under the naked stars because one has not the price of a doss.[23]

And there is no shortage of graphic descriptions of personal human tragedy to stir the reader's emotions:

> He had fought, and starved, and suffered for eighteen months. He got up one September morning, early. He opened his pocket-knife. He cut the throat of his wife, Hannah Cavilla, aged thirty-three. He cut the throat of his first-born, Frank, aged twelve. He cut the throat of his son, Walter, aged eight. He cut the throat of his daughter, Nellie, aged four. He cut the throat of his youngest-born, Ernest, aged sixteen months. Then he watched beside the dead all day until the evening, when the police came,

> and he told them to put a penny in the slot of the gas-meter in order that they might have light to see.[24]

Eventually, we arrive at the point in the book where London draws some wider conclusions from the months he spent living among the dispossessed of the East End of London. At the beginning of the final chapter, and in order to drive home his critique of the capitalist project, London poses the question, "*Has Civilisation bettered the lot of the average man?*" He makes the comparison between the Inuit who live along the banks of the Yukon River, with capital amounting to possibly to £2 per head, self-sufficient, and with no debts, and "the English folk … a consummately civilised people," whose capital amounts to at least £300 per head,[25] and who gain their food not by hunting and fishing, "but by toil at colossal artifices." The English folk suffer from lack of shelter, are vilely housed, do not have enough fuel to keep them warm, and are insufficiently clothed. "Many are to be found, winter and summer, shivering on the streets in their rags." Unlike the Inuit, many of the English folk die of starvation. London acknowledges that while "Civilisation" has increased man's "producing power" a hundred-fold, "the men of Civilisation live worse than the beasts, and have less to eat and wear and protect them from the elements than the savage Inuit in a frigid climate who lives to-day as he lived in the stone age ten thousand years ago."[26] London concludes: "Were the alternative presented to me, I would deliberately prefer the life of the savage to that of those people of Christian London."

London's Philosophy of Tramping

As this chapter focuses on London's contribution to tramping, his life having been more comprehensively recorded elsewhere, it is worth more closely examining his contribution to tramp philosophy.

The Art of Begging and Pretense

We are told how Diogenes the Cynic begged alms from a statue as practice in the art of being refused. Jack London likewise worked hard at the same art. He provides us with an excellent philosophy on begging that exhibits in his writings the Cynic's own literary and oral traditions such as irony, ridicule, satire and use of the aphorism as a means of getting his message across, for example, "upon his ability to tell a good story depends the success of the beggar." And in the same piece, "art is only consummate artfulness, and artfulness saves many a 'story.'"[27] London's thesis on begging mirrors that of Jim Phelan's in Chapter 13. For instance, he demonstrates his appreciation of the ancient Greek art of *kairos:* the "critical moment," in which, in his case, the beggar strikes a balance between seducing his target or losing the game, the following lecture ending with another arresting aphorism:

> First of all, and on the instant, the beggar must "size up" his victim. After that, he must tell a story that will appeal to the peculiar personality and temperament of that particular victim. And right here arises the great difficulty: in the instant that he is sizing up the victim he must begin his story. Not a minute is allowed for preparation. As in a lightning flash he must divine the nature of the victim and conceive a tale that will hit home. The successful hobo must be an artist. He must create spontaneously and instantaneously—and not upon a theme selected from the plenitude of his own imagination, but upon the theme he reads in the face of the person who opens the door ... I have often thought that to this training of my tramp days is due much of my success as a story-writer. In order to get the food whereby I lived, I was compelled to tell tales that rang true. At the back door, out of inexorable necessity, is developed the convincingness and sincerity laid down by all authorities on the art of the short-story. Also, I quite believe it was my tramp-apprenticeship that made a realist out of me. Realism constitutes the only goods one can exchange at the kitchen door for grub.[28]

Also like Phelan, it is worth noting that London was a fast learner on how to survive the brutalities of penal servitude. In his first extended spell in jail at the age of 18 (he had only spent the odd night in cells up until then), a 30-day trumped-up vagrancy sentence in Erie County Penitentiary, Buffalo, New York, rather than try to challenge the system, he learned quickly to earn favors from prisoners and guards alike (see chapters titled "Pinched" and "The Pen" in *The Road*).

London certainly had the gift of the gab, even if it did not always serve him. Having begged at a door where he spies an overfed glutton tucking into a meat pie, he is met with the usual prejudice about good-for-nothing hobos who are too lazy to work for their bread. The diner challenges London to earn his bread by meeting him tomorrow at a building site where he will be offered food in return for "tossing bricks." But our hero will not be dismissed in this way, telling his potential employer that it is now he is hungry and shall be even hungrier tomorrow, and how much hungrier when he has tossed bricks all day without anything to eat. "Now if you will give me something to eat, I'll be in great shape for those bricks." But the man was not so easily persuaded. "If I gave you something to eat now, I'd never see you again," adding that he knew London's kind, "idle and dissolute," unlike himself: "I have made myself what I am. And you can do the same, if you work and are honest." London then challenged the man as follows: "But if we all became like you, allow me to point out that there'd be nobody to toss bricks for you." This brought a flicker of a smile to the face of the man's wife, who had been observing the duel of words, but a roar of indignation from the man who sent London on his way without the hoped-for meal.[29]

There follows another hilarious tale when, to avoid arrest for vagrancy, London has to think on his feet after spinning a yarn to police in Winnipeg. He calculates that in the middle of that continent, he could safely make up a story to these landlubbers about being an English sailor, stranded from home after suffering tribulations at sea. To Livingston's dismay, the police return with an old sea dog sporting earrings and a sea-weathered face. A duel of words follows between London and the expert witness, with London always just one step ahead of discovery:

> "Do you remember the temple?"
>
> "Which temple?" I parried.
>
> "The big one, at the top of the stairway."
>
> If I remembered that temple, I knew I'd have to describe it. The gulf yawned for me.
>
> I shook my head.
>
> "You can see it from all over the harbor," he informed me. "You don't need shore-leave to see that temple."
>
> I never loathed a temple so in my life. But I fixed that particular temple at Rangoon.
>
> "You can't see it from the harbor," I contradicted. "You can't see it from the town. You can't see it from the top of the stairway. Because—" I paused for the effect. "Because there isn't any temple there."
>
> "But I saw it with my own eyes!" he cried.
>
> "That was in—?" I queried.
>
> "Seventy-one."
>
> "It was destroyed in the great earthquake of 1887," I explained. "It was very old."[30]

Time and again Livingston gets the better of the old mariner; not waiting to be caught out, he turns the tables and starts interrogating the sailor, asking if he'd ever come across old so-and-so in this port or that, until the weary matelot confirms to the police the veracity of London's story and he receives a night's lodging and breakfast for his trouble before being sent freely on his way.

On Morality and Human Vanity

On witnessing a gypsy woman being whipped by "the chief of the tribe," London makes the following observation on the defects of human behavior:

> I have sometimes held forth (facetiously, so my listeners believed) that the chief distinguishing trait between man and the other animals is that man is the only animal that maltreats the females of his kind. It is something of which no wolf nor cowardly coyote is ever guilty. It is something that even the dog, degenerated by domestication, will not do. The dog still retains the wild instinct in this matter, while man has lost most of his wild instincts—at least, most of the good ones.[31]

Interestingly, London's use of dogs to illustrate human beings' "unnatural" behavior is analogous to Cynic representations discussed in the introduction, both in their choice of name (the Greek *kynicos* being the adjectival form of the noun for dog) and their verbal and nonverbal discourse on the bankrupt state of human life. In his essay "The Other Animals" (1908), London refers to his own use of dogs to emphasize human failings:

> I have been guilty of writing two animal-stories—two books about dogs. The writing of these two stories, on my part, was in truth a protest against the "humanizing" of animals, of which it seemed to me several "animal writers" had been profoundly guilty.[32]

In direct contrast, then, to the humanizing of animals, London believes, like the Cynics, it is our very arrogance in elevating ourselves above "lower animals" that will prove civilization's nemesis. As he describes in his essay "The Somnambulists" (1900), civilization is no more than an illusion to disguise the fact that we are just animals:

> The mightiest and absurdest sleep-walker on the planet! Chained in the circle of his own imaginings, man is only too keen to forget his origin and to shame that flesh of his that bleeds like all flesh and that is good to eat. Civilization (which is part of the circle of his imaginings) has spread a veneer over the surface of the soft-shelled animal known as man. It is a very thin veneer; but so wonderfully is man constituted that he squirms on his bit of achievement and believes he is garbed in armour-plate.[33]

On the Effects of Alcohol

It is now worth noting just how London's relationship with alcohol seems to have sharpened his criticism, both of human beings' vulnerability and their banality. *John Barleycorn* catalogs London's transmutation from hobo to bourgeoisie, if not also bohemian, writer, and steady slide into alcoholism. Contrast the opening quotation at the top of this chapter from *The Road*, in which London identifies the surreal pleasures of living for the moment and having the whole world out there waiting to be discovered, with the world-hating introspection at the end of *John Barleycorn* where, having mined all the pleasures that life has to offer, he declares that true contentment can only exist in ignorance and stupidity. The diminishing of the world as a result of human civilization is wonderfully described by London in his 1900 essay "The Shrinkage of the Planet," opening with the words in the quote below, before proceeding to demonstrate how science and technology has brought us to a time where "the humblest clerk in any metropolis may place his hand on the pulse of the world"—how much more has the world shrunk since London wrote these words in 1900, and at an ever accelerating pace, than from the time of Homer up until then: "What a tremendous affair it was, the world of Homer, with its indeterminate boundaries, vast regions, and immeasurable distances."[34]

But in *John Barleycorn*, the shrinkage London describes is the disillusionment he experiences with the world within his own lifetime—the curse brought about by John Barleycorn on those with intelligence and imagination. For unlike the stupid man, he who "drinks himself into sottish unconsciousness" and whose "dreams are dim and inarticulate," the "white logic" that alcohol can produce in those with "imagination," exposes the sham illusions, frauds and corruptions that make up the entire human enterprise. What others hail as human accomplishments, London dismisses as inconsequential, "miserable little egotisms."

Here we have London the Cynic par excellence. And when London refers in the passage below to "a pessimistic German philosopher," he is likely referring to Nietzsche, whom he read and admired, although, unlike London, Nietzsche never touched alcohol. Furthermore, although Nietzsche represented naked Cynicism in its modern form, his was a positive, optimistic cynicism, not the nihilistic brand that he has often been misrepresented for. Whether London's cynicism is optimistic or pessimistic is not immediately apparent. Neither is it readily apparent whether London's expressed emotions at this period of his life were intrinsic, alcohol-fueled, or the result of the depression that inevitably accompanies chronic alcohol use. What is evident is that his thoughts and emotions are expressed with the clarity and poetry of the great German philosopher himself:

> ... to the imaginative man, John Barleycorn sends the pitiless, spectral syllogisms of the white logic. He looks upon life and all its affairs with

> the jaundiced eye of a pessimistic German philosopher. He sees through all illusions. He transvalues all values. Good is bad, truth is a cheat, and life is a joke. From his calm-mad heights, with the certitude of a god, he beholds all life as evil. Wife, children, friends—in the clear, white light of his logic they are exposed as frauds and shams. He sees through them, and all that he sees is their frailty, their meagreness, their sordidness, their pitifulness. No longer do they fool him. They are miserable little egotisms, like all the other little humans, fluttering their May-fly life-dance of an hour. They are without freedom. They are puppets of chance. So is he. He realises that. But there is one difference. He sees; he knows. And he knows his one freedom: he may anticipate the day of his death.[35]

There are many parallels between London and Nietzsche in the later pages of *John Barleycorn*. In exposing illusion and ridiculing human stupidity, both yet display a kind of envy for those who appear unconcerned at the world's imperfections and even appear to prosper on account of their freedom from intellectual preoccupations.

Nietzsche also described the price one had to pay for craving (as many of the tramp writers discussed in this book have) novelty and adventure over submitting to the civilizing effects of society. There is a terrible consequence, Nietzsche said, in "the attraction of the new and rare as against the old and tedious."[36] It is a curse characteristic of all forms of cynicism that cynics feel alienated from the society in which they live because they question the world's limits. This is why, unlike the spiritually enlightened who may exude a privileged smugness at their unique vision of the world, the modern cynic may at times feel handicapped, even tortured by it.

In an earlier discussion in Chapter 2, the contemporary German philosopher Peter Sloterdijk refers to this notion as "inner emigration": cutting oneself off from the fundamental values of society leaves the cynic on the horns of a dilemma, "Get out or collaborate? Flee or stand firm?"[37] In the latter part of his life, London seemed torn between the two to such an extent that he turned inward on himself, sinking into a pit of despair with nothing to look forward to other than his own death—although how much of this should be blamed directly on John Barleycorn is open to speculation:

> And now comes John Barleycorn with the curse he lays upon the imaginative man who is lusty with life and desire to live. John Barleycorn sends his White Logic, the argent messenger of truth beyond truth, the antithesis of life, cruel and bleak as interstellar space, pulseless and frozen as absolute zero, dazzling with the frost of irrefragable logic and unforgettable fact. John Barleycorn will not let the dreamer dream, the

> liver live. He destroys birth and death, and dissipates to mist the paradox of being, until his victim cries out, as in "The City of Dreadful Night": "Our life's a cheat, our death a black abyss." And the feet of the victim of such dreadful intimacy take hold of the way of death.

For a philosophic duel of words between London and John Barleycorn's "White Logic," the reader is urged to enjoy for themselves Chapters 36 and 37 of *John Barleycorn*. This leads us to London's own epitaph:

> I am aware that within this disintegrating body which has been dying since I was born I carry a skeleton, that under the rind of flesh which is called my face is a bony, noseless death's head. All of which does not shudder me. To be afraid is to be healthy. Fear of death makes for life. But the curse of the White Logic is that it does not make one afraid. The world-sickness of the White Logic makes one grin jocosely into the face of the Noseless One and to sneer at all the phantasmagoria of living.[38]

ENDNOTES

1 London, Joan. *Jack London and His Times: An Unconventional Biography,* Seattle: University of Washington Press, 1939, p. xii

2 London, Jack. *War of the Classes*, New York: Regent Press, 1905, p. 267

3 Joan London claims that, at the time of publishing her book in 1939, more than 40 movies (in different languages) had been spawned worldwide by London's writing, the people of the Soviet Union being among London's biggest fans.

4 London, Jack. *The Road,* New York: Macmillan, 1907 (Project Gutenberg ebook, no page numbers) from the chapter "Road-Kids and Gay-Cats."

5 1/ The term "John Barleycorn" is used as a personification of drinks made from barley, especially malt liquor. 2/ London's book *John Barleycorn* is the origin of the term seeing "pink elephants" when describing the hallucinatory effects of extreme drunkenness: "... [one] *who sees, in the extremity of his ecstasy, blue mice and pink elephants.*"

6 London, Jack. *John Barleycorn*, New York: Century, 1913 (Project Gutenberg ebook, no page numbers), Chapter IV

7 Ibid., Chapter V

8 Ibid., Chapter VI

9 Ibid., Chapter VI

10 Ibid., Chapter X

11 *The Road*, op. cit. from the chapter "Road-Kids and Gay-Cats"

12 Ibid., Chapter XIII

13 London, Jack. *The Cruise of the Snark*, London: Mills & Boon, 1911 (Project Gutenberg ebook, no page numbers), Chapter III

14 *The Road*, op. cit., from the chapter "Holding her Down"

15 Ibid.

16 Ibid., from the chapter "Hoboes That Pass in the Night"

17 Ibid., from the chapter "Two Thousand Stiffs"

18 *John Barleycorn*, op. cit., Chapter XXIII

19 London, Joan. *Jack London and His Times*, New York: Doubleday, Doran & Co., 1939, p. 134

20 London, Jack. *People of the Abyss*, Edinburgh: Thomas Nelson and Sons Ltd, 1903 (Project Gutenberg ebook, no page numbers) from Chapter I, "The Descent"

21 Ibid., "The Descent"

22 Ibid., Chapter V, "Those on the Edge"

23 Ibid., Chapter XVI, "Property versus Person"

24 Ibid., Chapter XXII, "Suicide"

25 At the time of publication the British pound was equivalent to 4.85 dollars.

26 *People of the Abyss*, op. cit., Chapter XXVII, "The Management"

27 *The Road,* op. cit., from the chapter "Confession"

28 Ibid., "Confession"

29 Ibid., from the chapter "Confession"

30 Ibid., from the chapter "Confession"

31 Ibid., from the chapter "Pictures"

32 London, Jack. "The Other Animals" from *Revolution, and Other Essays*, London: Mills & Boon, Ltd. 1910 (Project Gutenberg ebook, no page numbers)

33 Ibid., from the essay "The Somnambulists"

34 *Revolution and Other Essays*, op. cit., from the essay "The Shrinkage of the Planet"

35 *John Barleycorn*, op. cit., Chapter II

36 Nietzsche, Friedrich. *Thoughts out of Season, Part II* in *Complete Works*, London: George Allen & Unwin, 1909, pp. 25–26

37 Sloterdijk, Peter. *Critique of Cynical Reason*, London: Verso, 1988, p. 119

38 *John Barleycorn*, op. cit., Chapter XXXVI

Stephen Graham

(1884–1975)

So when you put on your old clothes and take to the road, you make at least a right gesture. You get into your right place in the world in the right way. ... What a relief to escape from being voter, tax-payer, authority on old brass, brother of man who is an authority on old brass, author of best seller, uncle of author of best seller, what a relief to cease being for a while a grade-three clerk, or grade-two clerk who has reached his limit, to cease to be identified by one's salary or by one's golf handicap.

Stephen Graham, *The Gentle Art of Tramping* (pp. 2–3)

Preamble

In the writings of these tramp authors—often well-read in philosophy, literature and the classics—is to be found their own personal philosophies on life and tramping. Furthermore, as the tramp is by nature an *individual*, the personal reflections on tramp life contained in the chapters of this book, although highlighting some common experiences, also draw on very unique insights. As personal accounts, they often also reveal the authors' personal prejudices. Graham was a confirmed Christian, yet an advocate of Jesus' original "peasant gospel," deriding, as did Nietzsche, Saint Paul's corruption of Christianity. And although Graham sometimes takes a moralizing and patronizing tone, this does not detract from his undoubted commitment to the poor and dispossessed, not to mention hugely informative insights into tramping in his remarkable prose style—even if he occasionally lapses (unconsciously perhaps) into the scornful homilies of his class and religion. But to be fair to Graham, he at least acknowledges these failings when he admits of himself, "There is much to learn [in tramping], there are illusions to be overcome. There are prejudices and habits to be shaken off." Later, Graham demonstrates even greater insight when he tells us:

> Class is the most disgusting institution of civilisation, because it puts barriers between man and man. ... But in the tramp's motley you can say what you like, ask what questions you like, free from the taint of class. It also puts you right with regard to yourself. You see yourself as others see you, and that is a refreshing grace wafted in upon an opinionated mind.[1]

Stephen Graham was a British writer, journalist, essayist, and professional tramp. His adventures and observations are documented in over 50 books and essays, many no longer in print. As it is impossible to do no more than summarize Graham's life in the following pages, those who wish to know more of the man should log on to *The Internet Archive* which has the most comprehensive collection of his extant works and can be read for free. A debt is also owed to unraveling Graham's life and times to Michael Hughes' excellent biography, *Beyond Holy Russia: The Life and Times of Stephen Graham* (2014).[2] The following summary of Graham's life and adventures is followed by a discussion on his important philosophy on tramping.

Graham spoke fluent Russian and many of his books concern his experiences of that country between the 1905 and 1917 revolutions, as did his work as a freelance correspondent for publications such as *The Times*, *Daily Mail*, *Harper's* and *The New Yorker*. Reading Graham is to be reminded of just what a different place Russia was over one hundred years ago. Yet Graham also tramped thousands of miles across America, including large stretches of the Canadian border where he tramped with American poet Vachel Lindsay (*Tramping With a Poet in the Rockies*, 1922). As well as tramping the American wilderness, Graham also tramped the streets of New York (*New York Nights*, 1927), Chicago and other cities. He of course also tramped Great Britain and large tracts of continental Europe, and published two accounts of his time as a soldier on the Western Front: *A Private in the Guards* (1919) and *The Challenge of the Dead* (1921).

Discussing Graham's philosophy on tramping will focus on two of Graham's better-known tramping texts. The first of these, *A Tramp's Sketches* (1913), is a travelogue and essays of Graham's various Russian pilgrimages totaling 5,000 miles of tramping between London and Jerusalem via northern Russia's White Sea port of Arkhangelsk (Archangel). He acknowledges that had he attempted such a journey in the normal way he would have failed. Only in the guise of a "Russian peasant I was enabled to go."[3]

The second is *The Gentle Art of Tramping* (1926), in which Graham shares his tramping experiences in a kind of "how-to" manual of instruction: the do's and don'ts of tramping, with chapters about how to attend to one's boots, clothes, fire, cooking, sleeping arrangements, et cetera, as well as philosophical reflections on subjects like companionship and idleness.

Early Life

Stephen Graham's father, the journalist and future *Country Life* editor Peter Anderson Graham, met and married Graham's mother Jane (née Macleod) in Edinburgh in 1881, having moved to that city with his family from over the border in England. Graham was born in Edinburgh in March 1884 and shortly afterwards the family moved to Cheltenham in England. In Graham's final work, the autobiography of his life, *Part of the Wonderful Scene* (1964), he dismisses his childhood in less than three pages, the most notable being his first tramp when he could barely walk. Describing himself as a toddler with "golden curly hair" and dressed like a girl, he was stolen away by gypsies to "begin a begging career." After being found and returned to his family by the police, his father cut his hair short and dressed him in a sailor suit, thereby ensuring he would no longer be mistaken for a girl.[4]

Not long afterwards Graham's father, described by Hughes as "a hard-drinking and driven man who resented having to spend his time doing "hack" work to support his family," abandoned his wife and children to live with a younger woman, with whom he later had two more children. When Stephen Graham turned 15, his father, now supporting five children, stopped paying for his education and so Graham was forced to take a job as a junior clerk in the civil service in central London. Graham would spend his time immersed in books, and on stumbling on a copy of Dostoyevsky's *Crime and Punishment*, soon became obsessed with Russia, acknowledging later, "I was on the trail of a religious philosophy more inspiring than Carlyle or Ibsen or Nietzsche." Graham's newfound interest in all things Russian, so intense that he started learning the language in order to read Russian literature in the original, coincided with a general resurgence of interest in Russia that would serve him later as a journalist.

Russian Adventures

Graham first traveled to Russia in 1906, even though the revolution of 1905 had taken place only the previous year. He traveled first to Warsaw, part of the Russian Empire at that time, and was arrested by the police who suspected that his camera might be a bomb. Following his release he traveled on to Moscow and then headed east to the provincial town of Nizhni Novgorod. Following his return to the U.K. from what was no more than a brief holiday from work, and unable to settle back into London life, Graham decided to quit his civil service job and return to live in Russia.

Graham returned to Russia in the New Year of 1908 where he planned to survive by teaching English, and to start a career as a writer. He stayed initially at the home of Nikolai Lebedev near Kharkov, a former student he had met in London who had helped Graham to learn Russian. The rail journey to Kharkov had been slow and his overcoat was stolen, necessitating the gift of a wolfskin coat from the Lebedevs on his arrival. Shortly afterwards Graham traveled to Moscow where he lived cheaply with friends, writing occasional articles for the British press and teaching English. It was at this time, after visiting the cathedral at Sergiev Posad outside Moscow, that Graham became mesmerized with the Russian Orthodox church, its customs, choirs and exotic architecture: "Even the air is infected with church odours and the multitudinous domes of purple and gold rest above the houses in enigmatical solemnity—they might be tents and pavilions of spirits from another world."[5]

But Graham's personal version of Christianity was unconventional even by Russian Orthodox terms. In his unpublished book *Ygdrasil* (the name for the great Ash Tree in Norse mythology that connects heaven and hell), Graham rejects the doctrinal tenets of Christianity for a spiritual belief based on the natural world received through one's feelings and emotions. One did not need to enter a church or listen to sermons to find God. God was present everywhere, even in the wildest places of the Earth. More on Graham and religion in "Graham's Philosophy on Tramping" below.

In March 1909, at the age of 25, Graham met and married a British woman in Moscow, Rosa Savory; she was 15 years older than Graham. Only weeks after marrying, Graham set off alone for what would be one of many extended tramping expeditions without Rosa. In his first book, *A Vagabond in the Caucasus* (1911), Graham describes in detail his 1909 tramp through the Caucasus, the adventures, the people and the places he encountered along the way. He had been warned that he would come across bandits in the region, a wild and lawless area at the time, necessitating Graham to arm himself with a gun and seek hidden refuges to sleep at night. In the Caucasus, he describes in detail kidnappings, murders and other violent events, noting that one did not have to be wealthy to be the target of robbery. One group of travelers he describes as being held up at gunpoint, relieved of all their clothing, and forced to town in "Adam's raiment."[6] Graham's base in the Caucasus, and where he spent much of his time there, was a mill near the town of Vladikavkaz. His neighbor there was a Muslim named Ali Pasha whom Graham describes as "a noble man, by far the most refined and courteous of the dwellers at the mill. I might also add, though it would sound paradoxical, he was the most Christian."[7] A telling line, acknowledging that it is the manner in which people behave toward their fellows, regardless of their religion, that defined for Graham their beneficence.

Graham believed it was the Russian peasantry who most keenly demonstrated Christianity in its true and natural sense. Their generosity in kind and spirit, for instance providing him with hospitality and a bed for the night throughout much of his travels, is discussed in his next book, *Undiscovered Russia* (1912). Following a brief return to Britain in 1910 to get interest from publishers and journalists for his next exploit, Graham returned to Russia to make his circuitous 1,000-mile tramp from Arkhangelsk in the far north of Russia to Moscow—a direct distance by road of 765 miles. In *Undiscovered Russia*, we are introduced to a fascinating variety of characters including aborigines from northern Russia and those still practicing paganism, all illustrated with Graham's photography.

Graham's next Russian adventure took place in 1911 when he tramped the length of the north shore of the Black Sea. In *Changing Russia* (1913) Graham talks about the changing character of Russia as a result of the industrial revolution in that country. It is in *Changing Russia* also that Graham starts to develop his philosophy, later discussed in *A Tramp's Sketches*, about human beings' loss of their connection to the natural world (see "Graham's Philosophy on Tramping" below). On reaching Constantinople at the end of his Black Sea hike, Graham boarded a ship full of five hundred Russian peasants on a pilgrimage to Jerusalem, becoming simply one of that group as they visited various biblical sites in that city. *With the Russian Pilgrims to Jerusalem* (1913) was a greater literary success than his previous books and no doubt increased interest in those also. *With the Russian Pilgrims* was followed by *Russia and the World* (1915) and *Through Russian Central Asia* (1916), and as with all Graham's books, these works were generously illustrated with his own photographs that provide their own unique testimonies.

Adventures in America and Asia

Due to the increasing popularity of Graham's books in America, in the spring of 1913 he boarded a ship from Liverpool carrying 1,500 emigrants in steerage passage, many exiles from Russia and Poland, including Jews escaping pogroms in those countries, whom Graham describes in his book *With Poor Immigrants to America* (1914) as "a strange gathering of seekers, despairers, wanderers, pioneers, criminals, scapegoats."[8] Disliking New York, after a few weeks in that city Graham began a series of tramps across the United States, eventually reaching Chicago after two months. But Graham was soon to return to London, anxious to continue promoting his writing at home. Not that he should have worried, for shortly after his arrival he received a telegram from Lord Northcliffe, proprietor of *The Times* and the *Daily Mail*, requesting that Graham write for his newspapers with the offer that he should "go where you like and write what you like." Although Graham had not yet completed the final manuscript of *With Poor Immigrants*, he started planning a new excursion to Central Asia after Northcliffe had handed him a contract for 26 articles.

And so by the end of 1913, Graham was back in Russia, first revisiting the Caucasus and by March 1914 back in Moscow. Graham's next trip was on board the steamer *Skobolev* for passage across the Caspian Sea, from there to Tashkent where he proceeded on foot to the small town of Kopal on the Chinese border. From there, Graham trekked to the Altai Mountains that form the border between China and Mongolia, some of the remotest areas of Asia. In September 1914, he arrived back in Moscow to report on the First World War that, at the time, was going badly for Russia. Many of Graham's dispatches were written close to the front line and within sound of machine guns and bombs dropped from German aircraft as the enemy advanced on Warsaw. At one point Graham was detained by the Russian authorities and only released following his production of a four-year-old letter written by the governor of Archangel testifying to his legitimacy.

In the spring of 1915, Graham set out in a ship from Marseilles bound for Egypt to report on early Eastern Christianity. He returned two months later via Athens to Sofia but was delayed on the Greek border for a week because the Bulgarian authorities had imposed a quarantine to prevent the spread of an epidemic in the region. From Sofia Graham traveled to Bucharest and then onward to the port of Odessa, blocked at the time due to hostilities in the straits at Constantinople, part of riots and unrest throughout the region due to Russia's poor handling of the war. Graham was to remain in Moscow and Petrograd for the summer of 1915 before returning to Britain in the middle of October, where he made a pilgrimage across Britain in the closing weeks of the year.

A Private in the Guards

By the summer of 1916 Graham was back in Russia, in spite of the U.K. Foreign Office's initial refusal to grant him permission for the trip, fearing that his tsarist sympathies might damage Britain's relations with the new provisional government. Graham had registered for U.K. military service shortly before this trip, but married men of his age were not at the time being called up for active duty. In September of the following year, due to the continuous slaughter on the Western Front and shortage of soldiers, Graham, then 33, received papers to report at the Caterham Barracks in Surrey, home of the 3rd Battalion of the Scots Guards. Concerned that a writer of such distinction had been conscripted for active service, friends of Graham's, including the Duchess of Bedford, made representations to the War Office to stop his draft. Graham was less concerned at the prospect of entering the war and even chose to enroll as a private rather than accept an officer's commission in order, he says, to see what life was like in the ranks.

On Christmas Eve of 1917, Graham was transferred from Caterham to Wellington Barracks in central London, only 20 minutes' walk from Graham's flat at 60 Frith Street. The three months he spent there prior to his departure for France included guard duty at Buckingham Palace. On Good Friday, 1918, his unit finally headed for the front, arriving in France on March 30. From Le Havre his unit traveled eastward for the battlefield. Difficult as Graham's life must have been during the months he spent in the trenches, he yet managed to keep a detailed diary of events, eventually published as *A Private in the Guards* in 1919. When it was first published, readers were shocked, and some outraged, by Graham's accounts of the brutalities meted out to its own troops by the British Army, including executions of men who were clearly suffering from shell shock, and also the mistreatment of soldiers by NCOs at the barracks in Caterham prior to them entering the war. In February 1919, prior to publication of *A Private in the Guards*, Graham had been discharged from the army with a disability pension due to heart problems and was awarded the British War Medal and the Victory Medal (given to all who saw service during that war).

Four Years of Travel in Europe and the Americas

In July 1919 Graham traveled with Rosa to Copenhagen and from there boarded a ship bound for the United States, returning in the spring of 1920. In February 1921, and still traveling together, they arrived in Rome before traveling on to Greece, Bulgaria, Yugoslavia and Serbia. Leaving Rosa in Belgrade, Graham headed off alone to Constantinople. After returning to collect Rosa in Belgrade, the pair then headed north for Budapest, Vienna, Prague, Warsaw, Munich, and finally Berlin. As well as his European travels, between 1919 and 1923 Graham traveled extensively throughout North America, from the East Coast to the Rockies, and Canada to Mexico. Rosa accompanied Graham on some of his less arduous treks in America as well as Europe, but not those Graham chose to make on foot such as tramping through Georgia in the path taken by General Sherman following the burning of Atlanta. In the South, Graham visited black schools and churches, gathering information for his book *Children of the Slaves* (1920) in which he highlighted the divisions between white and black America that had changed little since the abolition of slavery.

Late in 1919, Graham left New Orleans with Rosa, heading up the Eastern Seaboard by boat to New York where they rented an apartment across the street from Grand Central Station. It was during this stay in New York that Graham met and befriended the American poet and fellow tramp writer Vachel Lindsay after seeing him perform at the home of the political reformer Charles Burlingham. A few months later, Lindsay came to Britain on a recital tour and spent time with Graham planning a joint tramp through the Rockies. Lindsay's modus operandi as a vagabond poet had been to tramp vast stretches of the American wilderness surviving by exchanging his poetry for food and shelter, hence the title of his pamphlet "Rhymes Traded for Bread" and his moniker the "Prairie Troubadour." Graham, who had always preferred to tramp alone, was initially wary of the project but eventually consented, sharing the same strong affinity with nature and outlook on life as Lindsay. They met up in Lindsay's home town of Springfield, Illinois, and headed west to tramp through Glacier Park in the Rocky Mountains and northward into the Alberta plains in Canada. One of the highlights of this trek was Graham's discovery, in a remote valley, of the Doukhobors, the isolated Russian pacifist sect who had lived in the area since their persecution by the tsars and Russian Orthodox Church in the late 1700s. Their "crime": the rejection of the symbolism and texts of the Russian Orthodox Church for a simpler, more personal communion with God. Jim Christy, as part of his own tramping adventures recounted in *Jim Christy: A Vagabond Life*, describes a similar community at Gilpin, near Grand Forks, in the early 1970s. He had arranged to meet up there with a friend but left abruptly on finding the place overrun with hippies.[9]

Following his tramp through the Rockies with Lindsay, Graham and Rosa closed up Frith Street and set off for Central America via Spain. Graham took a strong dislike to Spain, being appalled by the cruelty he witnessed at a bullfight in Madrid. From that city they traveled to Cadiz and boarded a ship bound for San Juan, in Puerto Rico. His arrival there and onward travel to Haiti and Cuba is described in *In Quest of El Dorado* (1923). Graham and Rosa spent the summer of 1922 in an adobe house in New Mexico from where they explored the deserts and mountains of the Southwest. At the end of the summer, Graham left Rosa behind in Santa Fe to tramp through Panama in the footsteps of the 16th-century Spanish conquistador and explorer Vasco Núñez de Balboa. He was accompanied by two guides, one to carry his pack and gun, the other to hack a path through the jungle with a machete. The trio made slow progress, held up by rain and mud and tormented by mosquitos in spite of Graham wearing a full set of clothing including boots and gloves. Yet the poetry of Graham's writing was unaffected by his hardships and discomforts:

> Thousands of flaming fireflies lit the floating mists which along the edge of a jungle clearing looked like phantoms living in dark houses. ... Tongues of fire among white mists in intense darkness, howling of monkeys, the creaking and wailing and prolonged noise of insects in the trees, mosquitos as noiseless and attentive as breath, the air not vital, suffocating—such were the nights.[10]

Things got easier when they were able to join the *Camino Real*, a track carved through the jungle centuries earlier, until finally reaching an escarpment from which they could view the Pacific Ocean. The sight of the Pacific had no effect whatsoever on Graham's one-eyed guide, but prompted Graham to observe: "A warm current ran through my veins and something seemed to lighten heavy boots. Wings came out from my heels and I stood on tiptoe and stared."[11]

Domestic Difficulties

Following this trip, Graham and Rosa made an excursion through Mexico before arriving back in Southampton on the White Star Line's *Majestic* liner in April 1923, the culmination of three extended trips to the USA and two long tours of Europe. Most of the following year Graham stayed in London, writing and re-engaging in the cultural life of the city. In 1924, having rediscovered his interest in Russia, Graham headed out alone for Poland via Latvia and Lithuania. By this time, Graham's marriage to Rosa had started to disintegrate and, without the domestic and emotional anchor that 60 Frith Street represented, Graham was struggling to find a direction in his life. Initially he consoled himself in the cultural life of Paris but around this time Graham's father died and he had to commute back and forth between Paris and London to attend to his father's affairs. Early in 1925, at one of his Frith Street literary evenings, Graham met, and fell in love with, a young writer named Margaret Irwin. Irwin would later achieve literary fame for her historical novel *Young Bess*, a trilogy about Queen Elizabeth I.

Rosa left Frith Street in May 1926 and took up a room in a religious retreat, later returning after pleading from Graham. But he was unable to reconcile the two women in his life and by the summer he had become depressed, withdrawing from the London cultural scene then finally heading off again to New York in April 1927. *New York Nights* (1927) describes Graham's time in that city as a flâneur, walking the streets at night during New York's Prohibition and Jazz Age era in which he chronicles a world of flophouses and speakeasies in localities such as The Bowery, Bleecker Street, and Harlem.

Graham returned to America again in 1929 to visit his friend Vachel Lindsay, but it was his trip to Belgrade in 1930 that would change the course of Graham's life. He was staying at the home of Dimitrije Mitrinović, a Serbian philosopher, poet, and artist. Mitrinović had a younger sister, Vera, who was 27. Graham was 46 at the time but clearly smitten by Vera and maintained contact with her after his return to London. Returning to Belgrade shortly afterwards, Graham started to worry about Vera's health, sharing a tiny flat as she did with her tubercular brother Lubo. Graham was in Belgrade again early in 1931 when Lubo died, and remained there until the following year, writing prolifically and fussing over Vera. The only problem he encountered at the time resulted from unfounded rumors that he worked for British intelligence, but these were quickly resolved given his well-documented Serbian sympathies and contacts with Serbs in positions of power. Graham spent much of his time with Vera, both in Belgrade and Sarajevo, where he was developing a career in journalism.

Life with Vera

In 1935 Graham and Vera set off for an extended fishing and camping holiday to Lake Ohrid on the border of Albania and Macedonia. Not unexpectedly, given Graham's insatiable appetite for writing, even this trip produced a book, *The Moving Tent: Adventures with a Tent and Fishing-Rod in Southern Jugoslavia* (1939). A description of Vera in the book describes her as a "dark handsome girl with uncut black hair, merry eyes and one of those aquiline noses which the ancient Romans left behind on the Balkan peninsula."[12] Back in London, the pair set off for Cape Town, prompting Graham's novel *African Tragedy* (1937). Publication of the book resulted in a costly libel trial for Graham, who had too closely based two of the book's characters on a couple (including Lady Chesham) with whom Graham and Vera had stayed in Swaziland during their trip. The publisher was forced to pulp all unsold copies of the book.

At the beginning of the Second World War in 1939, Graham and Vera were living together at 60 Frith Street. Vera was working as the London correspondent for the Belgrade newspaper *Stampa*. Graham was 55, too old to be called up for military service but unable to continue his rambling due to wartime conditions on travel. By February 1941, we know that both Graham and Vera were employed by the British Broadcasting Corporation (BBC) at their London headquarters for their language skills. By the end of 1944 Graham was involved in production at the Serbo-Croat section, even making his own broadcasts in Serbo-Croatian.

Following the war, a problem presented itself for Vera because she did not have a British passport, neither was she married to Graham; the British authorities regarded her as a stateless person. Vera lost her job at the BBC and was at risk of being sent back to Yugoslavia but managed to avoid deportation until Rosa's death in 1956 when Graham became free to remarry. Graham was now well ensconced in the Russian section of the BBC where he remained until his hours were cut due to his deteriorating health and the proximity of his 70th birthday. In spite of his illnesses, Graham would live together with Vera for another 26 years.

Final Adventures

Although Graham continued writing profusely, the only work he published during his final years was his autobiography, *Part of the Wonderful Scene* (1964). Book sales had dwindled due to the reading public's changing tastes. Money became tight, yet Graham found money to travel to Yugoslavia with Vera in 1966, spending much of their time with her relatives on the coast. Receiving money from the BBC allowed Graham and Vera to return to the Adriatic for the following two summers. His final severance pay funded the first trip he had been able to make to America since 1930, 37 years earlier.

In November 1967 they left Heathrow on a flight to New York where they stayed in the Hotel Edison near Times Square. From there they took a plane southward and stayed for six weeks with a college professor friend in Tallahassee before traveling on to New Orleans, Houston, and then Chicago. Graham left Vera in Chicago while he went on alone to visit the home of his old friend Vachel Lindsay. Lindsay had died in 1931 and his former home in Springfield turned into a museum. From Chicago the Grahams returned to New York and also visited Graham's niece who taught at Howard University in Washington, before flying back to London at the beginning of February 1968.

In spite of his continually failing health, in the summer of 1970 Graham traveled with Vera to Spain and stayed with an old friend near Alicante, but this would be their last trip. The following year Vera found Graham unconscious in his bedroom, following which collapse he was only able to walk with the aid of two sticks. His eyesight was also failing, making it difficult for him to read and write. He was also beset with money problems. In this manner the couple somehow survived until Graham's death on March 16, 1975, four days short of his 91st birthday. Michael Hughs sums up his biography of Graham by describing him as a "neglected member of the British literary establishment." An acknowledgement that although at one time mixing in those circles, Graham and his writings have long since been forgotten, never achieving the recognition that they deserve.

Before discussing Graham's philosophy, it must be noted that, as well as tramping across continents by way of the remotest topography, in middle age Graham was also an extremely dedicated flâneur. In his books *London Nights* and *New York Nights*, his copious and detailed sketches on every aspect of nightlife in those two cities, not least the fascinating characters who inhabited them, make the much-lauded contemporary genre of "psychogeography" seem dull by comparison. Complementary to Jack Black's and Jim Phelan's insider observations on penology, *London Nights* includes sketches on prison life from several years of Graham's time spent as a nightly prison visitor in that city. The chapter titled "Prison Nights" concludes with the following words:

> It is a human Zoo, all the birds and animals of prey are in their cages and many of them have had their claws cut and talons drawn. They are harmless and defeated. There is only one lasting delusion, which is, that we can tame them and make them domestic and useful. They go out at given intervals, but are nearly always sent back. In and out they swarm, the many thousands of the "known to the police."[13]

His descriptions of markets, eating and drinking establishments, dosshouses, cemeteries, waterways, tunnels under waterways, red-light districts, theater-land and the high and low life attracted to these places for excitement, work, or simply survival, provide unrivaled descriptions of London and New York during the 1920s.

Graham's Philosophy on Tramping

Companionship

Here, the reader should be allowed to make up their own mind about Graham's literary skills by presenting the following extended section from *A Tramp's Sketches*, part of a longer chapter titled "The Wanderer's Story." No apology is made for relying exclusively here on Graham's own story of another tramp; the original is always more enjoyable and informative than secondary texts:

"THE WANDERER'S STORY: 1. MY COMPANION"

When star passes star once in a thousand years, or perhaps once in the forever, and does not meet again, what a tale has each to tell! So with tramps and wanderers when two meet upon the road, what a tale of life is due from one to the other. Many tramps have I met in the world. Far from the West I have met those who came far from the East, and men have passed me coming from the South, and men from the North. And sometimes men have suddenly appeared on my way as if they had fallen from the sky, or as if they had started up out of the earth.

One morning when I was dwelling in a cave between a mountain and a river I met him who tells this story. Probably the reader has never lived in a cave and does not appreciate cave life—the crawling in at night, the long and gentle sleep on the soft grey sand, the crawling out again at morning, the washing in the river, the stick-collecting and kettle-boiling, the berry-gathering, the lazy hours of noon, the lying outstretched on the springy turf, sun-drinking, the wading in the river and the plashing of the rushing water over one's legs; sunny days, grey days, rainy days, the joyous delight in the beautiful world, the exploration of one's own heart, the sadness of self-absorption.

It was on a grey day when I met the strange tramp whose life-mystery is here told. I came upon him on a quiet forenoon, and was surprised by him. He came, as it were, out of thin air. I had been looking at the river with eyes that saw not—I was exploring my own heart and its memories—when suddenly I turned round and saw him, smiling, with a greeting on his countenance.

It was long since I had looked upon a man; for though quite near the highway, no one had found me out in my snug cave. I was like a bird that had built a nest within earshot of a road along which many schoolboys ran. And any one discovering my little house was like to say, "Fancy, so near to the road, so unsuspected!"

"Good-morning, friend," said I, "and greeting! You are the first who has found his way to this cave. You are a wanderer like myself, I perceive. Come, then, and share my noonday solitude, and in return give me what you have to share."

"Forgive me," said he, "I thought I heard a voice; that was why I came. I thought I heard a call, a cry."

I looked at him. He was a strange man, but with something peculiarly familiar in his figure. His dark hair spread over a brow whiter than mine, and veiled two deep and gentle eyes; and his sun-tanned face and dusty hat made him look like a face such as one sometimes sees in a dream.

"You heard not me," I answered, "unless it was my thoughts that you heard."

He smiled. I felt we need not say more. I sat with my back to the sun and he lay stretched in front of me, and thus we conversed; thus two wanderers conversed, two like spirits whose paths had crossed.

"Now tell me," said I, "who you are, dear wanderer, stretched out at my feet like a shadow, and like a shadow of my own life. How long have you been upon the road, when did you set out, where is your home and why did you leave it?"

The tramp smiled.

"I am a wanderer and a seeker," he replied. "In one sense the whole world is my home, in that I know all its roads and am nowhere a stranger. In another sense I have no home, for I know not where I began or where I come from. I do not belong to this world."

"What!" said I, starting up suddenly and consequently disturbing my companion. "You are then an apparition, a dream-face, a shadow. You came out of thin air!"

I stood up, and he turned familiarly about me and whispered like an echo in my ear, "Out of thin air." And he laughed.

"And you?" he went on. "On what star did you begin? Can you tell me? Never yet have I found a man who could answer that question. But we do not know, because we cannot remember. My conscious life began one evening long ago when I stepped out of a coach on to a high road, this same road by which you have your cave. I had come from God-knows-where. I went backward, I came forward; I went all about and round about, and never found my kith and kin. I was absorbed into the world of men and shared its illusions, lived in cities, worked for causes, worshipped idols. But thanks to the bright wise sun I always escaped from those 'gloomy agreeable nooks.' It has now become my religion to avoid the town, the places where men make little homes which make us forget that in truth we have no homes. I have learned to do without the town, without the great machine that provides man with a living. I have sucked in a thousand rains, and absorbed a thousand suns, lain on many thousand banks of the earth. I have walked at the foot of mountains along long green valleys, I have climbed great ranges and peeped over them, I have lived in barren and in fertile places, and my road-companion has been Nature herself."

> I smiled upon my visitor and said, "How like you are to me, my friend! Stay with me and let us talk awhile. Grey days come, and rain, and we shall live in this cave together and converse. In you I see a brother man. In you as in a clear mirror I see the picture of my own soul, a darling shadow. Your songs shall be the words of my happiness, your yearning shall be the expression of my own aching heart. I shall break bread with you and we shall bathe together in the river. I shall sleep with you and wake with you, and be content to see you where'er I turn."
>
> That evening at sunset he crawled with me into the cave. And he slept so sweetly that I held him in my own heart. Next morning at sunrise we clambered out together, and together we gathered sticks, and together bent over the fire and blew into its struggling little flames. Life was rich. We hob-nobbed together. We doubled all our happinesses, and we promised to share all our griefs. Sitting on the rocks—there were many of them about, of all shape and size—we taught one another songs. I wrote songs; he sang them. I told him of places where I had been; he described them to me so that they lived again before me. I told him of beauteous women I had met; he had met them also and revealed to me their loving hearts. He could give the leaping love in my heart a precious name. I verily believe that when the sun was setting golden behind a great cliff, he could bid it stop and shine upon us an hour longer.
>
> Timid and shy at first, he grew more daring afterwards and interpreted my wishes even before I was myself aware of them. He was constantly devising some new happiness. His bird's heart was a fast overflowing fountain.
>
> Then when rainy days came we crouched together in the cave like night-birds sheltered from the day, and we whispered and recounted and planned. I scribbled in my diary in pencil, and he re-wrote my scribbling in bright-coloured chalks, and drew side pictures and wrote poems. Many are the pages we thus wrote together; some he wrote, some I wrote, and there are many from both of us in this volume.[14]

Here we have Graham at his poetic best. Here also are barely disguised external influences on Graham's writing: the legend of the Wandering Jew, appearing "out of thin air," the "whole world is my home"; and also Nietzsche, pitying the rest of the "human herd" from his lone and lofty perch of world-hating introspection. Graham is ambivalent about companionship. He craves it when alone: being "desolated by loneliness" and acknowledging "the need of loving human friends," but also resenting it when it impinges on his freedom to think and act autonomously. Yet it is also clear that Graham fully appreciated, and was preoccupied by, the dangers of tramping alone: "perhaps some one watched him as he smoothed out his bracken bed; or if he went into a cave a robber saw him and will come later in the night, when he is fast asleep, murder him, and throw his body into the sea."[15] Nonetheless, he also acknowledges that such feelings can be overcome, often inflamed as they are by non-tramping associates and dissipated as soon as he is on the road: "I half believed all the tales by which stay-at-home people tried to warn or frighten me. ... Then came my first week's tramping, and I emerged a different man. I felt bold."[16]

Religion

Graham's ability to overcome his fears is clearly also bolstered by his faith, even though, as already acknowledged, his is a personal compact between himself and his God, free from the trappings of organized religion. Like the asceticism of Cynics and early Christians, Graham's faith is a philosophy of the proletariat: "His [Jesus'] is a peasant's gospel, it seems to me, such a gospel as the peasants of Russia would take to themselves to-day if Jesus came preaching to them." Graham well recognized, as did Nietzsche also, the corrupting influence of the New Testament, and leaves us in no doubt as to which version of Christianity sustains him in his tramping:

> The cultured would disdain it, until a new St. Paul interpreted it for them in terms that they could understand, so giving it a "vogue." Both the peasants and the cultured would be Christians, but with this difference, that in one case the seed would be growing on the surface, and in the other from the depths. The peasant, of course, has no surface; he is the good black earth all ready for the seed.[17]

As with the Cynics also, Graham's personal philosophy is nurtured by contemplating and getting closer to the natural world beneath his feet rather than staring heavenward for moral guidance: "There is a way for the cultured: it is to discover the peasant down beneath their culture, the original elemental soil down under the artificial surface, and to allow the sweetness and richness of that soil to give expression on that surface. True culture is thus achieved; that which is not only on the surface but of the depths."[18] Graham was also a pragmatic Christian, one for whom sinning was a relative concept, as he explains in a chapter from *The Gentle Art* titled "Scrounging": "Who can resist robbing an orchard of a few apples? Oh, those Ohio apples! I've eaten many a one at dawn without paying for it, big as your fist, streaked with cheek-red, sweet as a kiss. ... One does not burn everlastingly for this in the hereafter. All I can say is, that if I settle on the land in my old age, some tramps may then rob me for my sins."[19]

But it is when Graham contrasts his spiritual God with the new, fast-emerging

"God of Capitalism" that Graham's unique philosophical fusion of Christianity and naturalism comes into its own. Ruminating on the fact that "it has become clear that the thirty pieces of silver not only sold the author of Christianity but Christianity itself," Graham recalls the words of a Russian deacon he had befriended: "Money has come between us and made us work more and love less. We are gathered together, not for love but for mutual profit."[20]

The Commercial versus the 'Natural' World

Graham is not calling for an alternative society in which we all go off into the wilderness and live on nuts and berries. "The tramp does not want a world of tramps—that would never do." He well understood that the role of his tramp, as was the role of the ancient Cynics, is a muted protest, a personal challenge (simply by demonstration of his own lifestyle) to the corruption of humanity manifested as greed and hypocrisy, advocating a return to a more natural way of being in the world. But as Graham points out, the tramp, like the Cynic, has no interest in changing the status quo, for such a change would negate their very need to exist. In this respect, both Cynicism and tramping are privileged and lofty positions to take; it is their raison d'être to hold up a ridiculing mirror to the rest of society *without* the need to offer an alternative. As Graham says, we can't all be tramps. Yet the impression of an ideological quest remains, if not a serious alternative model for society at large, certainly sound strategies from which individuals can learn to survive the increasing stress of living in today's world of hyper-reality and uncertain futures: "tramps—better call them the rebels against modern life—are perhaps only the first searchers for new life. ... Every one will benefit by a little more simplicity, and a little more living in communion with Nature."[21]

Unlike the Cynics, though, whose role in challenging human stupidity was for the most part limited to their physical and verbal "performances," Graham supplements his bodily protests with insightful philosophical writings, backed up by an erudite awareness of contemporary theorists—including, as though to underpin his own mission, the following words frequently attributed to Albert Einstein: "Only two things are infinite, the universe and human stupidity, and I'm not sure about the former." One can only speculate that the reason Graham's critiques on modern life at the start of the 20th century are not better known and respected today is for the same reason that Cynicism was not taken seriously in its own day: their eccentric appearance and lifestyle brought them into ridicule from those whose orthodox interests they dared to challenge. To sum up his thoughts on capitalism, let Graham speak again for himself. The following extract from *A Tramp's Sketches* on the sorry state of modern life is as acutely relevant today, perhaps more so, as it was when Graham wrote it over a hundred years ago.

> We are like people who have lost their memories on the way to a feast, and our steps, in which is only dimly felt the remembrance of a purpose, take us nowhither. We loiter in musty waiting-rooms, are frustrated by mobs, and foiled by an eternal clamour. We have forgotten the feast and occupy ourselves in all manner of foolish and irrelevant ways. Only now and again, struck by the absurdity of our occupations, we grope after our lost consciousness and feel somehow that somewhere out beyond is our real destination, that somewhere out there a feast is proceeding, that a cover is laid for us and dishes served, that though we are absent the master calls a toast to us and sends messengers to find us.[22]

Hospitality

It is impossible to ignore the similarities between Graham's personal philosophy, even his prose style, and that of Nietzsche, one of these being an expressed nostalgia and romanticism for past times and cultures. In Nietzsche's case it was the celebration of life as represented by pre-Christian Greece and Rome; in the case of Graham, it is the perception of a kinder, gentler society represented by simple, peasant, country life, before the arrival of either capitalism or Bolshevism. That both writers ignore the more brutal elements of the historical periods they romanticize does not detract from the power of their polemics. And one aspect of the greed and selfishness of modern times that Graham bemoans is the loss of hospitality. Paradoxically, his choice for a model of hospitality comes from the Middle Ages, one of the most tyrannical periods of history: "The doors of castle or cottage, of monastery or cell, were always on the latch to the wanderer, and not only to those performing sacred dues but to the vagabond, the minstrel, the messenger, the tradesman."[23] Graham decries that it is not possible to wander wherever he chooses and find free food and shelter. "I know no greater shame in national development than the commercialisation of the meal and the night's lodging. It has been our great disinheritance."[24]

For Graham, no one is kinder and more hospitable than the poor. He tells a story of seeking shelter at a prosperous house at night: he calls out from the dark, and hearing only a cultured voice they invite him to enter, only to be turned away again when his appearance is revealed. He ends up being given food and shelter in a one-room peasant shack, sharing what little the family have. But no one, according to Graham, is more hospitable than the tramp, recalling how a Caucasian tramp couple came upon him one night and sat for a while by his campfire. He was unable to converse with them because they spoke no Russian. The man produced some green tobacco leaves and dried them by the fire, ready to smoke. They were clearly starving and Graham gave them bread and beef and some hot rice pudding he had been cooking. "In return the man gave me five and a half walnuts! We seemed like children playing at being tramps, but I felt a very lively affection for these strange wanderers who had come so trustingly to my little home under the bridge."[25]

One further anecdote from Graham on hospitality worth noting—as it seems contradictory to his earlier observations—concerns an observation on hitchhiking (Graham was not averse to taking a lift, particularly through a boring stretch of countryside): "the man in the car is much more hospitable in America than in any other part of the world."

Motivation for Tramping and its Advantages

> He who sleeps under the stars is bathed in the elemental forces which in houses only creep to us through keyholes. I may say from experience that he who has slept out of doors every day for a month, nay even for a week, is at the end of that time a new man. He has entered into a new relationship with the world in which he lives, and has allowed the gentle creative hands of Nature to re-shape his soul.[26]

It is now time for Graham to answer a fundamental question, one that others in this book have answered in different ways. Exactly why was Graham drawn to tramping in the first place, and what kept him tramping into his advancing years? Maybe "advancing years" is a good place to start, for it would seem from studying Graham's writing that one of his motivations for tramping is to stay young, or rather, not to lose the innocence of childhood. In the chapter titled "The Boy Who Never Grows Old," Graham describes himself as "an old, bearded, heavy-going, wrinkled tramp, leaning on a stout stick; my grey hairs blew about my old red ears in wisps," before insisting that he is *not* old, nor will he ever be old, because even though aged in years, the tramp always remains a boy in his heart. "There is in him, like the spring buds among the withered leaves of autumn, one never-dying fountain of youth. He is the boy who never grows old."[27]

The childlike innocence of which Graham speaks also represents a resistance to the stupidity of adults: absorbed through a process of maturation; not acquiring wisdom, but rather losing it through false learning. Graham draws from the maxims of Nietzsche and others when he describes the "irreconcilables," those who feel alien everywhere but claim everywhere as their home—the Cynic cosmopolite, the Wandering Jew, the tramp:

> We are many upon the world—we irreconcilables. We cry inconsolably like lost children ... For perhaps we are kidnapped persons. Perhaps thrones

> lie vacant on some stars because we are hidden away here upon the earth. ... We are upon a deserted island and have no boats to take us from star to star, not only upon a deserted island but upon a deserted universe, for even the stars are familiar; they are worlds not unlike our own. The whole universe is our world and it is all explained by the scientists, or is explicable. But beyond the universe, no scientist, not any of us, knows anything. On all shores of the universe washes the ocean of ignorance, the ocean of the inexplicable. We stand upon the confines of an explored world and gaze at many blank horizons. We yearn towards our natural home, the kingdom in which our spirits were begotten. We have rifled the world, and tumbled it upside-down, and run our fingers through all its treasures, yet have not come upon the charter of our birth.[28]

Here we have Graham the postmodernist—before even the term modernism came into being, giving the lie to such "conditions" as fixed points in history. Graham could not have anticipated the new wave of philosophers such as Jean Baudrillard, who 80 years after Graham published "Irreconcilables" provided us with an identical description of a world stripped of any real meaning by science's attempt to understand, categorize, and control it. The curiosity of the scientist is a very different curiosity to that of the tramp. The tramp is not interested in discovering why or how something is; such knowledge would destroy the magic of the phenomenon or experience, rendering it mundane. Childish curiosity, which goes hand-in-hand with childish innocence, is claimed by Graham as the principal motive of wanderlust: "the desire to know what is beyond the next turning of the road ... the born wanderer is always expecting to come on something very wonderful—beyond the horizon's rim." Graham acknowledges that the joys of wandering are balanced by the pains, but that the desire to wander is incurable nonetheless. When taken to places he had never been before as a child, Graham refers to the experience as being a child of the "wander-thrill." "I remember from the age of nine a barefoot walk with my mother along the Lincolnshire sands from Sutton to Skegness, and the romantic and strange sights on the way. What did we not build out of that adventure?"[29]

Another attraction of tramping for Graham—one that provides a clue to his own unique cynical brand of Christianity—is the availability of heaven on earth. Graham derides those who sacrifice a life on earth in the hope of obtaining deferred happiness in heaven. In a dialogue between Graham and a fellow tramp, he proposes: "Many live their lives of toil and gloom and ugliness in the belief that in another life after this they will be rewarded. They think that God wills them to live this life of work." His companion responds, "Then perhaps in the next life they will again live in toil and gloom, postponing their happiness once more. Or on the Day of Judgment they will line up before God and say with a melancholy countenance, 'Oh Lord we want our wages for having lived!'"[30]

A clear indication is emerging from the chapters of this book—even for the tramp-*cum*-Christian—that a prime motive for tramping, as it was with the Cynics also, is to maximize life here on earth, as free as possible from painful preoccupations, and without deferring happiness for the later rewards of "heaven" in the full knowledge that such a place (in the supernatural sense) does not exist. The tramp knows that the most simple and fundamental pleasures in life can be obtained without the need of money. In the following passage, for example, Graham extols the virtues of the sun. And allowing that the targets of his diatribe are not the poorest in the world who suffer from the lack of rain, nor the modern victims of melanomas, his argument is a potent one. Interestingly, a stance also expressed over 2,000 years ago by Diogenes when sunning himself in a Corinth park after being asked by Alexander what wish he ("the Great") could grant him. The Cynic responded, "Stand out of my sun!"

> Have you not realised that we [tramps] have more than our share of the sun? ... That is because millions of people have lived without taking their share. We feel in ourselves all their need of it, all their want of it. That is why we are ready to take to ourselves such immense quantities of it. ... You must pull down the very sun from heaven and put it in your writings. You must give samples of the sun to all those who live in towns.[31]

If one of the advantages of tramping for Graham was greater access to the free benefits of outdoor life, another was the ability to jettison the unhealthy trappings and preoccupations of civilization. The example this time, one that requires no further explanation, is a diatribe from Graham ridiculing our obsession with time:

> The tramp carries no wrist-watch. ... In his cave he has no presentation timepiece mounted on lions or mermaids. ... He listens for no morning hooter; he boils his eggs without a measure of sliding sand; he punches no time-clock when he begins his day's tramp ... The most profound philosophers have been engaged for any number of years trying to explain time, and they are all agreed that it is an illusion.[32]

But significantly, Graham also observes from his invective on time that if an initial motivation for tramping is a rejection of, and a protest against, the forces of civilization, once on the road and free of such preoccupations, a different mindset takes over: "You will discern that going tramping is at first an act of rebellion; only afterwards do you get free from rebelliousness as Nature sweetens your mind. Town makes men contentious; the country smooths out their souls."[33] And yet for all Graham's warnings about city life and endorsement of living close to nature, as with the Cynic and for that matter the hobo also, he is continually drawn back to urban surroundings. He is both fascinated and repelled by cities. Yes, he admits to getting bored with nature at times, but then he seems to get bored by any condition that cannot sustain his desire for the extraterrestrial: "It is true the wanderer often feels bored, even in beautiful places. I am bored some days every year, no matter where I spend them, and I shall always be. I get tired of this world and want another. That is a common feeling, if not often analysed."[34] And so in spite of Graham's yearnings for the country, he is also well aware that metropolitan conurbations are not short on novelty and otherworldliness; and what's more, as an accomplished flâneur, Graham knows just how to profit from what cities have to offer. Countless examples are available of advice from Graham on how to get the most out of tramping, but one of the most fascinating is his "zig-zag walking," an entirely novel method of exploring both familiar and unfamiliar city streets: "taking of cross-sections of the world, the cutting across all roads and tracks, the predispositions of humdrum pedestrians, and making a sort of virginal way across the world." Zig-zag walking involves taking the first turn on the left and the next on the right, continuing in this manner to see where you end up. "In towns this gives you a most alluring adventure. You get into all manner of obscure courts and alleys you would never have noticed in the ordinary way."[35]

In summary, here is a list of some of the profits of tramping as seen by Graham:

- getting closer to nature to provide a rhythm both with yourself and the world that is right for you
- the satisfaction of partaking of the pleasures (and frustrations) of nature for free
- liberation from unnatural preoccupations with everyday life—such as worrying about time
- the ability to live in the present: taking pleasure now, not deferring it (whether for a pension or the promise of heaven)—something that eludes most other mortals
- not being defined by one's position or role in society—however exposing this may be
- sovereignty of the spirit and citizenship of the world, in contrast to narrow provincialism
- the ability to enjoy relationships without being bound by them
- maintaining youthful innocence, at the same time acquiring wisdom

ENDNOTES

1 Graham, Stephen. *The Gentle Art of Tramping*, New York: D. Appleton & Company, 1926, p. 29

2 Hughes, Michael. *Beyond Holy Russia: The Life and Times of Stephen Graham*, 2014. Hughes' website on Graham can be found at www.stephengrahamworldtraveller.com

3 Graham, Stephen. *A Tramp's Sketches*, London: MacMillan & Co., 1913, p. 303

4 Graham, Stephen. *Part of the Wonderful Scene*, Glasgow: Collins, 1964, p. 13

5 Graham, Stephen. *A Vagabond in the Caucasus*, London: John Lane, 1911, pp. 111–112

6 Ibid., p. 131

7 Ibid., p. 252

8 Graham, Stephen. *With Poor Immigrants to America*, New York: The Macmillan Company, 1914, p. 14

9 Cutler, Ian. *Jim Christy: A Vagabond Life*, Port Townsend: Feral House, 2019, p. 143

10 Graham, Stephen. *In Quest of El Dorado*, New York: D. Appleton & Company, 1923, p. 150

11 Ibid., p. 154

12 Graham, Stephen. *The Moving Tent: Adventures with a Tent and Fishing-Rod in Southern Jugoslavia*, London: Cassell, 1939, p. 106

13 Graham, Stephen. *London Nights*, London: The Bodley Head; John Lane, 1929, p. 121

14 *A Tramp's Sketches*, op. cit., pp. 243–249

15 Ibid., p. 31

16 Ibid., pp. 35–36

17 Ibid., p. 304

18 Ibid., p. 305

19 *The Gentle Art of Tramping*, op. cit., pp. 138–139

20 *A Tramp's Sketches*, op. cit., p. 174

21 Ibid., p. 41

22 Ibid., p. 179

23 Ibid., p. 174

24 Ibid., p. 86

25 Ibid., p. 92

26 Ibid., pp. 8–9

27 Ibid., p. 209. Also see "Peter Pan Phenomenon" in the epilogue of Ian Cutler, *Jim Christy: A Vagabond Life*, Port Townsend: Feral House, 2019

28 Ibid., pp. 258–294

29 *The Gentle Art of Tramping*, op. cit., p. 47

30 *A Tramp's Sketches*, op. cit., p. 285

31 Ibid., pp. 284–285

32 *The Gentle Art of Tramping*, op. cit., pp. 84–85

33 Ibid., p. 86

34 *A Tramp's Sketches*, op. cit., p. 40

35 *The Gentle Art of Tramping*, op. cit., p. 53

Jim Tully

(1886–1947).

The road gave me one jewel beyond price, the leisure to read and dream. If it made me old and wearily wise at twenty, it gave me for companions the great minds of all ages, who talked to me with royal words.

Jim Tully, *Beggars of Life*

Preamble

That he was a road kid for six years (although a tramp in spirit throughout his life) is just one of the remarkable facts about Jim Tully. At the age of six, following the death of his mother, Tully was left by his father in an orphanage where, even at that young age, he was determined to write. Tully was to become, among other things, a hobo, a chain maker, a pugilist and a tree surgeon, before becoming a minor Hollywood celebrity and finally a successful writer. As this book concerns tramp writers, it is Tully's tramping and writing that will be focused on here, but those who wish to discover all there is to know about Tully are urged to read his remarkable biography, *Jim Tully: American Writer, Irish Rover and Hollywood Brawler*, written by Paul Bauer and Mark Dawidziak. A debt is owed these two writers for much of the insight and chronology about Tully's life not available from his own writings. The researchers were helped and hindered in equal measure (the book was 19 years in the making) by the discovery in UCLA's archives of a never previously opened hoard of 117 boxes. The collection had been donated to the university in 1952 by Tully's third and last wife, Myrtle. Incredibly, the boxes were filled with Tully's unpublished works, papers, letters, magazine articles and other memorabilia.

Tully's Writing Style

As with most of the other tramp biographies in this volume, it is Tully's published works that will be principally relied on to get a sense of the man and his philosophy on life. But as noted previously, the magic and the frustration of this approach is the tramp storyteller's natural inclination to insert their life into their fictional works also—and occasionally, as in the case of Trader Horn, fictionalize parts of their life. Others have tried to categorize Tully's writings as either autobiography or fiction but as noted above, this is a somewhat pointless exercise as will be discussed, for instance, in the case of his third book, *Jarnegan*, below. In spite of the mountain of archives available to them, even Bauer and Dawidziak struggled to reconcile certain facts about Tully. But that is the price and the delight of engaging with Irish blarney.

As with Trader Horn, the deception is often deliberate and unabashed, and one must allow that, in any case, the truth is often more unbelievable than the fiction. Underneath a certain desire for celebrity, the books also reveal their author's extreme modesty, even self-deprecation. Tully's principal virtue is candidness, the brutal honesty that frightens those with more delicate sensibilities and threatens those who prefer the lie of idealism to human beings' baser instincts.

As H.L. Mencken, Tully's lifetime friend, editor and sometime publisher, said in his introduction to Nietzsche's *Antichrist*: "The majority of men prefer delusion to truth. It soothes. It is easy to grasp. Above all, it fits more snugly than the truth into a universe of false appearances."

It is for this reason that Tully's writing style has been described as "hard-boiled," and is best defended in the words of German philosopher Peter Sloterdijk, when he warns us, "Those who do not want to admit that they produce refuse . . . risk suffocating one day in their own shit."[1] Those tramps who choose vagabondage as a way of life—as opposed to those who have it thrust upon them—do so precisely to protect their integrity from what they regard as Mencken's "universe of false appearances." To quote Sloterdijk again: "In a culture in which one is regularly told lies, one wants to know not merely the truth but the naked truth."[2] This is Tully's considerable contribution to literature. He presents reality exactly as he sees it, stripped of sentimentality, and, considering the extreme censorship of the times, in the most unrestrained form he can get away with.[3]

Tully's response to his critics in his Introduction to *Blood on the Moon* reveals his contempt for self-appointed guardians of literature and his defiance against conforming to the literary tastes of the time. It also reveals just how aware Tully was that his writing challenged these literary conventions:

> While I am immune to the ink-stained bullets of the moral Social Soldiers who carry Truth as a mask, I have thought it best to change names in "Blood on the Moon" to keep them from shooting at those who are my friends. ... If I have not been able to invent a new medium in my picaresque books, I have at least been strong enough not to conform to one that is outworn.[4]

But Tully's writing style was not entirely unique for the time in which he wrote, even if it did upset literary orthodoxy. Other tramp writers display a similar gloves-off approach. Neither was he the only tramp writer to have engaged in the pugilistic arts (although he probably went further in the professional circuit than most). Jack Everson, W.H. Davies, Trader Horn, Bart Kennedy, Al Kaufman, and Jim Phelan[5] all boxed for money at some point in their tramping careers.

Tully's writing style is discussed further below, but after presenting a list of his published works, this chapter will move on to discuss the genesis of Tully's wanderlust and his love of words. The titles with an asterix below are all available free as electronic versions of their original editions:

*Emmett Lawler** (1922)
Beggars of Life (1924)
*Jarnegan** (1926)

Black Boy, with Frank Dazey (1926/ play—performed but no published script available)

Twenty Below, with Robert Nichols (1927/ play)

*Circus Parade** (1927)

*Shanty Irish** (1928)

Shadows of Men (1930)

Beggars Abroad (1930)

A Man of the New School (1931/ pamphlet)

*Blood on the Moon** (1931)

*Laughter in Hell** (1932)

*Ladies in the Parlor** (1935)

The Bruiser (1936)

Biddy Brogan's Boy (1942)

A Dozen and One (1943—13 profiles of Hollywood actors and acquaintances including his onetime friend and employer Charlie Chaplin, Raymond Chandler, Clark Gable, and lifetime friends, the former world heavyweight champion Jack Dempsey and publisher and journalist H.L. Mencken)

Early Years

Tully was the second youngest of six siblings, two girls and four boys. When his mother Biddy died, aged 35, giving birth to her seventh (stillborn) child, Tully's father (also named Jim) was unable to care for his six surviving children because he worked away from home for long periods digging ditches. The two girls, Maggie and Anna, the youngest, would go to live with their maternal uncle; the eldest son, Hugh, was able to work; but, at the suggestion of the local priest, the other three boys (Tom, Charlie and Jim) were sent to St. Joseph's Orphan Asylum in Cincinnati, over one hundred miles distant from their home in St. Marys, Ohio. There they would learn to read and write and be instructed in the Catholic faith.

Tully was six years old when he entered the orphanage and would remain there for the next six years. Not once did his father write or visit him during his stay at St. Joseph's. His misery was further compounded by the guilt of believing that he alone had caused his mother's death. As he later recollected in *Shanty Irish*, "Never did a criminal put in six more terrible years of torture."[6] The doctor had forbidden Biddy to drink water, yet when she begged Jim for a drink in her feverish state, he had obliged. The orphanage was run along prison lines with strict rules, beatings, and other punishments for infringements. But what Tully did get from his stay there was access to classical literature and a passion for reading and writing, often receiving rewards for his endeavors. Tully was not, however, a model Catholic. He admits to never having believed in God, although, like Nietzsche, he did have a soft spot for Jesus—though in the role of a fictional tramp activist rather than the living Christ. Tully was also to make some firm friends at the orphanage with whom he became reacquainted many times in the succeeding years.

In any event, Tully survived the orphanage and finally left its grounds for the first time in six years after being collected by his older brother and sister, who themselves had not traveled further than 10 miles from St. Marys in their lives. They had heard that by the age of 12, orphans who were not offered work on a farm, or whose family did not claim them, were sent to a notorious reform school. They persuaded a relative to write to the orphanage superintendent to vouch for Tully. This action was followed by him being passed around from relative to relative until, after a brief reunion with his father, he was placed to live and work with an illiterate farmer in a desolate part of Van Wert County known as Bear Swamp. And so, having escaped the reform school, Tully ended up incarcerated once again, this time in solitary confinement. The farmer did not provide the boy with warm clothing and when his father failed to send the required attire as promised, Tully spent two winters surviving sub-zero conditions in threadbare clothing. After tolerating these conditions for a year and a half, Tully took charge of his own fate and ran away, eventually finding shelter with a kind-hearted well-wisher named Joseph Blosser with whom he stayed for several months. Still aged 13, Tully later got work driving a team of horses between a quarry and roadworks for $3 a week plus board.

Road Kid

Most of the following accounts of Tully's adventures as a road kid come from his second book, *Beggars of Life*. There are also some powerful tales of tramping in his ninth book, *Blood on the Moon*, a work that includes some of the most unrestrained and ribald episodes of Tully's life, including drinking, whoring, stealing and fighting, as well as begging and tramping. As the *New York Post's* review of the book at the time states, "Mr. Tully writes with a sledgehammer." Other of Tully's books that include tales of his life on the road are *Emmett Lawler*, *Circus Parade*, and *Biddy Brogan's Boy*. A full reading of these books is recommended, as the following summary can only provide a brief account of Tully's seven years on the road, not the total immersion necessary to fully appreciate the joys and miseries of tramp life.

When the work finished in the autumn of 1900, 14-year-old Tully returned to his hometown of St. Marys with savings of $24. He found employment in the local chain factory at 50 cents for a 10-hour day, minus $2 a week for board in two rooms above a grocery shop with his older sister Maggie, aged 21, and Annie, aged 10. Work at the furnaces was hot and monotonous and Tully spent his free time around the bars and railroad yards of St. Marys. Here he met several hobos and road kids who captivated him with stories of freedom and adventure. His wanderlust was further fueled by the endless supply of magazines from his sister Maggie. Maggie intended these to encourage Tully's talent for writing. The act backfired when, seduced by images of exotic locations and the encouragement of a one-eyed road kid named Billy, Tully finally took to the road. He took with him useful advice from Billy, including warnings against jockers, whose exploitation and ill treatment have been described in other chapters of this book:

> ...don't you never let no old tramp play you for a sucker ... them old birds're too lazy to scratch themselves when they're crummy. So they gits young kids and teaches 'em to beg. They know people'll feed kids quicker'n they will them, so they make the kids do all the beggin'. Lotsa people pity kids at back doors.[7]

Tully admitted that he "made three unsuccessful journeys before I finally became even an amateur hobo." In *Blood on the Moon* Tully describes how he nearly lost a foot because he tried boarding a moving train from a standing position. A train wheel took off the heel of his shoe and left his foot painful and swollen for several days. Tully's first real trip started as a gentle 70-mile jaunt to Muncie, Indiana, in which he asked the freight crew if he could help them unload cargo in exchange for the ride: "I stood for long moments at the box-car door and gazed at the passing landscape. What did it matter though I lifted heavy boxes at every station—I was going somewhere."[8]

Tully daydreamed of being a writer; he thought about Edna from St. Marys' red-light district who had taught him all about sex for free while selling her body to older men at a dollar apiece; he thought of his brothers and sisters, and of the old farmer who had let him near freeze to death slaving on his farm, all the while nursing the intention to "trounce the hell out of him" the next time he met up with him.

On arriving at Muncie, Tully sought shelter in a shed full of hobos. The same night he was arrested for vagrancy, questioned by the police, and then sent to a dosshouse, only to have a sick tramp die in pain next to him during the night. After hanging around the town for five weeks waiting for the severe weather to break, Tully headed out in a boxcar and "hoboed about Kentucky and Indiana for several weeks, and then secured a job with Amy, the Beautiful Fat Girl ... the leading attraction with 'The One and Only Street Fair Company.'"[9] Tully's job was to crawl under a heavy glass stage on which the five-hundred-pound Amy danced, and shine different colored lights up through the glass to illuminate the angelic dancer—at the same time praying that the glass would not break.

Tully's other duties were as "Amy's liquor secretary," providing for her insatiable appetite for alcohol, for which he was entrusted with $60 a week. On one occasion Tully fell in with some men who had left the fair, and after getting drunk himself and being robbed of a portion of Amy's money, he fled to Chicago rather than face Amy's wrath.

On leaving Chicago with another road kid bound for Omaha, the pair were arrested at the first stop. After handcuffing them together, the railroad detective traveled with them at gunpoint in the blind baggage to Clinton where he had promised they would be put to work breaking rocks for two months. At one point, the detective turned his back to admire the landscape, whereupon Bill, holding tightly to the rung of the iron ladder, kicked the shack off the train. As he fell from the train, the man shot into the air, "then several more blazed up at the moon, but the train now sped through the open country at sixty miles an hour."[10]

After removing the handcuffs, the pair split up to beg food in Clinton, eventually coming across a tramp jungle near a river where, after enjoying the company and more food, they were approached by two armed detectives who tried to apprehend them. One tramp kicked over a lamp while Tully's companion Bill brought a stick down on the man's wrist. After a brief scuffle the two detectives were handcuffed to trees. One of the pair was the same lawman that Bill had kicked off the train earlier and so the tramps wasted little time in heading out of Clinton by train. Four departed at Cedar Rapids while Tully, Bill, and a tramp with one arm continued on to Boone. Eventually they reached Omaha before setting off for St. Louis where they had heard that good money was being paid for harvesting. The pair found work with a farmer and after finishing the harvest were paid $24 each.

It only took a few days of riotous living in St. Louis to deplete their funds and they moved on once more. But on returning in the direction they had previously traveled, they were warned that the country was hostile to hobos since two detectives were found beaten and handcuffed. Again Tully and Bill were arrested walking the tracks, and again they managed to escape. A short time later they were riding in a boxcar when they heard footsteps on the roof, then nails being driven into the door on one side of the train to prevent their escape. When they tried to escape from the opposite door they were confronted by the entire train crew but fought their way free, only to return to the train from the other side and ride the rods into the next town.

Having eventually said his farewells to Bill, Tully headed out on his own, standing precariously on the bumpers between two cars. Bill had warned him of the dangers of tiredness and how he had seen exhausted hobos fall to their death from trains. Tiredness did come over Tully and he gripped the brake-beam tightly until his wrists ached. "The roaring train lashed through the air. Wind blew viciously between the cars. It nearly blew the torn shirt from my body. My hair was wild-tangled and full of cinders." When his muscles started to ache and his head went dizzy, Tully unbuckled his belt and fastened it around his waist and the break-beam to prevent him falling. "A cold sweat came out on my forehead and body. The wind dried it quickly, and I grew chill." Five hours later Tully finally reached Rock Island, across the Mississippi River from Davenport, Iowa.[11]

Similar demonic train journeys are described by other tramp writers in this book, passages that reveal the very essence of the blowed-in-the-glass stiff and his relationship with life and death, such as Bart Kennedy's account of his frozen ride on a train's cowcatcher, and Leon Ray Livingston's ride on the rods with his face only inches from the gravel. There are also several accounts by tramp writers, including Tully, of the practice of removing tramps from the rods beneath trains by playing out a line with a heavy iron spike tied to the end. The spike bounces violently between the ties and the underside of the cars, mangling anything in its path.

Of Dreams and Other Adventures

Another distinguishing feature of Tully's writing is vivid dream sequences, revealing his early preoccupation with becoming a writer and his writer's imagination. There are several such sequences in *Beggars of Life*. For example, shortly after the train journey described above and a hearty breakfast in Davenport, Tully lies to rest under a tree by the Mississippi:

> I finally dozed off to sleep and dreamed that I had made a million in Alaska, and that I had returned to devote my time to having a reporter write books which I signed. ... The three trees danced like fantastic green bushes before my eyes. The river compressed itself into a tiny stream and swelled suddenly to a body of water as large as the Forty-Acre Pond near St. Marys.[12]

A train ride later finds Tully in a typhoid-induced sleep in a railroad camp:

> I dreamed feverishly until noon. I was an Irish general shot to death by the English and dying alone in my camp. I was a poet who recited many verses aloud.
>
> As the trains thundered by, all the hoboes I knew waved wildly at me, and danced, a ragged crowd of madmen on top of the cars. I saw the top of a bridge dash their heads from the train. They still danced, ragged and headless, with immense eyes gazing fixedly from the centers of their breasts.[13]

There then follows another nightmare train journey as Tully, burning with fever, his throat aching with thirst, risks riding lying flat on the roof of a cattle car in order to reach his friend Bill in Chicago and medical help. A friendly brakeman allows him to finish the journey in a hay manger inside a cattle truck. He slept fitfully, frequently aroused by the prodding of horns. "I dreamed I had a new blue suit, a striped tie, and bright tan shoes. I dreamed about Bill, and the farm in Missouri." Tully's thirst was so unbearable that he even resorted to chewing hay in the hope that the saliva would alleviate his parched mouth. Finally, unable to bear his thirst any longer, Tully relates his precarious passage across the tops of a dozen lurching carriages to make his way to the caboose where he begged for and was given water to drink. On his arrival in Chicago, Tully takes two further days to locate Bill in the Newsboys' Home in the South Side. He was taken the final mile by a kindly trucker who, on arrival at the boys' home, had to carry the sick road kid into the dormitory. From there, Tully was quickly transferred by ambulance to St. Luke's Hospital where, diagnosed with typhoid and malaria, he spent the next 48 days hovering between life and death. But Tully did recover, thanks to the kindness and attention of doctors and nurses, and unlimited reading material. "The boys from the Home made regular visits, and brought fruit each time. The matron came and lingered over my bed as though I was her own son." When the time came time for Tully to leave, the matron brought him new clothes and shoes. "I hated to go, and the last day was one of regret. ... I had been cured of typhoid and malaria, but the fever of the wanderlust still burned fiercely in my breast."[14]

But, on his discharge from the hospital, Tully did not immediately hit the road. Together with his friend Bill, they exploited election day in Chicago by picking up $3 every time they cast votes under false names given to them by bent election officials: "Let's see, your name's Abe Goldstein. You live at 422 Halstead Street. Go in an' vote." After taking part in the celebrations that followed the election victory in The Coliseum in Wabash Avenue, Tully spent the rest of the winter in Chicago before setting out for Cincinnati on a mail train with a fellow road kid named Dutch Vander. A strange choice of destination, given that Tully had been incarcerated in that city's orphanage for six years. The pair split up to bum food and drink which Tully found in abundance in a greasy saloon bar, courtesy of a generous benefactor. So well did he eat and drink that Tully fell asleep at the table, prompting another of his Bosch-like dream sequences, of which only fragments are included below—so much for those who criticize Tully's writing for not showing imagination:

> Countless numbers of girls of all colours, as naked as slender trees in winter, danced on an immense level and yellow stretch of sand, near a blue-green ocean under the light of the moon. Red, white, blue, and green angels flew above them scattering flowers. ... All of a sudden a horn of

> sand formed that reached to the moon. It circled round and round, as it was blown by the wind. Then millions of varied and brightly coloured birds and butterflies came as if from nowhere. Each bird and butterfly picked up a flower from where the sand had once lain, and each flower picked was of a different colour from the bird or butterfly that had picked it. ... The stars dropped downward from the sky, and the sun tore a great jagged hole through it in the east. Only the moon remained dancing, a mad fantastic orb of brilliant light above. ... Then the sun came quickly forward from the east, travelling faster than light. It rolled over the blue-green ocean and dried it up suddenly, as a hot flame dries a drop of rain. Fishes, sea-animals, and grotesque reptiles died slimy deaths in the kelp and coral of the ocean bed. Great whales lashed their dying tales and splashed mud for hundreds of feet, and then lay still. ... A great wind followed the sun, and swept the ocean bed clear of life, and sent all forms of it whirling, dead, among the flying angels, girls, and flowers. Everything moved with exact precision, and stars and sun and whales and even the tiniest bird carrying a flower, were in no more danger of striking each other than the planets ... A girl flew out of the confusing welter of confusion with some ham and eggs on a tray. I reached out for her. A hand grasped my shoulder. "Wake up kid, this ain't no lodgin' house."[15]

Blowed-in-the-Glass Stiff

Although still a road kid, Tully had served his hobo apprenticeship and was fast maturing in the ways of the road. After this brief stopover in Cincinnati, and not having met Dutch at the prearranged location, Tully boarded an express train hoping to reach Washington, D.C., over five hundred miles away, by the middle of the next day. He then found himself on the same blind baggage platform as Dutch. The pair clung to the Fast Flyer Virginia for 21 hours, over the Blue Ridge Mountains and roaring through tunnels. They had to forgo any food or drink because the express train did not stop at the small towns en route. At division points they had to hide behind boxcars or piles of railroad ties to avoid detection. "Passengers waiting for trains at depots would gaze in open-eyed astonishment as we flew past the stations gripping the iron ladders."[16]

After taking in the sights of Washington, including the White House and the Capitol building, the pair got themselves arrested while sleeping in a boxcar. After spending a night in jail, followed by a hearty breakfast in the company of other hobos, the pair were dismissed by the judge on the condition they leave town.

They continued their planned journey on to Baltimore where they begged a meal from fishermen in the Chesapeake Bay before traveling onward to Philadelphia. There they helped themselves to bread and milk from the steps of houses, then on to the Pennsylvania Railroad to continue their journey to New York via a detour to New Haven where they had been told "that Yale students often gave away fine suits of clothes." Instead, Tully lost his own coat when it was grabbed by a railroad detective as he leaped aboard a moving train departing New Haven. Dutch was less fortunate and, as Tully would learn later, spent 90 days in jail as a guest of that city. And so Tully continued on alone, one of his most perilous trips on the roof of a train being pelted by rain and unable to move from his perch. The cold air numbed his muscles and he "fought with a primitive lust for life," pounding on the roof of the car to revive his circulation. "I shook my head violently, as a pugilist does to drive the effect of a grueling smash from his brain. I longed for the train to stop."[17]

But he survived nonetheless, and on his arrival in New York City provides some insight into the paradoxical nature of tramping:

> For two weeks, I stayed in New York, living as a bird lives, though not as carefree. At times, I cursed the wanderlust that held me in its grip. While cursing, I loved it. For it gave me freedom undreamed of in factories, where I would have been forced to labor.[18]

As Tully next describes it, "I then went through a long siege as a hobo in the Central States." He picks up the story where he joins a party of 30 other tramps congregated around a wooden railway water tank at Cairo, where the states of Missouri, Kentucky and Illinois meet, but Tully seems to have been the only one capable of outsmarting the crew and jumping the train. At the next stop, Fulton, Tully switched trains to avoid capture and continued successfully on to Memphis. On the next leg of his journey, Tully had to share a boxcar with 17 other hobos. He was about to become acquainted with a hobo who had a powerful influence on him and confirm him as a seasoned hobo. Tully describes Oklahoma Red as heavily built with large hands like hams reaching nearly to his knees. "His hair fell in straggly red masses over his ears and neck. His coat was torn and gaped like wounds under his armpits ... His short neck bulged under his ears. ... There was decision and mastery about him."[19]

Tully was told, on asking another tramp about Red, "He's a b-a-d g-u-y." Oklahoma Red decided to build a fire in the boxcar to keep warm and, after swinging himself up onto the roof of the car, set out with two other tramps to collect wood from the moving train. By the time the party arrived at the next town, the fire had burned through the floor of the car and flames had worked their way up the sides to the roof. Escaping the inferno just in time, the hobos leapt to the ground, leaving the burning train to halt where it was hurriedly separated from the rest of the train. Only Tully, Oklahoma Red, and two other tramps were able or willing to board the same train as it departed once more. One of the tramps had a wooden leg but did not balk at jumping the train, by then traveling at 20 miles an hour: "Although all of fifty years old, he clutched the rung of the iron ladder I had climbed, his wooden leg sticking out from the car like the end of an immense broomstick." As the train started slowing down at Bald Knob, Arkansas, the four tramps left the train and headed for a large hobo jungle with half a dozen fires near a running brook. Just as the occupants of the camp were about to partake of their meal, a torrential downpour penetrated their rough shelters and soaked them all to the skin. Two barrels of stolen liquor lightened their mood until a serious fight broke out between black and white camp members. Oklahoma Red had been one of the main protagonists, and he, Tully, and Peg-leg made a quick exit from the scene, finally succeeding in jumping a train to Little Rock. Tully makes a distinction, by now already familiar in this book, that Red was a yegg ("a robber, a blower of safes, the aristocrat of the road, and the most dangerous man who travels it") rather than a hobo, and as such had money enough for the three of them to dine in the town.

After consuming a quart of liquor, Red told Tully his life story. He had been on the road since the age of five. His beggar "father" (Red was never sure he wasn't stolen) set Red and his sister begging with signs around their necks reading "motherless." Red was 12 when his father sold his 14-year-old sister to an old woman performer and got drunk on the proceeds for a week. Oklahoma Red had learned how to crack safes in prison and then spent two further long stretches in jail for burglary. He took to the road following his escape from the last prison after he'd broken a guard's jaw and been marked as one of the "bad guys"; he kept walking for a year to avoid being captured, not stopping in any town and growing his hair and beard long. Red promised to teach Tully the finer arts of safe-cracking but Tully never got the chance to become a yegg. Worse for the wear with drink, on the next train they jumped, Oklahoma Red slipped on the iron ladder and, with his foot stuck fast, fell backwards:

> He was dragging from the ladder of the second car behind me, his head bumping along the ties. ... I ran with the train and pulled his body loose. ... His arm was cut off at the elbow. It dripped, bloody and ghastly under the moon. ... "Red!!" I yelled, and grabbed frantically at his breast. His heart stopped in a dying flutter. I sobbed aloud.[20]

Although Tully later met many hobos who knew Oklahoma Red, he never told them the manner of his dying. After spending three days in Dallas, Tully beat it with a seasoned tramp to San Antonio in a "dead head" passenger coach (too dilapidated to remain in service) hitched in the middle of a freight train. Never mind the frayed and faded seats, this was the first time Tully had had the luxury of riding inside a passenger carriage. But he was not alone. Word had got around, and after entering the coach and passing some street lights that lit up the carriage, a bizarre sight, one worthy of Tully's dreams, was to meet his eyes, for every seat contained a hobo: "Some smoked, others talked, and some held their hands above their eyes and gazed out at the passing landscape."

After a difficult trip to El Rio then north again (he does not identify the town), Tully witnesses a horrific vigilante killing of a black prisoner. We do not know the alleged crime, but after being yanked by the mob from a third-story jail window by a rope around his neck, the terrified individual was then slowly burned alive propped above a fire already prepared for the ordeal. The scene is described by Tully in *Beggars of Life* in sickening detail, all the while, as though to normalize Southern culture, children were playing and laughing with the "death rope" around the fire. Similar "lynchings" are described by other tramp writers elsewhere in this book.

Circus Parade

After a particularly difficult time on the road tramping through Mississippi, not encouraged by the harsh Mississippi tramp laws that could consign a hobo to several years' hard labor, Tully decided to quit hoboing for a spell in a circus. He traveled for four months with "Cameron's World's Greatest Combined Shows" through Texas, Oklahoma, Missouri, Arkansas, Georgia and Florida. During his short employment with the circus he attended at least three funerals of close friends from among the troupe members. Tully was employed initially to help care for the animals with the lion tamer, work he seems to have enjoyed. Yet Tully's description of circus life is anything but romantic: "a canvas nest of petty thieves and criminals among the lower gentry." He describes the dregs of humanity engaged in acts of depravation and extreme cruelty; not only the circus folk themselves, but the trail of beggars who followed the circus for whatever scraps they could relieve from the crowd. The circus included "crawlers"—legless men strapped into small wheeled platforms propelling themselves along with their hands. Then there were "trailers," born double-jointed, twisting their bodies in every conceivable and grotesque manner. "Hard faces they had, and they moaned with pain when anyone drew near who might give them money."

The first chapter of *Circus Parade* concerns the African-American lion tamer who has to get inebriated before stepping into the lion cage. Yet he is mauled to death by a blind bear and two hyenas in a warm-up act after slipping and hitting the bear on the nose. The lesson for Tully is just how dispensable the circus performers were. The circus boss saw the event as valuable publicity and made sure the towns in the path of the circus tour were given a dramatic report of the event to increase box office sales. The many scams of the circus to swindle its paying customers are described by Tully in this book, prompting fierce lobbying from the "Circus Fans Association" that led to the movie version being shelved:

> Plundering and stealing, cheating and lying, laboring, fighting and loving; taking all we could and returning little, we went our careless and irresponsible ways, with laughter in our hearts and sneers on our lips—as anti-social as the hyenas who howled at the changes in the weather.[21]

But things did not always go the way of the circus. On one occasion, an audience, outraged at being swindled, started a brawl which resulted in the day's takings being stolen, the tent slashed and pulled to the ground, and serious injury sustained by several members of the troupe. But it would be a mistake to think of *Circus Parade* as merely an exposé of circus skullduggery. The remarkable feature of the book is its list of circus characters and Tully's tender and caring treatment of their tragicomic lives, portraits including The Strong Woman, The Moss Haired Girl, The Baby Buzzard, Goosey the elephant trainer, and the "African" lion tamer, Denna Wyoming. Then there was Whiteface the clown, of uncertain ancestry: "There were traces of Ethiopian, Caucasian and Indian in him. But in the South he was just another negro." Then there was the giant John Quincy Adams, a roustabout and stake-driver until the day he displayed his natural comedic talents and was promoted to the ring. John Quincy Adams was a simple and gentle soul; he shared a tent with Tully and Quincy's moth-eaten cat, Booker T. Washington. The trio would take walks together and discuss the meaning of life. But the fate of Whiteface the clown will not be revealed in this book. Those who wish to sample Tully at his storytelling best, not to mention the arbitrariness of circus life, human capriciousness, and the savagery of the South, should read the account in *Circus Parade* for themselves. Either the book's dramatic climax was written with a screenplay in mind, or Tully just has a powerful cinematic imagination, but thanks to the guardians of public taste and morality, moviegoers were denied the spectacle that *Circus Parade* might have offered on the screen. Neither do we know Tully's immediate movements following his time with the circus. Did he simply pick up tramping again where he left off—there is a dramatic description toward the end of the book of Tully re-boarding the moving circus train after being forced at gunpoint to jump from it—or did the circus mark the end of Tully's career as a hobo?

Whatever the case, because of the reference below to "crawlers and fakers," it seems reasonable to include Tully's four months with the circus as no more than a continuation of his experience as a road kid. In *Beggars of Life*, although it should be noted that he continued to hop the odd train for several years into his "working" life, Tully concludes his tramping adventures in Chapter 31 of *Beggars of Life* which proceeds as follows:

> There followed several years of wanderlust of which I eventually was cured. I lived in many a brothel where the dregs of life found shelter. I fraternized with human wrecks whose hands shook as if with palsy, with weaklings who cringed and whined at life, with degenerates and perverts, greasy and lousy, with dope fiends who would shoot needles of water into their arms to relieve the wild aching for an earthly Heaven. I learned the secrets of traitors and crawlers and other fakers. ... tramping in wild and windy places without money, food, or shelter, was better for me than supinely bowing to any conventional decree of fate.[22]

And here Tully introduces a new term to the lexicon of tramping, a designation that applies equally to many of the other tramp writers discussed in this book and one that would also assist his career as a writer: the "library bum." Tully stole books from libraries whenever he could, often carrying two or three with him but hiding them, as "It would not be wise for a bum to be caught with a library book. He would have to explain. Bums have so much to explain." As a final note on Tully's tramping career: according to his book *Shadows of Men*, Tully served five jail sentences during his six years on the road, terms varying from 10 days for vagrancy to four months.

Return to Chain-making and Writing

We know from *Blood on the Moon* that after taking a beating from three other vagabonds in 1906, being arrested, but having the good fortune to be able to rehabilitate himself rather than serving a custodial sentence, and still only 20 years old, Tully found work washing dishes at a school for $20 a month plus room and board. He then returned to St. Marys to pick up where he had left off at the chain factory, but a short time later the factory burned to the ground. After spending six weeks helping to clear the debris at 15 cents an hour, Tully made a trip to Chicago to visit his older sister Maggie, who had by now renamed herself Virginia. While in Chicago, Tully came across a news report that the tramp writer Josiah Flynt was staying in a Chicago hotel, seriously ill. Tully had heard of Flynt and was determined to meet the former hobo because he had achieved something Tully yearned for: to make a career of writing.

The meeting between the fan and his hero is evocative of Bob Dylan's meeting in the hospital with the ailing Woody Guthrie. It is recalled in *Blood on the Moon*. After sending a note to the hotel where Flynt lay dying, he was invited to visit his hero. "Josiah Flynt, the king of my world ... a withered little cigarette fiend burned out with the fever of wanderlust, the hardships of which had sapped his vitality." During the visit Flynt, true to his moniker, puffed one cigarette after another. Talking with difficulty and interrupted with coughing fits, Tully notes that Flynt was courteous even in dying. And the advice he gave Tully was to "get off the road"—something Tully was in any case already considering. "They're all snakes who crawl over it. It's not morals; it's nothing but protection." Before Tully left, Flynt handed him a few dollars, saying, "I haven't got much, Kid, and I won't need it long." When Tully left, Flynt was just staring at the ceiling. Tully notes that at the time of writing this piece, Flynt's books had been forgotten, "his name a hazy memory."[23]

Tully's sister Virginia had also given him a book of Jack London's, whom Tully was to meet later, further fueling Tully's writing ambitions, but he was not yet in a position to take up writing, needing money and somewhere to live. Shortly afterwards Tully got a job in a forge as a chain maker and worked at that trade several times over the coming years between writing, hopping the odd train, and boxing professionally. But back to the spring of 1907, and after a spell working in Racine, Wisconsin, Tully managed to secure a union card working as a chain maker in Columbus, Ohio, before jumping a freight train to Akron to join his brother Charlie who was working at another chain works in nearby Kent. Just as he had with his tramping, Tully started recognizing men he'd known at chain works in other towns. As he says in *Blood on the Moon*, "Chainmakers are the gypsies of manual labor."

Tully would spend hours in his cramped boarding house, writing prose and poetry with a pencil by the light of a kerosene lamp, his hands cramped and stiff from both forge work and writing. But eventually Tully got his first break in writing after befriending the Kent librarian Nellie Dingley. She encouraged his writing and also helped him get work as a reporter at the *Akron Press*. He did not take to the work, was fired, then got work at the rival *Beacon Journal*, only to be let go again after five weeks.

Prizefighter

Still in 1907, and shortly after his failure at journalism, Tully decided to take up professional boxing as a means to earn money. With a fake newspaper clipping of his "wins," he persuaded a boxing promoter to offer him a fight with Chicago Jack Tierney in Lima, Ohio. At 22, Tully was road-toughened. He knew he could take a punch and did not bleed easily. Disappointed that he did not win the fight, but praised for being the first person to go the distance with Tierney, Tully entered the Ohio boxing circuit as a professional featherweight. He recounts his first fight as a professional boxer in the chapter titled "A Change of Life" in *Blood on the Moon*. After two moderately successful years on the local boxing circuit, Tully's nerve was shaken after witnessing a boxer die in the ring. Then, after getting cut badly in a fight which was awarded to his opponent, even though he fought the same fighter to a draw in a rematch, Tully quit boxing and returned once more to the chain works in Kent.

This was not a happy time for Tully, not only because of the humiliation of having to ask for his old job back, but that his former workmates, having witnessed one of their own become a minor celebrity and local hero, now branded him as a coward for quitting the ring. But in December 1909 the factory burned down, putting four hundred employees out of work and prompting Tully to return to boxing once more. This time, instead of relying on his bulk and slogging it out as a bruiser, he decided to find a trainer and learn the finer arts of pugilism. But he soon aborted this plan and returned again to Kent, where, paradoxically, the former hobo found work washing down passenger cars at the railroad shops.

In 1910, Tully was introduced to tree surgery, a line of work he greatly enjoyed, not least because it took him to all parts of the county, he was out in the fresh air, and he had control over the workload which was often stretched out considerably longer than necessary. It was about this time also that Tully's thoughts turned again to romance. He had been pursued by a 17-year-old Kent high school girl, Florence Bushnell, but still nurtured strong feelings for the Kent librarian, Nellie Dingley—feelings that, in spite of their mutual love of books and writing, were not reciprocated. After proposing to, and being rejected by, Nellie Dingley, Tully started a romance with, and then married, Florence. He was 24, she 18. They rented an apartment above a wallpaper shop in Kent where Tully set to work on a rented typewriter in earnest. To make ends meet he continued picking up odd bits of work, including tree surgery and working the corner for boxers. But in the summer of 1911, Tully had his first poem published in the *Cleveland Plain Dealer*,[24] which was reprinted in several other papers including the *Chicago Daily News*. The *Kent Courier* published 11 more poems during the rest of that year.

Tully was at last the writer he had always wanted to be, but not yet able to support his family from writing alone. The birth of his son, Alton, put Tully under greater pressure to find paid work and he tried his hand again as a journalist for the two Akron newspapers who had employed him previously. Once more, he did not seem cut out for the work and ended up again in a chain factory, this time in Mansfield. In 1912 the family moved to California, where Tully worked again as a tree surgeon and also continued fighting for prize money. The same year Tully met Jack Dempsey in Salt Lake City. Dempsey was then an unknown kid who would challenge all comers in barroom brawls for money. Dempsey would later hold the World Heavyweight Championship from 1919 to 1926 but he and Tully remained close friends. Tully continued unprofessional prizefighting until an acquaintance, aware that Tully had been knocked unconscious for a night and half the next day, persuaded Tully to quit the ring for good. He returned to working as a tree surgeon by day and writing by night.

A Note on Tramp Rivalry

Around 1913/14 Tully met Jack London, two years before that writer's death. But rather than gain any inspiration from meeting one of the highest paid writers of the time, Tully was disillusioned both by the man and his tramping claims, which Tully concluded amounted to only eight months on the road. This is somewhat disingenuous as London was a sailor tramp from the age of 14 and did not return from his last tramp to the Klondike until the summer of 1898 at the age 22. Even allowing for some paid work and an aborted university education in between, London's time as a tramp equals that of Tully's. Claims that London's tramping memoirs were romanticized or fictionalized are not entirely fair either.[25]

In turn, Tully was himself criticized by other tramps, though this tramp rivalry does seem to have been in part fueled by the press. Al Kaufman (who had tramped with Tully) and Jeff Davis, already competing with each other for the title "King of the Hoboes," tried to minimize Tully's tramping credentials and even accused him of cashing in by publishing his memoirs. But these two vagabonds had their own business interests to protect; Kaufman claimed to have published two memoirs: *A Gentleman Hobo's Life* and *From 18 to 25*, although in researching this book no trace of this work has been discovered. Leon Ray Livingston had also claimed the title "King of the Hoboes" some years earlier. To be fair to Tully, and for that matter London and all of the other tramp writers featured in this book, bar Livingston, they were above such self-exaltation, being self-deprecating rather than boastful. True, many sought to publicize their writing, but that's a natural thing for a writer to do.

Writing and Hollywood

Throughout the next six years, Tully busied himself with his writing supported by various jobs including tree surgery and work as a government chain inspector. The most significant event during this time was the birth in 1917 of his daughter Trilby. But it was not until 1921 that Tully had his first real break in writing. He sent the first 5,000 words of his fledgling first novel *Emmett Lawler* to screenwriter, novelist and playwright Rupert Hughes—uncle of the tycoon recluse Howard Hughes, who had yet to make his own fame and fortune. The response was positive and Hughes provided Tully much-needed support and editorial advice. The book was completed in September 1921 and one month later was accepted by Harcourt, Brace & Company, whose list included Virginia Woolf, T.S. Eliot, and George Orwell.

Although not a runaway success, *Emmett Lawler* did help blaze the trail of subsequent more successful works, added to which, Rupert Hughes helped Tully get a job with the Samuel Goldwyn Production Company as a reader in the scenario department at $35 a week—only to be laid off a week later due to cutbacks. But as luck would have it, Tully had come to the attention of another benefactor, H.L. Mencken. Mencken was an influential literary critic and publisher, with a taste for cynical realism and a hatred of those revered established novelists who peddled sentimental idealism and the moralistic. The two would remain firm friends throughout the rest of their lives, but Tully was still not in a position to support himself by means of a literary career alone. He had discovered that a fast buck could be made writing short stories and features on movie stars, sports celebrities, and underworld figures for magazines. For the rest of his writing career Tully would receive a steady income from this less literary activity alongside his more serious published works. Tully was still struggling to support his family and after a 13-year marriage to Florence (living separately for the last two), the couple divorced, with Tully agreeing to pay $24 a week to support 12-year-old Alton and six-year-old Trilby.

Another break came in 1924 when a friend of Tully's, movie director and screenwriter Paul Bern, introduced Tully to Charlie Chaplin at a party. Chaplin was taken with Tully's tramping and writing achievements and drove him home from the party in his limousine. Bern and Hughes pulled some strings, and in February of 1924 Tully reported for work at Chaplin's Hollywood studio as the comedian's ghostwriter, composing articles that would go out in Chaplin's name, as well as being part of his inner court of cronies and hangers-on. Although the screen tramp and the real thing had a lot in common, both having clawed their way out of poverty and both sharing a cynical sense of humor, unlike most of Chaplin's sycophantic coterie, Tully always spoke his own mind, something that troubled his employer.

Tully's outspokenness included criticizing Chaplin for casting an inexperienced 16-year-old schoolgirl, Lillita McMurray (later Lita Grey), in the lead female role for *The Gold Rush*. Typically, Chaplin ignored Tully's advice, only to have to recast the role later with Georgia Hale when Lillita became pregnant with Chaplin's child. In order to avoid a charge of statutory rape, Chaplin was forced into a discreet shotgun wedding (Lillita's uncle was a lawyer) which took place in Mexico on November 24, 1924. Chaplin was 35. The marriage lasted less than three years but produced two sons, Charles Spencer and Sydney Earl Chaplin.

In spite of a certain friction between Tully and Chaplin, there was also mutual respect. At times Tully would be left alone in his office shack, free to write and dream, then he would get word that the boss wanted to see him and the two would spend time in Chaplin's office, his home, or a Hollywood restaurant. Tully's employment with Chaplin had coincided with production of *The Gold Rush*, on which Tully was in charge of publicity as well as some input into the script. Tully naturally delighted in the scene requiring six hundred vagabond extras to tramp through heavy snow in the movie scene of the Chilkoot Pass. No need for costumes or makeup, they were already attired for the part, complete with blanket rolls. The hobos, in turn, delighted in spending a day filming with the famous "little tramp." As Tully reported: "It was beggardom on holiday. ... They trudged through the heavy snows of the narrow pass as though gold were actually to be their reward, instead of a day's pay."[26]

In August of 1924, during work on *The Gold Rush*, Tully's second book *Beggars of Life* was published by Albert and Charles Boni, New York, who would publish a further four of Tully's books. Then in January of 1925, Tully married his second wife Marna, a 21-year-old society co-ed from the University of Southern California. He was now 38. Their difference in age and background mattered less than their shared passion for books and writing. *Beggars of Life* was received more enthusiastically than Tully's first book, followed by a stage production of the book in New York's Greenwich Village in September 1925. The part of Tully was played by the young James Cagney.

The popularity of *Beggars of Life* was assisted in part by Mencken, who heaped praise on the book. Mencken had founded the hard-hitting literary magazine *The American Mercury* the previous year. Tully suggested writing a piece for the *Mercury*, which Mencken enthusiastically took up. Being published by Mencken was the literary world's seal of approval for challenging, avant-garde writers such as William Faulkner and F. Scott Fitzgerald. Tully would regularly publish essays, biographies and short stories in the *Mercury* over the next eight years. At the same time, he also made a steady income from publishing non-literary sketches of Hollywood celebrities in the pulps and Hollywood gossip columns. This included a series of monthly profiles for *Vanity Fair* from March 1926 onwards, including profiles of Cecil B. DeMille, Mack Sennett, Greta Garbo, and John Gilbert, the latter resulting in a restaurant brawl in which Tully knocked Gilbert out cold. The publication of *Beggars of Life*, and Tully's insider knowledge of Hollywood and its luminaries, also resulted in his engagement in a series of lecture tours.

But it was a line from Tully's third book *Jarnegan*, a semi-autobiographical fiction about a Hollywood director named Jack Jarnegan, that would be the catalyst for his inevitable break-up with Chaplin. The manuscript was with the publisher in the summer of 1925, and a friend of Chaplin's who worked at the press reported to Chaplin that Tully had written something derogatory about him in his new book. Tully was given the choice of removing the offending line or losing his job. Naturally, Tully chose the latter. He was now approaching the peak of his own success, and so the break-up with Chaplin was timely; he was now free to lift the veneer off Hollywood and its celebrities with gloves off. No one was safe from Tully's ridicule, and according to Brauer and Dawidziak, Tully developed a "reputation as the most feared and hated man in Hollywood."

A Further Note on Tully's Writing Style—the "sentimental cynic"

By now, Tully had fully developed the role of a true Diogenean Cynic. It was not only in his writing that Tully attacked the vain and inglorious, but face to face at Hollywood parties, "puncturing inflated egos with a needle that could take the air out of the room."[27] Tully assumed the right to say whatever he wanted, in whatever way he wanted, and to hell with people's sensibilities. Yet in spite of being a master at the art of ridicule, Tully also had his friends and admirers; those celebrities who did not puff themselves up had nothing to fear from Tully's pen, and many complimented him on the manner in which he had portrayed them. This process of ridicule has been described by Sloterdijk as Diogenes' "truth test": ridiculing the claims of phonies to see just how much joking they can take, for whoever cannot stand satire directed against them must be false. As Sloterdijk further claims, not only can truth stand mockery, but it is "freshened by any ironic gesture directed at it."[28] A similar characteristic was described by Christopher Stone in 1914 in his book *Parody*:

> ...ridicule is society's most effective means of curing inelasticity. It explodes the pompous, corrects the well-meaning eccentric, cools the fanatical, and prevents the incompetent from achieving success. Truth will prevail over it, falsehood will cower under it.[29]

Such is the raison d'être of Tully's writing, although this would not necessarily have been a conscious characteristic of the man because true cynics are born, not made. He could not have written authentically in any other style, and he certainly did not write to preach to others, as he confirms in *Beggars of Life*: "Neither am I interested in sociology among tramps ... I am no reformer, but a weary writer who has been living in the memory of adventure."[30] And from his introduction to *Blood on the Moon*: "I did not study the people in this book as an entomologist does a bug on a pin. I was one of them. I'm still of them. I can taste the bitterness of their lives in the bread I eat today."[31]

Tully's writing simply reflects the writer's attitude to life and his own truth about those he encountered along the way, with no further agenda than to produce a good yarn and achieve prolific book sales—it is not expected that modern cynics should live out their entire lives in a barrel as did Diogenes, and certainly not in the harsh winters of the northern states of America. There is also evidence that Tully identified himself as a cynic philosopher. If, as Bauer and Dawidziak suggest, Tully modeled *Jarnegan* partly on himself, the following lines from that book give some insight into Tully's own personal philosophy:

> A man of no isms, he was tolerant of everything that did not touch his life. He knew nothing of nations or their rulers. He had never voted. Neither had he any theories about life. A cynical realist, he fought against the sentimentality that was his Irish inheritance. At times, in his cups, he ended by being that most ironical of humans—a sentimental cynic.[32]

There is no contradiction in being a sentimental cynic. The acerbic and forthright nature of cynicism is often interpreted as rudeness, and therefore misinterpreted as negative and sneering, even nihilistic. This is to misunderstand the cynic. To be positive, idealistic, even sentimental, especially when in one's cups, reveals the true soul of the cynic, who simply mourns the fact that human beings have made a mess of the world they inhabit and act so foully toward one another. As the cynic Raymond Federman wrote in his sci-fi parody *Twofold Vibration*, "true cynics are often the kindest people, for they see the hollowness of life, and from the realization of that hollowness is generated a kind of cosmic pity."[33] Note the parallel here between Federman's description of a cynic above, and a friend and fellow writer's description of Tully: "His loneliness is a burden he can't shake off. With a fire roaring through a brain mixed up with the futility of all things human and divine, he is at heart an artist frustrated and contemptuous."[34]

Further Success, and Failures

In 1926, as well as publishing *Jarnegan*, Tully wrote a three-act boxing play, *Black Boy*, starring Paul Robeson in the title role. Coincidentally, the other Irish tramp writer, Jim Phelan, subject of the following chapter, was a close friend of Robeson's—which begs the question of whether Robeson ever discussed one tramp with the other.

A less happy event than the premiere of *Black Boy* in October 1926, was the death of Tully's sister Virginia at the age of 49 from an unnamed illness. Yet Virginia had seen her dream realized that her brother would become a famous writer. The same year, Tully was preparing a four-part series titled "Charlie Chaplin: His Real Life Story" for the *Pictorial Review*, to be followed later by a book on Chaplin. In spite of Tully's reassurances to Chaplin that the biography would be written with sympathy and understanding, so terrified was Chaplin of what Tully might write that he took out a $500,000 lawsuit against the *Pictorial Review*, on the basis that his right to privacy had been infringed. Chaplin lost the case and the series was published, but the following year, when Tully tried to publish his book *Life of Charlie Chaplin*, the publishers ran scared of Chaplin's legal team. The book was killed and never published.

Tully had similar misfortunes with other projects. The film version of *Circus Parade* was shelved following fierce lobbying from the Circus Fans Association who felt that the film portrayed a negative image of circus life. But Tully had at last achieved the success he had dreamed of as a writer. 1928 saw the premiere of the movie version of *Beggars of Life*, the stage version of *Jarnegan*, and publication of his fifth book, *Shanty Irish*.

But those with tramping in their blood do not always flourish from material success. Celebrity did not fulfill all Tully had imagined it would. He was suffering episodes of depression and his second marriage was showing signs of strain. What one can say of Tully, though, is that neither money nor literary achievements went to his head. He never forsook his vagabond legacy, and later spent time in San Quentin and other prisons interviewing prisoners and encouraging them to write or tell their own stories.

Shadows of Men, published in 1930, is a biographical and semi-autobiographical work based mainly around the stories of those Tully encountered in prison and on the road. It is graphic realism at its most powerful, including descriptions of junkies shooting up and their crazed hallucinatory dreams that seem more familiar to later generations of readers than consumers of early 20th-century literature. As with Jack London's books, the bleak territory inhabited by Tully's writing was far more popular in Russia (where *Beggars of Life* and *Shadows of Men* were on the bestseller lists and, according to Tully, sold two million copies) than in America, even though no royalties could be received from the former. In 1930, also, *Beggars Abroad* was published, Tully's travelogue of the trip he made to Europe the previous year with Marna, partly in an attempt to patch up his ailing marriage. The trip included interviews with George Bernard Shaw, H.G. Wells and James Joyce.

Final Words

There is only scope here to provide a brief summary of Tully's later life. Those who wish to know more about this uniquely fascinating character should acquire a copy of Bauer and Dawidziak's excellent biography which, as well as carefully portraying all known aspects of Tully's life in detail, includes separate chapters concerning each of Tully's 13 published books.

Tully would go on to write a further six books and, in 1933, married his third wife, Myrtle Zwetow, secretary of his friend and MGM movie producer Al Lewin. Following the peak of his writing success at the end of the Roaring '20s, Tully's fortunes gradually declined, as did his health, although Myrtle would stay with him until his death. Tully's son, Alton, had been a constant drain on both Tully's finances and his emotional health. Alton was a serial rapist, and after several expensive court appearances financed by his father, following a rape in 1934 Alton was sentenced to one to 25 years at San Quentin. Even on this occasion he was eventually acquitted, but following a further rape the following year, Alton was finally imprisoned in San Quentin on a one-to-50-year sentence.

Devastating as the effects of his son's troubled life were on Tully, he remained surrounded by supportive friends, enjoyed the devotion of Myrtle, and to a lesser degree his daughter Trilby. In the last year of his life, Tully ended up in the same nursing home as another friend, former business partner and sometime neighbor W.C. Fields. After Fields passed away on Christmas Day of 1946, Tully was allowed to return home where he was cared for by Myrtle. He remained at home until he was admitted to the Cedars of Lebanon Hospital following heart failure, where he died on June 22, 1947.

Alton was released from prison before Tully entered the nursing home and, following a brief spell as a yeoman in the merchant navy, in 1946 married an army nurse named Margaret Becker. However, by 1949, two years following his father's death, Alton was again wanted for a rape and a 13-state alarm was put out for his arrest. Alton disappeared, but the following April, his and his wife's decomposed bodies were found in their car with the windows sealed and a hose running from the exhaust. From evidence shortly after Alton's disappearance, and later reported by the *Los Angeles Times*, the joint suicide was Alton's wife's proposal: "If I find him, I'll try a suicide pact. He hasn't the guts to do it by himself—he's not fit to live in this world."[35] At least Tully was spared this final drama by Alton.

Myrtle was aged 52 when Tully died, and although she was left Tully's entire estate, now diminished to $25,000, a lawsuit filed by Tully's daughter Trilby resulted in half that money being paid over to Trilby. Myrtle was forced to go back to work as a personal secretary until she was 67: five years for Judy Garland, three years for Greer Garson, and the last five years for Deborah Kerr. Myrtle moved to the Motion Picture & Television Country House and Hospital in 1975. She died on August 31, 1982.

It is thanks to Myrtle's efforts in finding a safe resting place for Tully's papers and unpublished works, and thanks to the authors of *Jim Tully: American Writer, Irish Rover, Hollywood Brawler* for discovering and researching them, that we know more about Jim Tully than many other tramp writers of the period. Nevertheless, as with many of these other literary vagabonds, Tully's writing remains relatively unknown today, even though his writing style was ahead of its time.

But the final word should be left for Tully himself. Other vagabond writers in this book have given their own view of the necessary ingredients that make for a successful tramp. In the following passage from *Beggars of Life*, Tully turns on its head the popular interpretation of a bum as someone who is lazy. Tully's bum is perceptive, enterprising, and indefatigable:

A clever young tramp, if he has that indefinable something called personality, can always beg money on the street with success. He must have a knowledge of human nature, however, and be able to distinguish one class of citizen from another. In the argot of the road a "good" bum is one who is always successful as a beggar. All in all, though, the most resourceful and energetic tramp gets the most food and money.[36]

ENDNOTES

1 Sloterdijk, Peter. *Critique of Cynical Reason*, London: Verso, 1988, p. 151

2 Ibid., p. 218

3 For responses to Tully's books at the time of their publication, one should read the numerous book reviews he attracted, and which are reproduced in Bauer and Dawidziak's biography. They make fascinating reading and provide much insight into the cultural and literary nuances of the period.

4 Tully, Jim. *Blood on the Moon*, New York: Coward-McCann, 1931, p. 11

5 Although one was American and the other European, there were many other parallels between Tully and Phelan. In addition to writing, tramping and fighting, both had poor Irish ancestry, both spent their early lives in steelworks, both wrote about crime and punishment, both were involved with screenplays, both had friendships with H.G. Wells and Paul Robeson (on different sides of the Atlantic), and both had three wives, one son, and one daughter—at least that they knew about.

6 Tully, Jim. *Shanty Irish*, New York: Albert & Charles Boni, 1928, p. 102

7 Tully, Jim. *Beggars of Life*, New York: A. & C. Boni, 1924, p. 15

8 Ibid., p. 19

9 Ibid., p. 41

10 Ibid., p. 50

11 Ibid., pp. 125–126

12 Ibid., p. 141

13 Ibid., pp. 152–153

14 Ibid., pp. 165–166

15 Ibid., pp.191–193

16 Ibid., pp. 197–200

17 Ibid., pp. 229–230

18 Ibid., p. 235

19 Ibid., p. 245

20 Ibid., pp. 271–272

21 Tully, Jim. *Circus Parade*, New York: Garden City Publishing Co., 1927, p. 122

22 *Beggars of Life*, op. cit., pp. 326–327

23 *Blood on the Moon*, op. cit., pp. 227–229

24 Coincidentally, Tully's biographer, Mark Dawidziak, is television critic for the *Cleveland Plain Dealer* today, in addition to his roles as a university professor, novelist and playwright.

25 See independent accounts of London's hobo credentials in the chapter on Leon Ray Livingston.

26 Robinson, David, cited in Paul Bauer and Mark Dawidziak, *Jim Tully: American Writer, Irish Rover and Hollywood Brawler*, Kent State University Press, 2011, p. 146

27 Parker, Ralph, cited in Ibid., p. 170

28 Sloterdijk, op. cit., p. 288

29 Stone, Christopher. *Parody*, London: M. Secker, 1914, p. 8

30 *Beggars of Life*, op. cit., p. 355

31 *Blood on the Moon*, op. cit., p. 12

32 Tully, Jim. *Jarnegan*, New York: Albert & Charles Boni, 1927, p. 131

33 Federman, Raymond. *The Twofold Vibration*, Los Angeles: Green Integer, 2000, p. 126

34 Scully, Frank, cited in Paul Bauer and Mark Dawidziak, op. cit., p. 270

35 "Author Jim Tully's Son Joins Wife," *Los Angeles Times*, April 20, 1950

36 *Beggars of Life*, op. cit., p. 334

Jim Phelan

(1895–1966)

... the central fact about vagabondage, which city people do not know as a rule. (How could they know? Their knowledge comes from books written by city men.) At one time nearly all the world was nomadic; the people who lived in houses were the few and the strange, the folks who were different.

Jim Phelan, *Tramping the Toby*

Preamble

Dublin-born tramp and writer James Leo (Jim) Phelan published the 25 books listed below and collaborated on others. He also wrote poetry, song lyrics, plays, film scores and narrated TV documentaries. His books include fiction, autobiographical works, travelogues, political essays, and memoirs on prison life, the Romani people and tramping. Phelan's original studies of prison life are second to none, but as this book is not principally concerned with penology, it is Phelan's tramping and writing that are the focus here.

Museum: A Novel (1937)
Lifer (1938)
Ten-a-Penny People (1938)
Green Volcano (1938)
Meet the Criminal Class (1938)
In the Can (1939)
Jail Journal (1940)
Churchill Can Unite Ireland (1940)
Murder by Numbers (1941)
Ireland—Atlantic Gateway (1941)
Letters from the Big House (1943)
And Blackthorns (1944)
Banshee Harvest: A Novel (1945)
Moon in the River (1946)
Turf Fire Tales (1947)
The Name's Phelan (1948)
Bog Blossom Stories (1948)
We Follow the Roads (1949)
Vagabond Cavalry (1951)
Wagon-wheels (1951)
Tramp at Anchor (1954)
Tramping the Toby[1] (1955)
Criminals in Real Life (1956)
Fetters for Twenty (1957)
The Underworld (1967)
Nine Murderers and Me (1967)

No other modern philosopher better demonstrates the premise that true cynics are born, not made, than Phelan. The use here of the term philosopher does not refer to the popular notion of a university-educated boffin who gives formal lectures and publishes treatises on the meaning of life; rather, it refers to those rare thinkers, like Diogenes of Sinope and Jesus of Nazareth (man or myth depending on one's preference), who not only preached their philosophy but lived it. Of course, if the fancy had taken him, Phelan could just as easily have become the university professor type of philosopher. An infant prodigy, he was already at school by the age of 21 months (with a photo and school certificate to prove it), reading better than most adults by the age of three, and in Sixth Form by the age of 10. Phelan was then stuck in the Sixth because the law did not enable him to progress further; he learned Latin and consumed classical works by the ancient Greeks, Shakespeare, Irish, English and French poetry, plus anything else he could get his hands on from magnetism to practical welding. We also know that during his lifetime, Phelan read the works of other tramp writers, noting that: "Until Jack London and Bart Kennedy, W.H. Davies, Jim Tully, and the rest set up real vagrant-literature against the other effusions ... only spurious writings on vagabondage were considered acceptable."[2] Phelan has now joined those other writers in providing a rich legacy of vagabond literature and philosophy to entertain and enlighten future generations.

Early Years

Much to the disappointment of his parents and his school headmaster, Phelan did not want to achieve the "genius" status that others had predicted of him. He already had the vagabond instinct at the age of four: "in that year and at that age I left home, deliberately and, so far as I was concerned, finally. That it was no infant stray-away I have been proving, in spite of myself, from that day to this."[3]

Born in Woodfield Cottages, Inchicore, now a suburb of Dublin, both Phelan's parents were storytellers from what Phelan describes as a peasant background. But they told stories of a very different kind. His father had a revolutionary background and had served time in prison, as had Phelan's grandfather and great-grandfather also. Phelan's father's stories (of which he sold a few) were of his adventures in far-flung places such as Sierra Leone, Guatemala and North America—a "vagrant at heart" now curbed by the responsibilities of family life. In contrast to his father's tales of travel and adventure, Phelan's mother's stories were more of the folk-tale variety, "timeless and place vague ... she did not believe in fiction, did not know of its existence ... there were no stories except true stories."[4] Phelan's mother Catherine had no understanding of the wandering urges of her husband and son: "Existence, as far as she was concerned, was an opportunity to work, save money, rear a family, love them and give them a chance in life, then die and go to heaven."[5]

And so at the age of four, fueled by the images of stories from both his mother and father, and drawn by the sights and sounds of Dublin and the countryside beyond, Phelan embarked on his first tramping adventure. He had planned for three days, with the penny his mother gave him for sweets on his way to school, to follow the railway line to Tipperary, a distance of over a hundred miles. Phelan knew that in Tipperary there lived a man named Jim Maher, "a kind of god or giant who had visited us once or twice"; Maher was actually Phelan's cousin. After proceeding through the village of Chapelizod, two miles from his home, he met an old, bearded man with a stick, "a tramp, I imagine," and walked alongside the man for some distance telling him stories about his home. But on the man questioning him further, Phelan let go of his hand and walked away. A woman at a farm gave him a drink of milk and urged him to hurry home, but Phelan lingered, playing with two kittens until a policeman arrived. Phelan spun the officer a yarn about having come from Tipperary—"that was the story I told him, in a lisping, sweetly-innocent singsong." After getting in touch with the district in Tipperary, described accurately by the young runaway, and discovering that there were several Jim Phelans living in the region, Phelan was put on a train with some cakes and milk to sustain him on his journey until wakened from a long sleep and handed over to another policeman in Tipperary. But this officer was not so easily fooled as the other: "That's no Tipp'rary chiseller." But Phelan maintained the pretense: "I stuck to my fibbing-voice story." Eventually, Phelan was driven to the location he had described and "exhibited to the several sections of the Phelan family." A woman who Phelan had never met before declared, "'Glory be to God—that's Jamesey Phelan's boy from Inchicore. And how did he get here?' The only bright spot, I remember, was that she blamed it all on the unfortunate policeman!" For his trouble, Phelan received "a terrific beating" on being returned home the next day, deciding him to leave home again at the earliest opportunity.[6]

But it would be over three years before Phelan ran away again, "Not because of the beating, but because I did not want to go." Phelan describes that, when in danger or difficulty, it is the tramp's natural impulse to "turn around and head for the horizon." And so at the age of seven, anticipating a beating for knocking his sister helpless with a clothes-brush and some trouble over missing apples, Phelan grabbed a bottle of milk and part of a loaf of bread and headed off to the canal basin. There he hid himself under a tarpaulin covering a barge, where he stayed until discovered by the barge-men the following day. He was handed over to a kindly priest who, after offering him food and a bed for the night, sent Phelan home by train with a letter to his parents. After another severe beating from his mother (he later acknowledges that there were only two such beatings, and had only praise and respect for both his parents) he was taken to a school run by the Christian Brothers. It was here that Phelan's full potential as a child prodigy was discovered and he received the aforementioned education.

First Job and First Tramp at Sea

Yet by the age of 13, Phelan had done with schooling and started working in the only job then open to 13-year-olds, that of a telegraph boy. At first, his headmaster Brother Redmond refused to provide the necessary reference, pleading with him and even offering to pay Phelan the equivalent of his wages for him to continue his studies:

> James Phelan, the greatest intellect it has been my privilege to train, in forty years of training famous men ... carrying wretched telegrams to grubby bookmakers and filthy people in sordid shops. Rubbish. Goodbye. Tell your mother to come and see me.[7]

But Phelan stuck to his resolve and dared the good Christian soul to lie to his potential employer when he told them that he was Brother Redmond's best pupil and ask them to write to him to confirm it: "That was the end of the attempts to make me a scholar; the end of Brother Redmond's mounting hopes." Phelan's job as a telegraph boy lasted about six months, not because he did not enjoy the work. He was dismissed for refusing to deliver a certain telegram and, in the aftermath, found himself on board a coal boat commiserating his plight to the crew with whom he had become friendly in his former occupation. The boat put to sea, without the crew realizing that Phelan was still on board, and by the time they did were already committed for their destination, Glasgow. A discussion took place as to how they would return the 13-year-old vagabond to Dublin, and in the end the crew had a whip-round to collect enough money for Phelan to return home aboard a passenger steamer. Phelan had no intention of returning home but took the money nonetheless. "To me Glasgow looked, smelt, and sounded like a dream-town. Now this was a real foreign city at last. I could not understand one word of the speech. Heaven!"[8]

Glasgow and Dublin Slum-Dog

Fortified with the severance wages from his job plus the fare money from the crew, Phelan set about wandering the streets of Glasgow, finally ending up in the Gallowgate district of that city. Phelan soon teamed up with some local slum boys where he "learnt to speak Scotch" and also the art of begging. His money, together with what he begged, lasted a month, requiring only four pence a night for lodging plus a penny for a breakfast of tea and bread. But just as Phelan was getting bored with the company he was keeping, he happened upon the crew of another boat out of Dublin who recognized him and offered him passage home.

This time on returning to his parents, there was no beating, no return to school, and no one mentioned work. Relieved that the prodigal son had returned alive, Phelan was free to become a Dublin slum-boy with, when he cursed loudly, a Glasgow accent. No longer did he think of books, "nor any nonsense about being a genius, I was a ragamuffin boy at last, and life was very good." The summer of 1909 was spent swimming, climbing trees, catching and selling pigeons, and going out into the country to collect mushrooms and blackberries. "For the rest of our time we fought and scrambled and I ran yelling through the streets. No one ever stole anything, I remember, nor did we smoke, and we never tried to 'line' girls, so that we were, in fact, fairly harmless. Just slum boys, in a slum."[9]

There then follows an interesting analysis from Phelan of the language of the slums, and that in spite of his declaration that he had no interest in books at this time; Phelan was always the scholar. He was fascinated by the words used in the slums, their origins and their meanings. The language never came naturally to him, acknowledging this was probably due to the fact that "the gulf between my father's pedantic English and what was later to be called 'Joycean prose' was too great." But whether or not Phelan was comfortable using it, he maintains, "I knew the language, though, as well as Dogger Dale and better than the author of *Ulysses*." And so part of Phelan's success as an author, consummate storyteller aside, clearly stems from his fascination with language:

> Nibbling in the dictionaries, for some clue to the words we used daily, I found that many of my companion's words were Gaelic equivalents of what one may, for politeness, call the strong "Anglo-Saxon monosyllables." But my companions did not know that. Nor did their parents. Hardly any adults, even in Dublin knew. I found out. Once again I knew something no one else knew!
>
> Joyce found out too. My belief is that he never discovered much besides, about those words, never got beyond the secretive-exultant stage.
>
> I can write the word "flah" here without offence. To print the English translation-word [fuck] would be illegal. Flah, flah, flah. ... my barefoot-running, my knowledge of the facts as well as the words of slumdom, saved me. Besides, I had had my magic words, in full measure, and the maximum thrill from them ... Of course I had—bloody hell, bloody hell, bloody hell![10]

The flip side of Phelan's use of slang was, in fact, his "ejjification." He became a hero amongst his companions following an incident when a policeman apprehended them raiding a strawberry patch. The slum boy switched to a polite educated apology, throwing in the Latin phrase "in flagrante delicto," twice for good measure. The same strategy used by a hobo in the American Midwest would probably have earned him a beating, but, as Phelan calculated: "An Irish policeman, in my reckoning, would know the phrase, [and] be proud of his Latin." And he was not disappointed. As he and the officer fell into conversation, with Phelan all the while flattering the policeman's conceit, the officer forgot the reason he had detained Phelan and his friends in the first place. As they walked along the canal toward Dublin, the policeman quoted a long poem to Phelan as his friends trailed warily behind, not a little impressed at their friend's learning and audacity.

Second Job and Fourth Tramp

Phelan's father must have eventually decided that his son had been a slum boy for long enough, and arranged for him to commence work in the steel foundry where he worked. Again Phelan actually enjoyed the work but, after a couple of months, fell afoul of a particularly bad-tempered foreman and was sent home. Rather than face the wrath of his father again, he jumped aboard a passing ballast train only to alight some 20 miles outside Dublin, again on the canal familiar to him from his previous adventure. Although still only 14½, due to his build and appearance, Phelan claims that he was easily mistaken for an adult of 18 to 20. This had both advantages and disadvantages. Phelan was already carrying a notebook and recording his adventures, as well as writing songs and poetry, which explains how he found later recalling details of his adventures in his autobiographies a relatively easy task. On his first night, Phelan slept alongside a hedge in a field, and after washing and drinking from the canal the following morning, set off once more. But by evening he was tired and ravenous, forcing himself to beg food. "It never once occurred to me that I might seek work as a way to avoid the ignominy of begging." But work he did, first collecting sheaves on a farm and on the second occasion finding casual work with a circus troupe—even though he got cheated of his money with the latter and beaten into the bargain. After getting as far as Limerick, and having recovered from his injuries, Phelan spotted a goods train in Limerick Junction bound for Inchicore, and, five weeks after he had left, returned home once again. It would be a further four, relatively happy, years before Phelan left home again.

Art School and Girls

Phelan's next choice of occupation seems a pragmatic one; not that he entered art school, but that he should choose the "Art Metal-work class" in which to enroll. This allowed him to engage in classical drawing lessons in the main art department, as well as consolidating his former skills as a blacksmith in the workshop with copper and steel. It was here that Phelan first came across snobbery and regretted abandoning his earlier education for a life in the slums. Phelan had always felt alienated from his companions, but his early attempts at courting girls reinforced that he was different from most people—working-class girls considered him too highbrow and the middle-class students at art school too rough around the edges. Though being more than interested in carnal pleasure, and he had been from a young age, these amorous encounters Phelan considered "sordid and embarrassing."

But, as is often the case, just at the point that Phelan had reconciled himself to a life of celibacy, an incident occurred that relieved his derangement. Tortured by dark thoughts and a toothache, and unable to sleep, Phelan went out for one of his nighttime excursions only to be accosted by a girl who, this time, was more than a match for his extreme awkwardness. After several attempts to resist her—considerations of hell and damnation from a strict Irish Catholic upbringing being the least cause of his aversion—Phelan recalls: "suddenly, as I tensed and worried and strained, with fear and revulsion and horror tearing at me, she put her arm round my neck and drew me closer."[11]

The inevitable accomplishment that followed had a powerful liberating effect on the confirmed vagrant: "I walked on air going home. I was not wrong and different at all; I was Jim Phelan, and I was a man." Unfortunately, his moment of triumph was marred by a nosy neighbor returning home late. They had followed Phelan and the girl to the lodging-house-*cum*-brothel and immediately reported events to his parents. "If I had been infected with leprosy and tuberculosis, had my arms and legs amputated, and was then carried off to a prison for lifelong torture, that would have been trivial in their eyes, compared to the story they had heard."[12]

On this occasion, although banished from home once more, and finding himself walking penniless 10 miles outside Dublin, a calmness, even happiness, and pity rather than anger toward his parents, had settled on Phelan: "there would be no more need for deception or pretense ... since I was three or four, I had had too much of both. ... For the first time I was not hurrying away from pain or fear."[13]

Adult Vagabond

Fifth Tramp and Taste of Hoboism

Phelan resolved that a week "would suffice to blunt the edge of my parents' grief," after which period they would be glad to welcome him home, and he in turn would fall in with their wishes and dreams and become a model citizen. But it would be a further 11 weeks and a transatlantic crossing before Phelan returned again to his parents' home.

Kilkenny gave way to Tipperary, and the 18-year-old tramp eventually arrived in Cork with three pence in his pocket. Enjoying the sights and sounds of that port city, Phelan formed an instant friendship with an American ship's engineer who, after getting drunk together, invited him to spend the night aboard the tanker *Narragansett*. Phelan was invited to work his passage and in two weeks had arrived in Galveston, Texas, from where he tramped to New Orleans, hobo-style. And there he stayed, finding life easy and people generous and friendly. "Everyone concerned knew I was a drifter ... but nobody minded much. A large tolerance in everything is the mark of New Orleans." Who knows what turn Phelan's life might have taken next, but, such as is the capricious nature of vagabondage, a ship's fireman from Lancashire persuaded Phelan to work his passage shoveling coal on a ship bound for Glasgow. Now armed with a seaman's union card for which he had paid $5, and after a brief visit to his former Glasgow haunts, Phelan had no trouble picking up a Dublin-bound ship, arriving at the port in the middle of the infamous Dublin strike of 1913. Thanks to his previous knowledge of crane-men, coal-heavers, and dockers, Phelan persuaded the strikers that he was only an illegal passenger and was allowed to disembark. "An hour later my mother was crying quietly but happily, saying nothing, and my father spoke in distantly friendly fashion of everyday trifles, before he left for work. ... there was a stirring of happiness in the thought that nothing whatever had changed except for the better."[14]

The events described above leading to Phelan's American adventure are as recorded in *The Name's Phelan*. In *Tramp at Anchor*, Phelan says that his departure to America was prompted by the threat of a "shotgun wedding" following the pregnancy of a woman his own age.

Further Troubles and Tramp Number Six

In *The Name's Phelan*, there then follows a fascinating social and political account of the Dublin labor troubles of 1913. Our hero, now an 18-year-old apprentice engineer earning seven shillings a week and living with his parents, traveled frequently between the iron works in Inchicore and the art school in Dublin (as part of his apprentice training). He deliberately took the route of the worst conflicts to participate in the street fights and battles that ensued. On one occasion Phelan came close to being expelled from art school after an iron bar, which he carried for protection in his sleeve, dropped noisily on the college floor, giving the appearance he had stolen the metal from the college workshop. Phelan had no desire to be expelled, particularly as he had at that time ardent intentions toward one of the female students, even though at the same time spending time with another girl from Inchicore.

What happened next is a bit vague, but from a cryptic discussion concerning the consequences of further unintended pregnancies, it seems that Phelan either had, or believed he had, been responsible for both women becoming expectant mothers: "even one christening-marriage or shotgun wedding would have nauseated me. With two on my hands—I drifted towards the main south road." Once again Phelan was to implement his strategy: when in difficulty head for the horizon. He goes on to describe how, although initially prompted by his "difficulties," after a few hours of padding, an involuntary existential calmness takes control of the tramp's psyche, altering his concept of time and place:

> Perhaps a Buddhist monk, or a Lama, might be able to explain. Every tramp I have questioned says it is just that a fellow goes quiet and blank, looking at the road and liking the sound of his footfalls, and then he's in the next town, without noticing. ... There has to be peace inside, a freedom from worry and strain which, for professional purposes, the tramp has to pretend he knows. Then contemplation, not of one's navel but of the tiny surrounding patch of road surface.[15]

This meditative quality brought on by tramping might go some way to explaining the addictive effects of wanderlust, even if, as in this case, there are sticks as well as carrots involved. On this occasion, after several adventures, including a farmer offering him two days' work milking cows, Phelan's tramp was interrupted by a group of traveling actors whose company he joined for three weeks as a baggage-man and bit-part player, only leaving the troupe on account of a drunken argument.

After tramping south to Waterford, Phelan persuaded the secretary in a shipping company to get him work on a ship, and two days later he arrived in Le Havre harbor in France. With no papers, little French, and in the full knowledge that "The professional tramp ... does not exist in France ... Hitch-hiking ... came about equal to rape in the French consciousness of that day,"[16] Phelan threw fate to the wind and headed south, eventually reaching Toulon on the Mediterranean, courtesy of a kind-natured lorry driver. The French adventure takes up a couple of chapters in *The Name's Phelan*, but for brevity's sake we pick up the tale where a crew member from an English ship in Marseilles allows Phelan berth to London in exchange for most of his remaining money.

As in his description of the Soho area of London from *Tramping the Toby* (discussed further below), Phelan was as captivated on his first visit to the city as he was on subsequent forays there as a writer. But it was also on this first visit, still aged only 18, that by sheer coincidence Phelan bumped into someone who would later become an important literary acquaintance. Outside a London bookshop, Phelan noticed a stout, middle-aged man watching and smiling at him. They started talking and within minutes Phelan had sketched out his life story, "except the two shot-gun weddings." After listening to Phelan's tramping exploits, the man asked him if he had ever read Jack London, then proceeded to give him a list of London's books on hearing he had not. They met again several times subsequently and below is a note Phelan received from his acquaintance after he published his first book, *Museum: a novel*, "perhaps the nicest line ever penned from an old writer to a young one": "DEAR JIM PHELAN, *I have just finished your novel Museum. If ever anyone else attempts to write a novel on the same subject, I shall re-read yours.* Cordially, H.G. Wells"

Not long after this encounter, Phelan was tramping up what would become the main thoroughfare of his adventures in *Tramping the Toby*, Watling Street, the route northwest from London via the Midlands to either Holyhead in north Wales or Liverpool, and Ireland beyond. And it was here that Phelan made close acquaintances for the first time with other tramps. On his first day out of London, Phelan learned about "parson-thumping" (begging at the doors of clergymen) and all manner of other tramp etiquette, ending that night sleeping at a "paddincan" (tramp hostel) in St. Albans. At breakfast the following morning, the familiar English tramp conference took place about who was taking which roads and in what order:

> Up the road I met and spoke to many tramps (they averaged one per five miles or thereabouts), but kept away from anything like companionship. The second night up from St. Albans I stayed at Towcester, having covered more than forty miles in two days. ... All the way up Watling Street I enjoyed myself. I had one lift from Weedon to Cannock in a big furniture-lorry, and one from Stoke-on-Trent almost to Warrington with a cattle-wagon, shortening my journey by more than a week. For the rest I walked, fadged, parson-thumped, and stayed at tramps' doss-houses.[17]

From Warrington, Phelan made his way to Liverpool, where he set about looking for a ship to take him to Dublin. As luck would have it, he spotted a crew member he knew on a Dublin-bound vessel who arranged free passage for Phelan. He had known Archie Anderson for several years through the Dublin riots and membership of the Irish Citizen Army.[18] As well as a sailor on the Liverpool run, Phelan would soon discover that Anderson was also a gun-runner for the Republican cause. On arrival in Dublin carrying five revolvers as the price of his ticket, Phelan cleaned himself up so that he could present himself to his family as an apprentice rather than a gun-runner or tramp. He also had unfinished business to attend to concerning the two women he had left behind. "I need not have bothered. One of the girls had been married a few weeks earlier. The other ignored me. Just when I wanted to be ignored."[19]

Republican Apprentice

The outbreak of the 1914 War had relatively little effect on Ireland, and Phelan threw himself back into his studies, read for pleasure, and wrote an account of his travels. The latter he posted to the *Daily News*—who sent it back. By 19, Phelan was writing poetry, songs, fiction, plays, essays, journals and travelogues, yet any literary success was still a long way off. By the age of 20, Phelan admits to having temporarily dismissed the idea of being a writer, or a blacksmith, but did continue with his apprenticeship, even though he used his time in the forge "illegally" making wedding presents for his friends such as sets of fire-irons, bronze ashtrays, and brooches.

By 1916 and the outbreak of the Easter Rising, the question of whether you were on the English or Irish side of the conflict tested friends and family alike; mistrust and secrecy crept into everyday life. Phelan was aware that his brother Willie and two sisters were members of the Irish Citizen Army (ICA), but was taken aback when his brother asked him what side of the conflict he was on. Phelan was, in fact, not only a member of the ICA but on its Secret Council, "was Willie's superior officer without his knowledge." Phelan had many Republican contacts during that time, including Archie Anderson who was still running guns between Liverpool and Dublin. But, although Phelan greatly admired many of the senior figures in the campaign, he did not closely identify with any of them. There were writers and intellectuals in the movement: "But many of these were before or after the time of which I write; most of the boys were unhewn granite, straight off the Dublin waterfront or out of its factories and foundries."

By now, Phelan's skills as a blacksmith were being put to good use in the repair and production of small arms—"Revolver springs were a speciality of mine." But settled though he might have been in the preceding three years, both as an apprentice and an activist, the fact that Phelan never fully identified with either now came to a head once more. With only months to go before his long apprenticeship would be completed and his future settled—"a fully-fledged craftsman, highly paid, able to support a home in comfort"—the wanderlust came upon Phelan for the seventh time. Perhaps panic at the idea that a settled life may soon be thrust upon him, at any rate, the catalyst for change again seems to have been another unwanted pregnancy: "My girl-friend wanted to get married. For the usual Dublin reasons."[20]

The Tramp Actor

Rathangan, some 40 miles out of Dublin, marked the beginning of a new episode in Phelan's tramping history, and the end of any possibility that Phelan would settle to a conventional life. Unlike the previous occasions that Phelan had headed for the horizon, this time he was dressed in a smart suit of clothes, had money in his pocket, and planned to earn more. At Portarlington in County Laois, Phelan caught up with the John Duffy Circus which he joined as a "lumper" (jack-of-all-trades): "Pay was good, food was excellent, conditions were thoroughly pleasant, and work was Titanic, unending."[21] But after 280 miles, and setting up and pulling down the big top 28 times, Phelan had to leave the circus after badly burning his hand on a paraffin lamp. After working for several weeks with a peasant farmer he had befriended, Phelan's next job was with another traveling theater, this time La Comédie Irlandaise. But after a fight with a jealous troupe member who (wrongly) accused Phelan of "poaching" his wife, Phelan had to quit that outfit also. Next it was the Roberto Leno Theatrical Company:

> Life in this particular company was a thoroughly jolly business for everybody. For me it was more than that. I swotted and read and enjoyed myself continually. I even wrote two plays! ... Often doing three-night stands, which meant double work but double pleasure for me, we drifted up and down Ireland until our big moment came. We were going to play the capital, do a repertory season at the Queen's in Dublin.[22]

After nearly a year away, Phelan's father had died. His mother "was uncertain whether, after all, an actor was not practically as good as a doctor or a judge, almost certainly better than a smith." But if she thought that Phelan was going to turn out a gentleman, some kind of genius after all, she was to be disappointed. At first Phelan was happy in his role, playing minor parts in the theater at night, and hanging out at the Citizen Army headquarters in Liberty Hall by day, but this clash of interests ended Phelan's acting career. A senior member of the Irish Citizen Army and Sinn Féin, Countess Markievicz,[23] known and greatly admired by Phelan, was being released from a British prison and a rally had been organized in her honor 15 minutes before the curtain was due to go up at the Queen's. Phelan made his choice and his acting career came to an abrupt end.

A Strange Choice of Occupation and First Marriage

There now follows a surreal episode of Phelan's vagabondage. First he tramped to Cork where he is followed and interrogated by the local Irish Republican Army (IRA) who were suspicious of his odd behavior: "What could I say? In the syllabus of Cork civic life there was no neat ruled space for such an entry as 'Drifting, unfocused, incipient writer.'"[24] After virtual house arrest under the watchful eye of senior IRA operatives in Cork, Phelan was eventually allowed to go on his way after the receipt of satisfactory character references from Dublin. Next comes a short spell in a boarding house in Dungarven, where Phelan learned to use a typewriter and produced two stories about slum life in Dublin. They were not even acknowledged by the agent. Next stop Waterford, where Phelan spotted an advertisement that blacksmiths were wanted to join the Tank Corps of the British Army. And so, bizarrely, given Phelan's role as an active Irish Republican, he made his way again to England, this time to a vast tank graveyard in the Dorset countryside, likely Bovington Camp south of the village of Tolpuddle (site of the celebrated 1834 trade union uprising of the same name). The camp was surrounded by a vast "heather-purple moor," the location of Thomas Hardy's fictional Egdon Heath. "In those days there were whole stretches where the heather could not be seen, because rows of fighter-tanks were lined up, side by side, thousands of them, thrown out on the Heath, unwanted and almost forgotten." Each tank had at least one removable quick-fire gun and loose rounds of ammunition were lying around for the taking. It was not lost on Phelan that "if the IRA had wanted tanks, a company of men could have driven away a machine each, across that heath, and in all probability no one would have noticed."[25]

Phelan does not describe the actual work he did with the tanks other than that he was a blacksmith. Although domiciled in the village of Wool, south of the tank cemetery, Phelan reports also being popular with the villagers of Bere Regis (Kingsbere in *Tess of the D'Urbervilles*), some six miles' distance away, remarking that he had slept at most of the two hundred houses in that village. Then suddenly in *The Name's Phelan*, not having mentioned Dora Mary O'Brien previously, on the occasion of a period of leave from the Army, Phelan announces a return to Dublin and marriage: "For some time Dora O'Brien and I had intended to marry 'when a chance came,' and we decided that this was a chance."[26] Phelan then goes back to Wool without Dora, eventually returning to Dublin having managed to secure his discharge four months early. But marriage did not curb Phelan's wanderlust, and Dora seems to have been remarkably tolerant of her vagabond husband: "When, after less than a month, I said I was going to Galway, she merely enquired if I should need one shirt or two."

In fact, Phelan headed for the town of Kinnegad, a kind of spiritual home for drifters, just as "a good Catholic turned to Rome, a good Moslem to Mecca." Although married, Phelan seems fully reconciled to a life of trampdom: "I knew what I wanted to be. I wanted to be nothing. I had never been anything and I never should be. … For nothing at all, anywhere, was I of any use." At 26, a confirmed vagabond Phelan might have been, but a sense of disappointment and regret is also discernible from his tone. As he later acknowledges, "Very well, then. What was the use of saying I wanted nothing? I wanted everything."[27] And Phelan certainly never gave up his ambitions to become a writer. His next port of call, a few weeks as a laborer helping to build the Vartry Reservoir at Roundwood near the Wicklow Mountains, provided the setting for what Phelan describes as some of his best stories. On his return to Dublin, Phelan again picks up with both married and political life. Of his marriage, although love and affection there clearly were, it was a partnership based on the mutual acceptance of two very different people. They hardly spoke of Phelan's wandering. "Each of us would have liked to be as the other, but neither could, and we did not niggle or nag."[28]

Of Phelan's political life, he had become captivated by the speeches and crusade of Liam O'Flaherty (cousin of Hollywood film director John Ford with whom Phelan would later work briefly), later one of Ireland's leading novelists. O'Flaherty was at the time engaged in raising a tramp movement along the lines of Kelly's Army, the protest march of unemployed on Washington, D.C., in 1894 described by London in Chapter 10. "O'Flaherty was a magnificent speaker ... This organising of a beggar's legion, comparable to the host of the beggar-syndicate described by Dumas in *Twenty Years After*, obviously appealed to him. It did to me too." There followed a trip with O'Flaherty and friends to Cork, but then Phelan's life takes another twist. Returning to Dublin, he met up again with the gun-runner Archie Anderson, sailed to Liverpool, and there he seems to have had a desire to make a new home and settle down. Phelan, now 28, took a job at an ironworks and sent for Dora to join him. Life in Liverpool was happy for a while. With a home and regular income, the couple settled into their new life.

On October 31, 1922, Dora gave birth to a daughter, Catherine Mary, and, as identified in Catherine's birth certificate, Phelan was at this time described as a dock laborer. Oddly, in spite of mentioning in *A Tramp at Anchor* that he had "raised me a son," nowhere in any of Phelan's autobiographical works does he mention his daughter Catherine. A possible explanation may have been the series of calamities that now befell the family.

Double Tragedy: sentenced to hang and Dora's death

The outbreak of the Irish Civil War in 1922 was to further alter the course of Phelan's life. Irish citizens in Liverpool were under constant surveillance and Phelan himself claims that at one time he was even wrongly identified as the operational commander of the IRA in Britain. Phelan maintained contact with former Republican acquaintances in Liverpool, and it was with one of these that he entered a post office in Hopwood Street, Liverpool on June 12, 1923, and was arrested a short time later. Both men were armed with revolvers, probably not unusual given their lifestyles, but Phelan denies that the incident that followed was part of any planned Republican mission. The following accounts come from various newspaper reports of the time.

After entering the post office, Phelan (giving the alias of Albert Finchley, a native of New Orleans) and John McAteer, the latter described as an Irish-American gunman with links to the IRA and American and Mexican underworld, entered the post office and demanded money from the postmistress' daughter. Instead of complying with his demands, she screamed out and her brother, 18-year-old Thomas Lovelady, came out from the kitchen at the back of the shop and confronted McAteer, whereby he was shot in the stomach by McAteer who then fled the scene. Phelan was then chased by a bystander named John Cunliffe, firing two shots that went wide but halted his pursuer. A separate report states that the pair "obtained their pistols and ammunition from members of the Communist Party in Liverpool." Lovelady died from his wounds in the hospital the same evening.[29]

Phelan's own account varies inasmuch as, although he does admit to participating in the hold-up, he claims not to have known the reason the pair went to the post office and, although he heard the shot immediately on entering the building, he was not aware of the shooting of Lovelady until the following day. He was arrested that night for firing a shot at his pursuer, not for the post office raid or the killing of the clerk. Phelan is also adamant that he fired only one shot at his pursuer, not two: "the police would know. Because only one shot had been fired from my pistol."[30] Had Phelan been a natural killer, he could easily have evaded capture, as had his accomplice. Although Phelan insisted to the police that he had no intention to harm anyone, a murder had been committed and justice demanded retribution. Both the police and the court[31] accepted that Phelan had not committed the murder but charged him anyway through the law of "joint enterprise," being associated with the actual killer. As Phelan himself identifies: "I had been present or in close proximity, had participated in the raid, was armed, was demonstrably willing to use firearms."[32]

Initially sentenced by Manchester Crown Court to hang on August 4, 1924,[33] on the eve of his execution Phelan's sentence was commuted by the Home Secretary to life imprisonment. That same year (about a year after Catherine's birth and Phelan's arrest) and aged only 27, Dora died after developing septicemia from a minor injury. The exact sequence of events is sketchy but can be deduced from a letter that Phelan's mother wrote to a member of the Irish Parliament in July 1926 seeking clemency for her son and referring to having to bring up Phelan's motherless child.[34] The letter also notes that the mother of the murdered man had herself pleaded clemency on Phelan's behalf, knowing him to be innocent of killing her son. Phelan had by this time been in prison for three years and his mother was caring for her granddaughter Catherine, but clearly struggling and concerned about what would happen to the child when she either died or was too infirm to any longer cope. After the death of Phelan's mother, Catherine was raised by her aunt, Phelan's sister Maggie Colgan.[35]

On Prison and Death

Phelan served a total of 13 years in Strangeways (Manchester), Winson Green (Birmingham), Wormwood Scrubs (London), Maidstone (Kent), Dartmoor (Devon), and Parkhurst (Isle of Wight), in that order, before eventually being released in 1937, vowing never to be confined by four walls again. But as this chapter is principally concerned with Phelan's tramping exploits, his experience of prison life will be dealt with only briefly. Those who wish to read the remarkable story of Phelan's prison life should read *A Tramp at Anchor*. The book is also an exceptional social critique on British penology of the period, just as Jack Black's *You Can't Win* is on the American penal system.

Phelan talks much in his prison memoirs of his difficulty, and that of lifers in general, in maintaining physical and mental health. The prison regime was designed to sap the will and create automatons out of healthy, autonomous beings. Even many of those who physically survived a long sentence were so emotionally traumatized by the experience that they were transferred to mental institutions on completion of their sentences. Phelan describes the professional criminal recidivist, those who had the animal resourcefulness necessary for survival inside, indeed, treated prison as their "place of work," as opposed to the "mug" or ordinary citizen: those whose outside skills or employment (banker, shopkeeper, schoolteacher, etc.) served for nothing in prison, indeed acted as a handicap because they used logic instead of cunning in the face of simpleminded and often brutal jailers.

While Phelan was more comfortable with, and accepted by, the professional crooks, he craved intellectual company and feared for the loss of his mind and spirit. His survival was at times severely tested, but he credits surviving his long sentence to his unique credentials. He was a scholar and a tramp, a blacksmith and a revolutionary; he had the intelligence to act dumb when required as well as smart when dealing with those who could make a difference. He became the head blacksmith at both Dartmoor and Parkhurst prisons, and, when he met a girl outside the prison that he took a liking to, got himself transferred to an outside gardening detail in order to consummate his desires. But this was much later in his prison career; he had suffered untold inhumanities before this happier respite. "In that summer [his last in jail] I wrote three hundred thousand words. In that summer, too, I escaped from the sex-thwarting that had torn at my healthy body for years."[36]

On questions of life and death, Phelan proposes that it is only when a condemned man is at the peak of good health that these two separate questions combine as a single philosophical problem, for: "Life does not really admit the existence of death."[37] At least, until one is on death row, then everything becomes about the existence of death, a "prosaic reminder that one's business in the house was to wait, until a certain day and hour, for a man with a rope."[38]

On death row, Phelan recalled tramping on long straight roads across the bogs of Ireland, "looking forward into mist and back into mist, the road running between like a narrow endless bridge." Now, at the end of just such a bridge, hurrying into the mist at one end, Phelan is forced to consider the following conundrum of his own existence with a heightened clarity:

> ... unlike the majority of men, I had time to think about it, because the mist had appeared while I was at my mental zenith, not when I was on my death-bed. Further, I was able to think clearly, with a keen, alert brain, because although dying I was not sick.
>
> Above all, I had nothing to distract me, no luring thoughts or plans or hopes, had no future to plot and not even a signpost to read ... Wherefore I could peer into the mist, and consider it, without fear of external influence and without need for self-deception.
>
> It is a time of great testing, the time when a man is to die without being ill. Mean, small hypocrisies and puny facile deceits of self are thrown away, count as nothing, and a man, if he has a healthy active mind, may look at himself and his world without blinkers or blinds.[39]

On the eve of his intended execution, Phelan wrote a sonnet to serve as his epitaph. But it is the commentary he added to the poem that reveals Phelan's philosophy on the world he was about to depart. He claims he had no wisdom to leave behind, knew nothing about the beginning or the end of the world, but did not approve of civilization. Human beings should not inflict their morality on each other because few were, in any case, "capable of sustained, conscious, logical thought." And the reason that vast numbers of people were unhappy is because they pretend this is untrue.[40]

Two Further Marriages and Writing

Sometime after his release from prison in 1937, Phelan married his second wife, Jill Constance Hayes, a political activist who had visited him while in prison. Their son Seumas was born the following year on February 4, 1938. Phelan settled down to his new career as a writer in spite of the commencement of the Second World War, but the following year, on September 8, 1940, tragedy struck for a second time when Jill was severely injured in the German bombardment. Details are available from a letter Phelan wrote to George Orwell on February 4, 1941, pleading for his friend to help him financially. Phelan explains to Orwell that he was broke, having spent all his money (including that paid for his recent writing) paying for the cost of Jill's care. Worse still, he was about to be evicted from his home and forced to sell all his possessions to pay his debtors: "five months' work of commissioned scripts, becomes waste paper, in the sale of 'effects.'" He continues that having been a tramp he "personally wouldn't care a curse," but "imagine what happens to a tramp with a baby and without a cent in the world." Phelan gives his address as Woodland Cottages, Wigginton, Herts. This is what he says about Jill in the letter:

> Jill Phelan knocked out first Sunday of blitz. ... Blood-loss and brain-injury. Alternately moribund and delirious. Now being better, is rapidly going crazy because practically incommunicado; no visits, no letters, no discharge, because "next of kin" can't call and demonstrate economic solvency.[41]

Phelan also wrote to Orwell about the shame he felt at no longer being able to pay for Jill's care, leaving her "a charge on the parish," meaning that she would need to be supported by public funds. Paradoxically, if Jill had required the same treatment only seven years later in 1948 when the National Health Service was established, Phelan may not have found himself in this situation as the state would have paid for her care anyway. Reports state that Jill Phelan died following a long series of mental health problems, but these must have been secondary to the original head injury. By the time Phelan wrote to George Orwell, Jill was a patient at Three Counties Hospital (for the mentally ill), Arlesey, Bedfordshire. In his desperate plea for help, Phelan also talks about the hardship of caring for his son Seumas, whom he describes as "dying of loneliness, as the result of living with a fellow who has to hammer a type-writer day and night."

A remarkable story written by Phelan using the voice and vocabulary of his five-year-old son, titled "Naughty Mans," provides a unique insight into Phelan's life at the time through the eyes of the young son:

> When me and Jim goes to Arlesey to see Jill, we go on the Luton bus from Tring. ... Once a time Jill was in bed with me. That was nice. ... Down the Oddy Hill you can roll, if your Jim isn't too rullied and too much thinking. When your Jim is thinking a lot, about the bloody words he is going to type, that's lousy. ... Your daddy goes off the deep end if you intersturb him when he's writing the bloody words. ... Jill is very nice. She kisses you plenty and says Hello Love and takes you in bed. Jill is broked now. That's lousy, because me and Jim lives on the Oddy Hill all by myself. The doctor won't let Jill come home. When I get a big man I shall shoot the doctor. ... Then you come to the hospital and Jill is in bed and Jim cries and you cry and that's not so good either. When I get a big man I shall shoot all

> the nurses and let Jill come home. The bomb came down. No more Jill. ... Sometimes I tell Jim to cry, and tend he has no mates and no toys and no sweeties. So I come in and tend to be a nice mans. Then when Jim cries I say What's The Matter Son? He says I Have No One To Play With Me. So I say I'll play with you because I am a nice mans.[42]

Sometime following this period of Phelan's life, approximately seven years after his release from prison, he met Kathleen M. Newton on the road, a partner who, for the first time, was fully prepared to embrace his unusual lifestyle and tramp alongside him—which she did until Phelan's death some 22 years later. The couple were married in Hampstead in 1944. Kathleen also helped Phelan bring up his son. Kathleen's story of how she met her husband is related in Chapter 15.

Phelan's tramp memoirs following his release from prison appear in *Tramping the Toby*. Some of these are discussed below under "Tramping in Britain" but are hard to place chronologically because the book shifts between stories and anecdotes about individual vagabond acquaintances and particular themes on tramping such as begging and places to sleep. Sadly, and somewhat surprisingly, they do not mention Kathleen, but an unpublished autobiography written by Kathleen, and discovered after her death, devotes itself to the couple's 22 years of adventures on the road and is liberally referred to in Chapter 15. Phelan was by now alternating his time between writing and playing chess in a gypsy-style caravan during the winter, and spending his summers with Kathleen out on the road. A feature in *Chess* magazine in 1964 reports him as saying, "I used to be a tramp pretending to be a writer. Now I'm a writer pretending to be a tramp."

Of Phelan's other activities, accounts are sketchy, but again there are some fascinating glimpses from "Naughty Mans," such as trips to the West End of London to visit publishers, buy sweets and visit the cinema. Phelan seems to have been just as comfortable among artists and writers as he was convicts and tramps, and often frequented bohemian circles around the bars and cafés of Soho and Fitzrovia. Seumas was clearly familiar with many famous celebrities—"My uncle Paul [Robeson] has black face"—and others less famous: "Once a time we were having tea with two chorus-girls. This is from the Coliseum, in Saint Martin's Lane, a jolly nice place."[43] Phelan also worked as a scriptwriter after the Second World War, making films for the Ministry of Information: "one day Dylan Thomas sat down beside me, to drink black coffee at the Madrid in Soho. Next day I was a scriptwriter in a film company, with Dylan and the rest of the boys."[44] More anecdotes about Dylan Thomas are recounted in Chapter 15. In 1964, two years before his death, Phelan made a four-part television documentary series for the BBC titled *Next Place*, which included interviewing Welsh tramps and discussing the Roma people.

Tramping in Britain

At the time Phelan wrote about tramping, he refers to there being 9,000 men padders and 3,000 women on the roads of Britain, with their own methods of subsistence and traveling. Today there may be increasing numbers of homeless and unemployed ever dependent on the life-draining institutions of the state, but across the West today, few still adopt the kind of lifestyle adopted by Phelan and the other vagabonds featured in this book, as Jack Kerouac observed as long ago as 1960 in his magazine article "The Vanishing American Hobo."[45] It should be noted here that Phelan's tramp moniker was "Dolcie Jem" (Sweet Jim), as confirmed by a friend of his wife Kathleen. Her moniker was "Convent Kate," "because she looked as though butter wouldn't melt in her mouth—but it would!"[46]

Phelan acknowledges that although the vagabond is one of civilization's rejects, it is not the natural or even the human world they reject. The world belongs to the vagabond and provides them with a means of survival. In contrast, the rest of civilization's rejects, in addition to being unfit for city life, are unfit to survive the rigors of the road also. Phelan understands that to keep a job and maintain a home for a lifetime requires tenacity and is "no vocation for a weakling." In response to the pressures of city life, such weaklings turn to religion, criminality, madness or death itself, and only the tramp—too strong to be killed by the hardships of unemployment, mentally too tough to be driven into madness, too honest to adopt a life of crime, and philosophically too shrewd to accept religion—has the strength to survive the tyranny of the civilizing process.

In the opening quotation of this chapter, Phelan nails the whole philosophy of tramping, reminding us that long ago we were all tramps. That those who lived in settlements were the odd and the different. Now we all live in settled communities (whether transient or permanent) and regard with suspicion the nomadic vagabond in our midst. But Phelan challenges many modern myths about tramping, starting with the myth of the tramp as lazy. "No wage-worker ever labored as hard as a tramp will, on occasion." He compares the degree of tenacity required to hold down a job by going to the office each morning with "that called for by a walk from Calais to Vladivostok or from New York to San Francisco"—emphasizing that tramps *have* walked those distances, not for pleasure or profit, but for the tenacity and will to do it.

Phelan also stands on its head the conventional view of tramping as a solitary profession, arguing that compared to city dwellers, the tramp has far more human contact and of a more intimate nature. The average city dweller, he says, will know one another's relatives but not the neighbors of those relatives. They will know a few friends from their workplace, but not those people's other acquaintances. They sometimes group together in big crowds such as a football match. "But on these occasions each citizen is just a lost unit, in the middle of a thousand strangers. A city is a lonely place."

> Now consider the padman. He knows—it is his trade to know—all the people in every good-sized house along his next day's road … Those people are not his friends, but he knows them … they are his benefactors, and may have been so for years, are interested in his survival and his strange way of life … He knows who is good-humoured, who is generous, and who is mean … who is away in London, or who has 'flu. … But all the above remarks apply only to one stretch of the padman's road, one day's journey.[47]

Phelan also dismisses the notion that just because the tramp can't stop wandering, that they do not have a longing for "home." The difference is that the tramp's home is everywhere, and to illustrate the point he talks about sauntering through country villages day after day, scrutinizing each one as though he had been born there: "It is the drifter's mentality, which a man either has or has not, that affection for a home which is not one place but may be a thousand places. … The trouble with people like me was that we had a nostalgia for everywhere!"[48] And here, Phelan describes the concept of the "lurk": a place to which the vagabond regularly returns for no particular reason than being drawn back to the spot. Every tramp has his favorite lurk, he says, a center to which he is drawn back in different parts of the world for rest and contemplation. Phelan's own lurks he describes as all very ordinary places: "A signpost outside Stockholm … in southern France, at Arles, there is a small bridge where … I have sat, for days on end doing nothing and being very happy … A cross-roads near Faringdon in England, a patch of green grass with a road-sign, where I can relax and go blank-eyed and feel that the world is a good place."[49]

Another contradiction of tramping described by Phelan is that although as "free as a bird," most tramps' movements are as anticipated as train schedules, adding, "A bird's movements are very predictable indeed, for anyone who knows birds."[50] While on the subject of birds, it is interesting to note that Phelan in Gaelic (*faoileán*) means seagull, that tramp of the bird world who scavenges for food and hitches rides on ships. Lastly, we have the observation made by Phelan on the tramp's lack of sentimentality: "A tramp does not have much emotional energy to spare in pitying other people. Pity, as a rule, belongs to the towns. (It is largely an excuse and a compensation for cruelty committed elsewhere—but, of course, it will be rather difficult to convince city folk of *that!*)"[51]

Classification of British Tramps

The various distinctions and categorizations writers have made of the American vagabond are contained in other chapters of this book. Below Phelan characterizes the uniquely distinct differences of the British tramp:

- the "padder" or "padman" covers only five to 10 miles a day because of calling at many houses along the way for a hand-out;
- the "wheeler" travels more slowly still, not being a genuine roamer or a rogue, but rather a city dweller or pauper, "killing time, like a little boy not hurrying home in case he might be whipped," calling from one institution to the next, clinging to "whatever civilisation has to offer him" and "greatly preoccupied about security as any suburbanite with a headache about last month's bills";
- the "topcock postman" is described as the opposite end of the scale as far as speed is concerned, hitchhiking in cars and traveling hundreds of miles a day; the postman is a restless tramp, always wanting to go a little further even than his intended destination, and unlike the padder, he only has time to call at a few selected houses where he is known and can rely on a decent hand-out;
- the "shuttler" comes between the postman and the padder: "They always keep to the same road, never vary their routine, hurry along their shuttle in one direction and hurry back in the other, up and down like a squirrel in a cage";
- the "drifter" is an amateur tramp;
- the "deener" (tramp slang for a shilling) is a miser obsessed with collecting coppers and converting them to silver which the deener hides about their clothing;
- and a "shellback" is a tramp who pretends to be a sailor.[52]

The Tramp's Attitude to Money

The distinction between the different categories of tramps described above can be understood further by Phelan's exposition on the tramp's attitude to money. And here we have another important link to the philosophy of the ancient Cynics, a mindset that Phelan tells us "will be difficult, almost impossible, for any normal citizen to understand." Phelan describes the vagabond as a person who, quite literally, "obeys the precept which is part of the Christian philosophy and many another." Taking no thought for tomorrow, the vagabond trusts that the road will furnish whatever he needs. It would be madness for the vagabond to buy clothing, a piece of leather strap, or even some copper rivets, even if he had the money. The road provides for everything he needs and he comes to regard it, "not only as his bank but also a kind of universal store."[53] And here Phelan uses the tramp's attitude to money and possessions to further distinguish between some of those distinct varieties of tramps listed above:

> There is one safe general rule; the bigger the load the cheaper the tramp. The professional vagabond carries as little as possible. It may be taken for granted that, if an alleged tramp is loaded down with bundles and garnished with packages, he is either an amateur or a wheeler. ... Some of the shuttlers carry a kit bag, with clothes in, but most of the padmen have only a small bundle or, more often, a soldier's haversack with a strap. The postmen carry nothing except a tiny attaché-case, like a child's school satchel. ... Even the posting-girls (there are not many) travel light, nearly always carrying a diminutive attaché-case like men. Yet they are always well turned-out, able to ask for a lift in a smart car ... It has been my great good fortune to ride the road for many thousands of miles with a posting-girl. But I have never ceased to be astonished by her ability to dispense with luggage.[54]

We may assume here, as Phelan refers to girl in the singular, that he is referring to his second wife Kathleen with whom he tramped until his death. He tells an amusing story of tramping with a woman he met in Looe, Cornwall, postman-style, each carrying no more than an attaché case 9 inches by 12. It was warm spring weather, and the pair were lightly attired in summer clothing. They did not stop their tramp until they eventually arrived in Bjirdnung, 800 kilometres north of Stockholm near the Arctic Circle. As they had been traveling fast and had made Bjirdnung from the south of England in only eight days, it was only the sudden realization that they were tramping in an Arctic winter in their summer clothes that they crossed to the other side of the road and tramped south again.[55] On women tramps generally, Phelan remarks: "Nearly all the girls on the road ... stick to padding. Also the majority of them are married or, as one might put it, engaged. Male vagrants outnumber the girls by three to one..."[56] This percentage of women to men, reinforced earlier, appears to be higher than that acknowledged in America; even so, many of those women who did tramp in America disguised themselves as boys or men to avoid the different kinds of hassles they would have attracted tramping openly as women.[57]

On Begging

Phelan further classifies the tramp's "mark" (person from whom the tramp begs) into the following categories:

- a "field day" he describes as "the psychological descendants of Good King Wenceslas—they will give money to anyone."
- the "soft mark": "yields no great largess, but will give a penny or two even to a wheeler."
- the "ordinary call": "is not by any means a fool but will reward a good well-told tale."
- the "hard mark": "can only be approached by the cocks of the road ... The work is more difficult and the line of guff must be really good, but the rewards are greater."
- the "dead mark": "is a person to be avoided by the normal vagabond. Outside his entrance gate will be the tramp-signs, warning the padman to get out of the district quickly, and stay out."[58]

Phelan compares the business of tramping to any other business venture. The employed person has an office or workplace in which they conduct their business, and a drawing room at home where they relax and become "themself." The tramp also needs to take time off from their "lark" and rest, smoke and dream: "a field [roughly equivalent to the hobo jungle in America] is the vagabond's drawing room, as against the road—which is his workshop or office." And here Phelan refers to the tramp's "line of guff"; this is the story (fact or fiction, but usually an element of both) that the tramp invents about his or her circumstances, often supported by some documentary evidence that tramps use to verify their claims: "the tramp lives on his story, and on his story alone, as a plumber lives by plumbing or a banker by banking ... and each tramp tells only one story." And each line of guff, Phelan maintains, is a work of art, often refined over a period of many years in response to what works best and what does not and, furthermore, the line of guff cannot be interpreted as outright begging for the reasons described below, so ingenuity is required:

> "Improvements and emendations are suggested—by the questions of his marks [intended victims]. Phrases and pauses which have not brought results are dropped. The devoted search for the right words! ... To begin with, the tramp must not be begging. In Britain and America it is illegal to beg. So the vagrant's story must not ask for anything; it must merely indicate the man's need and leave the mark to guess the rest for himself.

> Secondly ... the story must be true. Demonstrably true, that is, for an unsympathetic listener such as a policeman. That is because the telling of lies is a crime in Britain ... If a tramp tells lies, and someone informs the police, the vagrant may go to prison for false pretences. So the ... 'line of guff' must be documented.
>
> Thirdly, it must not be too sad, or too shocking. No mark will really listen for long, if a tramp tries to explain that he has tuberculosis, leprosy and dropped arches ... [it should give rise to] the atmosphere of the story, which is not meant to evoke pity for the road-wanderer but interest in that putatively-romantic background.
>
> As soon as the roadster has a basis for his tale, he goes over it day after day, altering it, adapting the tones of voice, making the pauses longer or shorter, putting a finish to it. At this stage the tramp has precisely the same job as the fiction-writer."[59]

In a six-page yarn to illustrate his point, Phelan gives the example of a tramp acquaintance named Jockey Merritt. Jockey, who had been on the road for 60 years, had a line of guff based on the fact that, although unsuccessful as a jockey, he had on two occasions ridden horses owned by a champion racehorse owner, not the champion itself (who had won both the Epsom Derby and Oaks in 1908) but no matter. The association was there and he had a much worn race-card from those far-off days to prove it. Jockey had learned by heart the names of famous racehorses, their owners, jockeys, and racing incidents, with which he would regale his racing aficionado marks.

Transformation from Tramp to Writer and Further Tramping

Although Phelan's preferred environment was the open road, he was also drawn to the bustling, cosmopolitan centers of capital cities. But his real writing apprenticeship took place in the various prisons in which he was incarcerated on the rare occasions when he had access to pen and paper. When Phelan was first presented a notebook and pencil, in Maidstone prison, he was overcome with the enormity of the opportunity that now presented itself:

> I was an explorer in a field of science which was almost untouched. ... I had an advantage over the orthodox penologists and commentators on jail-psychology. They dealt with reports, statistics, departmental accounts.

> … I had the men themselves, their chuckles and groans, their blood and sweat and excrement, the animal growl of the jail voices, the sniffing one another from afar, the lip-licking, saliva-drooling jungle technique of homosexual love-making, the fantasy hiss, the small sadism, the neurosis. Pioneering against my will, I had a whole new world to put on paper.
> I sharpened my pencil eagerly.[60]

But attached to the first page of the notebook were the customary prison regulations stating what Phelan was, and was not, permitted to use the notebook for. Bizarrely, these included "keeping a diary" and "writing about prisons." As all his writing would be closely scrutinized, it would take Phelan years of carefully crafted deception, sometimes discovered and punished (including using shorthand, prison slang, facts disguised with metaphor, and using foreign languages—including Gaelic and Latin—on alternate lines) to prevail in producing both his prison research and early drafts of short stories and novels. But in this he succeeded, which helped him in his later success as a writer.

Phelan's time at his last prison, Parkhurst, was his most productive. He had managed to secure, for his own betterment, a writing course with an external tutor, and nearing his release (he had been turned down for parole twice already) he reports having 30 stories, three-quarters of his first novel *Lifer*, and half of his prison memoirs, *A Tramp at Anchor*. When Phelan's post-prison writing career commenced, he had occasion to visit various publishers in the West End of London, and in the following passage describes his fascination for the Charing Cross Road (a description few would recognize today) on his way to sign his first book contract:

> It is a place of drifters, even if they live in cities. Bookshops crowd one another, and flocks of customers … bustle in and out. At one end all the shop-windows are filled with music sheets, and all the crooked small alleys are filled with gossiping musicians. … At the other side the narrow streets and alleys lead into Soho. Chinese and negroes, French people and Greeks and folks of a hundred nationalities move in and out of Soho … Brass plates, squares of wood, or visiting cards held in place by drawing pins, indicate the offices of a thousand specialists. Tattoo artists and private detectives, theatrical agents and dancing schools, Chinese laundries and dealers in "rare" books, all function side by side. There may be ordinary shops and offices, too. But I saw none of them that morning. I only saw the seething, multicoloured, polyglot, exotic crowd, like the populace of some giant paddincan [tramp hostelry], at a crossroads where all the highways of the world converge. It is a wonderful street for a tramp to walk through.[61]

Sign his contract Phelan did, but the problem presenting itself was where was he to write? In the event, his agent offered him the use of his house in the country, complete with typewriter and paper. The house was in the village of Stony Stratford, conveniently situated near the London end of Watling Street, the old Roman road (modern A5) that Phelan had tramped many times. Imagine Phelan's shock when he arrived at the gates of a manor house in wooded grounds, then was received in the drawing room by servants complete with a tray and whiskey decanter. And write Phelan did, until the word spread among his tramp friends that one of their own was now resident in his own "castle." The tramp visitors to Stony Stratford became so numerous that Phelan had a visit from the local constable and was forced to leave tramp signs at strategic entrances to the village to warn his friends of impending arrest should they re-enter the community boundary.

Phelan's transition from tramp to writer was not a straightforward affair. Spending weeks on the road at a time meant that letters from editors and publishers were often picked up after important deadlines had passed; for instance, a letter from an agent requesting Phelan to telephone Warner Brothers' studios at Teddington and a script on which he could have been put to work if he had received it in time. But conversely, his commitments as a writer also brought him legitimate scope to continue tramping. Naturally, he had to research an article he was asked to write on tramping to Loch Lomond: "One could not very well vamp up such an article." Similarly, when working on the script for the movie *Night Journey* (1938), a tale about lorry drivers working between London and Newcastle, Phelan spent three weeks on the road because, "I had to ride the road with lorry-drivers to get a feel ... into the thing." Phelan acknowledges being constantly torn between "the road and civilisation, between existence as a houseman-author and life as a tramp."

> The caged nightingale cannot sing, nor the captive buffalo breed. No tramp should have a master, and no writer should work for wages. That way the tramp and the writer cease to be. ... A tramp cannot carry a typewriter and a lot of reference-books along the road.[62]

But, in the end, Phelan did reconcile this conflict by acknowledging that he had no ties to one place, and that he could switch between tramp-writer and civilized person "at a minute's notice, and without disappointing anyone but myself." *Tramping the Toby* ends with this upbeat assessment of a man who had comfortably accommodated all his aspirations without further conflict to mar his pleasure in life—an enviable destination, out of reach of most "civilized" men and women: "I got out on the road a great deal, collecting material. It was the next thing to being a tramp—I had found the half-way house."[63]

Phelan's Writing Style

As with Leon Ray Livingston, Phelan was aware of what made a successful novel in purely marketing terms. Unlike Livingston, Phelan was a cynic, and knew just how to please the publishers and readers while having the last laugh at their expense. As did Trader Horn also, Phelan subverts the commercial with his own skills at storytelling. Of his short stories, he says, "There is always the central bit, which looks like the story. But never is." And like the contemporary fictioneer Raymond Federman, who claims that all of life is a fiction anyway, Phelan also refuses to engage with the fact/fiction dichotomy:

> It may be true, or perhaps barely credible. But it never sounds true. Not until it is "married" to some other possibly true narrative, quite unconnected with it.
>
> Then the result of that marriage, the third thing, which of course is not true at all, sounds vastly more credible and convincing than either of its parents. Then you have a good story. ... But it is far more interesting—because it is very unusual—to see the first bits, the parents, the originals. ... It is the difference between literature and journalism, to which many refer without being very clear of their own meaning. (But tramps know.)[64]

Here again, Phelan is referring to the tramps' "line of guff," the fiction that tramps create to persuade their "mark" to part with food or money. Ignoring the maxim that truth is stranger than fiction, which it often is, Phelan is clear that what is important from a tramping perspective is that "Good fiction always sounds true. That is why the tramp survives." But back to writing rather than "telling" stories, Phelan maintains that "the writer is satisfied, because he sees his creation come alive, and because he is paid for it. (Which he would not be, for crude stories ...) The reader is satisfied too, having been told the things he or she wants to hear."[65] But although Phelan claims that he played the publisher's game when it came to some of his novels and short stories, in his autobiographical works he fully exploits his cynicism, openly sharing with the reader his writing processes and satirical thoughts on the writing business itself. He achieves this through the use of diatribes, aphorisms and multilayered irony, and by the use of autobiographical fiction where he plays the central character in expositions on everything from politics, economics and civilization, to how to tell a good lie. These observations come from *Tramping the Toby*, but seven years earlier Phelan had noted the following in the opening passages of the author's preface to *The Name's Phelan*:

> For a teller of tales, a fiction spinner, such as I have been for most of my life, even before I was a writer, any attempt at a straightforward factual narrative

> is very difficult indeed. It is so easy, and the temptation is so great, to round off a passage or tidy up an episode, to make a neat story instead of the succession of inconsequentialities which a life story usually is.
>
> Add the fact that I have always rather tended to dramatise my own existence, as also that I would much rather forget a great many of the things which have happened to me, and that it will be plain that the ordinary difficulties of autobiography are for me multiplied.[66]

A tough character Phelan undoubtedly was, able to survive the hardships of the road well into his advancing years, but he did not escape a lifetime's enjoyment of smoking and drinking, eventually developing lung cancer and chronic obstructive airways disease. Two years after making the television documentary series for the BBC, Phelan discharged himself from the hospital against medical advice, true to his promise never to be confined by four walls again. But confined he eventually was, in bed at the home of his son Seumas in West London. Shortly before he died, and still anxious to pass on his wisdoms on life, Phelan called for his granddaughter, Amanda. "When she came into the room he took off his oxygen mask and they laughed together for a few minutes. He then told her his three rules for life: 'don't grass,' 'never lie to your loved ones,' and, most important of all 'stay alive.'"[67]

ENDNOTES

1 "Toby" here refers to the road, other British tramp designations of which are "the white," "the macadam," "the grit" (as in "hitting the grit") and "the pad."

2 Phelan, Jim. *The Name's Phelan*, Belfast: Blackstaff Press Ltd., 1993, p. 63

3 Ibid., p. 2

4 Ibid., p. 6

5 Ibid., p. 5

6 Ibid., pp. 7–11

7 Ibid., p. 47

8 Ibid., p. 57

9 Ibid., p. 67

10 Ibid., p. 69. In terms of putting the illegality of the first profanity into perspective, it was not until 1960 that the unabridged version of *Lady Chatterley's Lover* was able to be published. The latter profanity Phelan recalls as a "magic formula" his sister and he had learned at school to damn folk to hell.

11 Ibid., p. 119

12 Ibid., p. 121

13 Ibid., p. 123

14 Ibid., pp. 142–143

15 Ibid., p. 161

16 Ibid., pp. 173–174

17 Ibid., p. 197

18 The Irish Citizen Army had been founded by Jim Larkin during the 1913 "Dublin Lockout" to defend strikers from police brutality.

19 *The Name's Phelan*, op. cit., p. 205

20 Ibid., p. 224

21 Ibid., p. 228

22 Ibid., pp. 242–245

23 Markievicz was the first woman ever elected to the House of Commons in 1918—a year before Nancy Astor—though, like other Sinn Féin members, she refused to take her seat.

24 *The Name's Phelan*, op. cit., p. 252

25 Ibid., p. 257

26 Ibid., p. 259

27 Ibid., pp. 264–265

28 Ibid., p. 247

29 *Western Mail* (South Wales), June 13, 1923; *Portsmouth Evening News*, June 13, 1923; *Western Daily Press* (Bristol), June 13, 1923; *The Evening Telegraph and Post* (Dundee), June 15, 1923; *Liverpool Echo*, June 22, 1923; and *The Scotsman*, June 14 & 23, 1923

30 Phelan, Jim. *Tramp at Anchor*, London: George G. Harrap & Co. Ltd., 1954, p. 17

31 The presiding judge at Phelan's trial is reported to be the Right Honourable Sir George Arthur Harwin Branson, grandfather of business tycoon Sir Richard Branson.

32 *The Name's Phelan*, op. cit., p. 281

33 Letter from the Under Sheriff of the County of Lancaster, dated July 31, 1923

34 Letter from Phelan's mother, Catherine, to Alfred Byrne, TD (Teachta Dála, member of the Irish Parliament, who later became a member of the U.K. Parliament and Lord Mayor of Dublin), simply dated July, but would have been 1926 as she refers to Phelan's wife Dora having died two years previously.

35 Confirmed in a note received from Phelan's granddaughter Lillian Felstead, August 19, 2015

36 *Tramp at Anchor*, op. cit., p. 196

37 *The Name's Phelan*, op. cit., p. 284

38 Ibid., p. 286

39 Ibid., pp. 284–285

40 Ibid., p. 297

41 Letter from Phelan to George Orwell dated February 4, 1941

42 Phelan, Jim. "Naughty Mans" in the magazine *Horizon: A Review of Literature and Art*, July 1943, pp. 37–41

43 Ibid., p. 38

44 Phelan, Jim. *Tramping the Toby*, London: Burke Publishing Co. Ltd., 1955, p. 222

45 Kerouac, Jack. "The Vanishing American Hobo" in *Holiday Magazine* (Philadelphia, PA), Vol. 27, No. 3, March 1960, pp. 60–61

46 Jackman, Grace. Email to author, June 20, 2019

47 *Tramping the Toby*, op. cit., p. 185

48 Ibid., p. 39

49 Ibid., pp. 118–119

50 Ibid., p. 120

51 Ibid., p. 43

52 Ibid., pp. 40–42

53 Ibid., p. 113

54 Ibid., pp. 146–147

55 Ibid., p. 147

56 Ibid., p. 130

57 See comments in Introduction and also Ben Reitman's study of women tramps, *Sister of the Road: The Autobiography of Box-Car Bertha*, in which he provides an appendix with over 30 pages classifying women tramps alone.

58 Ibid., pp. 110–111

59 Ibid., pp. 88–89

60 *Tramp at Anchor*, op. cit., pp. 42–43

61 *Tramping the Toby*, op. cit., pp. 61–62

62 Ibid., p. 215

63 Ibid., p. 222

64 Ibid., pp. 48–49

65 Ibid., p. 49

66 *The Name's Phelan*, op. cit., p. i

67 Lees, Andrew. "The Rolling English Road," *Dublin Review of Books*, Issue 67, May 2015

Tom Kromer

(1906–1969)

You can stop a revolution of stiffs [hobos] with a sack of toppin's [food]. I have seen one bull [cop] kick a hundred stiffs off a drag. When a stiff's gut is empty, he hasn't got the guts to start anything. When his gut is full, he doesn't see any use in raising hell. What does a stiff want to raise hell for when his belly is full?

Tom Kromer, *Waiting for Nothing*

Preamble

This chapter detours somewhat from the theme of "tramping as a lifestyle choice" to discuss—even though the first train Tom Kromer ever beat was motivated by wanderlust—"the tramp of circumstances." Kromer was 29 years old when *Waiting for Nothing* was published in 1935. His series of dark, bleak, and very candid "essays" on hobo life (and death) are primarily an autobiographical account of human suffering and endurance during America's "Great Depression" of the 1930s. *Waiting for Nothing* is also a treatise on the extremes of cruelty that the "haves" are prepared to mete out on the "have nots," and the ultimate depravities to which humans are reduced simply to stave off hunger and death that at times seems a more welcome outcome than continued survival.

Thomas Michael Kromer was born in Huntington, West Virginia, into a harsh, working-class existence. His father had arrived in the U.S. from Czechoslovakia, aged two, and worked in the local coal mines from the age of eight, later becoming a glass blower, before dying of cancer at the age of 44. Kromer's beginnings were hopeful. He went through three years of college, taught for two more years in mountain schools in West Virginia, before one day jumping into the passing boxcar of a freight train and beating it to Kansas where the 23-year-old Kromer intended to work in the wheat fields—but the combines had come and gone:

> I got my first taste of going three days without food, and walking up to a back door and dinging a woman for a hand-out. It was a yellow house, but not too yellow, and I made it. Since then I have made a thousand such yellow houses and have never been turned down. Women who live in green houses will not even open the door for me.[1]

Kromer stayed "on the fritz" (down-and-out) for the following five years, looking for but failing to find work: "it was about that time that people started laughing at you for asking for work. After a while I stopped asking for work." He goes on to explain in the two-page preface of *Waiting for Nothing* how the book was written and why it was written in the style it was:

> I had no idea of getting *Waiting for Nothing* published, therefore, I wrote it just as I felt it, and used the language that stiffs use even when it wasn't always the nicest language in the world.
>
> Parts of the book were scrawled on Bull Durham papers in box cars, margins of religious tracts in a hundred missions, jails, one prison, railroad sand-houses, flop-houses, and on a few memorable occasions actually pecked out with my two index fingers on an honest-to-God typewriter.[2]

Some commentators of the time tried to throw doubt on the autobiographical validity of *Waiting for Nothing*, describing the voice as an "unnamed first-person narrator," but Kromer makes it clear that "Save for four or five incidents, it is strictly autobiographical." And, as with the other tramp writers featured here, even where fictional events are introduced, it is fair to assume that they are based on the author's first-hand experience—indeed, the actual lives and experiences of most of the tramp writers in this volume are beyond the imagination and audacity of most modern fiction writers.

Those who further criticize the book for its seemingly bleak, cold-hearted nihilism should consider the reality of the lives of those thousands of dispossessed Americans at the time. Kromer himself was crippled with tuberculosis for most of his life, a condition that put a premature end to his career as a writer. But Kromer is not indifferent either to the collective human misery around him or to individual suffering. Indeed, he often displays a surprising generosity of spirit in the midst of his renunciation. There is also some humor in the book, particularly cynical irony and the ridicule of absurdity, if one bothers to look for it. But Kromer's lack of sentimentality—a characteristic of tramps acknowledged by Jim Phelan in the previous chapter—does not negate emotion, nor his sense of outrage at the forces that created and sustained the Depression; it does negate, however, the political naïvety of the hobo revolutionaries he encounters on his travels. Kromer is a realist when it comes to understanding human nature, and simply frames depravity in the context of the reality it is. Kromer's brand of realism is reflected in the following two book reviews of the time. Roland Mulhauser, in the *Saturday Review of Literature*, noted, "There is a static calm in his point of view suggesting compression and numbness beyond pain. There is no sentimentalizing pity. There are no emotional outbursts. Nothing but hunger. Still, it is a shocking book: a picture of unmitigated depravity."[3] And Fred T. Marsh in *Books* observed that *Waiting for Nothing* was a "little piece of dynamite … [but one that would] accomplish nothing in its explosion because people will stuff up their ears with cotton and flee to their bomb-proof cellars."[4]

On Hunger 1

Chapter 1 opens with Kromer contemplating the practicalities of a mugging and sets out his uncompromising, staccato prose style:

> It is night. I am walking along this dark street, when my foot hits a stick. I reach down and pick it up. I finger it. It is a good stick, a heavy stick. One sock from it would lay a man out. It wouldn't kill him, but it would lay him out. I plan. Hit him where the crease is in his hat, hard, I tell

> myself, but not too hard. I do not want his head to hit the concrete. It might kill him. I do not want to kill him. I will catch him as he falls. I can frisk him in a minute. I will pull him over in the shadows and walk off. I will not run. I will walk.[5]

After waiting in the chosen spot for five to 10 minutes, a suitably well-dressed victim comes into sight. As Kromer observes, he has his head up and walks in a jaunty manner. A hobo doesn't walk like that. "A stiff shuffles with tired feet, his head huddled in his coat collar. This guy is in the dough." Everything goes according to plan until the moment the stick has to be brought down on his victim's head. Kromer acknowledges feeling sick in his stomach and losing his nerve. He starts sweating and shaking all over, feeling shameful for the act he had been about to commit but desperate nonetheless. "This will not do. This will not do. I've got to get something to eat. I am starved."[6] This brief, failed encounter provides a clue to Kromer's character. As with other such confrontations, such as the botched bank robbery related below, Kromer reveals his limitations as a natural born hustler, highlighting one of the differences between hobos who make out and those who remain humanity's casualties.

After failing to acquire cash by force to relieve his starvation, Kromer later describes staring through a restaurant window at an affluent couple in evening dress—she bedecked in diamonds—in a desperate attempt to attract some sympathy to his plight. It is not so much the image of the plump chicken dripping in gravy that arrests the watcher's attention so much as the fact that these two diners are more immersed in each other than the object of Kromer's craving:

> They are nibbling at the chicken, and they are not even hungry. I am starved. That chicken was meant for a hungry man. ... I will stand here until they come out. When they come out they will maybe slip me a four-bit piece.[7]

But Kromer will never find out, for he is roughly apprehended by a cop and moved on. After being turned away from several other restaurants and beginning to give up hope of getting anything to eat that night, a guy in a suit invites him to join him in a diner. His benefactor stumps up for a "beef-steak dinner and everything that goes with it," then another diner, not to be outdone, leaves him change for a "flop" (bed for the night). So it goes on the fritz: one minute you're so down on your luck you fear for your very existence, the next minute you're strolling along with a full belly and change jingling in your pocket. That's the serendipity of the hobo's life, and what most marks it out from the life of those with a home, family and steady work. There can be no knowing what fate will throw at the vagabond from one minute to the next, never mind the next day. Misfortune inevitably far outweighs the kind of good luck that befell Kromer on this particular night. In the event he spent the night in a 40-bedded flophouse dormitory surrounded by "gas-hounds" (down-and-outs who extract alcohol from gasoline to get high) at their messy and smelly business.

On Hunger 2

In Chapter 6, Kromer takes a more light-hearted approach to the topic of hunger, one of the few comedic episodes in what is otherwise a very bleak account of the Depression era. He writes of a writer friend he met in the park and in whose room he flops when the need arises. Karl works at carrying garbage out of a restaurant for two dollars a week. One dollar goes on his digs, the other on food. But Karl is always hungry. It is not certain that Karl is not Kromer himself: "Nobody buys the stuff he writes. ... He writes of starving babies, and men who tramp the streets in search of work."[8] One night, not wanting to freeze to death outside, Kromer turns the knob of Karl's room quietly. He cannot knock for fear of alerting the landlady to his presence, but he does not come empty-handed. On entering the room he observes Karl bending over his writing and knows from experience that Karl has not eaten that day.

> "Toppin's?" he says.
> "Toppin's," I say, "and more than toppin's. This is your lucky night."
> He takes the sack out of my hand and looks in.
> "Great God," he says, "a coconut pie! A real honest-to-God coconut pie!"[9]

Kromer and Karl—if one and the same—may not be proficient con men, but what they lack in cold cunning they make up for in generosity of spirit. They do not keep the feast to themselves but invite an artist friend, Werner, from the same apartment block to share it with them. Werner is another Kromer-like character, but unlike Kromer or Karl, instead of writing about deprivation, he paints it. That said, he has no more luck selling his paintings than Kromer or Karl do getting their writing into print. "They are good pictures," Kromer admits, but they don't sell. "I think it's because of the hungry look. ... I think if Werner took the hungry look out of the eyes of the people in his pictures, he could buy more hamburger steaks and take the hungry look out of his own eyes. But Karl and Werner say this would be sacrilege to art."[10]

Werner has less scruples than Kromer and Karl. When the latter have a bit of money they store up provisions for lean times. But someone is helping themselves to their stash of food so they prepare a deterrent. They buy 10 cents worth of croton oil (a fierce laxative) from the drug store and mix it into a bowl of beans which they then leave on the table of Karl's room. They go off for 10 minutes and on their return the bowl is still there but the beans are not. They double up in silent laughter as some time later Werner dashes for the toilet door with a "better-not-be-occupied" look of panic in his eyes. They know he will be dashing back to the toilet several times before the effects of the croton oil are exhausted. Kromer wants to go inside and lock the toilet door, but Karl is soft-hearted and thinks that Werner has suffered enough. They have pleasure enough from watching Werner dashing back and forth to the toilet through a crack in the door. Kromer rarely resorts to mirth in his predominantly dark treatise on human suffering and degradation, but on the occasions he does, it adds further to the authenticity of the text. This incident happened before Werner's friends invite him to share their feasts, which as well as the coconut pie includes enough doughnuts for each to have more than one.

> Tonight his [Werner's] eyes look even hungrier than ever. His eyes pop when he sees what is on the table. He licks his lips. We should not have put all this stuff on the table at once. A shock like this is not good for him. It might kill him. Werner's masterpiece will never be such a picture as this.[11]

As for the source of such a banquet, Kromer tells the others that he has befriended a baker's daughter. The other two insist he immediately marry the girl in order that they never need go hungry again. The reality is that there is no beautiful baker's daughter, just a soft-hearted baker with a straggly moustache who wheezes when he breathes. The feast now turns into a symposium on the merits of revolution in righting the inequalities and injustices of the times. But Kromer, a true cynic philosopher, scoffs at the fanaticism of his friends. One look at Werner's eyes coveting the doughnut crumbs elicits the thought, "If I was a capitalist, I would steer clear of Werner when the day arrives."

On the Hunger of Women and Children

In Chapter 6 Kromer observes the dehumanizing spectacle of women and children in the soup-line. They are old, he observes, these women in the soup-lines, because if they are smart and young they do not stand in the soup-line. "A good-looking girl can make herself a feed and a flop if she works the streets and knows how to play the coppers right." Those who don't work the streets don't stay young because they "get crows' feet under the eyes. The gnawing pain in the pit of your belly dries you up." The passage below is indicative of the kind of prose that Kromer's critics describe as causing his readers, those who choose not to be jerked violently out of the American dream, to block their ears:

> The eyes of these women you will see in a soup-line are something to look at. They are deep eyes. They are sunk in deep hollows. The hollows are rimmed with black. Their brows are wrinkled and lined from worry. They are stoop-shouldered and flat-chested. They have a look on their face. I have seen that look on the faces of dogs when they have been whipped with a stick. They hold babies in their arms, and the babies are crying. They are always crying. There are no pins sticking them. They cry because they are hungry. They clench their tiny fists. They pound against their mother's breasts. They are wasting their time. There is no supper here. Their mothers have no breasts. They are flat-chested. There is only a hollow sound as they pound. A woman cannot make milk out of slop.[12]

More such bleak images of the Depression are to follow, but in a separate story in Chapter 6, Kromer relates a story told by Karl about the fate of one particular young woman whom he meets on a park bench. He tells her to head for cover as there is a storm on the way, but she just stares blankly at Karl. "Storm?" she says. Karl repeats, "The baby will get wet … You had better get in out of the rain." "No place to go," she says. She tells Karl that she does not mind the rain, she is used to it. But the baby is only two weeks old, she tells him. She just sits there staring into the darkness. Karl says that if he knew what these women were thinking when they stare into the dark in that way he would write a book about it. A cop comes by and says to Karl, "Better get your wife and kid home, Jack. Regular hurricane blowing up." Karl fingers his last 20 cents and says to the girl that she must go to the coffee shop across the street, get a meal, and wait until the storm blows over.

Karl watches the woman slowly head for the coffee shop and then makes his own way to a pool hall up the street to wait for the storm to blow over. When he returns to the coffee shop the woman is still sitting there. He goes over to the table but she doesn't look at him; she is just staring out of the window across the road into the miserable, black and wet night. "Well, I see you got out of the wet alright." Karl says. "She turns in her seat quick. She jumps when she sees me. … She keeps staring out of the window. There is a wild look in her eyes." There follows some trivial conversation about the price of coffee but Karl observes, "I can see that she is talking batty. There is something wrong. … It is the baby. The baby is not there. She has not got the baby." Karl asks where the baby is but the woman does not answer, she continues to stare out of the window and Karl follows her gaze.[13]

> Great Christ! Through the blackness of the park I can see a white splotch on one of the benches. I know what that is. It is the baby. She has gone back after the rain and put it there. She waits here to see if anybody picks it up. We do not say anything more for a while. We just sit there and glue our eyes on this white splotch on the bench in the park.[14]

Karl asks if the baby can roll off the bench. The woman says no, she has pinned the bundle down. A tramp passes and looks down and the bundle, then hurries off and comes back with a cop who makes a call from a phone box. The woman gets up, she has seen enough. She thanks Karl for the coffee and hurries away not wanting to be recognized by the cop. Karl sits there finishing his coffee and observing the scene. A car pulls up and the cop hands the baby to a woman in the back seat. The cop looks around. He is hunting for someone. Several stiffs walk by and the cop talks to them before they move on. Then Karl panics; the cop had seen him with the woman and baby only a short time earlier. "That cop is hunting for me. He thinks that is my kid." The cop would not believe Karl's story if he told him. "They would put me in and throw the key away." Karl gets up from the table and sticking close beneath the awnings beats it home. Kromer concludes that Karl is soft-hearted. He is shocked and upset at the woman leaving her baby in a park because she cannot feed it. It reinforces his despair at a society that drives people to such desperation. But Kromer admits that he is not so soft-hearted. "That is nothing. I have seen worse than that. I know that that is nothing."[15]

On Hunger 4

Kromer is a fast learner, but does not always have the brass to pull off some of the stunts that come naturally to certain other hobos. In Chapter 5, he learns a scam from another stiff that involves sidling up to a rich-looking guy in the company of a girl. The assumption is that although the rich guy would never normally hand over money to a stiff—"Why don't you get a job. I ain't got no money for bums," et cetera—he has calculated that he will not want to appear mean and heartless in front of his date. Kromer acknowledges that he doesn't have the guts to hit on a guy with a girl but he does have the guts to "hit a high-toned restaurant." He describes walking into such an establishment with only tables, no counters. It is not evening, but women sit around in evening gowns, gold and silver slippers on their feet, and glittering with jewels. The men are dressed in tails and the tables "sparkle with the shine of silver dishes." Kromer stares at the scene in awe: "I cannot imagine people living like this."

The diners look up from their tables and stare at Kromer. "I do not blame them. I am a crummy-looking customer." The cashier asks Kromer what he wants. He replies he wants to see the manager. The manager comes over from one of the tables and asks Kromer what he wants. "I want something to eat. I am a hungry man." Kromer has calculated that it will not do the manager's business any good to turn down a hungry man in front of his well-heeled customers. "Sure, I can give a hungry man something to eat. Come on back in the kitchen with me." The customers smile in appreciation, but once in the kitchen and out of earshot, the manager shouts at the chef, "Hey Fritz, give this bum a cup of coffee and send him out the back way."

In Chapter 7, Kromer juxtaposes the Christmas of the "haves" with his own miserable Christmas. His Christmas present to himself is a threadbare coat he bummed from an undertaker who had to bury a stiff that died in the park of tuberculosis; "still a smudge of blood on the sleeve from the hemorrhage. I could have had his pants and shoes, too, but they were worse than mine." It is in this coat, bracing himself against a freezing wind howling around the corners, feet cold and soggy from the wet, that Kromer passes by the stores all lit up and packed with people buying gifts on Christmas Eve.

> Everybody is laughing. I wonder how it feels to laugh like that? That fellow and his girl in front of me have been laughing for a block. He has bundles piled clear to his chin. ... He is sporting a fur overcoat, and his shoes do not slosh as he walks. It is easier to laugh when you are warm and your shoes do not slosh.[16]

But Kromer finds some human comfort when least expecting it. He passes a dark doorway. Inside is a girl on the make. "You—you want to go with me?" she says. Kromer notices that her shoes are worse than his own, that she has runs in her stockings, and that she is not the usual type to be selling herself. He challenges her that she is not used to this and that she should go to a mission. She, in turn, admits to Kromer that he is the first man she has approached and acknowledges that she is clumsy at what she is trying to do but will learn. He is determined not to let her. She is on the street because she is starving. Kromer has four bits in his pocket and suggests they go to a restaurant and eat. She tells him that they would be better off buying groceries and going back to her room where she has a hot plate and can cook the stuff up. A plan unfolds to maximize what the two can get out of the four bits. Kromer describes the practice of "pennying-up." This involves going into various stores, pretending they are flat broke but still offering to pay rather than plain begging.

> We are hitting the red-light district. Her room is here. The red-light district is the only place where you can get a room for a dollar a week.

> I look at her. She looks at me. We are two people in the world. We are the same. We know we are the same. Our gnawing bellies and our sleepy eyes have brought us together. We do not say any more. We do not need to. I have these bundles piled up to my chin. She takes my arm, and we walk.[17]

Kromer describes the red-light district. A place where people live because they have no other place to live and where the cops don't bother anyone on the streets because that is what these streets are for. They arrive at the girl's room: "It is only a two-by-four hole, but it is clean. … It has a bed and a chair. A hot plate sits on a box." But to Kromer it is a mansion. They chat and laugh while the girl cooks. They understand each other and like each other. The girl had not eaten for two days, and had only eaten turnips and beets for three days before that. They talk of hunger and Kromer tells the girl that he got so hungry once that he tried to mug a guy and also rob a bank. "What did you think of me when I stopped you?" she says, "What do you think of a girl who will go as bad as that?" "I think she was awful hungry for a hamburger," he replies. They stand beside each other staring out of the window at the bridge all lit up to the right of town. Hundreds of stiffs live under that bridge, but Kromer will not be sleeping there tonight; he is invited to sleep at the girl's room "until the landlady kicks us out."

Bank Robber

Following the earlier tale from Chapter 5, after Kromer is thrown out the back door of the restaurant kitchen for begging for a meal, he takes off without even waiting for the coffee. Another lesson learned, a more desperate plan in the making. Kromer has acquired a gun which he now fingers in his pocket. He is slowly starving to death for the umpteenth time and hatches a make-or-break plan. He figures that things have got so bad that he has nothing to lose by risking his life to rob a bank. If his plan works he will have solved his problems once and for all; if not, he is ready to put an end to his suffering:

> They have starved me to death long enough. I am tired of walking the streets all day long asking for work. … I will stop asking for work. I will quit standing in the soup-lines for hours for a bowl of slop. I have made up my mind to take a chance. You can only die once. [18]

And so Kromer heads for the small branch bank he has chosen for his heist. He looks across the street. Through the window he sees the cashiers in white shirts with sleeves rolled up, passing cash to customers from piles of bills in drawers. There are plenty of such piles and Kromer calculates that just one of them will set him up for life. What does he have to lose? Only soup and stale bread. We learn the carefully thought-through details of Kromer's plan: the small alley near the bank that leads to several short streets; the picture show playing a short distance up one of these streets that Kromer will dive into until the hunt is over; into the toilet for a shave and change of appearance; then back to the mission, "the last place ... they will look for a guy with plenty of jack." Then off to the train station to buy a ticket out of there.

As he stands at a table in the bank pretending to write a check, deciding which cash desk to approach, that "sickish feeling" returns to the pit of his stomach, his hands start to shake, but he is committed. "I have made up my mind, shaky hands or not, I will sleep in no more lousy mission flops, I have whined for my last meal." He has a gun and will use it if he has to. "No one cares whether I live or die. They would let me starve to death on the streets without lifting a hand to help me." And so why should he care about the guys handing out piles of bills from their wire cages? "To hell with everybody I'm going to get mine." So Kromer gets in line knowing that the cashiers have guns also and will not hesitate to use them, even though it's not their dough they are protecting. He is sixth in his queue and describes the wrinkles on the back of the neck of the woman in front of him. She's fat and makes a good screen to hide the hand covering the bulge in his coat. Now there are only two people in front of him. The fat woman moves up to the window still shielding the bulge in Kromer's inside coat pocket. He observes that the guy in the adjacent cage locks up and retires to a back room; one less bank clerk to take pot shots at him.

Kromer presses his fingers around the handle of the gun, feeling its roughness, and hoping he will not have to shoot it. His hands are still shaking, and his knees too. The fat woman steps away from the window and Kromer and the cashier eye each other. "Yes, sir," the cashier says to Kromer. He gives his gun a yank but only the handle comes out; the rest is stuck in the torn lining of his coat. He yanks harder but still it does not come out. The cashier is suspicious now and steps closer to the window peering at Kromer. His face goes from pale to sickish green when he sees Kromer's hand pulling at his pocket but he has nothing on him yet, and although he realizes that a stick-up is in progress the two engage in an absurd and embarrassed conversation to pass the short time that elapses before Kromer's next move. "What are you pulling at your pocket for?" "Can't a guy put his hand in his pocket, if he wants to?" et cetera.

> He does not take his eyes of my hand that is in my pocket. I cannot pull at the gat while he is looking. He will yell or set off the alarm. I can feel the cold sweat that stands out on my forehead. Christ, but I am scared. I have to get out of here, but how am I going to get out of here?[19]

Kromer turns and starts walking fast toward the door, feeling the eyes of the cashier boring into the back of his head, and the eyes of everyone else in the bank staring at the bulge in his pocket still covered by his hand. When Kromer does turn around, he sees the cashier backing out of his cage to call one of the security guards. He cannot be caught with a gun in his pocket so he starts to run. "I must reach the alley before this cop gets to the street with his gat. I cannot have this cop filling me full of holes from behind. I run as fast as my shaking legs will carry me." As Kromer dives into the alley and headfirst into a coal chute, so too ends his failed career as a bank robber—but not, on this occasion, his life. His landing place reassures him of his safety. The place has not been used in a long time. Cobwebs stretch from ceiling to floor. As he lies still across the rafters of his basement hideaway, still clutching his gun, Kromer strains his ears for sounds of a commotion outside, but the only sound he hears is his own breathing. In his panic and paranoia he determines to shoot it out if he is hunted down.

Kromer crouches in his cellar hiding place for hours, aching in every joint, cramps shooting up his legs and back. He calculates that if he hides his gun he cannot be charged with attempted armed robbery. No one saw a gun, only a bulge. "You cannot send a guy up because you think he was packing a gat. You have to see the gat." Only when it's night does he dare emerge back into the open. He hides the gun under a pile of garbage after carefully rubbing off any fingerprints and walks down the street where he runs into a guy in a tweed suit: "Buddy," he says, "I am down on my luck with no place to flop. Could you spare me a few dimes to get me a flop?"[20]

Death on the Fritz

What follows are four very different descriptions by Kromer of hobo deaths: a suicide, starvation, old age, and the violent death of a teenager. In Chapter 3, Kromer describes being in a mission flop and noticing a middle-aged man in a suit, pacing nervously up and down. "He has not been on the fritz long. I can tell." The man goes into the toilet and blows his brains out.

> "What's he wanna bump hisself off fer?" says this stiff with blood on his face, "there ain't nothin' to bump yerself off fer."
>
> "He bumped hisself off because he's got the guts to bump hisself off," says this other stiff. "We are afraid to bump ourselves off, so we live in mission flops and guzzle lousy mission slop."[21]

Kromer notes that a clean sheet is brought to lay the man out on, observing: "This is the first time this stiff has had a clean sheet for a long time." Kromer then returns to his bed where he contemplates bumping himself off: "Why not? It don't hurt. I bet that guy never knew what hit him. Just a jagged hole, and a pool of blood mixed with black, and it is all over. He had the guts, and now everything is all right with him."[22] He looks out of the third-floor window at the hard concrete pavement below and considers how simple it would be to jump headfirst out of the window. In a few seconds it would all be over. But after considering the mess he has just witnessed on the toilet floor and contemplating the mess his own head might make, he pulls off his clothes and crawls into bed.

Chapter 8 opens with another description of the indignities of one of the many soup-lines that Kromer has witnessed during his time on the fritz. He has been standing in line for two hours, and in front and behind him are stretched hundreds of other men. A commotion up ahead in the line causes a distraction. An old stiff is stretched out on the pavement, eyes wide open and not moving:

> He is tired of waiting for this line to start moving. He is stretched out on the concrete, and as dead as four o'clock. I can see that this stiff is lucky. There will be no more waiting for him. ... There is no fuss when a stiff kicks off in a soup-line. There is no bother. They throw a sheet over him and haul him away.[23]

In Chapter 12, we are given a description of a stiff dying in another mission flop, as Kromer lies in bed listening to the dying man. Another stiff is complaining because he is kept awake by the rattle from the old man's hollow chest. Kromer is angered, showing his humanity when he says:

> This stiff has not always been a stiff. Somewhere, some time, this stiff has had a home. Maybe he had a family. Where are they now? I do not know. ... The fritz has made him alone. He will die cooped up in a mission with a thousand stiffs that snore through the night, but he will die alone. The electric light outside will go on and off in the dark, "Jesus Saves," but that will not help this stiff. He will die alone.[24]

Kromer yells to the mission orderly to call for an ambulance, "Are you going to let this poor bastard suffer all night?" "What do you think I'm goin' to do with him?" is the reply. "You're a God-damn mission stiff, and mission stiffs are sons of bitches." The argument continues and Kromer is told that he will be thrown out, but continues anyway. "You call an ambulance for this stiff or I will call it myself, and beat the hell out of you besides." Eventually a doctor and two guys in white coats with a stretcher arrive. The pathetic attempts by the doctor to get the dying man to tell him where he lives prompts the following diatribe from Kromer:

> This stiff does not answer him. He does not tell him, but I can tell him. He lives wherever he can find a hole to get in out of the rain. He lives wherever he can find a couple of burlap sacks to cover up his bones. He cannot tell him this, because he is dying. I have seen a lot of old stiffs die. I can tell. His bloodless lips pull back over his yellow teeth. It looks as though this stiff is grinning at this croaker who asks him where he lives. I shiver in my blankets. This stiff is a ghost. A ghost of skin and bones. A bloodless ghost. I try not to look at him. A dead man's grin is a terrible thing. A mocking, shivery thing.[25]

In contrast to Kromer's witnessing of this dying old man, in Chapter 11, we are given a much more violent description of death as it relates to the dangers of beating fast-moving trains. Similar such incidents are described elsewhere in this book, but here Kromer describes the scene as he and some other stiffs are waiting to move out from a hobo jungle. They have already gauged from placing their ears to the railway tracks that unless this train stops to take on water, it will be too fast to make it. "We are old-timers. We know by the sing in the rails when a drag is too hot." So they go back to their bindles and sit down to wait. If they can't make this one, another one will be along tomorrow. "What is a day to us ... We are not going any place." And when the train comes they know they won't make it, but they see a kid standing by the rails preparing to run. The cars whiz by and he runs alongside making a dive for the rear step. The other hobos look on hopelessly, knowing full well that it is impossible to make such a jump. But the boy jumps anyway, only to be swung high and thrown in between the cars. "He smashes against the couplings. He screams. He is under. Oh, Jesus Christ, he is under! He is under those wheels." The other tramps run over to where the boy is lying beside the tracks. "He is cut to ribbons. Where his right arm and leg were, there are only two red gashes. The blood spurts out of the stumps. It oozes to the ground and makes a pool in the cinders."[26]

They drag him away from the tracks and the kid has a sheepish grin on his face. "It hurts his pride to have a drag throw him." Kromer offers the kid a cigarette, leaning over so that the boy doesn't see that his limbs are missing. He just tells Kromer that his arm feels numb and tingly. "That old drag was balling the jack. I must have bumped it pretty hard." Kromer feels sick to the stomach as he watches the boy dying. "It is hard enough to watch anybody die ... But a kid is different. You kind of expect a kid to live instead of die."

> There is no color in his face now. All the color is on the ground mixed with the cinders. He closes his eyes. The cigarette drops out of his mouth. He quivers. Just a quiver like he is cold. That is all. He is gone. I unfold

> a newspaper and cover up his face. We sit there in the dark and look at each other.[27]

Kromer makes several references throughout his book to death being preferable to being on the fritz, even describing possible scenarios for ending his own life, yet the only hint that he may ever have attempted suicide comes from the book's dedication: "To Jolene, Who Turned Off the Gas."

On Hunger 5—and Homosexuality

Although it was of course natural that homosexuality would form part of tramp life, as it does any non-celibate culture, the only previous reference encountered to homosexuality among tramps is an obscure essay by Josiah Flynt in Havelock Ellis' *Studies in the Psychology of Sex (Vol. 2)*, titled "Homosexuality among Tramps" (1927); and even then, the essay had a negative focus on the habit of certain older tramps to prey on young runaways or road kids. Tom Kromer's autobiographical references to homosexuality among tramps is an essay on the mutually exploitative relationship between certain gay men with money and straight guys "on the fritz" desperate for money.

Considering the taboos and retributions around homosexuality that existed at the time, the notable feature of Chapter 4 of *Waiting for Nothing* is the remarkable manner in which the author candidly places himself at the center of a narrative that he must have calculated would scandalize the reading public of the time. Either that, or Kromer had no expectations of his writing ever being published, in which case equal tribute is due the press for having the courage to publish Kromer's raw and uncompromising work. Be that as it may, at the point of publication of the first British edition of *Waiting for Nothing* by Constable & Company (1935), the censor forced the publisher to remove Chapter 4 from the book. Because the book had already been typeset and printed, but not bound, the publisher decided to replace the gap between chapters 3 and 5 with eight blue pages which included an unusual disclosure at the front of the book (avoiding any direct reference to homosexuality) titled, "Why Chapter IV is missing from *Waiting for Nothing*." The publisher's lengthy explanation for removing the chapter, hinting that the edit was made under duress, ends as follows:

> We have cut out Chapter IV entirely—cut it out with reluctance and with shame, merely consoling ourselves with the thought that fortunately the continuity of the book is in no way affected. Were we wrong to cut it out? No one can possibly say. Would we have been guilty of corrupting youth had we left it in? Once again, no one—in advance—has the smallest idea.

> That is how things are in England these days; and that is why *Waiting for Nothing* appears in England in an emasculated form.

But to return to Chapter 4 itself, reintroduced in later editions, the following passage sets the scene and the modus operandi—incorporating slang terms for homosexuals that one would assume had a much more recent provenance:

> He lays his hand across my leg. I must not jerk my leg away. He is feeling me out. If I jerk my leg away, he will see that he is not going to make me. This queer will not put out for a meal until he sees that I am a good risk. I leave my knee where it is. These pansies give me the willies, but I have got to get myself a feed. I have not had a decent feed for a week.[28]

The game continues not only with the guy testing Kromer out, but Kromer trying to improve his own chances of a score by playing the virgin—well, as far as making it with another guy is concerned. Kromer's pursuer is a well-heeled and well-known local queen: plucked eyebrows, rouge, lipstick, the works. She invites Kromer to come back to her place later with the additional lures of a hot bath and some fresh clothes. Another stiff is curious to know if Kromer got a result:

> "Mrs. Carter," he says. "I see you out talkin' to her in the park."
>
> "So her name is Mrs. Carter?" I say. "Sure, I made her for four bits. I got a date for tonight."
>
> "You better fill it. She's in the dough. Lousy with it."
>
> "Any strings on her?"
>
> "Not now. She was livin' with a stiff she picked up off the street, but Geraldine, that big red-headed guy with the scarred face, took him away from her."
>
> ...
>
> "You are a lucky stiff making Mrs. Carter. There are plenty of stiffs in this town would give their eye teeth to make Mrs. Carter."
>
> "Where does she hang out?"
>
> "She lives up on the Avenue with the swells. The joint she lives in is lousy with queers, and what is more, they are lousy with jack. Mrs. Carter rooms with a cashier of a bank."
>
> "He queer, too?" I say.
>
> "Sure, she's queer," he says, "but you will not have a chance with her. Mrs. Carter would cut your throat if you tried to pull the wool over her eyes. She is a tough customer. She says she will scratch Geraldine's eyes out does she get the chance. My advice is stick to Mrs. Carter."[29]

When his date meets up with him in the park that evening, Kromer has to submit to the jealous scowls of the other stiffs in the park: "We walk down the street. We are going to this fairy's room. It is misery for me to walk on the street with this queer. People stop in their tracks and watch her wiggle." On entering Mrs. Carter's apartment, Kromer is confronted by a spectacle that could not be of greater contrast to his life on the fritz. He describes a room like that of a palace. Black satin drapes hanging in folds from ceiling to floor, a glass chandelier hanging from bronze chains with links "as big around as my wrist." His soleless, shabby shoes sink into a thick pile rug, and on a sky-blue lounge is sprawled Gloria, Mrs. Carter's roommate, in a peach negligée edged in gold, legs shaved and sporting a single silver ankle bracelet with a pink cameo the size of an egg: "'Have a good date, deary?' he says without looking up from his book."

The chapter concludes with the inevitable invitation to the bedroom and the following observations from Kromer. Mrs. Carter will stay awake until Kromer goes to bed and he has to sleep sometime so, "What the hell? A guy has got to eat, and what is more he has to flop. 'Sure,' I say, 'I am ready for the hay.'" From this interlude Kromer takes the following simple wisdom: "This is a funny world, and there are a lot of funny people in it. That is one thing I have learned since I've been on the road."[30]

The Doughnut Scam

One of the lighter aspects of *Waiting for Nothing* are Kromer's descriptions of the many scams employed by hobos either to acquire food or the price of a meal, or to hang on to what they have already got. In the following story Kromer asks a stiff why he walks around with a role of chicken wire under his arm. "The coppers," the stiff tells him. "What do coppers have to do with chicken wire?" Kromer asks. The stiff asks Kromer how he walks to avoid getting stopped by the cops and frisked for any change he might be carrying. Kromer replies that it's obvious, you go as fast as you can; if you don't go fast the cops will stop and frisk you. But the chicken wire stiff offers an alternative logic:

> "But I don't walk fast on the main stem or anywhere else, and the coppers don't bother me."
>
> "They don't bother you?" I say.
>
> "They do not," he says. "They don't think I'm a stiff. What would a stiff be doin' with a roll of chicken wire under his arm?"
>
> "You're a smart stiff," I say. "I have never tried that."

> "It's just as easy to be a smart stiff as a dumb stiff," he says. "All coppers are dumb. A smart stiff will fool a copper every time."[31]

Earlier the stiff had asked Kromer what he would do if he had a 10-cent piece, and Kromer replied that he would buy himself coffee and sinkers (a doughnut to dunk in the coffee). That is why you continue eating slop, the stiff replies. Impressed by the chicken wire stunt, Kromer now asks the stiff how *he* would use the 10-cent piece. His scam is predicated on his knowledge that while most men are hard-hearted, women "do not like to see a hungry stiff starve to death." The stiff buys a doughnut and walks down the street to where a group of women are waiting for a streetcar. He lets the first streetcar go by, then carefully plants the doughnut on the ground in sight of where the women would have been. The he backs off and waits for another group of women to assemble for the next streetcar. When his intended victims are in place, the stiff makes his move. He crosses the street, then stops and stares at the doughnut on the curb. "I expect to see him make a dive for it but he does not. … He just stands there and watches it." The women see him looking and wonder why will a guy stand on the street and stare at a doughnut. Then the stiff walks on by but stops a little way up the street, before coming back and snatching up the doughnut, swallowing it almost whole. "By the way he acts, you would think this was the first doughnut this stiff had ever snatched off the curb." The desired impression is to make the women watching believe the man is starving and has not eaten a proper meal for months. First one woman approaches the tramp, taking some change out of her purse. He shakes his head in refusal but holds out his hand for the money anyway, adding to the theater by giving the impression that his pride is hurt.

> Four or five of these women fish around in their pocketbooks and walk over to this stiff who hides behind the post. This is real money. This is not chicken-feed that this guy is taking in. One of these women shells out a buck. I can see the green of it from across the street. If I had the guts. … You just dive down on a doughnut, and these women do the rest.[32]

Kromer catches up with the other stiff later and compliments him on his performance. The profit from this one doughnut alone was $2.60. Sitting down later enjoying a meal with his newfound friend on the proceeds, Kromer is chastised for his own lack of resourcefulness: "Any stiff that eats mission slop ought to have his fanny kicked. There is too many doughnuts in this world for a stiff to eat mission slop." But Kromer has to admit to himself that although he has the brains and imagination to work such a scam, as with his other failed enterprises, he simply cannot do it. He just cannot summon up the guts.

On Beating Trains and Encounters with Rats

It has been acknowledged that Kromer was more a tramp of circumstances than he was a tramp of desire, yet in two chapters of *Waiting for Nothing* he describes the same sense of terror mixed with exhilaration as have other tramp writers in these pages. Read for instance Bart Kennedy's demoniacal ride perched on the cow-catcher at the front of an engine, and Jack London's account of outsmarting the bulls on a Canadian-Pacific cross-country epic in the chapter "Holding Her Down" from *The Road*.

Chapter 9 opens with Kromer crouched in the doorway of the blind baggage car of a passenger train. We are not told how, where, or why he boarded the train. He perches there for five hours, legs dangling beneath the car, blown this way and that by the freezing wind. But he cannot feel his swinging legs because they are numb with cold. He wonders how he will even get off the train if it slows down, as his legs would be unable to support him. He curses getting on the train in the first place. Like others who have traveled in this manner before him, sparks from the engine burn his back and neck. He tries every means to prevent falling asleep, as this would result in certain death, jerking himself awake when he feels himself doze: "You damn fool … you can't go to sleep here. You will fall under those wheels that sing beneath you. … Those wheels would make mincemeat of you. You would not be cold any more." Kromer starts to sing, yelling at the top of his voice to hear himself above the roar of the wind and the wheels. He can feel himself falling asleep and wonders if this is what it's like to freeze to death: "I know that a stiff is better off dead, but I don't want to fall under those wheels." He knows that he is drifting off to sleep, he sticks his head sideways for the wind to blast his face, tear away his tears, and keep him awake. All of a sudden he feels the brakes of the train hit and grabs at the sides of his perch with fingers that have lost all feeling. They slip but then hold. The train slackens speed and then he sees the lights of a town and knows that he must find a way to leave the train. "I laugh like a crazy man when I see that this drag is going to stop."[33]

When the train starts pulling to a stop to take on water, Kromer knows that the jerk of the stop could still throw him under the wheels. He has to get off before the train starts on its way again but is fearful that his frozen legs will not support him. He tries to move them and can see them move but feels nothing. He pulls himself to his feet and stands but cannot feel the car beneath his feet. Somehow he manages to climb down the ladder but it is still a long drop to the ground. He jumps and falls face-down in the cinders at the side of the track. The train whistles and pulls out leaving Kromer lying there in the cinders with a bleeding face, watching the coaches go by. His legs still have no feeling in them and he shivers at the roar of the wheels and the sound of the wind underneath. "I push my fists into the ground and get to my feet. I grimace at the pain that shoots through my legs, but I grit my teeth and walk."[34]

On entering a nearby café, the guy behind the counter backs away in fear at the spectacle of Kromer, one eye on the till. So Kromer glances at a wall mirror: "I do not blame this guy for being scared. What I see scares me, too. My face is black as the ace of spades. It is smeared with blood from the cuts of the cinders as they scraped my face." But, even though he begs nicely, he is thrown out without the much-needed cup of coffee. He goes in search of the town bull and begs to be locked up in jail for the night. But he is even denied that privilege and is chased out of town with threats of harm if he comes back. On the way out of town Kromer spies the lights of a shack in a pecan grove. He knocks on the door to beg for food and shelter but is greeted by an evangelistic psycho: "Son, do you believe in Christ?" Kromer is given no food but is led to a barn and buried up to his neck in pecans and given a burlap sack to put over his head to fend off the rats. Whereas on the train he could not keep his eyes open, now he is unable to keep them closed. He contemplates his lot in tragicomic style:

> Here I am covered with pecans. Before I went on the fritz, I was lying nights in a feather bed. I thought I was hard up then. I had a decent front. I had three hots [meals] and a flop. Can you imagine a guy thinking he is hard up when he has his three hots and a flop? That was two years ago, but two years are ten years when you are on the fritz. I look ten years older now. I looked like a young punk then. I was a young punk. I had some color in my cheeks. I have hit the skids since then. This is as low down as a guy can get, being down in a hole with pecans on top of him for covers.[35]

Kromer has had a fear of rats since waking up one day in a hobo jungle with two on his face. He has nightmares of rats as big as cats sitting on his face and gnawing at his nose and eyes. Another rat anecdote is related in Chapter 11 where Kromer protects himself from the creatures in a hobo jungle: no ordinary rats, big rats. But Kromer calculates that he is too smart for these rats. He has a big piece of canvas, "to keep these rats from biting a chunk out of my nose when I sleep." But it does not keep out the sound nor feel of the rats as they crawl all over him. "A good-sized rat tramps hard. You can feel their weight as they press on top of you. You can hear them sniffing as they try to get in." So he pulls the canvas tighter around his head.[36]

But to return to the shed where we left our hero up to his neck in rat feed: in spite of not wanting to offend the religious freak who offered him his pecan bed for the night, Kromer now extricates himself from the hole and hightails it down the road. He heads for the railroad yard and finds himself an empty wagon in which to spend the rest of the night, but shortly after turning in he is awakened by a sickly feeling that makes the hairs on the back of his neck stand out. The last six pages of this chapter describe the nightmare that follows with Kromer, in spite of his severely weakened condition, having to defend his life against a crazy guy with a knife determined to murder him.

In Chapter 10 we hear more on beating trains, and Kromer makes a reckless attempt to jump a high-flying express. He is one of several hobos in a rail siding waiting to board the next train through. But the next drag is an express and the more seasoned hobos slink back to the jungle knowing that this one is too hot to risk. The younger, more foolhardy hobos hang on to wait for the train to pass through. "I can see that a guy can't make this one. … The roar she makes as she crashes over the rails, and the sparks that shoot from her stacks, tell me she is just too fast. A stiff is foolish to even think about nailing this one."[37]

But first one and then another do try to make the train. The first one dives for the steps at the front of the carriage; it jerks his arm, spins and slams him against the car, but he hangs on and makes it. The second guy, less confident than the first, is likewise slammed against the car but then thrown headfirst into the cinders of the ditch at the side of the track; "Christ, but there's a stiff that's dead or skinned alive." Kromer does not have much time to make up his mind. "I've waited all night in the cold to make this drag, and I am going to make it. That first stiff made it. … I've nailed as many drags as the next stiff." Kromer makes sure that he goes for the step at the front end of the car. If he goes for the rear end and misses, he could be thrown between the carriages.

> I judge my distance. I start running along this track. I hold my hands up to the sides of these cars. They brush my fingers as they fly by. I feel this step hit my fingers, and dive. Christ, but I am lucky. My fingers get a hold of it. I grab it as tight as I can. I know what is coming. I slam against the side of the car. I think my arms will be jerked out of their sockets. My ribs feel like they are smashed, they ache so much. I hang on. I made it. I am bruised and sore, but I made it. I climb to the tops. The wind rushes by and cools the sweat on my face. I cannot believe I made this drag, she is high-balling it down the tracks so fast.[38]

Kromer spends two hours lying atop the car before he can disembark, stiff as a board from pressing down onto the frost-covered roof to protect himself from the relentless and freezing wind. He then finds a car already occupied by 10 other stiffs and jumps in before the train sets off again. There is a comical scene where the hobos set fire to a heap of tar paper on the floor of the carriage which they then feed with wood carved from the beams of the car with their knives, all the while huddling round the fire to keep warm. Black smoke fills the car but they keep the door shut to avoid attracting the shacks, putting up with the smoke to keep warm. Kromer describes pulling off first one sock and then the other to try and warm his feet on the fire before retiring exhausted to a corner of the car. In this case, smoke inhalation was the only result of the fire. Jim Tully describes a similar such fire in a boxcar in Chapter 12, one that burns through the floor of the carriage and has flames licking up the sides before the occupants are able to escape.

When the train pulls up to take on water, the door slides open. It is not the shacks. Two mean-looking yeggs climb into the car carrying flashlights and proceed to hold up the rest of the car's occupants at gunpoint. "I have got my opinion of any stiff who will hold up another stiff and take his chicken feed away from him. Any guy who will do that is a low-livered bastard. I do not say that out loud, though—not with those gats pointed at us like that." One by one, hands held high in the air, the stiffs are called up from the back of the carriage to hand over their meager possessions. "These are two of the toughest-looking mugs I have seen in a long time. One of them frisks this red-headed guy while the other one keeps us covered with the gat and flashes the light on us." These guys are pros; not only do they go through the stiff's pockets but they go through the sweatbands on their hats and the linings of their coats. The first guy says he only has chicken feed and he's right, but pinned to the lining of the next stiff's coat is five dollars, and, as Kromer observes, "he has been bumming smoking off the rest of these stiffs. A tight stiff like that deserves to lose his dough." He gets smashed in the face with the butt of a pistol for trying to hold out on the hijackers.

Eventually it's Kromer's turn to step forward. He owns up to having four bits in his pocket and they find nothing more in his clothes. "Where are you hidin' your dough? Come clean or you will get what that other stiff got." … "Four bits is all I'm holding. You've already got all the dough I'm holding." Kromer is sent back to the group feeling smug. He has hidden two dollars under a bandage on his arm smeared over with iodine. "It looks like I got a plenty sore arm. But there is nothing the matter with my arm."[39]

On Hunger 6

Chapter 11 opens in a hobo jungle strewn with tin cans and broken bottles. Between the piles of garbage are fires with folk huddled round for warmth, including women and children. A man and a woman huddle by a fire nearby and the woman is grasping a baby in her arms. The baby has croup and coughs until it is black in the face. Kromer can see that the woman is frightened as she pounds the baby's back, but it can only occasionally catch its breath. The child's father, shoulders hunched, paces up and down between the piles of garbage, helpless to be able to save his family from their certain fate. Kromer deduces the following from the hobo tableau confronting him: "Where are they going? I do not know. They do not know. …There is no work. He cannot leave his wife and kids to starve to death alone, so he brings them with him. Now he can watch them starve to death."

> When I look at these stiffs by the fire, I am looking at a graveyard. There is hardly room to move between the tombstones. There are no epitaphs carved in marble here. The tombstones are men. The epitaphs are chiseled in sunken shadows on their cheeks. These are dead men. They are ghosts that walk the streets by day. They are ghosts sleeping with yesterday's newspapers thrown around them for cover at night.[40]

Later Life

Kromer married the year after *Waiting for Nothing* was published, and settled in Albuquerque where he started writing his novel *Michael Kohler*, a political treatise on labor unions and the injustices of big business, drawn on the experiences and struggles of his father and others in the coal and glass industries. Kromer's only other short writings survived from his college days, including *Pity the Poor Panhandler*, a piece based on the bums in his hometown of Huntington. Together with his unfinished novel, these were eventually published in 1986 as *Waiting for Nothing and Other Writings* by the University of Georgia Press. Kromer became invalided with tuberculosis around 1940, never finished *Michael Kohler*, and had to give up writing altogether, eventually returning to live with his family in Huntington in 1960 where he lived until his death at the age of 63.

ENDNOTES

1 Kromer, Tom. *Waiting for Nothing*, New York: Hill & Wang, 1979, Preface

2 Ibid.

3 Mulhauser, Roland. "Bum and Mission Stiff," in the *Saturday Review of Literature*, March 30, 1935, p. 584

4 Marsh, Fred T. "Absolutely Down and Out," in *Books*, March 3, 1935, p. 2

5 *Waiting for Nothing*, op. cit., p. 3

6 Ibid., pp. 3–4

7 Ibid., pp. 7–8

8 Ibid., p. 95

9 Ibid., p. 97

10 Ibid., p. 98

11 Ibid., pp. 100–101

12 Ibid., pp. 93–94

13 Ibid., pp. 104–105

14 Ibid., pp. 106–107

15 Ibid., p. 108

16 Ibid., p. 111

17 Ibid., pp. 118–119

18 Ibid., p. 80

19 Ibid., p. 87

20 Ibid., p. 91

21 Ibid., pp. 56–57

22 Ibid., p. 57

23 Ibid., pp. 125–126

24 Ibid., p. 181

25 Ibid., p. 183

26 Ibid., pp. 174–176

27 Ibid., p. 177

28 Ibid., p. 61

29 Ibid., pp. 64–65

30 Ibid., pp. 73–74

31 Ibid., p. 129

32 Ibid., p. 132

33 Ibid., pp. 134–136

34 Ibid., pp. 136–137

35 Ibid., pp. 140–141

36 Ibid., pp. 165–166

37 Ibid., p. 151

38 Ibid., p. 153

39 Ibid., pp. 158–162

40 Ibid., p. 166

Kathleen Phelan

(1917–2014)

I am a bridge between the old style tramp with the stick and bundle and the backpacking drifter seen nowadays along the roads of the world. The tramps of yore took a year to walk from Penzance to Aberdeen. But as a pacy professional hitchhiking vagabond, I think of the Interstate 80 from New York to San Francisco, or the road from Scotland to Sicily as just another village street.

Kathleen Phelan, *What Lamp Has Destiny*

Preamble

An explanation is required as to why only one woman tramp writer is featured in this collection. There was certainly no shortage of women, explorers, naturalists, mountaineers, missionaries and journalists, who walked vast distances and wrote about their adventures throughout the period covered by this book. But for the most part, these women were funded for their expeditions and conducted them in the company of others, in some cases including a retinue of servants, in the manner of many of their Victorian male counterparts—not that this in any way lessens their incredible achievements with additional challenges faced precisely *because* they were women. However, unlike Kathleen Phelan, none of these women embraced the vagabond lifestyle, or espoused their philosophy of tramping, in the manner of those who are the subject of this volume. Indeed, Kathleen Phelan out-tramped all of the male vagabonds featured in this volume by virtue of spending 77 of her 97 years living on the road.

If the reader is aware of any other contender for the epithet of woman tramp writer, this writer would be very interested to hear from them. But for now, Kathleen Phelan will serve as the sole woman representative of this rare genus of humans. She will be referred to simply as Kathleen throughout this chapter to avoid any confusion with her husband, Jim Phelan (Chapter 13).

Early Life

Kathleen Phelan (née Newton) was born in Easington Colliery, County Durham, on the east coast of northern England, on November 28, 1917. Her father George Newton was the deputy manager of the local mine and, prior to her marriage, her mother had taught music and French at the Bede Collegiate School in Sunderland.

Kathleen had an older sister Norma, a brother Tom, and a younger sister (by 10 years), Elizabeth, who contributed to the writing of this chapter. Both Kathleen and Norma attended university in the early 1930s. Kathleen studied Physical Education and English at the insistence of her father who considered teaching to be the most appropriate profession for his daughter because, "If you don't get married then you'll get a pension at the end of it."[1] Kathleen's real passion had been to become a journalist and, as Elizabeth further recalls, Kathleen used to haunt Fleet Street, the journalistic center of London. Writers were also regular visitors at the Newton's house and as a child, Kathleen remembers sitting on George Bernard Shaw's knee.

Kathleen and her siblings grew up in a politically charged background that included having Ramsay MacDonald, the first Labour Prime Minister, and Lady MacDonald as house guests. This atmosphere had an influence on Kathleen who used to fool her father by going off with her sports gear on the pretext of furthering her career as a teacher, but instead made for the Fabian Society where she would listen to and join in political debate. Sadly, George Newton died just before war was declared and before he was able to witness his two eldest daughters graduating from university. After graduating, Kathleen got a job in Newcastle but shortly afterwards was evacuated to the Lake District. She did not return home following that event but taught in what Elizabeth describes as "all the 'way-out' schools like Rudolf Steiner." When at the Steiner School in Gloucester, Kathleen was already spending her time off and holidays walking and hitchhiking around the country. Discussing Kathleen's wanderlust, Elizabeth describes her as "the little girl who never wanted to grow up." Elizabeth also refers to possible Romani ancestry:

> She [Kathleen] always used to say that from way back we came from 'didicoy' on my father's side ... the odd ones, when you looked at them, with the jet-black hair ... and I think that has something to do with her nature and the wandering. ... I had an aunt who had a little shop, and when it was Spring, at fair time, all the gypsy people went to the shop.[2]

In spite of her yearning to stay forever young at heart, Elizabeth claims that Kathleen could have excelled in any conventional career of her choosing. Instead she chose the life of a vagabond and excelled at it, not least speaking 13 languages including Arabic, Urdu, Spanish, French, Italian and Scandinavian, all of which served her well during her global ramblings.

On one of Kathleen's trips to London as a teenager, she met a Californian named Joe Cassidy whom she describes as a "professional hitch-hiker." Cassidy had tramped across North and South America and was now tramping around Europe: "Until then I had never thought about vagabondage as a profession." From Joe, Kathleen learned that "if you did not like a place, you stood on a grass verge and jerked your thumb." Kathleen sums up the difference between the tramp and other mortals in the small typed pamphlet she wrote titled *Hiking a Hitch*. Kathleen produced many editions of the same work (the most recent in 2010), bound with cotton stitches and including individual acrylics hand-painted separately into each copy—half a dozen of which she always carried with her wherever she went and persuaded people to buy at £5 per copy, but frequently giving them away for free:

> Other people, when things went wrong or when they were being ground down—other people grinned and groaned and bore it. But Joe Cassidy—

> and I—merely jerked thumb over shoulder and opened a car door and moved on to nicer things and more pleasant people.[3]

Such sentiments have parallels with descriptions by other tramps in this book, including Jim Phelan himself who talks about heading for the horizon when things got tough. Kathleen opens her unpublished autobiography of her 22 years with Jim (discovered following her death) by providing her curriculum vitae: "Profession: — Vagabond. Money: — Nil. Address: — No fixed residence." Kathleen never took to the road with money or possessions. "Mostly I hitch the road without copper coin." Her early modus operandi was simply to stick out her thumb, and wherever the motorist was headed, that is the route she would take. She had also become a regular with the bohemian scene in London, spending weekends with friends in Covent Garden whose apartments were meeting places for writers and artists. One of these belonged to a Polish couple whose house was a regular destination for political activists. "I thought I was at the heart of the revolution—I was not sure which one—several in fact because all the speakers had such wildly differing viewpoints ... those days were the beginning of my real education."[4]

Married Life on the Road

This section draws mainly on Kathleen's unpublished autobiography with the working title *What Lamp Has Destiny*.[5] This manuscript was discovered following Kathleen's death and recounts her 22 years on the road with Jim Phelan. She would spend a further 48 years tramping solo following Jim's death. At the time Kathleen met Jim Phelan, 23 years her senior, she was already an experienced tramp spending most of her time out on the road. She had been hitchhiking out of Wales northward, when on the outskirts of Chester a motorist stopped to offer her a lift. When asked where she was headed, she just listed a string of cities to the north at random. The driver told her that he could take her as far as Garstang. Kathleen had no idea where Garstang was but hopped in anyway. When they reached the village, the driver pointed out the A6 road continuing north and said that he was turning off for Blackpool and that she was welcome to come the rest of the way with him. Kathleen declined and waited for another lift going on north. The story continues in Kathleen's own words.

> It was late afternoon and for a long while the road was very quiet. I began to regret not having gone to Blackpool.

> Then I saw a man sauntering towards me on the opposite side of the road. Occasionally he turned back to flag a vehicle southbound. Cars were few and far between in those days, but so were hitch-hikers, so we eyed one another plenty. When he was directly opposite, he stopped and stared across.
>
> About six feet tall, he wore a leather jacket and corduroy trousers. A large black hat was pushed to the back of his head and around his neck was knotted a red silk scarf. A duffel bag hung from his shoulder.
>
> He strolled across the road and stood in front of me and grinned. He looked as though he hadn't a care in the world. High, wide and handsome. I had never seen anyone more colourful or alive-looking.
>
> He stood and looked at me a while, I stared back. Then in a deep, lilting, Irish voice, he said, "And where might you be going."
>
> Me—I said nothing, just kept looking.
>
> Then he spoke again. "You didn't answer me. Where might you be going?"
>
> "Nowhere," I replied.
>
> "I'm going there myself," he said, "Do you mind if I come along a bit of the way with you?"
>
> We turned and headed out of Garstang together.
>
> I'm fond of saying that the road is like one great supermarket. Whatever you want is there for the asking.
>
> Even a husband.[6]

At the time Kathleen met Jim Phelan, he was already a published writer but, as he confessed to Kathleen, lived on the road and had no personal possessions apart from his typewriter and a few books which he kept at a friend's place in London. He spent a few weeks of wintertime writing his next book, sent it off to the publisher, and then hit the road again. That was good enough for Kathleen who was already familiar with the writings of Jack London and W.H. Davies. "Here was a carefree irresponsibility to match my own. So I went off with him—and married him—just—like—that." The pair were married in Hampstead, London, in 1944. Kathleen was then 27 years of age.

The first practicality of their relationship was to reconcile Jim's writing with their need to be forever moving along the road. The pair would stay in isolated, derelict buildings en route in order for Jim to type up his next book before returning to the road again. The first of these was a disused bakehouse off the beaten track in Gloucester recommended by a former hobo friend from America. "At first it sounded as if we would have to sleep inside the bakery oven, wrapped in sacks." But the place had been converted into a livable cottage, including an open fireplace and a portable gas ring burner for cooking. The bakehouse was surrounded by wild countryside, the tranquility of which was only broken by frequent visits to the Travellers Rest pub in Mawlswick two miles away.

And here Kathleen confesses that they "were not exactly penniless when we moved into the bakehouse." Jim had been put on a retainer of £5 a week not to write for any rival film company. "Surely a vagabond's dream—when they pay a man *not* to work." He had also been introduced to the wealthy philanthropist Henry Harben, "who liked giving money to writers with liberal views." He gave Jim £100 up front plus £10 a week to write his novel and, furthermore, would see that it was published on completion. After completing the novel, the pair headed for London to submit the manuscript and await the inevitable success that would follow. But Harben took an instant dislike to the book and wrote to Jim suggesting that he should give up writing and get himself and his wife a job.

Off they set, manuscript in hand, to drown their sorrows at several pubs around the West End, finally arriving at the Feathers in Oxford Street. The proprietor of the pub took an instant dislike to the two vagabonds ordering drinks at his bar and refused to serve them. An argument followed, Jim spat in the landlord's face, then a fight, someone screamed police, and the pair shot out of the bar and ran down the street. In their haste they had left the only manuscript of the book in the bar. The next day, Kathleen, pretending to be Jim's secretary, called at the Feathers to say that her boss had been there the previous evening worse for drink and had left a package at the bar—had they found the package? "No, naturally they had not. Jim had to rewrite the whole of the novel. A most expensive spit!" This was when Kathleen discovered that, even though he had lost scripts before, Jim never kept carbon copies of any of his writing. But he did have an incredible memory and could rewrite short stories verbatim. From that time onward Kathleen took over the typing from Jim, and made copies.[7]

Following the fracas in London, the pair arrived in Chester and then decided to cross the border into Wales and visit their friend Charles Beatty, who introduced three-dimensional chess into the U.K., of which game both Kathleen and Jim were themselves highly skilled practitioners. Jim regularly wrote for *Chess Magazine* and both he and Kathleen were able to beat champions of the game during the time they spent time playing chess at London's Mandrake Club. Returning to London on a bank holiday Sunday without a penny proved something of a challenge but a "line of guff"[8] to an American tourist paid for food and after being chucked out of Euston railway station, Kathleen secured them an undisturbed bed for the night inside one of the two hollow lion statues at the entrance to the British Museum—a secret respite known only to her.

There then followed a trip to Ireland and time spent in a converted cowshed 25 miles outside of Dublin where Jim was to write *Turf Fire Tales*, a collection of Irish short stories. At weekends the pair would hit the pubs in Dublin but the last bus back to Killincarrig departed at 10:55 p.m., five minutes before closing time. Leaving the Pearl Bar before closing time, a hangout for writers near the

Irish Times offices, was unthinkable but fortunately the editor of the *Irish Times*, Bertie Smyllie, who also lived in Killincarrig, would frequently persuade the driver to hold up the bus. The days that Smyllie did not frequent the bar Kathleen and Jim would walk the 25 miles home rather than leave the pub five minutes early. Bertie Smyllie decided that a tramp by the Phelans across Ireland from Dublin to Gallway would make a great series of articles for his paper. Of the characters and adventures related concerning this trip was a Guinness-loving horse who pulled the trap they rode in and got more drunk than they did.

A word here on the Phelans' relationship to money—not entirely divorced from their relationship to alcohol. True, there were times when significant amounts of money came to them, either from book and film deals or winning at the racetrack, but they attached no pleasure to acquiring money for its own sake, as illustrated by the following story from their stay in Killincarrig. Jim had received a hundred-pound royalty check for a previous book and went to the local pub to celebrate. Word got round and they ended up not only buying drinks all around but handing out "fivers" too. On this occasion they were afforded a second opportunity to enjoy the money because the local police constable had gone round the village demanding the fivers back, let himself into their house, and left 70 pounds in a kitchen cupboard. An even more extreme example of the Phelans' disregard for money concerns Jim's son Seumas later buying them a house in London. When some time later Kathleen asked Jim if he liked living there, they acknowledged to each other that they were not happy in the house, simply left the key in the door and walked off. Kathleen later told a friend that some lucky soul could just take it over.[9]

Another tale describing the Phelans' relationship to alcohol involves both Jim and Dylan Thomas working as scriptwriters for film companies in London. After work each evening they would meet up, often with Kathleen, at the "Back Bar" of the Café Royal from where they would move on to the Gargoyle Club. Dylan Thomas was living at the time in Staines but by the time the last train out of London stopped at his home station he was usually fast asleep and ended up in Reading. Every effort was made to solve the problem, including bribing train guards to put Thomas off at Staines, but in the end he resolved the problem himself by moving to accommodation in Reading. Another anecdote involves a drunken ride through the Scottish Highlands accompanied by a piper in a ragged kilt serenading them on their way, but Kathleen's autobiography must be acquired to read these delightful tales, told as only Kathleen can tell them.

Accounts follow of adventures in Cornwall, Devon and Dorset. Kathleen describes sleeping at Stonehenge en route, which in those days was not fenced off from the public. Other stories include a drunken Jim Phelan scaling the walls of Corfe Castle in Dorset "for the crack,"[10] and narrowly avoiding breaking his neck. During this time Jim finished *We Follow the Road* sustained throughout by half a pig given to them which they had to learn how to butcher and feed themselves on for the entire winter. The couple's next adventures are from the time they spent in the Suffolk and Norfolk countryside. This included their encounters with an infamous Romani family:

> One day we passed a long line of horse-drawn gipsy caravans near Ipswich, as we went hitchhiking to Felixstowe. Then that night when we got back to Assington, the same rake of wagons had pulled in about half a mile away, and people were making camp. Next morning we strolled over to the encampment, as we knew that these must be a family called Scampe, who kept to the Suffolk roads and we wanted some information from them.[11]

Kathleen goes on to relate a story that had occurred some years earlier when Jim had been arrested after a gypsy named Wallace Baker had escaped from Norwich Jail. The newspapers at the time, were full of print about sightings of the escaped convict. "Then one morning the headline was 'Gipsy Baker' arrested in Liverpool." A black-haired, brown-faced man with a gypsy scarf around his neck had been taken into custody after refusing to tell his name, but the authorities knew they had their man. The man had signed his name with an X but the prison warders supplied the rest which now read "Wallace X Baker." The arrested man was, in fact, Jim Phelan, but because Jim had a record for gun-running, he was not about to declare that he wasn't Gipsy Baker. It was not until his arrival back at Norwich prison that the warders declared they had the wrong man, by which time the real Gipsy Baker had had time to escape to Scotland.

Now the reason, years after this event, that Jim wanted to meet up with the Scampes, was to enquire after the welfare of the real Wally Baker, a relative of the family. On Jim announcing who he was, he was given the warmest of greetings for allowing himself to be arrested in place of Wally Baker and not snitching—something that was, in any case, part of Jim's personal code of ethics. What followed provided evidence that the story of Jim's arrest had already entered into Romani folklore:

> ... as soon as Jim's name was mentioned, an old woman turned and called out something in Romani. A small girl came out of a caravan, and the old woman indicated Jim. "That's Jim Phelan," she said, and paused. "Tell the say about Wally Baker." The child stood by the fire and recited the story about Wallace Baker and Jim in Norwich Prison.[12]

During the time that Jim was writing in the desolate farmhouse they had inhabited in Suffolk, Kathleen spent her time getting to know the local wildlife who were so unfazed by their human neighbors that one day, while watching a pair of partridges from a large window, she was joined by another local resident. An owl had come through the open window and perched on her head. Kathleen and Jim continued to spend time with the Scampes, Bakers and Kidds until one of the clan located a hundred-year-old, horse-drawn caravan which, after it was kitted out, became a mobile home. Sometimes they borrowed a horse to move the caravan on and on other occasions had it towed by a vehicle. In this manner they made for the Lake District via a spell in Lincolnshire. The caravan simply became the permanent home for Jim's typewriter and an office in which to write in between tramping exploits far and wide. It should be noted here that Kathleen returned to this mode of existence for the last 35 years of her life—albeit not in the same caravan.

It was in the Lake District that Kathleen and Jim first became acquainted with Kay Callaghan and her family in Skelwith Bridge. They pitched their caravan in a field opposite Kay's place and beside the "singing river," home to trout, otters, an abundance of wild birds and fowl, hares and rabbits cavorting along the banks. The story of this first meeting with Kay was related later by Kay's daughter Kerry in her book *Kay's Ark* (2016). As the back cover relates, Kay herself had arrived in Skelwith Bridge in the 1950s with "no money, a troubled marriage and an abandoned acting career." In her home Kay "created a café that became a much-loved haven for villagers, travellers, musicians, animals and animal lovers." And it was into this haven that the Phelans arrived by chance, Kathleen later maintaining correspondence with Kay (referred to later) from all over the world. The Phelan's arrival at Kay's Ark, as described in Kerry Derbyshire's book, took place when Kerry was only four years old:

> In the summer of 1952 there was a knock on the front door. When mum went to see who it was, I followed, clinging tight to the folds of her floral linen skirt. I remember this well because of the unusual couple standing on the porch step—a young woman with long dark hair and a flowing skirt, and a tall man. He appeared mysterious, like an ancient hawthorn surrounded by gypsy folk-lore. His complexion was craggy ... and from under a worn hat, white hair straggled his neck. His clothes were tattered like an autumn countryside. ... "Me name's Jim and this is Kathleen. I'll be wonderin' if you have a bite for us te eat? We' been travellin' days and this seems a most lovely place to stop and yer have a kindly face, you do so." And in they came.[13]

Kerry remarks that this meeting marked the beginning of how her mother's life would be lived in the quiet valley with the river running through it. "This was a paradise for us, and for the many who slept under our roof. I wanted everything to stay as it was. I was unaware of Mum's personal struggles.[14] Kerry also relates a much later visit by Kathleen around 1973, when Kerry had children of her own: "I asked my two daughters for any memories they had of Kathleen. They remember her taking them through the woods behind Kay's Ark to make camp fires and teach them how to smoke!"[15]

Next are related hitchhiking trips the pair made across Europe, including time spent in Paris in the company of Marcel Duhamel, Jean-Paul Sartre, Raymond Quéneau, "and others of the Gallimard Gang," who had by that time moved on from the Café Flore in the Boulevard St. Germain to escape the literary tourists and were now hanging out in a chess café in the Rue des Ciseaux.

> Naturally the chess habitués of the café did not know that the "pretty little Irish girl" (their description) had qualified for the UK's women championship ... Consequently in the Rue Ciseaux café, the regular chess players "played down" to me. God bless them! ... Suddenly all the chivalry for the pretty little Irish girl went out of the window.[16]

Then, after some time spent with a French traveling circus, a return trip to the Lake District, followed by a second trip to France, the pair spent a "pleasant summer" at the holiday home of Marcel Duhamel in the fishing village of Antibes near Cannes. Then back to the Lake District to move the caravan onward to its next destination, a "tiny rock farm" near the village of Blencow near Penrith, where they were forced to overwinter. Jim wrote the second volume of his autobiography, *Tramp at Anchor*, and Kathleen snared rabbits that would provide their main means of sustenance. Then onward with the caravan toward Scotland, only to leave it at a small farm near the Scottish border while the pair hitchhiked to Copenhagen and stayed with Jim's Danish translator, spending time there with various literary and radio folk. From there they hitchhiked to Stockholm using money from the Swedish translations of Jim's books (kept in Sweden because of the poor U.K. exchange rate) and continued all the way to Lapland.

> But it was so cold that one morning ... we looked at one another and shivered and without speaking a word crossed to the other side of the road and started to hitch south. We were like ghosts, cold, hungry and tired. Tired, because as it was light for twenty-four hours we had just kept on—waiting for night to fall. It didn't![17]

Kathleen and Jim then decide to move the caravan south again, not wishing to spend the winter in Scotland, but after a series of disasters with various horses acquired to tow the van, the pair were forced to overwinter in West Tanfield north of Rippon, still in the north of England. It was here that Jim wrote *Tramping the Toby* before getting the caravan towed south to York by a tractor. Then onward to Doncaster courtesy of members of the Baker gypsy family, and further again by a farm lorry to Leicestershire. The rest of the summer was spent fruit picking and betting on horse races, the latter being something that would sustain Kathleen for most of her life, becoming a virtuoso of the art. But in spite of continually getting tows for the caravan, the trip southward in this manner was becoming tedious and for reasons that Kathleen cannot remember they decided to head off hitchhiking to Trieste in Slovenia.

The Trieste trip starts with Jim being arrested in Paris for assaulting a gang of people after getting off the Metro, even though it was they who attacked him. Then on to Milan, Venice and much hospitality meted out en route. In the '50s, Slovenia was not geared up for tourism and after some odd encounters back and forth to Trieste, they returned sooner than planned and moved the caravan on south to Oxford. A great time was spent frequenting the pubs of that city with Jim's Oxford publisher and his wife. Then on with the caravan down the Thames Valley into Berkshire, broken by trips to Cheltenham and other racecourses. "We had lots of luck with the horses and made *lots* of money. We backed the winner of the Gold Cup, Gay Donald at fifty to one … Happy, happy days." Their good fortune was made all the more so by *Tramping the Toby* being published that year. It was a long hot summer and more money was made at Newbury and Salisbury racecourses thanks to hot tips from jockey friends. There was also a great Romani gathering for the hop picking season at the end of that summer, involving much drinking and more time at the races.

Fetters for Twenty was written during the Phelan's next overwintering stop north of Brighton, then more adventures and a variety of tedious journeys with the caravan the following summer across the south of England, culminated with a decision to be done with the cumbersome beast once and for all. The caravan's final journey started at the Barford Park estate of Sir Dudley Forwood and his wife Mary, in pastureland alongside the River Avon near Salisbury. Mary Forwood owned "several beautiful Arab horses, given her as a gift by King Ibn Saud. … These beautiful silver grey horses used to visit us at the caravan. It is all like a fairytale in my head—some other life—some other time." During their stay at Barford Park, Dudley Forwood bought from a Lady Lucas the near-derelict Old House, Burley, situated in the center of the New Forest. He drove the Phelans over to Old House, showed them around, and offered them the option of pitching their caravan on site and having full run of the house. The caravan was duly put on a low-loader and moved to the completely isolated house, miles from human habitation.

> It is not easy to describe the peace and loveliness of that lone glade in the heart of the Forest. Sometimes I felt I knew every deer, badger, pony, fox, rabbit, woodpecker and squirrel for miles. When winter came, one of the hardest for years, there was deep snow and ice everywhere. We were totally isolated.[18]

One day they walked the three miles through the snow to the nearest village and arranged for a forester to deliver sacks of cattle feed and bales of hay for the animals whose only food had been the small patch of unfrozen grass beneath the caravan. Kathleen spent weeks feeding the local wildlife who joined her each morning for breakfast. She describes how during the big freeze, the locals in the village—who had expressed concern for the Phelans' situation—had no water or electricity, while Kathleen and Jim were able to continually draw water from the 20-foot-deep well and enjoyed huge log fires in one of the house's grand fireplaces.

The caravan remained at Old House until it eventually fell apart. The Phelans would visit it occasionally between hitchhiking jaunts, being at a loss what to do with, or without, it. It contained the typewriter and all their possessions. But a chance meeting with a publisher who was very familiar with Jim's writing and who owned a caravan park in Charmouth, Dorset, solved the problem. The man's wife was Irish, besotted with Jim, and happy to provide them with a new caravan free of charge. Over the next two weeks, Kathleen hitchhiked back and forth daily between Charmouth and the New Forest—alone because Jim had a deadline to write a script for a BBC film—with a large suitcase, "to transfer their goods and chattels from the old wagon to the new." On the last trip Kathleen threw paraffin into the old caravan and watched it burn to the ground.

That summer, Kathleen and Jim were involved in writing and narrating two documentary radio broadcasts for the BBC on Welsh gypsies, involving much tramping through the Welsh countryside. On returning to Charmouth at the end of the summer they decided to move the caravan on to a farm near Axminster in Devon. A different film company, Westward TV, then decided to make a series of films which involved moving again deeper into Devon and another idyllic pitch, a secret place surrounded by towering rocks, the only entrance being a hedge that opened and then closed in behind them. In spite of earlier references to Kathleen playing the harp in the minstrel's gallery of Old House, here we have confirmation that Kathleen did indeed play the harp, and also must have owned one. Stories sprung up around the area that the place was haunted by strange music:

> In the night time I used to sit on the steps of the wagon and play my harp. The rocks echoed the music so that there was a great resonant sound. Like an organ. It could be heard all the way to the Totnes Road, but no one knew where the sound came from. Hence the legend.[19]

Soon the pair had to move on again to Wales with the caravan because the BBC now wanted to follow up the radio documentary with a TV series about Welsh tramps and gypsies. It was broadcast in 1964, titled *Next Place*. A farmer towed the caravan to Raglan Castle. "Once again we had a wonderful few weeks touring the Welsh Countryside courtesy of the BBC." When the filming was finished, further offers of films for Newcastle and Glasgow came in, and with plenty of funds available, Kathleen and Jim decided to return with the caravan to Cornwall and then make a tour of Europe. However, sometime after filming the TV series, Jim became ill with lung cancer and chronic obstructive airways disease for which he was eventually hospitalized. We do not hear from Kathleen whether they made the European trip or not.

Jim discharged himself from hospital—having vowed following his prison sentence never to be confined by four walls again—and died in his son's house in London in 1966 surrounded by Seumas' family. The effect on Kathleen of Jim's death is recorded in notes she made for Part 2 of her autobiography which was never completed:

> When Jim died I walked out of London and for two weeks I hitched blindly all over England. It was November, so the weather must have been pretty bad. I have no recollection of where I went, or where I stayed, or much of what I did. ... I had no time to worry about Jim having died. On the road whatever happens, one still has to cope with the ordinary problems of survival, and my sense of survival has always come first. Rule one. Stay alive.[20]

One of the first things Kathleen had to do was to reshape her "line of guff" as she was now hitching as a widow. "I must have managed to formulate a fairly plausible tale, because I survived without being charged with vagrancy and without being committed to a lunatic asylum." One day, from a car that was giving her a lift, she saw a caravan parked in a field. "I suddenly remembered that was where I lived." She had borrowed the caravan some weeks before Jim became ill so that he could finish writing a book. Kathleen then proceeded to empty the contents of the caravan into the field where, "except my own clothes, some letters and scripts ... I made a bonfire in the corner of the field and burned the lot." Then she got a driver to tow the caravan to Glastonbury where she pitched it for the winter. There she set about completing and handing Jim's overdue last two books to the publishers and reconnecting with friends who were relieved to hear that she was okay.

Now equipped with a large basket on rubber wheels that she describes as being the size of a wine barrel, and complete with a tent, her easel and paints, Kathleen set out for France, later writing in a letter to the author Dan Davin: "When Jim died I had about twenty pounds so I hitched to Morocco and then when I had nothing left decided to cross the Sahara. It seemed like a good place to go without money."[21]

Tramping Solo: Nepal via North Africa and the Middle East

The trip about to unfold proceeds through France, Spain, Morocco, Algeria, Tunisia, Libya, Egypt, Lebanon, Turkey, Iran, Iraq, Afghanistan, Pakistan, India and Nepal; adding to Kathleen's return journey, Kuwait, Cyprus, Greece, and Italy. Somewhere in a Nepalese rainforest, Kathleen reports that she came across a young Scottish man who was whistling "The Skye Boat Song." So overcome was Kathleen with nostalgia for Scotland than she made an about-turn and hitchhiked back to the Isle of Skye.

Highlights of the trip, lasting almost three years, were obtained from typewritten notes for a book which Kathleen prepared but never completed, together with journal entries and also letters to friends. A summarized version of the trip appeared in a magazine article, complete with photographs, and published circa 1972.[22] The following passage from the article provides a good insight into Kathleen's personal philosophy of tramping and in the last paragraph a description of the manner in which she traveled:

> Fine weather or foul I am out on the road. I own nothing but what I stand up in and can carry with me; I rarely have more than a couple of copper coins to rub together and yet you'd have to go far to find a happier woman.
>
> There is nothing to compare with the excitement of walking each day and never knowing who you are going to meet and where you are going to find yourself by nightfall.
>
> Sometimes I walk from dawn till dusk and other times I get a lift in a car and just go wherever the driver is going. Once, I started out with the West Country in mind and landed up in North Wales; another time, I started out from Tehran in Persia with a vague idea of heading to Afghanistan, and 12 hours and 300 miles later, I was on the shores of the Caspian sea. But what did it matter.
>
> For 25 years [in reality 22] I travelled the road with my husband Jim Phelan and when he died, 6 years ago, friends told me: "You must settle down now and get a secure job. Tramping the road was alright with a man, but it's not something you can do on your own."
>
> But never for one moment did I consider changing my way of life, although I did want to get away from the British roads for a while. I had come to know them so well when travelling with Jim; we had made hundreds of friends up and down the country and grief was too sharp to visit them yet.

> …
>
> Rarely does it happen that a person giving me a lift doesn't want to take me home and introduce me to their family. People are so intrigued by my way of life and fascinated by the stories I have to tell. Because every vagabond is a storyteller—that's how we live. On my passport, my profession is given as storyteller.
>
> It's a myth that tramps of the road go around telling a whole lot of lies. We belong to a fast vanishing band of minstrels who sing (and talk) for our supper. We are performers, entertainers, and we may have to talk for eight or nine hours a day without repeating ourselves and all for a cup of coffee, a meal, a space on the floor to sleep or a few coins. There are not many trained actors who would want to do this and write their own script! People reward us not because we're poor, but because they like the tales we tell.
>
> I have had so many fascinating experiences that I don't have to make up stories. For instance, take the morning I found myself in Ataba Square in the centre of Cairo. I had arrived as usual in my jeans, blouse and barefooted (I wear canvas shoes when necessary but prefer to go without any shoes at all when I can).
>
> …
>
> As always I travelled light: a sleeping bag with a built-in ground sheet, a small tent in case the weather is rough, slacks, jeans, a change of underclothing, a dress and two or three blouses. I take woollen socks and tights but rarely wear them, toilet things of course, scissors, a knife, a torch—and a chess set. That is the one truly international game. You can enter a café practically anywhere in the world and by setting up your chess board, you'll soon get to know people.[23]

The story of Kathleen's arrival in Cairo's Ataba Square will be related later, but her journey begins in France after crossing from England to Dieppe early in February 1967. Noting how expensive France was, and frequently being mistaken for a "French lorry girl" (prostitutes whose principal customers were truckers), Kathleen determined to get to Spain in all possible haste.

The obvious dangers of a single woman hitchhiking alone through around 35 countries (let alone her own) cannot be underestimated, and there are many hints in Kathleen's narrative of some dangerous encounters. However, as a friend of Kathleen's confided,[24] she only wanted to tell the good stories. It was her wish to keep the unpleasant experiences to herself as they were far outweighed by pleasant ones. Be that as it may, the trip through France was not without its lighter moments: a lift from a professional cyclist (in his car), a picnic with another lift, being supplied with sandwiches by another, sleeping in catacombs in the Garonne Valley, being stopped by the police, and getting drunk on wine and pastis, courtesy of a young woman owner of a hotel who took a liking to her vagabond visitor, before finally arriving at the Pyrenees.

At the border, one of the customs officials commented on Kathleen's easel, that Salvador Dali had been the last artist to cross the border and had drawn the border guard as an ant: "Will you draw me too." Now Kathleen had her new line of guff, offered to her by a border guard; she would become a "vagabond artist." This encounter was followed by a lift all the way down the Costa Brava to Barcelona, where, knowing no other part of that city by name, she ended up in the Ramblas and drank wine in a local tavern until dawn with some newfound friends.

Morocco

On her arrival in Morocco and headed for Tangier, Kathleen assumed that she had arrived in the middle of a festival as the roads were thronged with people wearing "brilliantly coloured dresses of silk or satin." It took Kathleen a while to get used to the fact that these were the clothes people wore every day to work in the fields. Although there were very few cars on the road, and those that did exist belonged to government officials or the very rich, everyone on the road wanted to walk and talk with Kathleen and help her flag down the few cars that did pass. Not only *did* all the cars stop and give her a lift—it was rare for a woman to travel alone in North Africa—but she would also be fed. If she was not bought a meal at a roadside café she would be given the addresses of friends in towns she might visit, so always had somewhere to sleep for the night: "it would be a very rare occasion that the motorist would not take you along to meet his family." Kathleen says she made another "delightful discovery":

> On my passport I give my profession as "Storyteller," claiming that all tramps and vagabonds are like the bards or minstrels or troubadours. We sing for our supper, as it were. ... In Morocco that made me something very unusual and turned out to be very lucky for me.[25]

Kathleen made her way toward the south of Morocco because she had always wanted to visit the town of Goulimime on the edge of the desert. "The people lived in tents looking out on miles and miles of pinkish sand, unbroken but for stark stumps of stunted trees. They wear their own distinctive costume, long blue robes with white turbans, and they welcomed me warmly but with curiosity." As hospitality to the wayfarer was part of everyday life, Kathleen stayed in Goulimime for a few days in order to see the famous weekly cattle market. People came from miles around, "dressed in their colourful robes and weaving around the thousands of camels which fill the market place."[26]

Kathleen traveled part of the return journey to Marrakesh with a party of Berbers and one of the women gave her a small portable charcoal stove made from clay that was to prove useful on her onward journey. Kathleen resolved to learn to speak Arabic, which by the end of her Middle Eastern travels she did tolerably well, but she managed to get by during initial stages of her trip speaking French. On reaching Marrakesh, Kathleen went to the address of a friendly café owner in a poor quarter of the casbah. The people were kind and let her sleep on the floor. She chatted with the customers and would go round the market where she got scraps of food from the stall holders to cook on her little stove. After living with the family for about 10 days she was invited to a meal with the owner and his family, consisting of a huge dish of couscous and vegetables. They were sitting on the floor, eating with their fingers, when suddenly there was a great commotion outside and a knock on the door:

> ... a beautiful horse-drawn carriage pulled up outside. The driver in resplendent uniform entered and to my surprise made straight for me.
>
> "Are you the lady who travels the road and calls herself a vagabond and storyteller?"
>
> "Yes," I said.
>
> The driver then said, "We would like to offer you better accommodation."
>
> I said thank you, but I was learning much about Morocco and the people from talking to customers here, and the owners had been more than kind.
>
> "I think you had better see the accommodation before refusing," he replied and there was an air of authority about him, and so I followed him into the carriage. We drove across the town and eventually he pulled up at a place that looked a cross between Windsor Castle and an Arabian Nights palace. There was a huge wooden door and he gave me an enormous key to open it.
>
> I entered into wonderland. A tiled courtyard was surrounded by beautiful gardens filled with geraniums and bougainvillea and in the distance, I could hear a fountain playing. Inside, the rooms were just as palatial with mosaic tiles and ironwork as fine and dainty as lace.
>
> "You are in a palace which belongs to King Hassan II and we will be happy for you to stay here for five or six weeks." he said courteously.
>
> I was stunned but I managed to stammer. "But why?"

> "Storytellers are welcome and respected in our country and we have heard of your fame. May you be happy here."
>
> After he had gone, I had to have a quiet laugh to myself. The luxury was fantastic but not much help when you haven't got any money or any food. I had actually been a lot better off at the café where I might eat with the owners and customers bought me the odd cup of coffee. Each night I let myself into my palatial quarters with the massive key, sat in solitary state in the courtyard and cooked scraps from the market on my stove.
>
> I stayed there for about four weeks and then came the call of the road. There is never any denying it. I gave the key to the caretaker, said farewell to my friends in the casbah and set off for Algeria . . .[27]

After sheltering from a sandstorm in terror, Kathleen spent the next night in a filthy Moroccan dosshouse near the border with 60 men, "old, poor, sick and hopeless." She sat up all night until dawn relating her stories to the assembled company.

Algeria

Kathleen's first lift after entering Algeria was from a border guard who drove her to the first town, Maghdia, because he wanted her to meet his wife and baby. Early the next morning, a lift in a van full of apples and melons took Kathleen to the market in Oran. After spending one night in the Oran public library, Kathleen hitched on to the small fishing port of Tenes where she spent two days sitting on the balcony of a small youth hostel overlooking the sea, frying fish on her charcoal stove, and listening to the waves pounding on the rocks. "The street is lined with date palms, the little boats are clonking, there's quite a sea tonight and directly opposite the harbour lights are flashing red and green."[28] Kathleen describes the little villages she passed through, beautiful woods, deserted beaches, and everywhere ripe grapes being harvested, then stopping off at a cave to watch wine being made. Following a lift in a market van to Algiers and arriving at the market at four in the afternoon with no money, Kathleen "parked" her basket on wheels at a little café in a backstreet near the waterfront and did what she had done many times before, but in reverse. She gazed across the Mediterranean at Marseilles.

Then onward through many more small fishing towns and the same routine: begging fresh fish from the boats, a lemon from the market and bread from the boulangerie, then down to the beach with her little clay stove to cook breakfast, receiving curious stares and smiles from others with whom she shared her meal and people coming out of shops with something to replace what she was giving away. Finally, there was a long ride inland of 400 kilometers in a huge car, with lunch en route in a mountain restaurant, arriving at the tourist city of Constantine at four in the afternoon. Her lift then took Kathleen on a tour of the town built on two sides of a huge gorge that would have taken her days to sightsee on her own. "Unfortunately, at eight o' clock my companion said, 'And now we will go to my apartment.' Poor me. Pitchforked out once again onto the side of the road ... Casanova disappearing into the darkness cursing me."[29]

Kathleen then did what she always did when stuck in a town in the middle of the night. She knocked on the door of the first house with a light on and declared that she was from Ireland, it was her first time in the town, she wasn't sure where she was, and could the person help her. A girl of about 18 answered the door and when Kathleen asked if her mother was in, she discovered that she was at a boarding school run by Norwegians for girls orphaned following the revolution. There she was made welcome and stayed for nearly a week in a beautiful room, eating with the children and helping to cook, clean and teach English. Then onward to the town of Annaba, 150 kilometers from the Tunisian border. On arrival at the town, one of the wheels on her basket broke outside a building named Jeunesse des Sports. Kathleen left her basket in the care of the commissionaire and was ushered in to a board meeting in progress where everyone wanted to repair her basket and offer her a bed for the night. She stayed with a young couple who lived with their parents and grandparents, sleeping out on the roof under the stars after "a smashing supper." The following night it was back to pick up the now repaired basket and the offer of a room with a young French woman who lived alone.

Kathleen acknowledges that she found Algeria the most interesting of the north African countries because of the lifestyle and attitude of its young people who, having been orphaned in the war, had taken to the roads as individuals. "They had a great understanding of my way of life and I enjoyed travelling with them part of the way."

Tunisia

Kathleen arrived in Sfax, Tunisia, at the beginning of December 1967, where she occupied the smallest hotel she had ever encountered. Opening onto a tiny courtyard were nine doors, behind each of which was a small room with no windows or ventilation, only big enough for a small bed. Kathleen joined the market traders the first evening, each sitting in front of their charcoal stoves preparing and sharing what little food they had. Kathleen took her stove back with her into her room and, as she always did, retired to bed naked. Some time later she woke coughing and gasping for breath—not realizing how lethal charcoal fumes were—yanked open the door, called out for help, then fell backwards knocking herself unconscious. When she came round she was lying naked on the bed with a line of men passing bowls of water one to the other to throw over her.

Kathleen describes her further adventures in Sfax in her journal: "Met a journalist—went to see a Russian film dubbed in French. Spent the night in an all-night café. Staying with a Tunisian family in Sfax. A crowd of guys gave me a lift and I spent the journey explaining about contraception!"[30] While staying with the aforementioned family, Kathleen ended up being locked into the driver's home with his wife and children under purdah.[31] As for the contact with the journalist, a further journal entry notes that: "La Presse (Tunis) did an article about me. I got paid! Journalist spoke only French and Arabic—quite a feat for me to cope. Photo with article of me gazing into a dustbin."[32] Kathleen stayed in Sfax for the month of Ramadan and the three days and nights of festivities that followed. She celebrated with student friends from Sfax—who did not keep Ramadan but fully embraced the festivities—and also with friends from Morocco who drove over to visit her and took her to Djerba (Circe's island) which Kathleen described as a "Beautiful place. Like a south sea island." From there she went on to stay with a French couple:

> Lovely house with hundreds of books and discs, piano, sports room—table tennis ... two or three weeks of luxury before I hit the hard road for Libya. ... Quite a few artists and writers hang out there [Sfax]. I spend a lot of time down at the harbour. Nice sailor's café there which floats on the sea, and the coffee is excellent. In a mad moment I took a boat to the Isles of Kerkennah.[33]

Kathleen spent three months in Tunisia before crossing into Libya, and it was here also that she started formal Arabic lessons. She had met a student in a café who asked her if she wanted to see his school. In the event it was a shack by a river with 20 little desks and the student taught children from poor families there for "a shilling or two a week." "The student indicated a chair, gave me a notebook and Arabic reader and within minutes I had joined the class. This is what is so exciting about my life. When I had got up that morning, I didn't dream I'd be taking Arabic lessons a few hours later!"[34]

Libya

A car had deposited Kathleen in Tripoli at 10:30 at night. The driver had given her a postal order for one pound in order that she could have a bed for the night, it being unsafe to sleep out in that city. As there were no small hotels in sight, Kathleen walked into the largest and asked for the manager, showed him the postal order and asked if he had "a small room you could let me have for the night for one pound? I will cash this tomorrow." The room cost £2.40 but after listening to Kathleen's story the manager showed her to a beautifully furnished, huge double room with a private bathroom.

> I hadn't been there five minutes when there was a knock at the door and a waiter came in with a four-course dinner on a tray. Oh heavens, I thought, he really doesn't understand I've only a pound, so I rushed downstairs and said to the manager, "Is the meal included in the pound?"
>
> He nodded, "Of course. I thought you might be hungry."[35]

The next morning, on cashing her postal order and returning to the hotel to pay, the manager refused to accept any payment at all. "We are not busy at this time of the year. I shall be pleased if you will stay a week in that room. I was in England a few years ago and people were kind. This can be my way of saying 'thank you.'" And so she did. On hearing of the unusual guest, Kathleen was besieged with offers from "very rich oil people" fascinated with her stories; "they took me everywhere in great limousines and we ate in some of the finest restaurants."

A young couple on holiday at the hotel were appalled to hear that Kathleen intended to cross the desert on foot to Benghazi and offered to buy her a ticket to accompany them to that city by plane. "I thanked them warmly but privately I thought: I haven't hitch-hiked all the way here from Casablanca to look down at the desert from a plane. I should be frustrated all the way wondering what it was like down there." So she accepted their address to look them up and set off with her basket across the desert on foot. After walking for two days she came to a little oasis where she joined two Bedouin families who were going south with their camels. They traveled together for five or six days with Kathleen riding one of the camels. "I can recall those glorious nights under a sky full of stars and the breathtaking sight of the sun coming up." Then halfway to Benghazi she got a lift with a large convoy coming up from one of the oil wells: "about 20 lorries, a benzine truck which 'tanked up' the lorries across the desert, 100 Libyans, two New Zealanders, two Australians, an Austrian, a Frenchman—and me!" Kathleen rode beside the driver of the benzine truck. Each night the trucks drew up in a large circle and set up bivouacs and portable huts, lit fires and cooked the evening meal. Each night, they erected a little wooden hut for Kathleen to sleep in and a different group invited her to join them to eat. "When the fires died down, the lovely, graceful silhouettes of gazelles would appear and stand all around watching us." Kathleen was eventually dropped off at the small town of Agedabia from where she managed to hitch rides the remaining distance to Benghazi and then regale with her adventures the surprised couple who had offered to buy her a plane ticket. After Benghazi, on arriving in the town of Beida (Al Bayda), Kathleen was trudging down the middle of the main street with her basket while crowds of people were lining the sides. "I knew they couldn't really be for me—I hadn't known I was going to Beida." A policeman called her over and asked if she would mind moving herself and her basket onto the sidewalk. She was holding up the cavalcade of the Turkish president who was in town on a state visit. One of the cortege stopped as he was passing and offered Kathleen a lift to Tobruk, another 300km closer to the Egyptian border. After spending a night in Tobruk, Kathleen continued to the border where she stayed in the small frontier town of Sallum.[36]

Egypt

The next day Kathleen headed for Alexandria, not realizing that it was a 600km distance and mostly desert. The first lift took her 200km. "Some nurses fed me in a hospital and a man gave me some money for a hotel—the manager wouldn't take the money." On the third day in Egypt, a truck took Kathleen to El Alamein—only 110km from Alexandria. There she noticed a group of buses and asked if any of them were bound for Alexandria. On being told they were, but that it was a faculty outing of 150 university students, Kathleen asked if she could join the faculty and was invited to accompany them. Kathleen stayed five days in Alexandria, including being taken out by the chief of tourism and later watching a play with the director of the theater. The director gave Kathleen radio contacts in Cairo which she would exploit later. Then on to Cairo with two lifts: one with a guy who had visited Ireland and gave her a pound, the other "to the centre of Cairo in a fast car with a young Egyptian who had been educated in Eton." And below, the story of Kathleen's arrival in Ataba Square referred to earlier.

> One side of the square small streets led past the Opera House and widened into boulevards with fashionable cafés and shops, luxury hotels, and beyond that, the Nile. On the other side, the narrow streets disappeared into a network of lanes and alleys which held the noisy, colourful bazaars and markets, thronged with people.
>
> Suddenly there came a thudding of hooves and warning shouts. Lorries braked, a tram bell clanged urgently and men, women and children scattered swiftly. Swooping into the square came a herd of about 40 camels headed by a small one on which perched a laughing young Arab.
>
> He sat proudly showing off his ability to control and direct the herd between the traffic. The crowd roared their admiration for this man who had ridden straight in from the desert.
>
> As he swept across the square to pass me, I made the age-old sign holding up my right hand palm outwards on a level with my face. It is

> known as the "show-out" which means "Good luck to you." He then lowered his hand but immediately swept it up and this time, he held his hand still palm outwards but farther away from his face, which meant "Need any help?"
>
> I at once crossed my arms, hiding my hands, which indicated to him that I did not need anything. These greetings were made swiftly and unobtrusively and he nodded gravely and was gone.
>
> That was a great moment. There I stood, a stranger in Cairo, coming from the other side of the world, and yet I was able to change greetings with a wandering Arab camel-driver. He probably had centuries of nomadic history. I had only my lifetime, but we were able to communicate because we both follow the road.[37]
>
> My reaction to Egypt was quite simple—I fell in love with it. I stayed six months—a lifetime to a vagabond's way of thinking. I wandered up and down the road alongside the Nile from Cairo to Aswan until I came to know every inch of the way. I became famous in Egypt through broadcasting and television and with the money I received from the talks.[38]

Kathleen's madcap adventures up and down the Nile as well as around Cairo included trouble with visas; dating guys and getting drunk with her friend Rita Zulpo (another woman vagabond, from San Francisco); crazy encounters, including with an ex-con who had been in every prison in Egypt and an escaped lunatic; and then all of the "performances" that Kathleen made in cafés, clubs, on radio and TV—indeed becoming a recognizable local celebrity for the time of her stay in Egypt, as testified by several Arabic newspaper clippings found in her caravan following her death. During this time also, Kathleen took more formal lessons in Arabic from several teachers, including one who taught her how to use profanities. Reluctant to leave, but driven by her wanderlust, Kathleen eventually continued on her travels.

Lebanon

The Six-Day War with Israel had taken place the previous year and so Kathleen was unable to continue her journey around the Mediterranean as planned, instead having to take a 44-hour boat trip from Alexandria to Beirut, in Lebanon, via Cyprus. Kathleen talks about starting to get sick of the responsibility of her basket and wishing someone would "rip it off." She had left it in cafés and the backs of lorries innumerable times without it ever being tampered with. But on arrival in Beirut and leaving the basket alongside the wall of a dock building to enquire how to get out of the city, she returned to find the basket intact but its contents ransacked, including her scripts and all of her clothing. Her easel, paints and tent were all that remained.

> BEIRUT. JULY 9TH. The Lebanon is very beautiful. Did a broadcast for Radio Beirut also TV, they put me in the news bulletin. Something about the UN—then Nasser trotting up the steps of the Kremlin—then me! ... A glossy magazine published an article a photograph of me with Mohamed Abdulwehab.[39] The editor said, "Don't you know he's the most famous musician in the Middle East."—oh well, I'm the most famous vagabond—so that makes us equal![40]

Graham Marriott was a 22-year-old Englishman taking a traveling break from work when he met up with an American friend and "an Irish woman hitchhiker" in Beirut Airport on August 1, 1968. The "Irish woman" was Kathleen Phelan, then aged 51, and on her way to Istanbul where she intended to stay with some young Americans whose address she carried. As Marriott recorded in his journal: "All her worldly goods were done up in a huge shapeless bag."

> I spent a couple of days with Kathleen and the Americans. We had a high old time! It was an eye opener for me listening to Kathleen's stories. We went our separate ways hoping to meet again. I said I would leave a message for Kathleen under the corner of a specific carpet in the Blue Mosque in Istanbul, hence the reference in Kathleen's letter [below]! Sadly we never did meet again.[41]

But Kathleen later wrote to Marriott and below is a copy the letter he received the same year they met. The letter provides further descriptions of Kathleen's outward and return journeys to and from Nepal.

> Kuwait, December 27th
>
> Dear Graham,
>
> Many thanks for your card posted from Spain which I collected at Tehran when I was outward bound for India. I am now on my way back along a different route. I hitched from Tehran all through Afghanistan and Pakistan to India, then visited Kashmir, before going on for Khatmandu, the Himalayas and a view of Everest. Khatmandu is fantastic. You mustn't miss it Graham. I had a wonderful time there. I think often of our few days in Adana. I met John again in Istanbul and we crawled all over the Blue Mosque turning up the mats looking for a message. We then took a trip up the Bosphorus towards the Black Sea. Landed at a little place which was

> beautifully forested, so we climbed a hill in the woods and 'turned on'! Rita, my American friend also arrived in Istanbul so we stayed around for a week at Gülhane. Rita just couldn't get into the Blue Mosque. The guy at the door kept sending her back to wash her feet. After washing them three times, she decided they were clean enough for a 'white' mosque and said "Oh, fuck off" or something, it was really quite funny. Rita went back through Europe from Tehran. I was so sorry, we had had such wonderful meetings all the way from Libya. She should be back in the States by now. John also will be back in America. I wrote him from Nepal. I loved the Persian people. ... I'm really intending to get to England by the early summer. India was great. I only stayed in the Northern part. I didn't dare venture south. I'd have been there for another two years! And it's over 2 years since I was in Ireland. So in early December I left India, came across the dust in lower Pakistan and Persia and have been in Kuwait for 2 weeks (28 dollars for pint of blood). I am staying with an Egyptian doctor and his family. I met them in Cairo. Kuwait is no place to stay if you don't know someone. The hotels are vilely expensive. I don't know my next address yet. I'm going to hitch up to Baghdad on Sunday but shall only stay there a day or two, then I'm heading for Beirut again. I'll drop a card when I know my next Poste Restante and I hope you will then write me all your news. Eventually I expect to hitch to England via Greece, Italy, etc. Sorry, but this is all for now. Hope to see you in England. I forgot your surname!!
>
> Love and Happy New Year, Kathleen PHELAN

Turkey

From Beirut Kathleen took a plane to Adana in Turkey for £10 from where she hitchhiked westward around the Mediterranean and Aegean seas to Istanbul, and where she describes some amazing scenery and towns en route. "I got a visa for Iran—had a weird evening with the consul and Rita and got totally smashed on top of cholera injections." And here Kathleen describes that having come all the way across North Africa and the Middle East without any serious incident, it was traveling eastward through Turkey that she encountered her most terrifying experience:

> I remember accepting a lift in a car and immediately the two men pointed their guns at me and demanded money. I said I only had a few pounds and then proceeded to talk non-stop about my travels. This is all I can

> do when I find myself in a tricky situation. Eventually they lowered their guns but every two miles or so, they would stop at a water tap and say, "You are thirsty." I had to be! So I got out and they amused themselves by firing over my head as I drank. Most unnerving.
>
> I walked a lot on that road which was surrounded by wild, rugged countryside. As always when you're on such lonely paths, you feel you must be miles away from another human being—but you're not. There are always shepherds or goatherds, woodsmen or farmers, who come out to meet you because a stranger walking alone is such a very rare happening. Usually they take you back to their homes—often wooden huts or even caves in the hillside, and here you'll meet their families, have a few dates, some fruit and a drink and perhaps sleep the night.[42]

From Turkey to Iran, Afghanistan, Pakistan, India and Nepal

And so onward to Tehran where Kathleen experienced an earthquake, met Geoffrey Sumner at a party—the Cairo correspondent of the *Sunday Times*—and stayed in his huge apartment in the city center for a few days where she contributed to a newspaper article, the beginning of which is as follows:

> People usually ask Kathleen Phelan, a 46 year old [Kathleen was in fact 51 in 1968] Anglo-Irishwoman who arrived in Tehran on Tuesday, whether she is a tourist or working in the place where they meet her.
>
> She tells them "Neither," and says "I'm a vagabond. And that's what I am and proud of it too," she told me yesterday. "For the past 23 years I have been on the road, without a home or any other material possessions and that's how I intend to go on."[43]

And from Kathleen's journal: "An Australian girl is here too [at Geoffrey Sumner's apartment] so have a chance to relax and clean up for a few days ... [before] heading for Afghanistan, Pakistan, Kashmir via the Khyber Pass."[44] Then, getting on the wrong road out of Tehran, Kathleen got a lift with an army doctor all the way up to the Caspian Sea.

> But it was beautiful. ... Decided recklessly to take one of the mountain roads. Climbed on a donkey cart with a woman and 4 kids. Plodded up the mountain road all day. Stayed with the woman's family on the top and a few days later a taxi took me down to the main road again.[45]

Then another side trip to Nishapur and Mashhad in Iran before crossing into Afghanistan. From here Kathleen hitched south to Herat which she described as "strange and lovely … no mechanised transport. I saw three cars! Just wonderful horses and carriages." Then 500km of desert to Kandahar from where an engineer, who had studied at Moscow University, drove her north again to Kabul in his Land Rover. "My Moscow man also took me up into the Hindu Kush mountains and to Bamiyan the stupa outside of Kabul. Kabul thrilled me." From that city Kathleen was given a bus ticket to take her to the Pakistan border. From here Kathleen's notes are brief and muddled:

> Next address Rawalpindi [September 27th]. Don't need a visa. What a mistake that turned out to be. … Some French people gave me a lift to the Pakistan frontier [with Afghanistan], then I lived in the Khyber Pass for what seemed like weeks over some mix up at the border. Kept running up and down to Kabul slept out several nights with the tribes people—could talk perfectly to them using all the gipsy words I know! Eventually a taxi took me for free all the way to Peshawar ignoring the border.[46]

From Peshawar Kathleen got a lift with a man and his wife who took her on a picnic to a local beauty spot where the Indus and Kabul rivers meet. The man worked in the courts and knew of Jim Phelan's prison books. They gave Kathleen enough money to stay in Rawalpindi for a couple of nights. "Pindi is not a bit like a city. So green. Like one huge garden." Then on to Islamabad where Kathleen met the Egyptian ambassador, whose sister she had known in Cairo, and because he was departing for Karachi, he gave her enough money to last a week in Islamabad. The next recorded entry in Kathleen's journal is from September 30th, leaving a medical college in Lahore and catching a bus to the Indian border. Things then seem to become manic but only a small sample of Kathleen's notes are related below (some place name spellings corrected for purposes of identification):

> *October 4th*. Early walk out of Delhi … lift to Chandigarh … lift with school-girl to Shimla. …
>
> *October 5th*. Cold. Left for Narkanda—jeep—school—jeep border policeman and family to Narkanda for lunch—fantastic view … down road to track—walk to Lusi? bridge—old bus … rest house for night—outside! Buddhist vagabond.
>
> *Oct. 6th*. Early start up the pass. Tea at house of peasant. Travel with Tibetans and ponies. Jeep to Jelori Pass 10028 feet. Smoke at cafe. Descent to Banjar. … Kullu Valley. Festival. … Tourist office—sleep. Idols, dancing, fires by river—stoned. Rain.

Oct. 7th. Up early—rain. Left for Mandi. Beautiful walk in valley—jeep, luggage lost at crossing. Poxy room. 2 rupees. Girls next door. Procession—wet.

Oct. 8th. Left Mandi at sun-up. Cold, Tea in Sikh shack … Ludhiana—stay night. …

Oct. 9th. 30 rupees. Bus to Jalandhar. Sikh on motorbike. …

Oct. 10th. … Pilgrimage—border Kashmir … Up mountain. Groovy beggars … nightfall—rest house. … Chapatis. Ate too many.

Oct 11th. … coconuts and marigolds—temple—water hose—hysteria … young singing girls—cave—row … back over mountain. …

Oct. 12th. Bus to Srinaga—all day—army on roads. Dark arrival house boat. Lake Dal—very cold.

And on continue Kathleen's journal entries in a similar vein (exhausting to read, never mind live through) up until November 11 where they run out following an entry that ends "Boat across the Ganges. Smooth still and glassy. Nostalgia for Nile. 3rd class train to Siganta [?]. Sleep waiting for train to Raxaul." Kathleen is now at the border with Nepal and the next (extended) journal entry reads as follows: "KATHMANDU. November 19th.

"Had a beautiful view of Everest the other day from the top of a truck owned by the Head of the Forestry Commission. Must tell this episode in detail later. I'm concluding my trip easterly soon." Which brings us back to the story related at the beginning of this section, of how in a Nepalese rainforest Kathleen meets a young Scottish man who was whistling "The Skye Boat Song" and, overcome with nostalgia for Scotland, turns around and hitchhikes back to the Isle of Skye, this time varying her homeward route. The only other reference to Kathleen's time in Nepal comes from "I am a Vagabond": "I met two Tibetan families with 40 ponies and travelled with them over the Himalayas, climbing to over 12,000 feet." The rest of the magazine article comments on tramping in general but is worthy of note:

> I have made dozens and dozens of friends in each country I've visited, people I write to and others with whom I know I can have a meal or spend the night whenever I happen to be where they live.
>
> They come from all walks of life, from the humblest peasant in a mud hut to an oil merchant in his magnificent air-conditioned house.
>
> Civilised people who live under a roof tend to ask me the same questions: what things do I travel with, how do I keep clean and am I ever afraid, sleeping out?
>
> Well, the professional vagabond always stays clean, otherwise he dies. There are streams in the country or you can go into the washroom of a

> café in a town. Failing that, I would guarantee I could go to any house and say, "Look, I'm travelling the road. Is there any chance I could wash out my undies and blouse?" and they'd invite me in at once.[47]

In the same vein, the following two excerpts from Kathleen's pamphlet *Hiking a Hitch* add to her philosophy of the road:

> People often ask me, "What happens when you're ill?" That's easy. You sit by the side of the road and you hitch a car. It stops, you get in, and the driver is always a doctor! And if you didn't have that kind of faith, you wouldn't last a month on the road.

And below, the end of a tale from the penultimate page of *Hiking a Hitch* of when Kathleen, requiring urgent dental treatment following her return from Nepal, finally attends a dental surgery near Cambridge in England:

> When everything was done, he [the dentist] said, "You know, I am a very proud man. Do you realise that I am the only dentist who can boast to his colleagues that he has a patient who travels all the way from the Himalaya Mountains to Newmarket for his services!"
>
> From such encounters springs the faith of a vagabond. A complete and unquestioning reliance on the road. Somehow one's needs are fulfilled.[48]

But we are still in Iran on the return leg of Kathleen's trip and here her notes become very jumbled, with one record saying that she was in Isfahan on December 9th from where she went on to Kuwait where she stayed for two weeks. A friend, Mohamed, took her to the outskirts of Kuwait City, then in a small truck across the desert, and "a large Kuwaiti car" to the border with Iraq. From there it was a free taxi ride to Basra and on to Baghdad in a large truck where she spent the night with an Iraqi family in a "house on wheels." From there, Kathleen returned to Lebanon, but not being able to use Beirut Airport in January because it "was smashed," she hitched north to Byblos from where she got a plane to Nicosia in Cyprus. The plan was to get a boat from Cyprus to Greece but, in the event, Kathleen decided to revisit Egypt before returning through Europe to the U.K. She sailed on an Italian boat back to Alexandria, from where, and still with her basket on wheels, she caught a train to Cairo where she visited many of the acquaintances she had made two years earlier.[49] Kathleen did eventually keep to her plan, finishing her trip with a visit to the Isle of Skye.

Return to Morocco and a Lasting Female Friendship

In whatever way Kathleen spent her time following the adventures just related, by January 1970, just over a year following her trip to the Isle of Skye, she was back in Morocco. Kathleen herself has not recorded this trip but kept an Athens newspaper report of it written by a Dutch woman named Lilly Batta, whom she met in Morocco. The article is notable for Kathleen's objection to being described as a "tourist" and again having to educate the author on the finer points of vagabondage. A more detailed account of this second visit to Morocco comes from the vagabond writer Jim Christy,[50] when he describes how he and Kathleen met and then tramped around Morocco together for several weeks before continuing on their separate ways.

> In early January, 1970, twenty-four years old, I was on a ferry, traveling to Morocco from Spain. Most of the passengers appeared to be Arab, many in western garb; the rest, or so it seemed, were young western men and women, hippies, in other words. But walking the deck half an hour after boarding I saw a white woman, older than the rest, and certainly no hippie. She had grey hair, a lined face and to me, she was nearly ancient, fifty, at least. She must have seen me look her way because a minute or so later a voice at my side said, "You look different from the rest of them."
>
> "I could say the same about you!"
>
> She smiled and told me her name was Kathleen and we began talking as if we were old friends who were continuing a conversation we'd been having just the other day.
>
> After a few minutes, she asked me what I did. I shrugged, told her I worked various jobs.
>
> She nodded, and said, "Yes, but what do you want to do?"
>
> "Well, I guess I want to be a writer."
>
> She nodded, as if she'd known it all along. "My husband was a writer. He died a few years ago."
>
> "A real published writer?" Writers were an exotic species to me.
>
> "Yes, widely published."
>
> "What was his name?"
>
> "You've probably never heard of him, coming from North America. Jim Phelan."
>
> "'Bell Wethers' [title of a short story by Phelan]."
>
> Her eyebrows shot up in surprise, rearranging the deep lines in her face. Her eyes which I remember as grey-blue seemed to sparkle.

"Yes, that's Jim's."

We talked about books and traveling and by the time the boat docked, we might have been the closest of friends. Kathleen suggested we could set out together, and I readily agreed. We avoided Tangiers, tramping the roads and calling at small towns, and all along the way people seemed drawn to her. I saw men who would ignore other foreigners, approach her, smiling, it was as if they wanted just to be in her presence. People offered us rides on camels and in donkey carts. We had tea sitting in the fields with shepherds. Men and children approached to tell her things. The women regarded her from a polite distance.

A man stopped Kathleen along the road and began talking earnestly. She nodded and turned to me, "This man's son has gone to Casablanca and he is worried about the boy." And while she translated the man looked at me and nodded his head solemnly, as if acknowledging the sound advice she had given him. I nodded back and we all pondered the problem. After the man went on his way, I asked if he was an old friend of hers. It was possible, I figured, if not probable; I'm sure she had dear friends down in the Kalahari.

"Just met him," she laughed.

In one town, we stopped to have tea on an outdoor patio, and soon a small crowd gathered around us. Kathleen was the focus of attention for children, teenagers and adults.

...

We stayed in other small towns, in lodging places that were unadvertised, beautiful rooms behind unmarked doorways, rooms arranged around mosaic courtyards with fountains.

...

Finally, I felt I had to go on my separate way. I should have stayed with her. I have often regretted going off. Before we parted, she gave me a pamphlet of writings by Jim Phelan that she sold along the road to support her travels. She inscribed it on the cover, to recall a meeting on the road in Morocco.[51]

Another chance meeting, on the return leg of this trip, would lead to Kathleen's seven years of tramping the Americas[52] from Alaska to Tierra del Fuego and many points east and west en route.

In 1970, a young woman named Grace (Gracie) Jackman was traveling from Paris to Dorset in the U.K. to be fitted for a bridesmaid's dress for her cousin's wedding. When she boarded the ferry in France, Grace realized that she had forgotten to bring money for her fare. As luck would have it, she encountered Kathleen Phelan returning from Morocco who, paradoxically, as our vagabond heroine usually traveled without money, on this occasion was able to buy Grace's ticket for her. Food and wine were provided by a group of Frenchmen on their way to an international rugby match in Wales, and the two women became the closest of friends—a friendship that would continue until Kathleen's death 44 years later. Grace describes Kathleen as having "a nostalgia for everywhere" and, adding to Kathleen's list of talents already described elsewhere, and presumably related to her earlier career as a sports and PE teacher, that she was a contortionist, able to put her ankles behind her head.

Grace also refers to her and Kathleen having a psychic connection. She gives the example of having a premonition one day that someone was coming to her home in the 16th arrondissement of Paris. Proceeding to make a snack from the contents of her larder, then laying up the table for two with a bottle of wine and two glasses, the doorbell rang and in walked Kathleen. Kathleen later told Grace how Jim taught her some kind of telepathic mind-reading. Grace recalls how she had started to tell Kathleen about a dream she once had. Kathleen stopped her, picked up a pad and wrote a series of words from the end of the dream exactly as Grace would have finished it. In 1971, Grace moved from Paris to Vienna where she stayed for three months and then moved to Geneva where she sat her formal exams as a translator in French and Spanish. On passing her exams in 1973, Grace was transferred to work in the United Nations headquarters in New York. Shortly afterwards she was visited in that city by Kathleen.

Tramping the American Continent

Originally intending to visit Grace in America for three months only, Kathleen ended up staying on that continent for nearly seven years, from early 1973 to late 1979. Kathleen used Grace's apartment in New York as her permanent postal address and Grace as her guarantor for visa purposes, managing to constantly renew her three-month American tourist visas for seven years by crossing over into Canada or Mexico (at least 25 times and by different border crossings) and reentering the U.S.—something she later acknowledges as causing her no little anxiety.

As distinct from the more or less progressive journey to Nepal and back, Kathleen's American adventures radiated out from Gracie's apartment north as far as Alaska, south as far as Tierra del Fuego in Argentina, and included many trips to the West Coast of America—Grace telling how Kathleen could easily hitchhike from the East to the West Coast in less than four days. Unlike the more extensive notes of her Middle East and Asian trip, the only extant accounts of

Kathleen's American adventures are letters she wrote to others. Even so, these include some detailed descriptions of many of Kathleen's adventures across that continent. However, as Kathleen's modus operandi as a vagabond has already been clearly established in the preceding pages, undoubtedly leaving the reader somewhat breathless, the following accounts of this much longer trip will be confined to its more defining aspects.

As for Kathleen's writing style, there is no question that she attempted to emulate her husband's achievements by formally publishing her stories—the notes and unpublished manuscripts later found in her caravan testify to that—but she was not prepared, at this time at least, to be tied down to deadlines and commitments in the way that Jim had. Grace tells how one day Kathleen brought home the editor from Knopf who, interested in her life story, told her that he wanted a total outline within a month. Grace describes how when Kathleen sat and started to write, not a word would come to her. It made her so ill that she did what she always did in stressful situations: headed for the horizon. Another loss to Kathleen's literary legacy, of this trip in particular, resulted in Kathleen writing to Grace and pleading with her to post back all of the letters she had written to Grace from Latin America. Grace reluctantly posted the letters to the poste restante address Kathleen had given her but the package never arrived; as a result of which, the only accounts of Kathleen's Latin American adventures are from the few letters referred to below. Even so, these letters testify to the energy and charm of Kathleen's writing when not straitjacketed by publishers' deadlines.

While staying with Grace in New York, Kathleen had befriended numerous foreign diplomats from Latin America who were to later offer her hospitality in several countries on that continent. Grace refers to Kathleen's ability to charm all comers from whatever social background. She tells a particular story about a diplomat from Afghanistan who, on Kathleen asking him where he was from, told her that she could not possibly have heard of the place. When Kathleen described not only his own village but all the surrounding towns and villages, Grace recalls how "that guy's jaw just never stopped hitting the floor."

Paradoxically, Kathleen found New York City more dangerous than many of the remoter places she visited in the Americas. When staying with Grace, Kathleen would sometimes take off with her bedroll, ignoring Grace's pleas that Central Park was no place for a lone woman to be sleeping out at night. When attempting to sleep one night on a subway bench, Kathleen also discovered just how brutally the police could behave toward those they regarded as vagrants: "They literally just kicked her, and I mean she was a tiny woman, they just kicked her off that bench on to the platform."[53] Fortunately, Kathleen had her own set of keys to Grace's apartment and so had a safe bolt-hole to return to when things got rough.

Kathleen had an incredible way of always seeing the brighter side of any situation, described by Grace as "dancing through life," something described by others also (see testimony of Jan Bond below) whether on the road in a rainstorm or in the "Green" Irish bars of the Upper West Side. Grace explains that Kathleen's moniker, Convent Kate, belied her feistier side when raised to anger. But she was savvy enough to know when to challenge and when to back off. One guy she was drinking near at a bar kept brushing his hand against her breast when raising his whiskey glass. The first time, Kathleen knocked his glass to the floor. When he touched her for the second time she knocked his glass to the floor again, waved her finger in his face, and declared: "That's two that made it to the floor. One more like that, the whiskey goes in your face and the glass goes after it." Grace also related how Kathleen had a sixth sense with lifts and would never get in a car with anyone she felt unsure about. Once a car stopped that she thought was being driven by a woman but when she got in she noticed it was a guy with long hair and had a bad feeling about him. At the next set of lights she simply excused herself, opened the door and got out.

The following selection of reports from letters, electronic messages, and old newspaper articles simply give a flavor of the time spent by Kathleen in the Americas and some of the places visited. The following letter Kathleen wrote to Kay Callaghan (referred to earlier) is not dated but the content speaks for itself and gives a summary of the first years of this trip:

> I don't really believe that it is 4½ years since I came over here. ... I was coming for three months ... but I'd want to return to the States. I just love it here. I've hitchhiked to Argentina (practically the South Pole) and Alaska (practically the North Pole) but I still haven't managed the fare to Europe and back. ... Nice thing is I have made lots of friends all over the States—Canada too. That year I spent from May 'till September hitching across Canada from Quebec to Vancouver—side-tripped up through the Rockies to the Canadian Yukon up the Alaska Highway to Dawson City and Fairbanks, Alaska. ... While waiting for lifts, wolves would cross the roads, black bears in packs of 6 or 8 (no grizzlies thank God) ... herds of deer, 50 or so at a time in the early morning, moose and elk coming down to the stream in the dawning, coyotes calling ... I am currently in Hollywood staying with an actress friend ... I've been in California since January for the winter—nice and warm ... I oscillate up and down between Los Angeles and San Francisco ... hitch it in a day on the freeway. Lots of insanity over here—walking for instance up a beautiful canyon road about 2 weeks ago—lots of cars—no other maniacs on two feet. Kay, believe this ... THEY SENT THE SHERIFF OF MALIBU IN A HELICOPTER WITH A PILOT TO LAND AND FIND OUT WHAT I WAS DOING. WALKING, I SAID. W-W-WALKING—HE SAYS! ...

Latin American Adventures

In an earlier letter to Kay Callaghan, dated May 3, 1974, Kathleen describes her first visit to Mexico City.

> Dear Kay,
>
> That letter you sent to Florida finally caught up with me. ... I've been on the road (hard) for some weeks with not a chance to write to anyone. Got into Mexico City a few days ago—and wonder what I'm doing here ... huge smog sprawled spread. But it's interesting. Lots of things to do and see but they all cost money ... No special plans. I was sorry to leave San Francisco—I was there for 6 weeks—I think it's the best city I was ever in. I had such an exciting time there—so I may go back! I've got the cheapest possible room here ... 3 dollars a night—which isn't cheap really—but anything less than this is very dirty. I can last here another week with luck, then I'm going to sleep outside of the city for a while and pop in & out to collect mail ... I was in a very pretty little town (Morelia) over Easter ... I went to a party with a lot of French people the other evening & got absolutely paralytic on tequila ... it's really quite alright once you get used to it ... Tourists get in free to Mexico City race-course. Guess who's always at the gate first! ... I've lost quite a bit of weight on the road. It was terrifyingly hot down in the tropical jungle area of the coast and I was infested with ants—mosquitos—sand-flies & dust. None of that up here in the mountains. Incredible—this city is over 7000 ft above sea level.
>
> I was invited to do a stint on TV here last week, but the money was so abysmal I refused. ... I'm not sure which direction I shall head in ...[54]

Following this trip, Kathleen did return to San Francisco before heading back to Mexico City at the end of November and then proceeding on to South America, but not before giving a report to a Mexican newspaper in which she described vagabonds as follows: "Those of us who are drifters are too strong physically to die, too strong mentally to go insane and too chicken to be criminals. Not that it doesn't take some guts to be a professional vagabond."[55]

In a long letter to Grace Jackman describing her onward journey from Mexico to Peru, Kathleen gives her return address with a Peruvian diplomat introduced to her in New York. Oswaldo de Rivero's home was in Santiago de Surco, Lima, where Kathleen stayed with Oswaldo's wife Juliette for "at least 3 weeks." Kathleen admits how grueling her trip through South America was. She had entered Mexico the previous November with only $20 and a few of her booklets, traveled all over Mexico, then on to Guatemala City where she arrived on New Year's Eve. From there, on to El Salvador from where she got a lift to a small Indian village and she stayed a week then "skimmed through Honduras and Nicaragua in a camper with some young Americans." Kathleen further describes in the letter that she "negotiated most of the Central American borders successfully but everyone told me Panama and Colombia would be the most difficult. Most drifters were avoiding Panama by flying direct from Costa Rica to Colombia, but as I didn't have any money I couldn't do that.[56]

And Kathleen did experience problems crossing into Panama. First she joined a bus queue pretending to be a passenger and had her passport stamped along with the others but, as she could not board the bus, had to walk across the border and down the road in full view of the border guards, who sent a squad car after her. But being Kathleen, she persuaded the cop to give her a lift to the first town from where she hitched a lift in an open truck the 500km to Panama City: "a furniture truck, so I sat in the back in a rocking chair and rocked along the road for ever and forever." Kathleen had an address of an American family living in the Canal Zone and stayed there for two weeks, enabling her to organize her onward passage to Colombia. One night in Colombia, walking alongside a coffee plantation and planning to go into one of the fields to sleep, she was met by the farmer who warned her not to sleep near the coffee fields as he lived some distance away and before he left would be unleashing his dogs to patrol the property. "But why, I wondered, it's just fields and fields of beans. It would take more than a week to pick one row."[57]

Kathleen had more border problems entering Ecuador, and on being asked how much money she had, she lied, saying "700 dollars." "I totally freaked out when the guy said 'Show me.'" When Kathleen blurted out it's in Quito, the border guard said, well, how much on you, to which she confessed to only having 10 dollars whereupon he stamped her passport. In fact Kathleen did not have a single coin, could not get a bus or taxi, and was forced to walk the two miles to the first bend in the road before being out of sight of the bemused gazes of the border patrol. And here Kathleen contemplates, "What happens I wonder if when I come to a country which won't let me in and having exited from the previous one, they won't let me back. Interesting—but I hope I don't have to find out." But she *was* in Ecuador. "All that nonsense about the equator being hot and jungly and humid, etc. Christ, I walked across the centre of the earth (penniless, can't be many who've done that) at a height of roughly 7,000 feet and it was freezing."

To make up for her discomfort, Kathleen was to find Quito the most spectacular of the cities she had encountered thus far and provides a fascinating description of it in her letter, following which she "hitched a sensational road right up in the Andes and then down, down, down, to hot, tropical Guayaquil, the main port of Ecuador on the Guayas river, a big, brown, treacherous, devouring slice of water in flood like the Mississippi." On arrival in Peru Kathleen had to show her onward ticket and fill in another form about how much money she was carrying. "I blithely wrote 800 dollars and they never asked to see it—thank heaven (had only 6 dollars)." Then two days crossing the desert "with lovely isolated beaches the whole length of the coast." Kathleen's stay in Lima is described in another letter that finishes by stating, "I'll be here 'till April. Want to go to Cuzco and Macchu Picchu, etc.—then Bolivia."[58] In another long letter, written to Kay Callaghan from La Paz, Bolivia, May 12, 1975, Kathleen describes her onward journey and how difficult hitching was becoming:

> "I walk for miles—and wait for hours—recently I saw only one car in 11 days & only a few trucks. And it's a very long time since I saw anything but rough dirt roads—and I arrive in places thickly encrusted with dust. ... Some days I've walked for miles along roads running between thousands of purple lupins—they grow wild in Peru—just gorgeous."[59]

Kathleen promises to write a longer letter soon and gives her onward address as a travel agency in Buenos Aires. No independent accounts are available of Kathleen's onward southbound trek to Argentina and Tierra del Fuego, or the inevitable return trip, although, as one of those who knew Kathleen relates a story of her playing "football with Pele in the streets of Brazil," we can assume that her return journey was made via that country.

Canadian Adventures

From the few surviving letters and postcards that Kathleen posted from Canada, we know the following about one of her extended trips through that country. In a letter to Grace from Sherbrooke, Québec, June 25, 1977, we hear that after two lifts that took her to Buffalo, she walked over the Peace Bridge on Midsummer's Night into Canada to be met by two border officials from Ireland who were so busy swapping tales with her about Dublin that her three-month visitor visa was stamped without any further formalities. From there, it was two trucks to Toronto, arriving at two in the morning and sleeping in a deserted park. Then a five-mile walk to the city center and on to the Woodbine racetrack where Kathleen "happily" lost eight dollars—being in-pocket for having sold three of her booklets on the way. A free night at a campsite in her sleeping bag then back into town to pick up her pack and out on the road to Montréal.

Kathleen continues her description of this trek in a letter to Grace from Banff, Alberta, July 6, 1977. She refers to a day and night in Montréal where she found an Irish bar with live music: "Danced and drank myself stupid ... they'd never seen a liberated 'Irish-American' female fresh from her triumph at the Glocca

Morra, etc." After sleeping off her hangover in a city park Kathleen got on the road for Ottawa, and in spite of the "hundreds of hitch-hikers," got a lift with a guy to Ottawa driving at 90 miles an hour. Due to a temperature of 93 degrees, Kathleen headed west through the city from ice-cream shop to ice-cream shop, reaching the highway going west around 6 p.m. By the time Kathleen reached Sault Ste. Marie she had been drenched in a thunderstorm and found herself surrounded by other hitchhikers trying to get a lift around the north of Lake Superior, "some had been there for 7 days!" But a lift bought her a meal and a room in a motel and the next lift had relatives in Thunder Bay where another meal and bed were provided. From there, a lift with two women students to Winnipeg and a trip to the fairground. Next Kathleen stayed over at the parents of her friend, the photographer Cherie Westmoreland, in Regina. Kathleen had first met Cherie, prior to her American trip, at the Ambleside Pottery, eight miles from the aforementioned "Kay's Ark," Skelwith Bridge in the Lake District. Next a lift to Calgary with a senior, plainclothed, Royal Mounted Police officer. "Am now in the Rockies which is beautiful."[60] The letter continues to describe Kathleen's onward journey to Dawson City.

In another letter to Grace from Penticon, British Columbia, Kathleen describes looking forward to receiving letters in Vancouver. She then tells more of her Yukon trip, the wildlife and scenery, sleeping next to the Yukon River, and enjoying the 24-hour daylight. Kathleen stayed with her friend Cherie in Edmonton for 10 days and headed for Vancouver, describing the warm, fertile lake country around the Okanagan Valley with its ripe peaches and apricots.[61] There is no mention of the trip up the Alaska Highway to Fairbanks, mentioned in her earlier letter to Kay Callaghan.

The only reference to Kathleen's return trip to New York is contained in a rather woeful letter, written to Grace in the Calgary public library. This letter offers a rare glimpse of the melancholy face of Kathleen. Grace is on her way back to New York from a trip to Nigeria and Kathleen is clearly missing her companionship. She reports staying two weeks in Vancouver and that she is:

> ... back again heading east towards who knows where. ... Starting my 'border paranoia' any minute!! ... Have enjoyed and am enjoying my sojourn in Canada in many ways, but am also very unsettled. Miss the States and Americans very much. ... Still managing to get by with my little books by a series of miracles.[62]

Kathleen also reports that a combination of the Alaska Highway and bad weather have worn out her shoes, and finishes: "This is such a boring letter. I'm looking forward to talking to you ... I am pretty disorientated—don't know which way I'm going—and not a clue as to how and when or where I tackle my re-entry? Will write again soon. Love you. Much love, Kathleen."

Return to the U.K.

The following correspondence is from someone who encountered Kathleen shortly before her return to the U.K. "I met Kathleen Phelan in a bar in New York in the late '70s-early '80s. … I would go Sunday nights to the Eagle Tavern on W. 14th Street and listen to her tell stories."[63] Kathleen left America in 1979, now a mature vagabond in her early sixties. She would continue to tramp the roads of Britain for the next 35 years, always returning to her caravan which she had towed around the country, gypsy-style, from one farm and campsite to another as described below by Grace.

> Kathleen did live in England once she had finished the huge swather through the world. Yes, she joined me in Holland et cetera when I was in a hotel for work but mostly she went the roads here, flipped up to Scotland and back, and moved the van from farm to farm and pitch to pitch.[64]

We know from the following extended account from Jim Phelan's grandson Liam (now a successful newspaper editor in Australia, as was his father before him) that Kathleen (Kaye, as he and others referred to her) and Grace visited Jim's son Seumas and his family at their home in Howth, outside Dublin, in 1981. Liam was around 13 years old at the time of Kathleen's visit, his sister Amanda was older, and Liam recalls an old photograph of Jim, Kathleen and Amanda at an airport in North Africa in the mid-1960s, taken shortly before Jim died. Liam's family left Ireland in 1984 shortly after a second visit from Kathleen. The family settled in Australia in 1990 and Liam never saw Kathleen again. As an aside, we know that Kathleen was in Dublin again in late 1985 from a sheet ballad signed to Kathleen by the folksinger Peggy Seeger. Here are Liam's recollections of Kathleen:

> I remember Kathleen as always having a jaunt in her step. She seemed so exotic to me, a young boy growing up in suburban Dublin. She brought tales of the outside world—Europe, North Africa, the US—and the knowledge that you could access it without money by using your nous and some road skills.[65]
>
> At the time I was reading widely—Jack London, George Orwell, Steinbeck—but Kaye brought this wider world into our lounge room. I only partly understood at the time how adventurous she was, and what a trailblazer she was in a sexist world as a single woman. She was indefatigable, and just seemed to see opportunity where other people saw risks and obstacles.
>
> She stayed at our house in Howth for a week or two at a time, turning up randomly and disappearing again. She would tell some amazing travel

tales. One that stands out is of her hitching, I think in North Africa somewhere, and she got held up at gunpoint in the back of a pickup truck. But her captors didn't want to rob her. They just wanted her to walk above them as they took turns lying underneath her and looking up her dress. Looking back on this as an adult I realise the danger and humiliation of such a situation, but at the time, Kaye somehow turned it into a humorous tale, sidestepping the risk and emphasising the absurdity of it all. She laughed when she told it.

We had one of her paintings on our wall, of a market scene from North Africa. My mum still has that painting today. It featured a woman in full headdress and flowing robes walking down a cobbled street surrounded by old buildings.

As I think I mentioned to you before, she took me on my first hitchhiking trip across Wales and into England. We caught the ferry and then hitched from Holyhead through Chester and over to where she had her caravan, somewhere near Sherwood in Nottinghamshire. I remember her teaching me to not get in a car without first looking the driver in the eye. If you didn't get a good vibe of them, you apologised, closed the door and waited for the next mark. I later used this technique when hitchhiking from Sydney to Central Australia and up to Queensland.

...

I remember her taking me to the bookies on our hitchhiking trip, and showing me how she gambled, carefully while always trying to protect her initial stake. I would have been about 14 years old then.

I also remember her extraordinary optimism as we got rained on, battered by cold winds and stuck on bad stretches of road. She always managed to stay positive and skipped along, walking on the fronts of her feet like a dancer. A rainstorm was an opportunity to get a cup of tea from a roadside café.

I remember her telling me about New York and Gracie Jackman, and I remember getting a book from New York which I treasured at the time. It was like another window opening on another side of the world. I also remember how neat she was—her small caravan was meticulously ordered and her booklets and sketches and papers kept in neat piles and drawers. Her clothes were simple but always extremely well looked after, folded neatly.

I loved watching her working a mark, telling her tale in such a seemingly random way to the drivers who picked us up, all the

> while calculating what they might be worth. They might buy one of her booklets, or give us a few pounds extra, or provide a night's accommodation, or lend their tow-bar to move her caravan. I loved the idea of her owning a caravan without a car. Kaye made that life look easy, and I would sit in the back of the car awestruck at her ability to read people, ingratiate herself and ask for something when she needed it. For a slightly shy, cerebral teenager, this was a revelation.
>
> Kaye got a mixed reception at our house. My mum wasn't really a fan. She saw Kaye as a "hard woman," a taker and thought she was always after something. Which I guess at some level was true, her life was built on relying on people's kindness and need to help others. But she gave plenty back in return. My dad liked having her around, but there was a bit of tension at home and so she would just drift in and out of our lives.
>
> I did write to her for a while and she would write to me, long letters full of great details of where she was at the time. Unfortunately I am not a great keeper of things so those letters are long gone now.
>
> I went travelling myself aged 16: picking grapes in Greece; driving across Europe in a camper-van; going over to Australia and New Zealand; to Canada skiing and tree planting; walking along Franciscan trails in Italy; sailing from New Caledonia across the Pacific to Australia.
>
> In later life we lost touch and looking back now I realise I should have done more to keep in touch, and to look after Kaye as she aged. I realise now, as an adult and a parent, what a tough life it must have been for her behind all that cheeriness. But I also realise hers was a life well lived, that she would not have chosen another path. That she was influenced by Jim, but was not defined by him. She was an amazing feminist before I even knew such terms existed, making her way in the world on her terms, having to hustle for daily survival and living by her skills as a storyteller, a writer and an artist.
>
> She taught me to be adventurous, to dream big, to stay sharp and to enjoy the art of conversation. To look people in the eye and to hold your head high. I was glad to know her.[66]

Following Kathleen's return from America, with the exception of rare testimony such as the email from Liam above and that from Jan Bond below, all that we know about Kathleen comes from correspondence, now reduced mostly to postcards, to friends and her sister Elizabeth (whom Kathleen visited at regular intervals) and occasional letters to Grace. The following account is typical of others who communicated with the author of this book and who met, and were captivated by, Kathleen in the course of her long vagabond life.

Kathleen Phelan and I met in London in 1983 and reconnected in Paris the following year. I was then a 23-year-old Australian taking the traditional post-university overseas tour. Kathleen was some decades older. Her base was a caravan in the English countryside, from which she hitched and sold or exchanged handmade, illustrated booklets of her writing. Kathleen financed her London stays by placing bets on horse races.

One winter evening, in the common room of a youth hostel in Holland Park, Kathleen initiated conversation about the book I was reading ... We talked all night, smoked copious quantities of cigarettes and became firm friends.

Kathleen was petite, probably not many inches over five feet, dynamic and lively. Her face was handsome, by that time quite lined, with large, hooded and engaging (emerald green) eyes, a hawkish nose and strong jawline. She kept her hair coloured dark and wore it neatly parted and at neck length. She dressed simply in jeans, jackets and walking shoes, without embellishment, but with a nod to Bohemian style in perhaps a scarf or '60s style shoulder bag and a dash of scarlet lipstick. She told me, with a laugh, that she couldn't imagine being attracted to the young backpackers who populated the London youth hostel because, while she may have lived quite a wild life, and made love on wine-splashed sheets, these guys just didn't look CLEAN.

In the daytime, we were turned out of the youth hostel. We'd linger outside in the cold mornings to chat and drink coffee. At intervals, Kathleen would disappear to listen to the racing results on a small transistor radio. Then Kathleen and I would go our separate ways.

In the evenings, we'd reconvene to continue the wondrous extended conversation of which our friendship largely consisted. Kathleen was an expert storyteller; without this skill she couldn't have hitched the roads as extensively as she did. She possessed a rich sense of humour, formidable intelligence, a well-honed interest in and understanding of humanity with all its foibles, strength of character and joie de vivre, and great warmth without effusion.

From Kathleen I learned much about the "tramping" lifestyle—non-consumerist, sustainable, highly principled and free. We kept in touch for close to twenty years, though neither of us seemed to stay in the same place for very long. In 2002, I moved from Hong Kong to Hangzhou in mainland China. Kathleen's last postcard, in her familiar writing and with her current address, was sitting on the ledge of the bay window on my last evening in Hong Kong. In Hangzhou, I looked for it in vain.

> On many occasions, over the years, I have tried to locate Kathleen but never succeeded. I am comforted by the knowledge that Kathleen would never have been without companionship and the fact that she was both a highly independent spirit and a survivor par excellence.[67]

If there has been little mention of Jim Phelan throughout the telling of Kathleen's foreign adventures, it should be emphasized here that he remained ever-present in her letters and storytelling. For instance, letters to Grace Jackman included copies of all the publisher's contracts for Jim's books. We also know that, during the later years Kathleen spent in her caravan when not out on the road, she produced two full-length fictional manuscripts that, according to her sister, she tried (unsuccessfully) to publish. The real loss to literature—because Kathleen's own stories are more fascinating than her fiction—is that although she did complete her unpublished autobiography recounting the time spent on the road with Jim (*What Lamp Has Destiny*), she never finished a final manuscript from the notes she made of her adventures in the Middle East and Asia, and failed to produce any significant record at all of her American adventures. Following Kathleen's return from America, what the postcards and letters written to Grace alone *do* reveal—although most with the year of postage absent—is the huge variety of places around Britain (some on more than one occasion) to which Kathleen had her caravan hauled and parked, and also details about trips she made to Europe between her times spent at the caravan. Not included in the list below are the dozens of poste restante addresses on postcards and letters Kathleen sent from around the U.K. (many from racecourse towns—Newmarket in particular) and Europe.

List of Some of the Sites Kathleen Pitched Her Caravan Between 1979 and 2014

Kings Head Park, Newport, SHROPSHIRE
Summerhill Caravan Park, Quatford, Bridgenorth, SHROPSHIRE
Castelton Motel Caravan Site, Stamford, LINCOLNSHIRE
Road End Farm Caravan Site, Great Casterton, Stamford, RUTLAND
Witchford Caravan Park, Ely, CAMBRIDGESHIRE
Appleacre Caravan Park, Fowlmere, Royston, HERTFORDSHIRE
Wolvey Caravan Park, Villa Farm, Hinkley, WARWICKSHIRE
Newlands Caravan Park, Wellesbourne, WARWICKSHIRE
Marston Caravan Park, Marston, WARWICKSHIRE
Twilite Moorings Caravan Site, Banbury, OXFORDSHIRE
Templars Court Country Club, Sanford-on-Thames, OXFORDSHIRE
Southend Farm, Wooton-under-Edge, GLOUCESTERSHIRE

Briarfields Caravan Park, Cheltenham, GLOUCESTERSHIRE
Bury View Caravan Park, Corston Fields, Bath, AVON
Loddon Court Farm, Spencers Wood, Reading, BERKSHIRE
The Merry Harriers Caravan Site, Hambleden, Nr Godalming, SURREY
Maynards Caravan Park, Cross Bush, Arundel, SUSSEX (November, 1993—February, 1994)
Loveders Caravan Park, Nutbourne, Chichester, SUSSEX (April, 1994)
Bat and Ball, Wisborough Green, WEST SUSSEX
Ellerslie Caravan Park, Fareham, HAMPSHIRE (October, 1994)
Whiteparish, Nr Salisbury, WILTSHIRE (May 1995)
Alderbury, Nr Salisbury, WILTSHIRE (July—September 1995)
Longfield Caravan Park, Christchurch, DORSET (January, 1996)
Springfield Caravan Park, Corfe Mullen, DORSET (June, 1996)
Moreton Glade Caravan Park, Moreton, Nr Dorchester, DORSET (October, 1996)
Warmwell Country Touring Park, Dorchester, DORSET (January—April, 1997)
East Fleet Farm Caravan Park, Chickerell, Weymouth, DORSET (June, 1997)
Clay Pigeon Caravan Park, Wardon Hill, Evershot, Dorchester, DORSET (October, 1997)
Waterloo Cross Caravan Park, Uffculme, DEVON
Manleaze Caravan Park, Cannards Grave, Shepton Mallet, SOMERSET (July—September, 1998)
Somerset View Caravan Park, North Petherton, SOMERSET
Isle of Avalon Caravan Park, Glastonbury, SOMERSET
Hogsdown Caravan Park, Lower Wick, GLOUCESTERSHIRE (May, 1999)
Lickhill Manor Caravan Park, Stourport-on-Severn, WORCESTERSHIRE (December, 2000)
Alderbury Caravan Park, Whaddon, Salisbury, WILTSHIRE (July, 2008)
Mayfield Caravan Park, Perrotts Brook, Cirencester, GLOUCESTERSHIRE (2005, 2009–2014)

Apart from where the years are dated on Kathleen's correspondence, it is not possible to know in what order her caravan moved around the country but the list is presented roughly clockwise around England starting in Shropshire, taking in the Midlands, the South East and finally the West-country from the south, then northward to Gloucestershire. Of course, Kathleen's road trips away from the caravan were far more wide-ranging, taking in Ireland, Scotland, Wales and also France, Switzerland and other European destinations.

Final Words

The email below from Jan Yates, then joint owner of the Mayfield Caravan Park in Cirencester, England, includes a summary of Kathleen's final decade and the manner of her dying.

> It was high summer 2005, not long after we'd bought our caravan and camping site that Kathleen turned up at the door to interview us. She wanted to see if we would be a suitable place to bring her caravan for a few weeks. It seemed we were, as shortly after her van was towed in and put on pitch by a gentleman who waved her goodbye as he left her to settle in. Kathleen soon became friends with everybody, including us, and we were often entertained by tales from her past. Frequently we'd be kept from work by how she met her husband Jim on the road: how they'd drunk with Dylan Thomas in London and Picasso in the south of France, then after Jim died played football with Pele in the streets of Brazil, and telling stories to the Shah of Iran—tales we were to hear more than once! In fact Kathleen's favourite phrase was 'Did I ever tell you about ...?'
>
> Describing herself as a tramp and vagabond, in the true sense of the word, we learned a lot about life on the road, the welcome signs such travellers would leave on people's gate posts, the kindness she found from both rich and poor. She would leave us for days and weeks at a time to hitch a ride—to wherever! Itchy feet meant time to move on and in February 2006 we found ourselves towing her caravan to the next chosen site and pitching it for her before it was our turn to wave goodbye.
>
> Several years, sites and letters later (she wrote beautifully, long newsy letters in her careful script) she once again turned up on our doorstep in October 2009—could she come back "for the winter." Of course we welcomed her back and here she stayed until she passed away asleep in her caravan (as she would have wished) in the early hours of Wednesday 26th November, 2014—two days before her 97th birthday.
>
> We have many memories of Kathleen: the way she would dance everywhere rather than walk; her immaculate dress code; her carefully coloured hair; her pride in keeping her home clean and shiny, inside and out; her fierce independence; swapping cigarettes with our regulars; her light burning late into the night as she painted her little horsy booklets she would sell to raise "a few bob"; listening to her radio; her dislike of tv, computers, internet and any such modern contraptions; the friends she made with people on the bus (when nobody stopped for

> her outstretched thumb), at the bookies and, in the last years, the local taxi drivers (delivered to her door!). But most of all it's her stories we remember, we begged often for her to write them down—I even bought her a posh notebook. It was found empty after she died and returned to me. However, what was found was file upon file of notes and memories. How I would love to read those tales again—maybe someday.
>
> One of life's great characters, the world is a richer place for Kathleen. She touched the life of everyone she met and will be remembered by many around the world. Certainly I will never forget her![68]

Then the following email was received from Jan in 2019 on being asked whether Kathleen remained active until her last days and if she suffered illness prior to her death.

> Yes, you're right, Kathleen wasn't so sprightly in her last days, though still fiercely independent. Peter (our business partner) took her to the doctors a couple of times but there was nothing major. The site we owned was on the market confidentially and we didn't tell anyone, especially Kathleen, as we didn't want her to worry but someone clearly got wind and told her. We would never have sold to anyone without making sure she was welcome to stay but I think it rattled her a little. We moved her caravan to several different pitches in the last few years as she seemed happy to stay with us. She still went off on her haunts for days on end and we'd take her to the bus station in Cheltenham to catch the bus to visit Elizabeth (Kathleen's sister)—she always insisted on paying.
>
> My husband and I were on holiday when she died. Peter noticed he hadn't seen her for a day or so, so went and knocked on her caravan. When he got no answer he looked through her window, saw her inside and went in to make sure she was OK—found her curled upon her bunk dead. She was cremated. There was no service—on her orders no one was to attend.
>
> Once Elizabeth had emptied her caravan, which by now was in some disrepair (though always immaculately clean) a local man came and took it away to repair for family holidays—Kathleen would have approved.[69]

The obituary appearing later in *The Times* newspaper reads as follows: "PHELAN Kathleen Tramp and Vagabond died peacefully in her sleep, in her caravan ... once met never forgotten."

ENDNOTES

1 Interview with Elizabeth Holdsworth, Kathleen's sister, Sunday, June 9, 2019

2 Ibid.

3 Phelan, Kathleen. *Hiking a Hitch*, self-published, printed and illustrated pamphlet, p. 1. Kathleen gives her version of the origin of the term "hitchhiking" on page 3 of her pamphlet: hike refers to holding onto something, and hitch refers to the rope that hangs down from the rear of a horse-drawn wagon. The origin of the term thus refers to asking a driver's permission to hold onto the rope to ease one's passage up an incline. After wagons became motorized, the term was still used to refer to getting a lift on a truck, but later became the general term it is today for getting a lift with the driver of any vehicle.

4 Phelan, Kathleen. *What Lamp Has Destiny* (unpublished autobiography). Feral House plans to publish this work in 2020 but not under Kathleen's working title.

5 The only similar reference to this strange title is the gambling video game *Lamp of Destiny*.

6 Ibid.

7 It should be noted here that following Jim's death, and even though she continued to dote on Jim and promote his books throughout her life, she acknowledged to her friend Grace Jackman that there were aspects of the relationship that were unequal and that her own talents had taken second place to Jim's writing career—not of course without Kathleen's full cooperation. Interview with Grace Jackman, July 16, 2019

8 The tramp slang "line of guff" is fully described in Chapter 13 but is a story (part truth, part fiction) the tramp invents to acquire money, food, shelter, etc., from their "mark": the person who is the target of their story.

9 Interview with Grace Jackman, July 16, 2019

10 From the Irish "craic" meaning doing something for the fun of it.

11 *What Lamp Has Destiny*, op. cit.

12 Ibid.

13 Derbishire, Kerry. *Kay's Ark*, Sedbergh (Cumbria): Handstand Press, 2016, p. 41

14 Ibid., p. 43

15 Derbishire, Kerry, email to author, September 7, 2019

16 *What Lamp Has Destiny*, op. cit.

17 Ibid.

18 Ibid.

19 Ibid.

20 Phelan, Kathleen, notes for unpublished autobiography Part 2

21 Phelan, Kathleen, letter to Dan Davin, September 21st, year not written

22 Phelan, Kathleen, "I am a Vagabond," *Woman's Own*, no date visible but believed to be 1972.

23 Ibid.

24 Interview with Grace Jackman, July 16, 2019. Grace is introduced later in the chapter.

25 Notes for unpublished autobiography Part 2, op. cit.

26 "I am a Vagabond," op. cit.

27 Ibid.

28 Phelan, Kathleen, journal entry, September 21, 1967

29 Notes for unpublished autobiography Part 2, op. cit. There are other similar references in Kathleen's memoirs to rejecting unwanted sexual advances but this is the first referenced.

30 Phelan, Kathleen, journal entry, December 8, 1967

31 Purdah is the practice of female seclusion in certain Muslim and Hindu practices.

32 Phelan, Kathleen, journal entry, January 11, 1968

33 Ibid.

34 "I am a Vagabond," op. cit.

35 Ibid.

36 Notes for unpublished autobiography Part 2, op. cit.

37 "I am a Vagabond," op. cit.

38 Ibid. This included a program with the musician and composer Mohamed Abdul Wahab.

39 See note 22.

40 Notes for unpublished autobiography Part 2, op. cit.

41 Graham Marriott's journal, August 1968

42 "I am a Vagabond," op. cit.

43 Clipping of article among Kathleen's possessions excludes source or date of article.

44 Notes for unpublished autobiography Part 2, op. cit.

45 Ibid.

46 Ibid.

47 "I am a Vagabond," op. cit.

48 *Hiking a Hitch*, op. cit.

49 Kathleen Phelan's handwritten notes.

50 See Cutler, Ian. *Jim Christy: A Vagabond Life*, Port Townsend, WA: Feral House, 2019

51 Christy, Jim. "The Name's Phelan," unpublished short story.

52 Kathleen's sister Elizabeth mentions that Kathleen spent nine years on the American continent and the writer Dan Davin that she spent 10 years, yet, unless Kathleen traveled to America more than once, archive material confirms this was seven years.

53 Interview with Grace Jackman, July 16, 2019

54 Phelan, Kathleen, Correogramma (telegram) from Mexico City to Kay Callaghan, May 3, 1974

55 Phelan, Kathleen, cited in Vromen, Galina. "Song of the Vagabond," *The News* (Mexico City), December 3, 1974

56 Phelan, Kathleen, letter to Grace Jackman from Lima, Peru, March 12, 1975

57 Phelan, Kathleen, from unpublished notes on trip to Nepal

58 Phelan, Kathleen, letter to Grace Jackman from Lima in Peru, March 12, 1975

59 Phelan, Kathleen, letter written to Kay Callaghan from La Paz, Bolivia, May 12, 1975

60 Phelan, Kathleen, letter to Grace Jackman, July 6, 1977

61 Phelan, Kathleen, letter to Grace Jackman, August 7, 1977

62 Phelan, Kathleen, letter to Grace Jackman, August 29, 1977

63 Gallagher, Mary Cate, email to author, March 6, 2019

64 Interview with Grace Jackman, July 16, 2019

65 Nous is a U.K. slang term for common sense.

66 Phelan, Liam, email to the author, July 8, 2019

67 Bond, Jan, email to author, January 2, 2015.

68 Yates, Jan, email to author, January 10, 2015

69 Yates, Jan, email to author, August 6, 2019

ACKNOWLEDGEMENTS A special thanks to my publisher, Jessica Parfrey, for her support in bringing this book to life and producing a series of other books to foreground tramp literature as part of Feral House's "Tramp Lit Series". Thanks also to Sara Powell for her forensic editing skills, Laura Smith for proofreading and production, and Jacob Covey for his stunning design and layout of the book. A special thanks to my sons: Max for the book's character illustrations and Seth for his support and encouragement throughout. Chapter 1: Thanks to Linda Fluharty, West Virginia Genealogy Coordinator for obituaries on Page and company information; the writer Dave Lossos of 'Genealogy in St. Louis' for probate and business records; Adele Heagney of St Louis Public Library for information from the *Encyclopedia of the History of St. Louis*, probate records, and articles from the *St. Louis Post-Dispatch*; and Jason D. Stratman and Kay Thurman of Missouri History Museum for their very helpful assistance in tracking down and posting the clippings cited above. Chapter 3: Thanks to Zoe Stansell, Maps & Reference Service, and Lee Taylor and Adrian Shindler, Humanities Reference Service, all of the British Library, for their very helpful assistance in tracking down key documents relating to Bart Kennedy. Chapter 4: Thanks to the late Professor Tim Couzens, author of *Tramp Royal*, for his helpful advice on Trader Horn. Chapter 12: Thanks to Mark Dawidziak, co-author of *Jim Tully: American Writer, Irish Rover, Hollywood Brawler*, for his help and advice on this chapter. Chapter 13: Thanks to all those who provided valuable advice and archive material for the chapter on Jim Phelan. Seumas and Liam Phelan (Phelan's son and grandson with his second wife Jill), Les Singleton and Lillian Felstead (Phelan's grandson and granddaughter with first wife Dora), David Cowell (who provided copies of rare archive material including the letter from JP to George Orwell and the clemency letter from JP's mother), Jim Christy (author, artist and vagabond, who met JP's third wife and widow Kathleen on a boat from Spain to Morocco in January 1970 and tramped with her for a week in the Moroccan countryside), and Jim Phelan (no relative, who is also researching his namesake). Thanks also to Prof. Andrew Lees' for discussing his essay on Phelan, 'The Rolling English Road', Dublin Review of Books (2015), and to Michael Gill of Liverpool University who was completing a PhD on Phelan at the time of writing. Chapter 15: Thanks to Elizabeth, Adrian and Paul Holdsworth (Kathleen's sister and nephews), Seumas and Liam Phelan (Jim Phelan's son and grandson), Grace Jackman (Kathleen's friend of 44 years), Kerry Darbishire, Cherie Westmoreland, Yiannis Gabriel (for translating the Greek newspaper article), Graham Marriott, Jim Christy, Mary Cate Gallagher, Jan Bond, and Jan Yates.

PHOTO CREDITS: Page i: Tramps Fighting Between Railroad Cars. Library of Congress; Page ii: Railroad Yards, circa 1921–1940. Photo by Mathew Brady, U.S. National Archives; Page iv: NY Police Dog Treeing Tramp, 1921. Library of Congress; Page v: Tramp Standing On Porch With Food and Drink Given To Him By Woman Standing Inside House, circa 1919. Library of Congress; Top Front Cover: Freight-Hopping Youth Near Bakersfield, California, 1917. Rondal Partridge, U.S. National Archives and Records Administration; Bottom Front Cover: Hobo On Tracks. Photo by Will Bickner, Credit Lake Oswego Public Library; Top Spine: James River Landing, James River, Virginia. Photo by Mathew Brady, U.S. National Archives Collection; Bottom Spine: Two Hobos Walking Along Railroad Tracks, After Being Put Off a Train. Library of Congress; Back Cover: The Clearing Yards Of The Belt Railway Company Of Chicago, 1943. Jack Delano, Library of Congress.

A special thanks to the following publishers for granting permissions to use extended quotations from the following titles still in print: Blackstaff Press Ltd., Belfast, *The Name's Phelan*, 1993; Witwatersrand University Press, Johannesburg and Pan Macmillan, *The True Story of Trader Horn*, 1994

ALSO BY IAN CUTLER

"The Cynical Manager", *Management Learning*, Sage, 2000

Cynicism from Diogenes to Dilbert, McFarland & Co., Inc., 2005

"Old Dogs New Tricks: a cynical legacy", *Think*, Royal Institute of Philosophy, 2006

"A Tale of Two Cynics: the philosophic dual between Jesus and the Woman from Syrophoenicia", *The Philosophical Forum*, Inc., New York, 2010

"On the Author of Christ and the Author of *The Anti-Christ*: Nietzsche's Diatribe on Paul and Affinity with Jesus", *Philo*, Centre for Enquiry, New York, 2012

Jim Christy: A Vagabond Life, Feral House, 2019

Original illustrations by Max Cutler

The Lives and Extraordinary Adventures of Fifteen Tramp Writers from the Golden Age of Vagabondage is part of the Tramp Lit Series for Feral House. For further information about these titles, see www.feralhouse.com

Feral House
1240 W Sims Way #124
Port Townsend WA 98368

Design by Jacob Covey / Unflown

ISBN: 9781627310840
Printed in the United States of America
10 9 8 7 6 5 4 3 2 1